Caledonian Jews

Caledonian Jews

A Study of Seven Small Communities in Scotland

NATHAN ABRAMS

McFarland & Company, Inc., Publishers
Jefferson, North Carolina, and London

LIBRARY OF CONGRESS CATALOGUING-IN-PUBLICATION DATA

Abrams, Nathan.
　　Caledonian Jews : a study of seven small communities in
Scotland / Nathan Abrams.
　　　　p.　　cm.
　　Includes bibliographical references and index.

　　ISBN 978-0-7864-4285-0
　　softcover : 50# alkaline paper ∞

　　1. Jews—Scotland—History.　2. Small cities—Scotland—
History.　3. Scotland—Ethnic relations.　I. Title.
DS135.E55S3523　　2009
941.1'004924—dc22　　　　　　　　　　　　　　　　　　2009017959

British Library cataloguing data are available

©2009 Nathan Abrams. All rights reserved

*No part of this book may be reproduced or transmitted in any form
or by any means, electronic or mechanical, including photocopying
or recording, or by any information storage and retrieval system,
without permission in writing from the publisher.*

On the cover: Celia Wolfe in front of her store, Greenock
(courtesy of L. Alexander Wolfe); background ©2009 Shutterstock

Manufactured in the United States of America

*McFarland & Company, Inc., Publishers
　Box 611, Jefferson, North Carolina 28640
　　www.mcfarlandpub.com*

Acknowledgements

I would like to acknowledge the assistance of many people whose advice, support, comments, suggestions, and revisions were invaluable in helping me to complete this book. They include: Michael Abrams, Ben Braber, Terry Brotherstone, Ramsay Brown, Kenneth Collins, Chris Croly, Peter Davidson, David Ditchburn, Vinciane Duperthuy, Nicholas J. Evans, Graeme Harper, Howard Hotson, Albert Jacob, Harvey Kaplan, Dovid Katz, Lorna Kay, Walter Kress, Iain Macinnes, Andrew MacKillop, Helena Miguélez Carballeira, David Rose, Etti, Yonni, and the Shoshan family, and Debby Taylor.

An earlier version of Chapter 1 appeared in *Northern Scotland* as "The Jews of Aberdeen: a revolving door community since 1893 and its antecedents" (27 [2007]).

The research for this article was made possible by grants from the University of Aberdeen, the Carnegie Trust for the Universities of Scotland, the British Academy, the Hanadiv Charitable Foundation, and the Society of Antiquaries of Scotland.

I dedicate this book to those in Aberdeen who made me feel so welcome during my short stay there, in particular my former colleagues in the Department of History at the University of Aberdeen and the Aberdeen Hebrew Congregation.

Contents

Acknowledgments	v
Preface	1
Introduction	5
1. Aberdeen	15
2. Ayr	41
3. Dundee	65
4. Dunfermline	95
5. Falkirk	110
6. Greenock	123
7. Inverness, the Highlands, and Islands	142
Conclusion	167
Appendix A: Figures for the Size of the Communities	189
Appendix B: "A New Letter"	192
Appendix C: Burials in the Jewish Section of Grove Cemetery, Aberdeen	194
Appendix D: Burials in the Jewish Section of Bow Road Cemetery, Greenock	196
Appendix E: Burials in the Jewish Section of Tomnahurich Cemetery, Inverness	197
Appendix F: List of Children Enrolled in Falkirk Schools	198
Glossary of Hebrew and Yiddish Terms	201
Chapter Notes	203
Bibliography	223
Index	231

Preface

I became interested in Scottish Jewish history following my move to Aberdeen to take up a position as a lecturer in American history at the University of Aberdeen in September 2005. A question often asked of me during my time there was, "Why did you choose Aberdeen?" I replied that I didn't choose Aberdeen at all but that it chose me. Does this sum up the position of Aberdeen's Jews through the ages, I wondered? How many of them chose to move there, or arrived as a consequence of the usual push and pull factors that bring Jews to any part of the world? The sixtieth anniversary of the consecration of the Aberdeen Hebrew Congregation's synagogue in June 1945 gave me an opportunity to look back at the history of the Jews of the Granite City.

As I dug deeper, it became clear that not only had Aberdeen's Jewish history not been unearthed to any great extent, but also that this was true of the other small Jewish communities in Scotland—namely, Ayr, Dundee, Dunfermline, Falkirk, Greenock, and Inverness. Up until fairly recently, Anglo-Jewish historiography has paid little attention to Scotland, the center of its focus being primarily on England rather than Britain as a whole. When Scotland has been looked at, the focus has been on Glasgow and Edinburgh. This book, then, aims to fill that gap in our understanding of Scottish history in particular and British history in general.

The work of Kenneth Collins has been an invaluable starting place. More than anyone else, Kenneth has begun to undertake the task of mapping Scottish Jewish history in his various books: *Aspects of Scottish Jewry* (Glasgow: Glasgow Jewish Representative Council, 1987); *Go and Learn: The International Story of Jews and Medicine in Scotland* (Aberdeen: Aberdeen University Press, 1988); *Second City Jewry: The Jews of Glasgow in the Age of Expansion, 1790–1919* (Glasgow: Scottish Jewish Archives, 1990); *Be Well! Jewish Immigrant Health and Welfare in Glasgow, 1860–1914* (East Linton: Tuckwell, 2001). Kenneth's pioneering work has been built upon by a new generation of scholars who are helping to flesh out different aspects of Scottish Jewish history. They include Henry Maitles, William Kenefick, and Harvey Kaplan, among others.

However, in spite of the spread of Jews throughout Scotland, those that chose not to live in its two major cities have received scant scholarly interest.

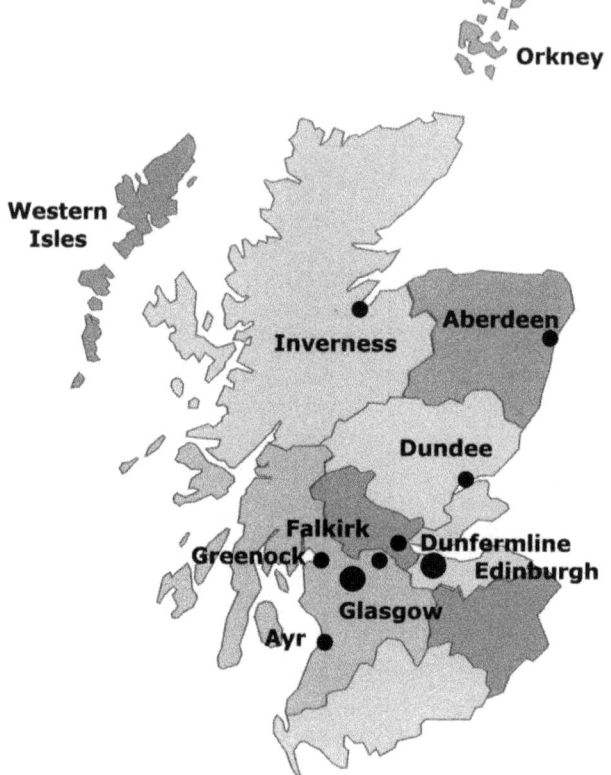

The Jewish communities of Scotland.

This book is an attempt to rectify that situation, focusing on seven Jewish congregations (those that were able to establish a synagogue and related Jewish infrastructure)—namely, Aberdeen, Ayr, Dundee, Dunfermline, Falkirk, Greenock, and Inverness—as well as individuals and families who lived even further removed from their co-religionists in those cities.

A wide range of primary resources have been consulted for this study. These materials are located at research libraries and archives in Scotland and England, including the Special Libraries and Archives at the University of Aberdeen; the Scottish Jewish Archives Centre in Glasgow; the British Newspaper Library in Colindale; the British Library in London; the National Archives in London; the archives of the Chief Rabbi's Office and United Synagogue at the London Metropolitan Archives; the Hartley Library at the University of Southampton; and local public libraries. In addition, a number of newspapers and other publications were used, primarily the *Jewish Chronicle*, the *Jewish Echo*, the *Jewish Telegraph*, and the *Jewish Year Book*, as well as local newspapers specific to each community. Finally, these written materials were supplemented with interviews and correspondence from the surviving members of those communities and their relatives.

It is my great hope that this book will contribute to the picture of Scottish and British Jewish history that has already been built up, and will inspire future students and scholars to continue to research into this important field.

Introduction

Mystery, Myth, Rumor, and Conjecture: Scottish Jewish History

Very little is known about Jewry in Scotland because of the small numbers, and what little evidence there is has often been handed down by word of mouth. Much of Scottish Jewish history, therefore, is surrounded in mystery, myth, rumor and conjecture. According to Rabbi Salis Daiches, once the *de facto* head of Scottish Jewry, "Scotland remained for the Jew throughout many centuries a *terra* incognita."[1] There seems to have been hardly any Jews in Scotland at all prior to the nineteenth century, and it is only in the early decades of that century that Jews began to settle in its two principal cities. Individual Jewish traders and merchants did, however, have commercial interests in Scotland without actually settling there, as shown by an official regulation passed between 1181 and 1187 by the Bishop of Glasgow forbidding "Churchmen to pledge their benefices for money borrowed from the Jews or other usurers."[2] Cecil Roth adds that no Jews "are encountered in Scotland in pre-Expulsion times, but Jewish financiers did business from time to time with the Scottish sovereign."[3]

Yet, many feel that there might have been a trickle northwards after the expulsion of the Jews from England in 1290. The Royalist author and translator James Howell wrote in 1653 that it "is thought divers families of those banished *Jews* then fled to Scotland where they have propagated since in great numbers; witness the aversion that Nation hath above others to hogs flesh."[4] Similarly, John Toland, an early enlightenment thinker, opined in the early eighteenth century that a "great number of 'em fled to *Scotland*, which is the reason why so many in that part of the Island, have such a remarkable aversion to pork and black-puddings to this day."[5] A. M. Hyamson, in his *A History of the Jews of England*, quotes the Jewish historian Josippon as stating that many Jews "are also said to have taken refuge in Scotland."[6] Abraham Levy adds, "It is natural to surmise that some of these refugees may have made their way northwards."[7] Those Jews who escaped from York after the expulsion by Edward I in the thirteenth century may well have traveled to Berwick on Tweed, which was then Scotland's main port.

Despite these rumors, no reports of any such Jewish movement survive of which we are aware. This is not helped by the fact that most of Scotland's public civil records prior to 1340, if any escaped the campaigns of Edward I, were destroyed by the English during the military operation of the Lancastrian kings. *The Universal Jewish Encyclopedia* records the following: "There is legendary reference to Jewish children having been transported north to Scotland during the persecutions that preceded the Expulsion in 1290, in the effort to effect their thorough conversion. Of such migrations, however, there is no record."[8] Furthermore, following the massacre of Jews in York in 1190, a royal army came to punish the perpetrators. "But," wrote William of Newburgh (1136–c.1201) in his *History of English Affairs*, "the chief and best known actors of the deeds done, leaving everything they had in the country, fled before his face to Scotland."[9] Would Jews have subsequently moved to a country which harbored their killers? More doubts have been thrown on these surmises. A. Levy has written, "This route of escape could have hardly have commended itself to many. Despite the 'golden age' in Scotland that preceded the wars of independence, Jews had not yet spread into that country from the south and lacked Scottish experience and connections. Following the expulsion, England no longer provided a stepping stone for immigrants by land, the disturbed Scottish scene was not such as to encourage direct immigration by sea from the continent."[10]

Patricia Skinner adds:

> It is tempting to speculate that Jews fleeing England in 1290 might have looked northwards rather than across the Channel, but the combined factors of their distribution prior to that date (none further north than York, apparently, Newcastle having expelled its community in 1234), and Edward I's invasion of Scotland in 1296, massacring the inhabitants of Berwick before ruling the country until 1306, render the likelihood of a post–1290 Scottish Jewish community somewhat remote.[11]

Skinner notes that a "Thomas fil Isaac" was recorded in Aberdeen in the fourteenth century,[12] but, although Elizabeth Caldwell Hirschman and Donald N. Yates feel this is "an undeniably Hebrew surname,"[13] Skinner adds that he was "unlikely to have been Jewish," as he married a daughter of King Robert I.[14] David Ditchburn is clear that later medieval Scotland had no Jewish communities.[15] And according to Harvey Kaplan, director of the Scottish Jewish Archives Centre, in any other place where Jews once lived, there remains traces of Jewish infrastructure, such as synagogues, *mikvaot* (special baths), or Jewish cemeteries. "To the best of my knowledge," Kaplan goes on to say, "not a single stone from a medieval Jewish building or cemetery has ever been found or authenticated. In addition, even in medieval times, Jewish community leaders and rabbis corresponded extensively across Europe and the Middle East on matters such as religious law. Had there been Jews in Scotland at this time, one would have expected references in Jewish correspondence and writings of the period."[16] Indeed, it has also been claimed that Jews were never made welcome in Scotland,[17] and William Cunningham goes so far as to suggest they were intentionally excluded.[18]

Nonetheless, unconfirmed rumors that there was a Jewish presence in Scotland during medieval times, mainly down the east coast of the country, still circulate. According to Sidney Caplan, Nigel Tranter, the famous Scottish historian and author, said that after the Battle of Stirling Bridge, when Edward I's army was defeated by the Scots under William Wallace, the Jewish merchants gave Wallace letters of credit to buy arms in Europe. Sadly, as mentioned above, Edward came north again and captured Berwick, slaughtering all the inhabitants, Jews and gentiles alike. Caplan further maintains that Jews were merchants trading with the city states of Northern Europe, amounting to about thirty families. As evidence, he refers to the initials "I M" carved on an engraving of Moses on a wall of John Knox's house along the Royal Mile in Edinburgh, which refer to Isaac Mossman, a goldsmith to Mary Queen of Scots and also her financial advisor. It is thought he came to Scotland from Lorraine with Mary when she returned from France. Mossman was executed when Mary fled to England—not because he was Jewish, but because he had backed the wrong side.[19]

Similarly, a 2006 book, *When Scotland Was Jewish*, also seeks to argue "that much of Scotland's history and culture from the 1100s forward is Jewish."[20] The authors' thesis is based on the notion that Jews fleeing from medieval persecution and the Inquisition in continental Europe arrived in Scotland in large numbers, and were the ancestors of the Scottish ruling class: "We believe that the first members of [the Campbell family] ... arrived in Scotland as a result of anti–Jewish pogroms in France and Spain in the middle of the fourteenth century."[21] They continue to assert that Jewish influence enabled the rapid growth of the medieval Scottish economy. Aberdeen's economic growth in the Middle Ages is attributed to the authors' idea that all the major families in the town were of Jewish descent. "We believe a compelling case can be made that Aberdeen did serve as a centre of Jewish worship and culture during the time period 1100–1750 C.E."[22]

The first actual record of any Jews in Scotland is not until the seventeenth century. Kenneth Collins has pointed out an entry in the matriculation album of Marischal College in Aberdeen in the session of 1634–35 for Samuel Suecus, whose name was similar to that of Samuel Suero, the son of Menasseh ben Israel, the Jewish scholar who negotiated with Cromwell the return of Jews to England in 1656. Suero claimed to have a doctorate from Cambridge, but the university refuted this claim.[23] Caplan also claims that at the end of the sixteenth century the Earl of Huntly gave money to found the University of Aberdeen on the condition that the University enrolled three Jewish students; however, there is no evidence for this.[24] In the middle of that century, isolated individuals who were converted European Jews began to arrive in the capital as Hebrew teachers. Levy gives examples, such as Julius Conradus Otto, a converted Jew from Vienna who became professor of Hebrew and Oriental Languages at Edinburgh University in 1641, and also Paulus Scialitti Rabin, c.1665.[25] However, the first openly-practicing Jew to settle in Scotland appears to have been David Brown, who applied to the town council of Edinburgh for permission to trade in the burgh in 1691. Although Brown initially met some resistance on the grounds that only Christians could be granted such privileges, he was defended by the treasurer, Hugh Blair, who argued that the Jews were "the ancient people of God and the seed of Abraham," and thus "to them belongs the promise."[26] Such tolerance, however, did not last long, and the town council denied the privilege of trade to Jews unless payment of £100 was made, the sum finally being paid by Isaac Queen in 1717. "Due perhaps to this bigoted and mercenary policy," William Ferguson points out, "no further references to Jews in Scotland occur until near the end of the century."[27]

Throughout the eighteenth century, Jewish individuals and families settled in Edinburgh, but there is no evidence of there being an actual community. Joseph Hart Myers was the first Jew to study as an undergraduate at Edinburgh University, and graduated M.D. in 1779. Herman Lyon, a dentist and "corn operator," came to Edinburgh from Prussia in 1788, and obtained a burial plot for himself and his family on Calton Hill in 1795 (lost for many years, the site was rediscovered in 1994). It is not until the nineteenth century that we see the establishment of the first Jewish communities in Scotland. The distinction of the first Jewish community in Scotland belongs to Edinburgh, where the first synagogue opened in 1816 in a lane off Nicholson Street, serving twenty families. In 1820, Scotland's first Jewish cemetery was opened in Braid Place (now Sciennes House Place), which was used until 1867. The members of this nascent Scottish Jewish community were primarily wealthy merchants and businessmen of German origin, as were those who were also beginning to settle in Glasgow and Dundee.[28] Up until the 1870s, the community numbered about one thousand, and was concentrated in the three cities of Edinburgh, Dundee, and Glasgow. It was only during the last third of the nineteenth century that Jewish immigration to Scotland reached significant levels, with the mass migrations from Central and Eastern Europe prompted by anti–Semitic persecution in Russia, a desire for economic betterment, and the improvements in steam and railway transportation.[29]

"Anglo-Jewish" History

Accurate records of Scottish Jewish existence before the eighteenth century are hard to come by because no systematic study of Scottish Jewry has been undertaken. Until such time that it is, the subject will remain shrouded in mist. This is explained by the unfortunate fact that, up until fairly recently, *soi-disant* Anglo-Jewish historiography has paid little attention to Scotland, the center of its focus being on England rather than Britain as a whole (as is indeed indicated by the discipline's very name).[30] Often the terms "Britain" and "England" are used synonymously, as in Miri J. Freud-Kandel's book, *Orthodox Judaism in Britain Since 1913: An Ideology Forsaken*, where, despite her title, she begins with the words, "The Jewish community in England...."[31] Indeed, given the high degree of geographical concentration of British Jewry into six communities (London, Manchester, Leeds, Glasgow, Birmingham, and Liverpool), the history of Jews in the United Kingdom has, in fact, primarily been the history of these centers of population, despite a number of studies that have focused on other smaller communities.[32] No doubt this will remain the case until "British-Jewish" historiography becomes the preferred term, since the *Oxford English Dictionary* defines "Anglo-Jewish" as "English, of England."

Unfortunately, there is still some resistance to changing it. Harold Pollins, for example, in wanting to avoid using "such clumsy terms as 'Jews of the British isles,'" instead, by his own admission, "loosely" refers to "Anglo-Jewry." But he is at least aware that "this is a dangerous step."[33] Nevertheless, his book is still called *Economic History of the Jews in England*, even though it refers to Jews in the whole of the British Isles! Tod Endelman, on the other hand, justifies his unwillingness to discard the term because "it is conventional to use the term 'Anglo-Jewish' to refer to Jews in Britain as a whole, including Jews in Scotland and Wales, even though they were not, in a strict sense, 'English' Jews. This usage is too well established to be dropped. Moreover, since the number of Jews who lived in Wales and Scotland was never large, folding them into 'Anglo-Jewry' does not distort the overall picture."[34] One cannot help feeling that the term is continued to be used out of laziness; however, it does contain a sort of honesty, for, by and large, the histories of the Jews in Britain have largely been the histories of the Jews in England. In contrast, William D. Rubinstein uses the term "Anglo" in its linguistic sense, as the title of his book demonstrates: *A History of the Jews in the English-Speaking World*. This is an acceptable usage, for it is accurate, but it is not one that is widely shared. Furthermore, the emphasis will still continue to be on the major metropoles, for the historiographical attitude is summed up by Endelman, who maintains: "What happens elsewhere, however piquant or arresting in human terms, reveals little about the main currents of Anglo-Jewish history."[35]

Fortunately, not everyone shares Endelman's point of view, and a pleasing sign is that the work in the field of Scottish Jewish history, which has already been completed by scholars such as Kenneth Collins, Henry Maitles, William Kenefick, and Harvey Kaplan,[36] among others, is now growing and being added to by many younger scholars undertaking fresh work.[37] Nevertheless, the much smaller field of Scottish Jewish history is itself prone to the metropolitan bias manifested by Endelman, for much of it is primarily focused on the experiences of Jews in the West of Scotland—in particular, Glasgow, and, to a lesser extent, Edinburgh.[38] It is, as Kenneth Collins, the pre-eminent chronicler of Scottish Jewish life, has written, "a tale of two cities."[39]

As a consequence, although Jews are literally and liberally dotted across the length and breadth of Scotland, those Jews who lived outside of Glasgow and Edinburgh have attracted little attention from historians and researchers.[40] And what *has* been done is largely anecdotal. For example, only three pages in Collins' *Aspects of Scottish Jewry* – itself only a brief pamphlet – are devoted to the communities outside of Glasgow and Edinburgh, and this same information is also repeated in his book *Go and Learn*.[41] Further, the information contained therein is largely factual, giving no sense of the texture and peculiar idiosyncrasies of Jewish communal life in Scotland in its smaller communities, and does not extend much beyond the Second World War. As a consequence, the life and history of the smaller communities has been neglected.[42] It is an unfortunate irony, then, that we probably know more about the far-flung communities of the world than we do about those in our own islands. Until a detailed study of Scotland's smaller Jewish communities is undertaken, the picture of Jewish life in Scotland in particular, and the British Isles in general, cannot be considered complete.

I attempt to begin such a study here. This book deals with the peculiar and particular experiences of Jews outside of those mainstream communities of Edinburgh and Glasgow, who are often overlooked and forgotten. It focuses on Scotland's seven small Jewish communities—that is, those communities which were of sufficient size and affluence to form themselves into a congregation with a functional synagogue: Aberdeen, Ayr, Dundee, Dunfermline, Falkirk, Greenock, and Inverness. It will also consider, albeit briefly, those Jews "isolated from other Jews in towns and villages throughout Scotland from the Shetlands to the Borders," where such information is available.[43] Examples of this include the Jewish Network of the Argyll and Highlands, established to bring those Jews scattered in the West of Scotland together, or those Jews who chose, as we shall see, to settle in Lerwick on the Shetland Isles or the Isle of Skye. It is a reminder that there always has been and continues to be a significant Jewish presence throughout the British Isles.

These small communities also provide an opportunity to study the experiences of all of Scotland's and Britain's small and remote Jewish communities. Not only were, and are, some of these communities small, but, in the case of Aberdeen, Argyll and the Highlands, and Inverness, they are geographically isolated. Aberdeen is situated some seventy miles from the nearest community, Dundee, and nearly one hundred and fifty miles from the nearest organized center, Glasgow. Inverness is even further, and Argyll and the Highland areas even further still, lending them "a special character and entail lifestyles and interests that can distance [them] from any urban community."[44] Interestingly, the medieval Jewish name for Britain literally translates as "the end of the earth," and this seems most apt for these places that provide a starting point or prism for considering the position of what I shall call "remote Jews"—Jews who chose and choose to live far from a Jewish community and Jewish practice—and why they moved there in the first place, and the particular problems and difficulties that they faced once they had arrived there.[45] They provide a standpoint from which to study Jews physically and psychologically removed from the major centers of Jewish life.

I shall use this remoteness not only to refer to physical distance but also to psychological aloofness. By this I do not mean that remote Jews have deliberately detached themselves from the center or mainstream of Jewish life, although this is clearly the case with some individuals and families; on the contrary, remote Jews have been kept apart. Their isolation from mainstream Jewish life has been compounded by the attitude of those who form the latter. Jewish newspapers do not circulate unless by individual subscription. The United Jewish Israel Appeal may have an Office for Small Communities whose ministers try to visit regularly, and student chaplains also drop in, but the various incumbents holding the position of Chief Rabbinate have been conspicuously absent. Chief Rabbi Dr. Hermann Adler conducted a tour of Scotland that took in the small communities of Aberdeen, Inverness, and Greenock in 1907.[46] Interestingly, he had deemed the newly-established community of Aberdeen worthy of a visit almost a decade earlier, too.[47] Yet, since 1907 no chief rabbi has visited these small Jewish communities. A chief rabbi was not even present in 1945 for the consecration of the Dee Street synagogue in Aberdeen. This has justifiably led to a perception of aloofness, if not indifference, on the part of the Chief Rabbinate by some congregants of these congregations. When, in 1992, the Chief Rabbi's Council requested a sum of £120 from the congregation, the president suggested responding with a "no."[48] The president then contacted the Scottish representative on the Chief Rabbi's Council, requesting that it ignore Aberdeen and Dundee in future, and not send any more bills, which would be ignored if received.[49]

Furthermore, these small communities have been referred to with an unfortunate and overwhelming sense of pessimism and negativity, as if they were inexorably doomed from their very beginning.[50] The fortunes of such places have never been looked upon with much favor. They are often perceived as insignificant anomalies, irritants almost, that buck the dominant trend of Scottish (for which Glasgow is often used as a metonym) Jewish history. Even in the information age, communications between these small and remote communities and the center in Britain remain tenuous, although this has not always been the case over the course of the nineteenth and twentieth centuries. This book, then, hopes to answer the questions: If Jews tend to cluster, then what happened when they didn't? And what was the nature of the relationships with the centers of Jewish life in Britain?

How "Small" Is "Small"?

According to Lee Shai Weissbach, there is no "previously developed and widely accepted definition of what constitutes a small Jewish community." In its absence, he has chosen as a paradigm any urban Jewish community with reported Jewish populations of at least 100 but fewer than a thousand individuals in 1927.[51] This decision was motivated, in part, by "the premise that in the late nineteenth and early twentieth centuries ... settlements of fewer than 100 Jews were unlikely to have attained the critical mass necessary to constitute full-fledged communities."[52] Since the records for this year are incomplete in the *Jewish Year Book*, such figures can't be given for Scotland. The earliest year for a complete set of figures for all of the small communities is 1939, during which the size of Scotland's small Jewish communities ranged from thirty to one hundred and seventeen. In terms of their overall history, the size of the communities ranged from twelve at their smallest to one hundred and sixty at their greatest. Obviously, Scotland's small Jewish communities do not fit Weissbach's (or probably any other, for that matter) model of a small community, even taking into account the fact that not only was he referring to the United States, but his lack of definition of what he meant by the term "full-fledged." Yet, in light of this, and the fact that "[t]hese small communities, usually numbering a dozen or so families, nevertheless managed to retain a remarkable infrastructure with a synagogue and religion classes, and employing a rabbi and a minister who would lead the congregation in prayer, provide the kosher meat and teach the children," we might have to revise what we mean by a small Jewish community.[53] And given such small numbers, it is remarkable that not only did such communities form congregations in the first place, but they maintained them, too.

Statistics

Accurate statistics of Jews in smaller Scottish Jewish communities are difficult to come by. The statistics we do have are based on the *Jewish Year Book*, the *Jewish Echo*, and the *Jewish Chronicle*. However, for a variety of reasons, they are not entirely reliable. Often conflicting or confusing statistics are given. For example, population figures can be stated as seat holders, families and individuals, if given at all; and the *Jewish Year Book* relies on obtaining accurate and up-to-date figures not from official data but by writing to the communities themselves to provide statistics. As Ursula Henriques put it, "The figures for Jews rest on the *Jewish Year Books*—that is, largely on guesswork" because "compilers seem to have depended on irregular reports from the provinces; and if, as seems likely, the reporters counted only synagogue subscribers, they omitted many families without synagogue affiliation, producing a serious underestimate."[54]

The number of seat-holders, for instance, does not tell the whole story. Only the relatively well off and the Orthodox would pay for a seat. Nor can it be assumed that all Jews who came to Aberdeen became involved in congregational life at all; and we have no statistics to determine what percentage did. Some Jews, too, would have lost their name upon marriage or changed it. Name changes are a particularly complicating factor. If a Jewish man marries a non–Jewish woman, according to Jewish law his children are not Jewish, although the name would suggest otherwise.[55] Conversely, if a Jewish woman marries a non–Jewish man, her children would remain Jewish even if their name does not. Another problem for identification lies in the practice of adopting names familiar in the community; it was noted in the *Aberdeen Free Press* in 1904 that the names Gordon and Cowan had been assumed by Russian and Polish Jews in Aberdeen.[56] There is, therefore, no accurate way of determining just how many Jews there were in Aberdeen. And the problem is compounded because Aberdeen would probably have followed the pattern of intermarriage that can be established for other small and remote communities, such as Inverness. There also has been considerable deracination, so that some may have retained no visible signs of Jewishness, or perhaps nothing more than a Star of David necklace or a piece of Judaica on a mantelpiece.

The statistics are further complicated by contradictions in the sources. For 1909, for example, with regards to Aberdeen, the *Jewish Year Book* repeats its 1907–1908 figure of twenty-three seat holders, whereas Alexander Gammie reports that the population was officially returned as twenty-four families, of which there were twenty-six seat holders.[57] In the following year, the *Scotsman* claimed that the Aberdeen "Hebrew community at present consists of 23 heads of families and three single men, the total number of individuals being under 100; whereas the *Jewish Year Book* puts the figure at twenty-five seat holders.[58] From 1927 onwards we have some figures for the total number of individuals: twenty-five are listed in that year, rising, by 1936, to fifty-six in twenty-five families—a figure that remained fairly stable until 1945. One factor that may have contributed to the growth in Aberdeen's number is the decline of the Jewish community in Inverness. Certainly the few families that remained in Inverness, as well as other individuals scattered as far north as Shetland, migrated to Aberdeen over the High Holy Days.[59]

Census data is not fully accurate either. As Kenneth Collins has pointed out, "It is probably that the Scottish Census of 2001 underestimated the number of Jews in Scotland. Jews, and especially older members of the community, have a strong reluctance about volunteering their identity to any government list. The thought of a fascist government rounding up the Jews of Scotland would seem far-fetched, indeed paranoid, but the Jewish people have long memories and the precedent of the twentieth century is not a good one."[60]

The problem is compounded by the partial nature of records of the communities under study. At present, the fullest records are those of Ayr and Aberdeen, and even those of the latter are incomplete, as the pre–1930s records were lost in a fire. As for the rest of the communities, the records are patchy, consisting of the odd clipping, letter, and so on. Furthermore, the high degree of intermarriage, as well as population turnover caused by intra–Scottish migration and transmigration, means that figures for these communities were continually changing as members married out or moved from one community to another. Thus, I have included figures from the *Jewish Year Book*, *Jewish Echo*, and *Jewish Chronicle* as a guide only.

Structure

The book is simply structured in that it examines each community in alphabetical order. Some chapters are longer than others, reflecting the lifespan of that community and where there are a greater number of sources, namely Aberdeen, Ayr, Dundee, and Inverness. Nonetheless, it is hoped that the reader will draw significant comparisons across the communities with regards to a number of themes, including, but not limited to, their history, size and character; trades and occupations; religious ritual and internal dynamics; education; Zionism, charity and social activities; community and communal life; and relations with the non–Jewish world and anti–Semitism.

In doing so, a wide range of primary resources have been consulted for this study. These materials are located at research libraries and archives in the United Kingdom. Furthermore, physical evidence of other kinds, such as prayer books, Judaica and Hebraica, and other items, were essential to this research. I also undertook field trips to the small communities to research the local records and newspapers, as mentioned above, as well as to identify synagogue and burial sites and to photograph them. The latter helped to flesh out the demographic details of each community. Where the community was either too small to have its own burial site or in close proximity to a larger center of Jewish life, burials took place in Glasgow and Edinburgh, which were also visited. This material was supplemented with oral and written evidence from members of those communities which still exist, and those who once lived in those communities that no longer survive.

This study intends to provide as full a snapshot of these communities as we currently have in order to facilitate further study. It is hoped that *Caledonian Jews* will begin to dispel some of the mystery, myth, rumor, and conjecture surrounding Scottish Jewry, and transform the existing "tale of two cities" into a narrative of nine (but without forgetting those who are scattered elsewhere, too).

1

Aberdeen

As with much of Scottish Jewish history outside of Glasgow and Edinburgh, the history of the Jews of the Granite City—currently "the most northerly place of Jewish worship in the British Isles"[1]—is surrounded by rumor and conjecture. At some point the story was propagated that no Jews stayed long in Aberdeen because they felt that there was no livelihood to be made there. The *Jewish Chronicle* reported in 1910, for example, that "an old jibe says that a Jew cannot flourish in Aberdeen, and there is a well-known case of a wealthy Lord London Mayor who first tried his fame in the northern city and failed. Probably the truth is that few try."[2] According the historian and Celtic scholar William Skene:

> In "Reynolds's Miscellany," which was very widely read fifty years ago, appeared a short history of Aberdeen, in which it was stated that there were no Jews in the city, the following story being given as a reason. James VI had been under some obligation to the Jews, and as recompense to them, granted charters to settle where they pleased in the country. A few came to Aberdeen but were not long in returning whence they came. His Majesty got word of it, and sent for them to know the reason. They seemed diffident to answer, and His Majesty thought it might be the cold climate; still, he thought it could not be that, for there were Jews in St. Petersburg. In a lot of fencing, they said the reason why they came back was because they could not make a living, "as the people of Aberdeen were all Jews together."[3]

Skene provides no detail of the few Jews he states came to Aberdeen, nor does he explain his final comment. An observation from Israel Zangwill, who visited the city, however, does shed some light, noting that "the Aberdonians are hard-headed, close-fisted and logical," and adding with "sardonic amusement" that "there is a proverb that no Jew can settle among them."[4]

As we have seen, a "Thomas fil Isaac" was recorded in Aberdeen in the fourteenth century—his name pointing to possible Jewish origins—but he was "unlikely to have been Jewish as he married the king's daughter."[5] Elizabeth Caldwell Hirschmann and Donald N. Yates propose the existence of a "Judaic colony" in Aberdeen which expedited that burgh's "phenomenal growth as a trading center and financial capital."[6] Yet there is no known, verifiable record of Jews visiting before the nineteenth century.

Boats of Jews and Jewish Doctors

Leaping ahead to the seventeenth century, there is an entry in the matriculation album of Marischal College in the session of 1634–35 for Samuel Suecus. His name is similar to that of the son of Menasseh ben Israel, the Jewish scholar who negotiated with Cromwell the return of Jews to England in 1656, Samuel Suero.[7] Cecil Roth places the first record of Jews in Aberdeen in 1665 when he reports "to the effect that a barque with silken sails and cordage, manned by a crew speaking only Hebrew, had been sighted off Scotland."[8] This seems to refer to "A New Letter from Aberdeen in Scotland, Sent to a Person of Quality Wherein is a more full Account of the Proceedings of the Jewes Than hath been hitherto Published." This letter reported that a ship, with white silk ropes and white-branched satin sails emblazoned in red letters with the words "THESE ARE THE TEN TRIBES OF ISRAEL," put in at the port of Aberdeen. Aboard, stated the letter, was a large party of Jews, dressed in black and blue and with stores of rice and honey. The professor of Tongues and Languages was supposedly sent for. He determined that the crew spoke broken Hebrew and that they held a letter in High Dutch which said that they were bound for Amsterdam to correspond with their brethren there. Probably they would have been on their way to join the pseudo-messiah Shabbetai Tsvi in the Levant and would not have stayed in Aberdeen. Arthur Williamson identifies the author of this letter as Robert or Richard Burton,[9] but nothing more is known about it or the story

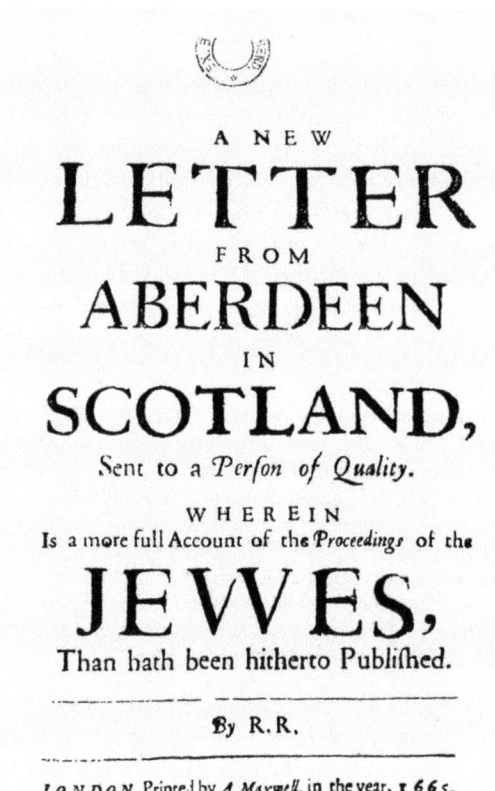

"A New Letter from Aberdeen"

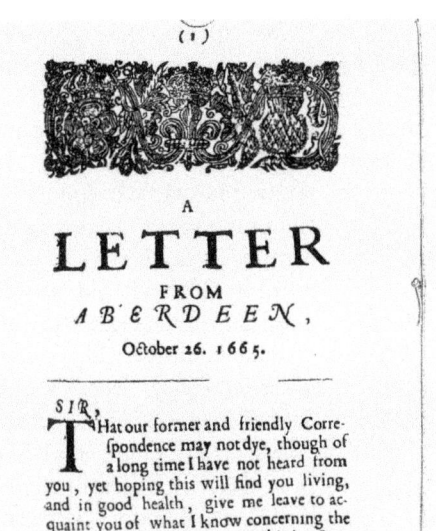

"A New Letter from Aberdeen"

it tells. We cannot even be certain that those aboard were indeed Jews; or indeed that the letter is anything other than a fiction, the product of a then-fashionable flight of a London imagination playing to a London audience and using Aberdeen as a convenient location because its remoteness made verification more difficult. Interesting in itself, rather than as evidence for the story this article puts on the record, "A New Letter..." is examined further in the appendices.[10]

There appears to be no further mention of Jews in Aberdeen until the eighteenth century. In their book *Gordons Under Arms; a Biographical Muster Roll of Officers Named Gordon in the Navies and Armies of Britain, Europe, America and in the Jacobite Risings*, Constance Oliver Skelton and John Malcolm Bulloch mention that the youngest son of John, Third Earl of Aboyne, born in 1732, married Isabella, "a Jewess, dau[ghter] of Elias Levi, with whose relations he had a lawsuit in 1769."[11]

Kenneth Collins has shown that medicine attracted Jews to Aberdeen. Between 1739 and 1829, sixteen Jews graduated in medicine from Aberdeen's two universities. They were largely foreign-trained refugees from the Portuguese Inquisition, and Aberdeen offered them a British medical qualification and a degree from a Scottish university that would have helped to "enhance their standing in society and to attract patients."[12] The standard of Aberdeen's two medical schools—Marischal College and, to a lesser extent, King's College—was considered to be on par with the best international institutions of higher learning. Unlike Oxford and Cambridge, moreover, there was open entry and religious toleration; and the fees and living expenses were relatively low. Consequently, the first Jews in the English-speaking world to graduate with degrees did so from Aberdeen.

The first Jew to graduate from Aberdeen was the *converso* Jacob de Castro Sarmento—already a medical graduate from the University of Coimbra. He received his M.D. in July 1739. But of the sixteen Jewish medical graduates, all but two were based in England; and, as was normal up until at least 1825, all of them took their degrees *in absentia*. They were Ralph Schomberg (1745), David Cohen (1755), Gumpertz Lewisohn (1775), Benjamin Lyon (1783), William Brodum (1791), Samuel Solomon (1796), Benjamin Lara (1802), Joseph da Cuhna (1814), Jacob Adolphus (1816), Daniel Baruch (1816), Emmanuel Pacifico (1817), Nathaniel Wallach (1819), Judah Israel Montefiore (1824), Daniel Garcia (1824), and Samuel Cardozo (1859).[13] In this period, degrees were conferred by recommendation from at least two patrons attesting to the candidate's medical standing, without written or oral examination; and, according to A. Levy:

"A New Letter from Aberdeen"

This was especially true of Aberdeen. It was the custom both at the university of Aberdeen at King's College, and at Marischal College and University to confer the degree of M.D. on anyone who was prepared to pay the fee and who could find two members of the senatus to sponsor him. Many Jewish physicians in London and elsewhere thus secured Aberdeen degrees but ... none of them are thought ever to have resided there.[14]

This *modus operandi* did not always produce the desired results. Both Solomon and Brodum turned out to be quack doctors. Solomon's affidavits, from two Liverpool doctors, were possibly forged, and he ended up making a fortune in that city selling his patent medicine, the Cordial Balm of Gilead. Having also tricked the medical authorities, Brodum successfully sold his Nervous Cordial and sexually explicit writings on the dangers, prevention, and treatment of sexually transmitted diseases.[15]

The first bona fide Jewish medical student who did move to Aberdeen was Ernest Henriques of Kingston, Jamaica. He came to study medicine, graduating in 1898, but left soon afterwards to practice in Lancashire—as did all other Jews who graduated with medical degrees from Aberdeen. Henriques's daughter, Stella, however, also studied in Aberdeen, graduating M.B.Ch.B. in 1923.[16]

As we move into the nineteenth century, there is yet more rumor and conjecture. In *East Neuk Chronicles*, William Skene's personal recollections of life in the nineteenth century, a short section on the "Jews in Aberdeen" claims that

> Another to whom the Townhouse door was a favourite rendezvous was Lazarus Myers. I can fancy I see him yet—wizened, round face and stubble beard, keen eyes looking through spectacles, and everlasting blue cloak, with brass chain at the neck ... by all accounts ever I heard he found money-lending, etc., profitable, and, like his great prototype "Shylock," he always secured his pound of flesh when it was obtainable by possible means. The late Sheriff Watson had a few of Lazarus's customers before him in his time. I believe Lazarus was the only Jew in Aberdeen for many years. He ultimately left the city, I understand, to end his days in his native Germany.[17]

But, as there is no record of Lazarus Myers in the 1881 Aberdeen census (which, incidentally, does record an "Isaac Myres" from Russia and a "Lazarus Lubon" from Poland), it may be that he was either the product of the dim recollection of a real Jew or a concoction, based heavily on anti–Semitic stereotypes, of Skene's imagination.

On surer ground, we do find evidence of Jews settling in Aberdeen from the 1840s onwards. The *Aberdeen Directory* for 1840–41 listed H. Rosenberg and Company as manufacturing furriers and importers of foreign skins at 115, Union Street. In the spring of 1842, the proprietor Harris Rosenberg, together with his wife Alethia Rosenberg (née Barnett), furriers described as "foreigners," were convicted of "wilfull fire-raising" at their shop premises.[18] Although there is no precise evidence to confirm their Jewishness, their first and last names certainly indicate a high probability of this being the case. Another possible Jew who lived in Aberdeen at that time was M.A. Levy, a tailor, clothier, and outfitter listed at 26, Union Street during 1849–50. At about the same time, Alfred Edersheim, born in Vienna in 1825, arrived in Aberdeen. Although Edersheim was born a Jew, he converted to Christianity and, after preaching for a time in Aberdeen, was appointed in 1849 to minister at the Free Church, Old Aberdeen. In 1861 health problems forced him to resign, and he left for Torquay.[19] Joseph Levenston was also living in Aberdeen at that time, as his son, Solomon Alexander, was born there in 1858. Until his death in 1897, Joseph practiced as a medical herbalist all over Scotland.[20]

The Growth of the Modern Community

Though individuals had been in Aberdeen previously, Jews did not start arriving in significant numbers until the later part of the nineteenth century. The Jewish painter Josef Israels, for example, visited his patron J. F. White and met the Scottish painters Chalmers, Reid and Cameron in Aberdeen at the end of May 1870. He stayed about two weeks, during which time he sat for a portrait which hangs in the city's Art Gallery.[21] The following year, Master Gunner J.C. Lyons of the Royal Artillery, who had survived the Crimean War and was a decorated soldier, was stationed at Fort Torry in Aberdeen when his daughter was born.[22] In 1873, however, he died suddenly in Aberdeen and was buried with full military honors according to Christian rites, despite being Jewish.[23] The years from 1881 to 1914 witnessed large-scale immigration into Britain from Eastern Europe and Russia by Jews either fleeing persecution or seeking economic betterment, a process eased by quicker and lower-priced mass transportation via railway and steamship.[24]

The 1881 census lists several Jewish families already resident in Aberdeen. Isaac Barnett (36) from Russia was a "Master Picture Dealer" living with his three children, Abraham (12), Jacob (10), and Elizabeth (7), at 42, East North Street. Myers Barnett (26) from Prussia, also a Master Picture Dealer, lived at 39, George Street with his wife Theresa (an unusual name for a Jewish woman) and their children Frederick (1) and Ernst (three months), both born in Aberdeen. Samuel Dreyer (55), an unmarried peddler from Prussia, was boarding at Chronicle Cottage, as was twenty-four-year-old Louis Reelman, another unmarried peddler. At 10, Justice Lane, Lazarus Lubon (21), a glazier from Russen, Poland, was boarding. The Myres family was living at 52, Hadden Street. They consisted of Isaac (35), another Picture Frame Maker, from Souvalk Stakie, Russia; his wife Leah (33) from Souvalk Servent, Russia, listed as a "Picture Frame Makers Wife" [sic]; and their children—Hannah (14), a wool millworker who was also born in Russia, Sarah (12), born in Hull and listed as a "scholar," Ellen (11), born in Aberdeen, Rebecca (10), Rine (8), Esther (6), and Moses (five months). Given that Ellen was born in Aberdeen, the Myres had arrived there c.1870. These Jews were engaged in a limited number of immigrant trades and were living mainly in the less salubrious areas towards the east of the city center, like Constitution Street, Hadden Street, Justice Street, East North Street, and Guest Row. The *Aberdeen Directory* similarly contains entries for Jews such as Alex Zamek, the future president of the synagogue, who is first listed in 1884–85. Zamek, who was from Poland, was naturalized in 1887.[25]

Religious Concerns

Religious concerns were central to Aberdeen's Jews. But as they were a small group and were, "with very few exceptions, of the poorest class,"[26] a synagogue was not immediately affordable. They may have worshipped in private or met informally in someone's home, but we have no evidence of this. Evidently, it took a great deal of debate to form the community.[27] An 1893 report in *The Scotsman* stated that a "feeling was said to have existed for a considerable time among the Jews resident in Aberdeen that a synagogue should be established in the city," and that unsuccessful attempts had been made to form a congregation.[28] As Kenneth Collins put it, "The small group of Jews had been there for many years but had hesitated to take the step of formalising a community structure."[29] Then, in the fall of 1893, "[t]hey took the plunge" and found suitable premises, and the formal community was established on September 7 when the synagogue was consecrated by the Russian and Polish Jewish community of Aberdeen.[30]

Because the community was not wealthy, the *shul* was not purpose-built but located in two rented rooms on the first floor of a house at 34, Marischal Street, opposite Trinity Quay in the dockyard area of Aberdeen. It was described as "one of the lowest quarters of the town."[31] A later congregant recalled the overwhelming fishy smell that would blow in off the North Sea. It cost £400, and because the congregation consisted of eight members "of whom only five can be looked to for substantial support," the community looked to wealthier Jews in London and the provinces for financial support.[32] The *Jewish Chronicle* reported that the "synagogue has been furnished in a handsome manner and presented a bright aspect."[33]

According to the *Aberdeen Journal*, the synagogue's president, Alex Zamek, expressed the optimistic feeling that although the synagogue

> was not all that could be desired as yet, ... in the course of fifteen or twenty years, when they were more prosperous than they were at present, they would have a synagogue similar to those of Glasgow and Edinburgh. [T]he congregation would not be a large one for some time and he did not think they had any reason to be ashamed of their little synagogue.[34]

At the same time, provision was made for a minister, the Reverend James Littman, who was also the teacher of the Hebrew classes, circumciser, and slaughterer.[35] Charitable and welfare organizations were set up to assist poorer Jews; even the General Assembly of the Scottish Church noted that Aberdeen's Jewish "poor are well cared for by their own rabbis and the better-off people."[36] There was also a keen interest in Zionism. A Shekel Group was formed in 1900 with five members, and Aberdeen's Jews bought six shares in the Jewish Colonial Trust established by Theodore Herzl in London in March 1899 as the financial instrument of the Zionist movement, promoting colonization schemes in Palestine.[37]

Immediately after the congregation was formed, the Minister and *Shochet*, the Reverend James Littman, together with its president, Alexander Zamek, were put on trial. The local branch of the Society for the Prevention of Cruelty to Animals persuaded the procurator fiscal to prosecute Littman and Zamek for "the slaughter of a bullock after the Hebrew manner, in connection with recent celebrations in the opening of [the] synagogue."[38] It was also alleged that the pair had "cruelly ill-treat[ed] and torture[d]" said bullock.[39] Just days before Littman killed his first bullock in Aberdeen, the Swiss had voted in a nationwide referendum to ban *shechita* (the Jewish method of slaughter). The evidence did not support the charges, and the Magistrate found the case not proven. It was dismissed and the judgment given that the *shechita* had been properly and skillfully carried out. *Shechita* resumed in Aberdeen during the following year, and a special delivery of Scottish beef was sent daily to London.[40]

"There was a widespread feeling, both within the Jewish community and beyond," according to Kenneth Collins, "that antisemitic motives had been prominent, and that if Littman had been found guilty then further shechitah in Aberdeen would have been hard to sustain."[41] Indeed, Collins feels that if the prosecution had succeeded, "a defeat in Aberdeen might have led to attempts to ban shechitah in other parts of the UK."[42] But this assertion flies in the face of the available evidence. Chief Rabbi Dr. Hermann Adler expressed his confidence that "in Scotland, where the Hebrew scriptures are so deeply venerated, nothing will be done to prevent Jews from obeying *kashrut*."[43] Furthermore, the case was probably brought because of a genuine concern for the welfare of the animal and because it was the first time that *shechita* had been practiced in Aberdeen, rather than from motives of anti-Semitism.[44] The Aberdeen Association for the Prevention of Cruelty to Animals was at pains to point out that the case was not brought about by a desire to question the Jewish method of slaughter in general, but because of the lack of "proper care and skill" on this particular occasion. A century later, a similar incident occurred when the Grampian Goat Club's magazine published "a biased article on ritual slaughter." However, this time it invited the president of the congregation to reply, and as a result, a "continuing and amicable relationship" ensued, and the society even asked if the Jewish community could make use of unwanted kids![45]

Unable to afford a permanent rabbi, Aberdeen's Jews engaged a series of visiting ministers on short-term contacts, a practice fairly typical of the smaller Scottish communities. Often, such ministers were required to perform multiple tasks and were not well paid. Littman stayed in Aberdeen for several years and was succeeded by the Reverend Morris Cohen, who likewise only remained for a short duration before being replaced by the Reverend A.E. Hirshovitz.[46] By 1907, the minister was the Reverend Itzig Ostrow (known as Isaac Ostroff) from Russia.[47] One of the reasons for this high turnover of ministers, a trend typical of all the small communities in Scotland, was, in the words of Kenneth Collins, their "notoriously low" salaries; but he is harsh in suggesting that this reflected a lack of respect for the religious leadership rather than a simple lack of funds. Nevertheless, the low pay "led to the need to augment income by means of teaching or accepting gratuities for the rendering of religious services."[48]

As Aberdeen offered little opportunity for large-scale employment for Jews, its community was never large. According to the *Jewish Year Book*, there were twelve seat holders in Aberdeen in 1896–97, although the *Aberdeen Journal* reported fifty present at the inaugural Jewish New Year services in September 1893;[49] and the community was sizeable enough to merit a visit from the then Chief Rabbi of Great Britain, Dr. Hermann Adler, in 1896.[50] He exhorted the congregation to keep the Sabbath more strictly than several were in the habit of doing, implying that religious standards were somewhat lax in Aberdeen.[51] Even though it was small, the community had made a large enough impact for the seriously misinformed Emanuel "Manny" Steen to recall, in the late nineteenth century, that "there's a big Jewish settlement in Aberdeen"![52] By 1907–1908 the community had almost doubled to twenty-three seat holders, and Adler paid it another visit, the last time the incumbent of that position has visited the city.[53] At that point, the 1905 Aliens Act had reduced the numbers entering Britain, and this would have limited further growth in Aberdeen to internal migration.

A cemetery was founded in 1913 when a portion of the public Grove Cemetery was sectioned off for use as a Jewish burial site as dictated by Jewish law. Up until that point Aberdeen's Jews were buried in Glasgow or Edinburgh, most likely at great expense and difficulty given that both cities were about one hundred and fifty miles away. Stella Edelshain, for example, was interred in the Jewish section of Newington Cemetery (formerly Echobank), Edinburgh, when she died in 1909, and Alexander Zamek was buried in the Western Necropolis in Glasgow in 1908. It was only in 1913 that a Jewish burial site within Aberdeen's public cemetery was secured (although Samuel Edelshain was also buried with his wife in Edinburgh when he passed away in 1917).[54]

Shortly before the outbreak of the First World War, for example, the Reverend Israel Frankenthal, born in Meah Shearim in Jerusalem in 1889, and thus still officially a Turkish citizen, came from Trieste to act as cantor, circumciser, butcher, teacher, and visitor to His Majesty's Prison Peterhead, where, incidentally, he met the wrongly-convicted Oscar Slater. His salary of £1/12/6 per week was so meager for a family of three children that he learned cabinet-making and opened a store in Guest Row. Eventually he left for a presumably better-paid ministerial post in Glasgow.[55] The First World War also had some impact on the community's figures. The number of seat holders dropped from twenty-five in 1911 to twenty in 1914, and eighteen by the end of the war. Jewish enemy aliens in Aberdeen were threatened with internment or repatriation, and the *Jewish Chronicle* reported that the congregation "lost several members owing to the present crisis." [56] E. Hyams, for example, resigned as secretary because he had been called up for military service.

The Reverend Israel Frankenthal

Eking Out a Livelihood

What, then, attracted Jews to such a remote and isolated place, especially one that "enjoyed the reputation, rightly or wrongly, of being the only town in Scotland where Jews could not eke out a livelihood"?[57] Since Jews had primarily been town dwellers in Eastern Europe, and were restricted to certain trades such as finance, tobacco and clothing, Jewish immigrants to Britain tended to migrate towards urban rather than rural areas.[58] Furthermore, they "gravitated towards occupations requiring skills they already possessed, or which could be easily learned, and where language problems could be minimized."[59]

By the late nineteenth century, Aberdeen was a fair-sized city, ranking as the twenty-second largest provincial town. Its population in 1871 stood at 88,198, almost doubling to 163, 891 by 1911.[60] Its economy was based on a number of industries. Paper-making, granite quarrying and polishing, Aberdeen Angus beef cattle rearing, and shipbuilding were all in existence, but by the last third of the nineteenth century the city's main reputation was based on fishing. Unsurprisingly, given its location, Aberdeen had always been a thriving port, but from the 1870s onward it underwent something of a herring boom; "'Aberdeen herring' became a mark of quality in the Baltic where the burgh's seaborne commerce had long been active."[61] In 1882, the fishing industry was transformed by the arrival of the first steam trawler, and white fish stocks, primarily cod and haddock, began to be exploited. As a result, Aberdeen flourished; the trawlers were mainly built there, and subsidiary industries, such as ice provision, fish processing, and box making, flourished, bringing in more and more wealth. By 1914, Aberdeen was the third largest fishing port in Britain and the largest in Scotland.[62] Such a destination would have proved attractive to the mainly poor, newly-arrived Jews.

When the Aberdeen Hebrew Congregation was formed in the 1890s, the majority of its members were self-employed, working at home or in backstreet workshops in crafts such as cabinet-making, tailoring and shoe- and hat-making. Or they were petty shopkeepers and poor peddlers and hawkers—traveling salesmen who traveled widely to the villages of the northeast, selling their wares and returning home for the Sabbath.[63] Their language and accents would have been a mixture of Yiddish, English, and Scottish. These first commercial travelers would have settled in Glasgow and other Scottish towns in the central belt, venturing north by train to Aberdeen and returning home for the Shabbat. Some eventually settled there, taking advantage of the economic opportunities thus explored.[64] Beginning as peddlers, many bought properties and settled down as shopkeepers. Most enjoyed a modest living, though they were probably "not infrequently ... tempted to accept payment in kind."[65] Aberdeen's Jews retained a fairly homogenous occupational status until the end of the First World War. They were concentrated in a fairly small number of trades and retail businesses—tailoring, furniture, shoes, fish, clothing, fur, and fruit. One of the more unusual occupations was that of Alexander Zamek, the founding president of the Congregation who was cited in the Aberdeen Small Debt Court in 1896 as a "Jewish usurer."[66]

The size of Aberdeen's Jewish community was also boosted by the seasonal influx of commercial agents. The *Scotsman* reported that "[d]uring the herring season Jewish salesmen from Russia, who do business at Aberdeen, Peterhead, and Fraserburgh, augment the resident Jewish community."[67] In the days before the First World War, Jews were involved in, or with, the firms that handled the herring trade with Russia, through ports such as Riga, Memel, Saint Petersburg and Königsberg.[68] Others may have worked or traveled on the fishing fleets during herring season, such as Leon Harris (Charap) from Sokolufka, Galicia. Indeed, since "the herring is an ambulatory fish" (the shoals move on), it stands as a particularly apt metaphor for the Jews of Aberdeen in general.[69]

There is evidence that the pioneering Jewish peddlers did not stop at Aberdeen but used it as a base for going further afield. Harry, Louis, Hyman, and Woolf Greenwald (né Pochapovsky) traveled from Gorodea (a Belarusian *shtetl* near Minsk) to Glasgow and then Aberdeen, before settling in Lerwick. After having landed in Glasgow, they trudged along dirt roads to Aberdeen, attempting to sell jewelry along the way and picking up the occasional lift on farm wagons. From Aberdeen they took the *S.S. St. Magnus* to Shetland, where they eventually settled.[70] Julius Quint, another peddler who made his living trudging along the roads of Shetland, probably also arrived there via Aberdeen.[71] Around 1879, according to the 1891 census, Isaac Salberg and his wife Annie passed through Aberdeen (as two of their children, Barnett and Abraham, were born in the city) before they relocated to Glasgow.[72] Another example was Hartze Kahan, a Lithuanian immigrant who, as the family story is told, intended to emigrate to America but stopped in Aberdeen to do business for his father, who was an importer-exporter in Lithuania. At the boarding house where he was staying he met Sophia Livingstone, the owner's daughter, and they married. Sophia's family was Russian, originally named Levi, who had previously moved to Aberdeen. Sophia and Hartze then moved to Dundee, where they settled.[73]

Professionalization

Between the wars Aberdeen's Jews benefited from a United Kingdom-wide trend in which, in the words of William D. Rubinstein, "provincial Jewry now became more important in the lives of their towns than before the Great War, as the community became acculturated and as the gentile manufacturing dynasties of Britain's industrial revolution years often sold out or demonstrated profound entrepreneurial decline."[74] As a sign of this, some of the more successful began to branch out. Ernest Bromberg was the proprietor of Aberdeen's first public dance hall, the Palais de Dance, situated in Diamond Street. As Bromberg was an avid cinema enthusiast, he began to hold cinema-oriented events there from 1926, such as the Aberdeen Cinema Ball. Bromberg subsequently opened Aberdeen's first News Cinema in September 1936 (it ran until 1963, when he sold the cinema).[75] Other Jewish professionals also arrived in Aberdeen, such as Bennett Teff in 1936, a civil servant in customs and excise.[76]

Around this time, native-born Jews began to graduate from university, entering professions such as medicine, law, and teaching. Their economic success led to their movement away from original areas of settlement towards the more affluent West End. Aberdeen–born Dorothy Gershon graduated in medicine from the University of Aberdeen in 1928, as did Montague Franklin, of Argyll Place, born in Aberdeen in 1915, ten years later in 1938. Both qualified as doctors. Aberdeen–born Jews began to be joined, from 1923 onwards, by foreign Jews, such as Theodore Chanoch, a South African medical student at the University of Aberdeen who tragically died in a car crash at age eighteen.[77] From 1927 onwards, American Jews, unable to gain places in medical schools in the United States where a *numerus clausus* had come into operation, began to study in Aberdeen.[78] Eleven Americans were admitted in 1928, and in 1930 there were two hundred and three applicants for places in medicine. Virtually all of those who applied were graduates of either New York University or the City College of New York (the "Jewish" university). Other overseas Jews came from South Africa. Most of these graduates, however, only stayed temporarily, returning home to practice medicine, sometimes taking (non–Jewish) Scottish brides with them.[79] A survey conducted by Geoffrey D.M. Block in 1936–37 found that out of a population of 1,272 students at the University of Aberdeen, two Jews (or 0.16 percent) were enrolled there.[80] Rubinstein points out, however, that "this figure is an underestimate" because Block's results relied upon data "provided by the Secretaries of the Inter-University Jewish Federation," and hence any student who did not belong to that organization was most likely excluded.[81]

By this time the character of the community was Eastern European. Indeed, Aberdeen has never had a strong Sephardic influence—if Sephardim did visit, it was only temporarily as students or visiting scholars—and those Sephardic Jewish students who took degrees never even came to Aberdeen. This Eastern European Ashkenazi flavor remained, but members of British birth began to predominate—with the "exception of an element of elderly foreign immigrants"—until, in 1936, a trickle of the German Jews who came to Britain as refugees from Nazism began to arrive in Aberdeen.[82] In 1938 the Aberdeen Refugee Committee was established and was "instrumental in bringing a number of Jewish families into Aberdeen."[83] One of those was the Kress family, who had left Vienna after their father was imprisoned in Dachau.[84] Other notable figures also arrived, including the eminent philosopher Emil Fackenhim and his father Julius; the academic Peter Landsberg; the academic and Soviet expert Rudolf Schlesinger; and the educators Kurt Hahn, Karl König, Trude Amann, Barbara Lipsker, Thomas Weihs, Peter Roth, Alix Roth, Marie Korach, and Alex Baum. Many came to the University of Aberdeen as either staff or students, or set up educational institutions, such as Gordonstoun School, founded by Hahn, and the Camphill–Rudolf Steiner schools, established by König and others.

In Glasgow there is evidence that similar arrivals created divisions within the Jewish community, but in Aberdeen the newcomers were integrated quickly and fully into what was a small community. Julius Fackenheim, who was to become president of the congregation, was a good example. Furthermore, the arrival of these more assimilated, educated, middle-class German Jews assisted the increasing *embourgeoisement* of the indigenous community.

Fascism in Aberdeen

Although Fascism came to Aberdeen in the 1930s, it did not seem to affect the Jewish community. When Oswald Mosley attempted to organize a rally and march in Aberdeen in the 1930s, little mention was made of it by the Jewish community, perhaps because the congregation wanted to maintain its typical low profile. It certainly didn't stop the aforementioned German–Jewish refugees from moving to the area. According to Colin Cross, Aberdeen was "the real centre of Scottish Fascism, where W.K.A.J Chambers–Hunter, a former planter from Ceylon, who had lost an arm in the war, ran a keen, lively group."[85] Under the guidance of Chambers–Hunter, British Union of Fascists (B.U.F.) policy classes were well attended in Aberdeen (at least according to the B.U.F. itself), and Fascists were in the streets selling pamphlets and canvassing voters (for which, in September 1936, the Aberdeen Branch was the first Scottish branch to be awarded the Oswald Mosley Cup for paper sales). A propaganda campaign was launched throughout the northeast of Scotland and public meetings were held in Aberdeen, Banchory, Kemnay, Inverurie, Forres, Peterhead, Turffif, Oldmeldrum, and Stonehaven. At all of these meetings the fascist newspaper *Action* was sold and other literature distributed.

Nevertheless, Mosley made little headway in Aberdeen outside of the local group. Liz Kibblewhite and Andy Rigby explain that the reasons why "the fascist campaign in Scotland between 1936 and 1939 was centered on Aberdeen was not due to any firmly held belief that the population was particularly susceptible to fascist propaganda," but rather down to the "commitment and determination" of Chambers–Hunter himself.[86] B.U.F. meetings were often heckled and its rallies disrupted. In July 1937, the press reported the abandonment of a B.U.F. meeting and the escape of its members under police protection when 7,000 to 8,000 people gathered to chant, "Down with Fascist murderers.... Mosley shall not pass.... One, two, three, four, five, we want Mosley dead or alive."[87] The following year a lorry used as a platform by five Fascist speakers was mobbed by a crowd of six thousand, and three B.U.F. members, including Chambers–Hunter (by then the prospective parliamentary candidate for North Aberdeen), were taken to hospital. B.U.F. activity ended in Aberdeen in 1939.[88] In general, this fitted the trend in Scotland whereby the B.U.F.'s advance was slow; as Cross states, "The most difficult area was Scotland where, throughout its existence, the B.U.F. found it impossible to make headway."[89]

The Second World War and Beyond

During the Second World War the size of the community was temporarily boosted by the influx of London medical students who were relocated to Aberdeen along with other evacuees, refugees, and military personnel. One refugee, Walter Kress' father, was employed by Mitchell & Muil bakery to produce continental and Jewish specialties, and another, Emil Fackenheim, was hired to tutor the children in Hebrew. As a result of the greater numbers, Friday night services were resumed, and one Aberdeen resident recollected that in order to make up the required numbers, "the secretary of our tiny little synagogue would go up to Union Street and try to find Jewish servicemen" from Australia, Canada, France, South Africa, occupied Europe, and other parts of the world.[90] Services for members of the Armed Forces also took place on alternate Sundays, officiated by H. Brookfield.[91] Service personnel were also entertained by the local residents. Joseph Bordoley, who was stationed at an R.A.F. radar station near Aberdeen, recalled meeting at Bennett Teff's house, as well as at Ernest Bromberg's dance hall. Coincidentally, Joseph's son Allen at one point dated Teff's daughter, Elizabeth.[92] The community was involved in the British Red Cross Society.[93] James Leo Rosengarten of Huntly celebrated his bar mitzvah in 1942, the "first to be held in the synagogue for many years."[94] The Scottish Union for Justice for the Jews was set up in Aberdeen, led by various non–Jewish local notables such as Mrs. W. Moncrieff Paterson and Major Malcolm Hay of Seaton. Its purpose was to put the Jewish case before non–Jews and to disseminate accurate information. To this end, a shop front exhibit explaining the Jewish contribution to the Allied course was opened.[95] Members of the community also fought in the war: Flight Sergeant (Navigator) Henry Max Bittiner of the R.A.F. was recorded as missing in 1944.[96]

The post-war era saw the community grow and become wealthier and more established. One of those who arrived was Louis Cohen, born in Glasgow in 1913. After finishing his military service, Louis came to Aberdeen to marry a local girl. He stayed and set up a barber's shop. From then on, Aberdeen's permanent community was primarily located in the professional and business classes, especially academia. Fittingly, in 1945 the congregation acquired a Georgian terraced house for use as a synagogue. The principal ground floor room was adapted and furnished along similar lines to those found in all Orthodox synagogues. In June of that year, a new and larger synagogue—incorporating a sanctuary as well as communal areas and living space for the minister—was consecrated at 74, Dee Street with the name "*Ohel Yaacov*" (Tent of Jacob), where it remains as such to this day. This involved a move from the two unsuitable rented rooms near the docks into an entire building—converted for sacramental use—in a relatively affluent part in the center of the city. The renovation of the building, and its adaptation to the community's requirements, was assisted by a Jewish architect from the Chief Rabbi's Office. The new synagogue sat approximately sixty. The plan was enthusiastically supported by Aberdeen's Jewish population of fifty residents, who contributed more than fifty percent of the £1,600 costs.[97]

The community advertised its new profile by holding a consecration ceremony, described by one witness as "pretentious," attended by local dignitaries such as the Lord Provost, the Bishop of Aberdeen, other leading churchmen, press reporters and photographers, and key Jews like Sir Maurice Bloch, Rabbi Kopel Rosen (then the communal rabbi of Glasgow), the Reverend Israelstam of Bradford (acting padre for Scotland), and Mr. H. Brookfield (the Minister to the Congregation). A gold key was specially cut for the occasion and pre-

Consecration of 74, Dee Street, 1945. (Photograph courtesy of the Aberdeen Hebrew Congregation.)

sented to Sir Maurice during a reception in the communal hall.[98] Aberdeen's Jews, clearly, had become well integrated into the civic life of the city and of Scotland in general.

In addition to the Aberdeen Hebrew Congregation, in 1946 Aberdeen had a Jewish Literary and Social Society which met on at least a quarterly basis at the synagogue's chambers. Two years later, in 1948, a Women's International Zionist Organization (W.I.Z.O.) group was formed, with fourteen members, and when it ceased activity, the Zionist work was taken over by the Ladies' Guild. In that year the *Jewish Echo* contained the report "Aberdeen is Proud" and a letter from one of its Jewish residents: "Aberdeen's little Jewish community are feeling quite proud of themselves, and we feel, rightly so. With a population of not more than 50 souls, we have raised a total amount of £610 for the Joint Palestine Appeal."[99] Despite this clear Zionist feeling in Aberdeen, the establishment of the state of Israel in 1948, which led to the emigration of some British Jews—in 1947, this was recorded as fifty, rising sharply in 1955 and 1956 to one hundred and eighty one and one hundred and seventy five respectively—had no discernable impact on the Aberdeen population.

In 1953, during his report at the annual general meeting of the Aberdeen Hebrew Congregation, President Dr. Julius Fackenheim reported that the congregation "had increased in size."[100] Although the community lost one of its oldest members with the death of Israel Lann, and the Teff family had moved to London in 1950, it grew with the arrival of two new families. The congregation was also able to appoint "for the first time" a full-time minister, Harry Jacobi, to take charge of the services and the education of the "growing number of children."[101] At age thirteen, Jacobi was the last boy to be bar mitzvahed in the Friedenstempel synagogue in Berlin before it was burned down on *kristallnacht*.[102] He stayed in Aberdeen from 1953 until 1956. The preceding year, however, the community suffered a decline in membership, as several families had left Aberdeen. Friday and Saturday services were still well attended nonetheless, and a monthly children's service was now being held. A new education committee to improve religious classes and adult education had also been set up.[103] By 1955, the congregation held a monthly *Oneg Shabbat* (and continues to do so today).[104]

Despite the decline in membership, the congregation was still able, and sufficiently prosperous, to appoint in 1956, for the first time, a permanent rabbi. This was a rare occurrence for such a small and isolated community, and, as we shall see, only Dundee and Dunfermline were able to do the same (incidentally, by hiring the same person). The Aberdeen appointee was Dr. Gustav Pfingst, who was born in Germany in 1900. He studied at the University of Wurzberg and then in Berlin under Rabbi Leo Baeck. His last post in Germany was in Landsberg, where his synagogue was destroyed by the Nazis in 1938 and he was thrown into a concentration camp. He managed to escape and emigrate to Great Britain in 1939, and held posts in Cheltenham and Leeds before moving to Aberdeen with his wife Rosa and their two children.[105] Rabbi Pfingst was active in not just the congregation's affairs, but also in those of the wider non–Jewish community. In November 1956, for example, he addressed an interfaith meeting with the Aberdeen Unitarians.[106] In a visit to Aberdeen, the Reverend Dr. I.K. Cosgrove of Glasgow praised Pfingst for his work "knitting the Community together" during the short time he had been in Aberdeen. As a result, Cosgrove observed, the "Aberdeen Jewish Community clung to their beliefs and put them into practice despite many difficulties." He added, for good measure, that this "was a sign that the 'Northern Jews' were determined not to let out the light."[107] Unfortunately, Rabbi Pfingst died in 1957.

The congregation found it impossible to replace Pfingst. This was most likely in part because of the congregation's decreasing ability to afford one—in 1957 its figure dropped dramatically to seventy, never thereafter rising higher than eighty-five in 1959–61—and the remote northerly aspect of the city, which would not appeal to the more religious members of the British Jewish community from whose ranks a minister would be drawn. From then on, the community entered a period of statistical decline, dropping to a low of twenty in 1964–65 (the comparable *Jewish Year Book* figure for the middle of the first decade of the twenty-first century being thirty). A number of factors accounts for this falling away: an aging population; intermarriage; emigration, as children moved away to university, in search of employment, or to find a suitable marriage partner; and families with young children moving to a location with a more developed Jewish infrastructure. The community's situation was not helped by the downturn in the city of Aberdeen's fortunes after the Second World War. As Robin Smith has pointed out, "Aberdeen remained primarily a major fishing port, and generally was not really thriving in the half century up to 1970. This was due to the decline of the local textile industry ... to falling demand for granite in buildings and tombstones, to overfishing of the North Sea, and to the drift of population towards central Scotland with its New Towns."[108]

Decline and Revival

In 1960 the Jewish population of Aberdeen was eighty-five.[109] Eight of those were children who were now being taught by the Reverend Ordman on Sundays and twice during the week.[110] When Dr. Julius Fackenheim retired as president of the congregation in 1959, his role was taken over by Phil and Sarah Orkin from Canada. Phil taught zoology at the University of Aberdeen, while Sarah was the first registered dietician in the city. Phil led the services and the Seders, and their house became the focus of the community, as they opened their home to members of the community, visitors, and students who met for activities and Friday evening meals. Two of those students were Valerie and Frank House, from London, who visited Aberdeen as part of an academic conference in 1963. They later returned to study in Aberdeen and stayed for five years when Frank became a lecturer in pharmacology and statistics at the University of Aberdeen Medical School. Their two sons were born there, and their *brit milot* were performed by a rabbi from Edinburgh. High Holyday services were led by a trainee rabbi. Kosher meat was obtained from Glasgow or Edinburgh, and occasionally from London, sent by train.[111]

During the 1970s the congregation continued to be quite vibrant. Classes for the children continued, and the Jewish Students' Society ran regular events. Some of the students also attended synagogue services. The community and students in Aberdeen were also looked after by the Student Chaplaincy Northern Region. During a fundraising meeting for that body it was said: "Aberdeen with its Jewish community of 13 to 15 families had given more than the Glasgow Jewish community with 15,000 people."[112] The congregation also attempted to foster education about Jewish matters in the general community, hosting visitors to the synagogues or giving lectures on Judaism. In 1979 the Orkins left for London after thirty-one years in Aberdeen, when Dr. Orkin retired from his post as senior lecturer.

The following year, in 1980, the community was advertising kosher accommodation, following the opening of a Jewish student flat, or a "mini-Hillel," located on the top floor of the synagogue.[113] Rabbi Dr. J. Weinberg, minister of the Edinburgh Hebrew Congregation, visited the community and urged them to keep the synagogue open for Shabbat services even if it was not always possible to obtain a *minyan*, indicating that declining numbers in Aberdeen had taken its toll on attendance.[114] According to the then Secretary of the Aberdeen Hebrew Congregation, "Within a radius of 15 miles, the number of known Jewish inhabitants comprises 25 adults and eight children."[115] One of those was Ben Collins, a stalwart of the community who, at the age of eighty-one, was possibly the oldest active commercial traveler in Britain.[116] Services were held on Friday nights, followed by a beginner's course in Hebrew conducted by Adrian Foreman. Shabbat morning services took place on the first Saturday of every month, a practice that continues today.

In 1983 the synagogue was refurbished, and the Fred Gold Youth and Community Centre was opened above the sanctuary on the first floor of 74, Dee Street.[117] The help of Alfred Dunitz, an expert at restoring Georgian synagogues and cemeteries in isolated Jewish communities, was enlisted. He recalled writing to about thirty wealthy individuals in Glasgow, eventually receiving only £25 from Goldberg's departmental stores. Instead, much of the money was provided by charitable trusts and local donations.[118] A consecration ceremony, led by the Reverend Malcolm Weisman, was held, at which he expressed the wish that Aberdeen's oil boom would see the restored building become a focal point for the expanding community.[119] Four years later, the "small but active" congregation celebrated its first bar mitzvah in over a decade, that of Steven Shrago, at which more than seventy people literally packed out the synagogue.[120] By the end of the decade the community was still able to attract a *minyan* for Shabbat services.[121]

By 1990 six people typically attended the monthly Shabbat service. Jonathan Shrago's bar mitzvah attracted eighty people, doubling the size of the community, albeit temporarily. The Students' Jewish Society was still running and held a bagel brunch in 1994.[122] One of those in attendance was Berty Matus, a pharmacy student from Israel, who was also a referee in the English premier basketball league. Three years later, Shir Moaz, the son of Israeli architecture student Dror, was circumcised by Rabbi Moderchai Bamberger, Scotland's only *mohel*.[123] In 1998 the stalwarts of the community, the Shragos, left Aberdeen. Lionel and his wife Sandra were the president and secretary, respectively, of the congregation, and Lionel also took the services and continued to act as lay reader over the High Holy Days. At that point membership stood at fifteen families but swelled to about forty over the festivals as a result of a high number of Israeli and Jewish university students. Dr. Leslie Stankler replaced Lionel Shrago as president, and Yonni Shoshan, Ramsay Brown, and Ehud Reiter joined the committee as treasurer, deputy chair, and secretary, respectively. All three men remain on the committee at the time of this writing.[124]

The 2001 census recorded one hundred and seven people putting Jewish as their current religion, and one hundred and fifty five as their religion of upbringing. But the census is not entirely reliable as a guide to those who identify and affiliate with the community; in addition to the caution mentioned in the Introduction that the census most likely underestimated the number of Jews in Aberdeen because Jews, and especially older members of the community, have a strong reluctance to volunteering their identity to the government, not all Jews choose to join the local congregation.[125] It pointed to a fairly affluent, professional community engaged in business and academia as the largest concentrations of those who gave Jewish as their current religion in Aberdeen, a community located in Old Aberdeen, where the University of Aberdeen is situated, and the West End, the wealthier area of the city. In that same year, Daniel Shoshan celebrated his bar mitzvah, the first since Jonathan Shrago's in 1990. Two days later, Rotem Gelfer was circumcised.[126]

Aberdeen Hebrew Congregation synagogue, exterior. (Photograph by Nathan Abrams.)

From 2004 the community has witnessed something of a mini-revival. At this point the *Jewish Year Book* listed the congregation as having thirty members, which amounted to fourteen paying units of membership, incorporating both individuals and families. This figure belies the actual number of non-members who participate in at least one of the community's activities during the year, which is around one-third of the one hundred and seventy four Jews recorded in Aberdeenshire and Aberdeen in the 2001 census, according to its vice-president, Ehud Reiter.[127] In July 2004 David Taylor celebrated his bar mitzvah. Unfortunately, that same year the community's oldest member, Louis Cohen, passed away at the age of ninety one and was buried in the Grove cemetery. Prayers are held every Friday, although attendance is usually low (sometimes a lone individual), and a Shabbat service is held on the first

Aberdeen Hebrew Congregation synagogue, interior. (Photograph by Nathan Abrams.)

Saturday of the month, which attracts higher figures, as does monthly Friday night suppers held in the synagogue. Rabbi David Rose of the Edinburgh Hebrew Congregation visits on a monthly basis to deliver a *shiur* (informal lecture) and also to teach the children. Other events have been held, such as a celebration to mark the sixtieth anniversary of the consecration of the synagogue in June 2005, and a joint Purim celebration with the University of Aberdeen in which a fourteenth-century *Megillat Esther* (Book of Esther) was read, with eighty guests in attendance. During that period the Aberdeen University Students' Jewish Society was re-established, reflecting a small but growing number of Jewish students choosing to study there.

A City of Tolerance

The surviving records suggest that overt anti–Semitism was not a major feature of Aberdeen Jewish life. Jews were generally tolerated and welcomed by their gentile neighbors. Non–Jews were recorded as being present at various Jewish events, and entry to golf clubs was not denied to Jews, as in other British cities such as Glasgow. Indeed, in 1909, Leopold Bittiner won second prize in the Christmas competition of the Balnagash Club.[128] The following year Louis Bittiner was unanimously elected as the candidate for Aberdeen Parish Council; he went on to become the vice-chairman of the local ward committee.[129] Other than the *shechita* case mentioned above, and which was not specifically motivated by anti-Semitism, the only sour note was a motion proposed by the Aberdeen Trades Council critical of alien workers in the garment trade in 1881.[130] Since the end of the Second World War, only a few mentions of anti-Semitic incidents have been found. Just outside Aberdeen, an issue of the *Banffshire Journal and Northern Farmer* in April 1954 contained an advertisement which read, "You do not need to deal with Jews. Order from your own people at..." The editor, John Meldrum, wrote to the *Jewish Echo* explaining apologetically that the "advertisement went through our advertisement department without either the manager or myself being informed of this deplorable statement.... I am surprised that Mr [name not given] should have done this since he must meet a lot of Jewish people in his very wide business travels and have considerable dealings with them."[131]

Some three decades later, in the 1980s, there was evidence of some anti–Zionist and anti–Semitic activity in Aberdeen. Moves to twin the University of Aberdeen with one in the West Bank, as well as attempts to block visiting Israeli delegations, were attempted, but generally these reflected the wishes of a small minority of political activists rather than being the result of any general feeling. Such efforts were in no way comparable to the events that were to take place in Dundee, as we shall see, in the same decade. Nevertheless, there were still some uncomfortable moments. In March 1988 an offensive letter appeared in the *Press and Journal*.

This continued into the 1990s and beyond. In 1992 the minutes of the congregation referred to the "circulation of racist literature going around Aberdeen in the past few months," some of which had reached the *shul* and Jewish households; members were urged to beware and be vigilant.[132] In the wake of the Hebron Massacre in 1994, the congregation was concerned that extremists might attack soft targets, like Aberdeen's synagogue. After the bombs in London later that year, it was proposed to remove the plaque from the front of the building, but this did not happen. In August 1997, five drunken football fans traveling by train between Glasgow and Aberdeen were arrested and subsequently convicted for screaming, "We hate the Jews," and for giving Nazi salutes.[133] In March 2001 Aberdeen University Jewish Students joined in a protest to demonstrate their opposition to the National Front's planned "Day of Action" in the City. In 2002 the synagogue caretaker, Gladys Marshall, although not Jewish herself, was plagued by menacing telephone calls, which she ascribed to "a rise in anti–Semitism" caused by "the Israeli/Palestinian conflict."[134] In 2003 it was reported that the National Front had decided to target football fans in Aberdeen. In 2005, a swastika was spray-painted on a bus stop, but there is no indication that the act held any specifically anti–Semitic intent. And in the same year, it was reported in the Aberdeen press that a man had made anti–Semitic comments to his Jewish neighbor.[135]

There were also other expressions of prejudice. In 1929 Rabbi Salis Daiches commented, "People persist in speaking of the miserly Aberdonian and especially of the avaricious Aberdeen Jew!"[136] Perhaps he had in mind two books published in Dundee in 1926 and 1927. Using a combination of caricature and stereotype, Allan Junior's *The Aberdeen Jew* and his *Canny Tales Fae Aberdeen* recorded specifically Aberdonian "Jewish jokes," with illustrations by Gregor McGregor that depicted the Jew in typical anti–Semitic caricature. A typical example reads thus: "Two American Jews happened to be travelling together on a train which was held up by a gang of desperadoes. Word reached them that all the passengers were being despoiled of their dollars. At this Isaac turned to Maurice and exclaimed: 'Maurice here is the hundred dollars I vas due you. Now don't forget I've paid you, Maurice.'"[137] Both books were so popular that they were published in multiple editions.

Altogether, however, these few and relatively trivial events add up to a handful of incidents in more than a hundred years, with no record of physical violence against Jews—a record very different from that of many larger conurbations. These minor incidents aside, how should we explain the relevant tolerance displayed towards Jews in Aberdeen? There are several possible, and probably interrelated, factors. The number of Jews in the city was small, at times scarcely achieving two figures. Even today many Aberdonians are unaware of the existence of their city's synagogue. Small numbers, however, do not guarantee tolerance. David Ditchburn has pointed out that, although later medieval Scotland (c.1215–1560) had no Jewish communities, "If the views of chroniclers were at all typical, it shared some of the Latin West's anti–Semitic and anti–Islamic prejudices."[138] There does therefore seem to be force in the idea that Aberdeen and its region have manifested a tradition of "open commonwealth" productive of an especially marked tolerance. As Nicholas J. Evans has put it:

> In the North East of Scotland, Aberdeen in particular, religion has been seen as a strictly personal thing. Whether Jew, Christian, Mormon or Muslim, it has been possible to observe one's own religious holydays as local holidays are rarely linked to Christian festivals (the notable exception being Christmas Day). This is particularly true of Good Friday and Easter Monday (observed throughout the rest of the UK). Such high holy days are not public holidays in the City of Aberdeen.[139]

Residents in nearby Forres, for example, were enthusiastic supporters of the removals of Jewish disabilities in February 1848 following the election of Baron Rothschild for the City of London—long before we know of any Jews venturing that far north.

A Revolving Door

A major characteristic of a small and remote Jewish community like Aberdeen has been its "revolving door" nature; and the significance of population turnover has to be seen as a very complex and important element in its history. There has been no systematic study of this, but it may be assumed, on anecdotal evidence, that the rate of Jewish population turnover in Aberdeen since the 1880s has been high. Kenneth Collins has pointed out how the 1881 Census shows "the ease with which the Jewish population travelled round the immigrant areas of the country seeking employment," with quite a few children born in Aberdeen and Dundee.[140] Aberdeen's Jewish community in the post–Second World War era in particular can be characterized as a transient, drifting, and fleeting community that never intended to settle. In light of this, it is remarkable that such a congregation has endured for more than a century while other smaller communities have closed, notably in Ayr, Dunfermline, Falkirk, Greenock, and Inverness.

Yet it is precisely this turnover and revolving door nature that has allowed Aberdeen to survive continuously. Workers, traveling salesmen, military personnel, students, and others come and go, boosting numbers at some points, draining them at others, but these figures supplement the backbone of more permanent Jewish residents. It was reported in 1998, for example, that the one hundred-strong community, of which fifteen families were members of the synagogue, was swelled at the High Holy Days and festivals by about forty students from Robert Gordon University. The increasing urbanization of Scottish society in the post-war period surely helped, in that Aberdeen, Scotland's third largest city, grew by twelve thousand between 1931 and 1961.[141]

Given these trends, it is surprising that, unlike the other small communities in Scotland (with the exception of Dundee, as we shall see), Aberdeen has maintained its community, based on a congregation, in the post–Second World War era. Several factors explain this relative post-war stability. While Aberdeen has not managed to stem the tide caused by death, a low birth rate, and departure (accelerated by periods of economic downturn in Scotland), it has managed to balance the outgoing figures with incomers. There was certainly a constant coming and going of Jewish families in Aberdeen, as they have been attracted to the city as a result of various employment opportunities. For example, in 1951 Julius Fackenheim stated, "New members had balanced the losses by the community in the past year."[142] Students and staff have been recruited to higher education in the city—to the University of Aberdeen and to the Robert Gordon Institute of Technology (after 1992, the Robert Gordon University). In 1951, one of those included David Daube when he was appointed as a professor of jurisprudence at Aberdeen University. Other Jewish students and staff have come from England, the Isle of Man, Israel, the Netherlands, America, Canada, Barbados, South Africa, Spain, and elsewhere.

A significant proportion of Aberdeen's twenty-first century Jewish population is composed of students and staff at both universities. This growth, which could also have taken place in Dundee (as we shall see), was possibly a result of people coming to Aberdeen to take up a position at the University; but it could also have been a result of the growing demand for labor in Scotland, resulting from a period of economic prosperity which started after the war and lasted broadly until the 1960s. The vacant jobs may not have been filled by Jews, but it is possible that Jews catered to the needs of the new laborers and the existing population, which saw incomes rise.

Employment opportunities for the professions—for example, in hospitals and finance—have also been an attraction, and there has been some presence of personnel from military establishments in northeast Scotland (and, for a while, one of the few local places selling kosher food was the PX at RAF Kinloss). The discovery of commercially viable oil in the North Sea in 1969, which transformed Aberdeen's economy by reversing the previous trend of relative depression, low wages, and large-scale emigration from the city in search of better employment elsewhere, has also been a factor in the Jewish community's survival. It attracted new Jewish employees, lured by a well-paid job (at one point in the 1970s, three of the congregation's members were flying British Airways helicopters over the North Sea to and from the oil rigs). Furthermore, Aberdeen's North Sea oil-based (relative) prosperity in the last quarter of the twentieth century attracted other Jews in related or ancillary industries.[143] Indeed, in an item entitled "Growth and Opportunity," the *Jewish Chronicle* reported "considerable activity" in Aberdeen in 1982.[144]

Pragmatic Compromise

Alone, however, this high population turnover does not explain Aberdeen's longevity relative to the other small Jewish communities in Scotland. It must be taken into consideration alongside the consistent maintenance of the community's social and cultural activities, in addition to synagogue attendance. Importantly, the Aberdeen Hebrew Congregation has operated in a spirit of compromise in accommodating the religious needs and desires of all the members of the community and not just an exclusive few. Aberdeen's Jews have achieved this by taking a pragmatic approach to religious matters when necessary. Several examples shall suffice here. When the congregation was formed, while all the usual holiday and Friday night services were held, regular Saturday morning services were not possible because most congregants were engaged in the retail business. Instead, Shabbat services were held on Sundays and were generally well attended.[145] Later on, non–Jewish partners of Jewish men were often approached to persuade their husbands to attend the synagogue. When a minister was needed, Harry Jacobi, despite being Liberal, was hired for three years.

Furthermore, as befitting an Orthodox synagogue, seating arrangements were separate. Later, as numbers declined, however, the seating arrangements were designed in such a way as to accommodate the feelings of those who attend. Although the genders are segregated—women are clearly separated from the men at the front—there is no partition (*mehitzha*). When complaints about the seating arrangements were received from less Orthodox congregants, the president ruled that there was "a case for retaining tradition whilst adapting to changing circumstances." Since the *shul* ran as an Orthodox one, men and women would continue to be separated, but he had no objection to any man who wanted to sit in the women's section.[146] In July 2008 the first ever Bat Mitzvah at Aberdeen *shul* took place. Although the synagogue functions on Orthodox lines, the service was a Liberal/Progressive one, with large chunks in English, and with women leading part of it.

Together these were the ways the collapse of Jewish communal life was avoided. In his capacity as minister to the small Jewish communities, Malcolm Weisman observed the following reasons for the survival of a small community: looking forward, optimism about its activities, and "[t]he more services, generally speaking, the better the other activities." Such qualities, he stated, enable "even a tiny congregation" to "project a Jewish identity in its members."[147] And it is the projection of such an identity that has helped Aberdeen Jewry to survive continuously from the 1880s to the present. As the records of the Congregation report: "We are sure that many of us, even if not religiously inclined, still wish to promote and maintain some form of organised Jewish activity." Meetings, talks, socials and so on were deemed to be the best "hope of retaining a Jewish communal identity in Aberdeen"; and, judging by its coverage in the *Jewish Chronicle*, *Jewish Echo*, and *Jewish Telegraph*, Aberdeen maintained a vigorous and active community.[148] That this issue was of perennial concern and thought helps explains why the remote Jews of Aberdeen continue to survive to this day.

2
Ayr

The first mention of a Jew in Ayr that we can find is Max Michael Maier (known as Michael Maier) from Bavaria, who was naturalized in 1890. The following year he was joined by twenty-three-year-old Miriam (known as Marion or Mary) Michaelson. Miriam was born in Warsaw in 1868 but moved with her parents to Edinburgh (as well as Glasgow for a short while around 1881). However, in 1886 Marion's father, Harris, died, causing family hardship. So, as the eldest child, Marion was sent out to work as a general servant; she was recorded in the 1891 census as working for a family in Ayr. Her income helped pay for lessons for her younger sister, Sarah, who was listed in the 1901 census as a twenty-three-year-old "student of singing." Two years later, in 1893, Harris Freeman, from Russia (naturalized 1897), arrived in Ayr. In 1902, David, the eldest son of Mr. and Mrs. E. Zive, became engaged to Leah, the only daughter of Deborah and Julius Slevansksi, of Grimsby.[1] On 2nd June of that same year, Kate (née Cohen) and Mitchell Roch gave birth to a daughter at Craigie Avenue.[2] In the September of the following year they had a son, as did David and Leah Slavinski.[3] Prior to the late nineteenth century, Hirschman and Yates claim that Ayr's cemeteries contain the graves of Jews of Sephardic ancestry whose names derived from Hebrew antiquity or tribal or given names.[4] Given that from the sixteenth century onward Ayr functioned as a busy port, exporting wool, fish and hides while importing wine and salt, there might well have been contact with Jewish merchants. One such connection was the failure of the Ayr bank, when Alexander Fordyce, one of the partners, was prevented from discounting on a bill on a Dutch Jew who had engaged in speculation in British stock.[5]

The Foundation of the Congregation

The exact date of the congregation's formation is somewhat of a mystery. According to the *Jewish Year Book* (although not until much later) and the JCR-UK website (probably based on the former source), a sufficient number of Jews had settled in Ayr by 1902 that a congregation was formed.[6] Rather unusually, the *Jewish Chronicle* did not report on this occurrence, which was certainly usually the case when a new congregation was either set up or in the process of being so. At the very least there is a letter from a disgruntled Jewish resident complaining of the lack of such provision, but this wasn't even the case with Ayr. Further confusing matters is a report in the *Jewish Chronicle* which states that Harris Freeman "was chiefly instrumental in founding the congregation *towards the end of the last century.*"[7] Kenneth Collins, however, points out that a "Jewish community in Ayr was already in existence in 1904 when a Zionist society was formed there."[8] The text of the report in the *Jewish Chronicle* certainly seems to indicate the existence of a congregation:

> The circle of Zionist societies is slowly but surely increasing in Scotland; the latest addition being the Ayr Zionist Society, which was established, thanks to Mr. Percy P. Baker, of Glasgow, this week. Mr. Baker addressed the gathering. The entire congregation (both ladies and gentlemen) were enrolled, 30 names being entered. The office-bearers have decided to canvass amongst all co-religionists in the surrounding districts for additional members and for support for the movement.[9]

The first mention of Ayr in the *Jewish Year Book*, however, is not until its 1910 edition (meaning that, if its details are correct, the congregation was most likely set up some time during the previous year, in 1909; however, the address is wrongly given as "45, Kyrle Street" until the correct entry for "Kyle Street," appears in 1917, where the synagogue remained until 1923).[10] *The Third Statistical Account of Scotland* noted in c.1950, "[F]or the last forty years there has been a Hebrew Congregation in Ayr."[11] One Jewish resident of Ayr, Cecil Freeman, recalled that there was a synagogue "which was not only a house of prayer but a social and cultural centre."[12]

In addition to the town of Ayr itself, there was also Jewish settlement in the surrounding area. Jews often traveled from Glasgow to the mining communities of Ayshire.[13] Joel Slonimsky was born in Slonim in Russia in 1882. He was registered as living in Old Cumnock, Ayrshire, when he naturalized in 1905.[14] At some point he went back to Slonim where he found a wife before returning to Ayrshire, where he had five children. He later changed his surname to Dunetz. Chaya Links was the eldest daughter of Mayer and Simie Links, who came over from Brzezany in Galicia in 1907 before settling in Glasgow. Chaya married Naphtali Baim, and they lived for some time in villages in Ayrshire. Their daughter Ettie (Cahif) was born in Cumnock, Ayrshire, in 1909 where Naphtali was a sponge traveler. Later the family settled in Glasgow. Samuel Yacobsen and Lionel Polson arrived from Russia in 1911. Lionel was born Yehudah Polyevensky (or Polyevansky or Polyavinski) in Byten. In order to avoid conscription into the Tsar's army, he took the name Polson and emigrated to Scotland, eventually settling at 20, St. John Street, Prestwick in Ayrshire, where his three children, Moses, Joshua, and Fannie (or Fanny or Fay), were born. In 1934 he left Ayr for Montreal with his son

Moshe (born 6th February, 1917), where he died in 1954. His daughter Fannie (listed as Fay) lived with him for many years.[15] Daniel Rosenbloom temporarily settled in Kilmarnock as a "Scotch draper" in 1889. He had left Russia as a ten-year-old, possibly in the early 1880s. Arriving in Liverpool, he lived in Southport, Newcastle, before marrying his boss's daughter in 1889 and moving to Kilmarnock. They had three sons, and a teacher came especially to Kilmarnock to teach them. Rosenbloom traveled the countryside with his drapery, dressed in frock coat and top hat. The family eventually moved to Glasgow where Daniel naturalized in 1931.[16] He remained a traveling salesman but swapped drapery to sell wine and spirits. Later he became a distiller and a prominent communal leader.

The Attraction of Ayrshire

Ayrshire proved attractive to newly-arrived Jews because it provided business opportunities away from the Jewish concentrations in Glasgow. The main reasons accounting for remote and isolated Jewish settlement within Scotland in its initial years in the late nineteenth century were commercial opportunities. As Kenneth Collins has pointed out, Ayr "grew as a result of internal migration within Scotland with Jews looking for locations from which trade could be conducted with less competition than could be found in the larger centres."[17] Although Ayr did not become a manufacturing center during the industrial revolution, remaining a county town (unlike much of Scotland, which was transformed), it possessed quietly prospering industries, including iron foundries, shipbuilding, and a flourishing port from which large amounts of coal were exported. By 1885, Ayr was among Britain's top ten ports for the coastal shipping of coal.[18] Its long sandy beach made it a popular family seaside resort since Victorian times, and thus Ayr also developed as a holiday town, facilitated by the development of the railway from Glasgow, which opened in 1840 and which made it easier for tourists—and Jewish immigrants—to reach Ayr and nearby locations. And despite its failure to industrialize, Ayr grew rapidly. By the end of the nineteenth century its population stood at 31,000, and it continued to grow throughout the subsequent decades. From 37,000 in 1931 it rose to 42,000 in 1951, and 48,000 in 1971.[19] Such a center would have proved attractive to Jewish peddlers wishing to find a more competitive base from which to operate. Indeed, Collins has noted how Jews traveled from Glasgow to the mining villages of Ayrshire, selling laces, picture frames, and other goods, sometimes returning home only for the Sabbath.[20]

The resort of Dunoon on the Clyde was one of the first popular destination of choice of the Garnethill community, seeking to escape the filth and commotion of Glasgow during the summertime. As early as 1871, a "Mr. Cohen" wrote to the *Jewish Chronicle*, but it's not clear if he was a resident or vacationer.[21] Two years later Philip Lucas had a house there.[22] Sam Getlin, a clothier from Glasgow, took his family on outings to Dunoon.[23] And Michael Simons maintained a second home at Hoop House for many years. In the summer of 1890, the *Jewish Chronicle* reported, "This beautiful Scottish watering-place has of late years become increasingly popular among our coreligionists, and the number of Jewish visitors this season will probably be the highest on record."[24] From that summer onward, services were held at the Dunoon Burgh Hall, conducted by the Reverend E.P. Philips, beginning, in the words of Kenneth Collins, "a tradition of Jewish holidays at the coastal resorts which remained popular until the advent of travel to warmer resorts."[25] Collins also points out how the presence of Jewish services during July attracted visitors from as far afield as London.[26]

A Low Profile

At the outset of its existence, it seems that the Ayr Jewish community kept a rather low profile. Some events of note were recorded in the *Jewish Chronicle*: engagements, marriages, births, and deaths, as well as fundraising activities, services and synagogue meetings. In 1904 the Ayr Zionist Society was set up, composed of the entire congregation of thirty individuals (but this did not include Jews in the surrounding districts, as the office bearers decided "to canvass amongst all coreligionists … for additional members and for support to all the movement')[27] The following were elected: Mr. Harris Freeman, president; Mr. S. Freedman, vice-president; Mr. M. Levy, hon. secretary; and Mr. H. Zive, treasurer. A Ladies Zionist Society was also set up in Newton-on-Ayr in June of that same year.[28] Five shares of the Jewish Colonial Trust, at the cost of one pound each, were bought by the community in Ayr.[29] The following July the services of a minister had been secured: the Reverend Abraham Dove, who had only arrived in Britain the previous year. However, the temptation to leave for a bigger community (in this case Stockport) proved too great, and by 1905 Dove had been replaced by the Reverend A. Edlin, a Chazan from Tiktin in Poland who conducted the High Holyday services of that year. Relations with the non–Jewish community must have been good, as many non–Jews were reported as being present at the services.[30] The community was of sufficient size by 1907 to warrant a visit from the Chief Rabbi, but, strangely, as with the circumstances of the congregation's establishment, there was no report on it in the *Jewish Chronicle*—unlike with the other small communities he visited, namely, Aberdeen, Greenock, and Inverness.[31] At some point Ayr proved unsuitable for Edlin, as the Reverend D.L. Halpern was conducting services by the end of 1909, when he led a Chanukah service. Hebrew classes were also being held by that point and must have been of a fairly high standard, for Halpern was assisted by the Hebrew School children.

By 1910 the *Jewish Year Book* finally took note of Ayr's existence, thereby catching up with the *Jewish Chronicle*. Milla Levy, the daughter of the president of the congregation, presented mantle for the *sefer Torah* to the *shul* that year. At the end of the year a service was held in memory of the late Reverend S. Alfred Adler, who three years earlier had accompanied his father, the Chief Rabbi, on his pastoral visit to the small communities in Scotland, including Ayr. A Relief Society was established in his memory, bearing the name the "Alfred Adler Memorial Fund." Two weeks later a Chanukah service took place, followed by the annual examination of the Hebrew School children. Relations with the local community continued to be good, as many Christians were reported as being in attendance.[32] At that point the Reverend Halpern had left Ayr for Aberdeen, to be replaced by the Reverend Leib A. Falk, who in turn departed to join the community in Inverness. This seems a strange decision for Falk to have made because ministers of such small and remote communities typically left for bigger and more accessible ones, and Inverness, as we shall see, can hardly have been any bigger or less remote than Ayr at that point. Nevertheless, whatever the reasons for Falk's decision, the community carried on regardless, and by May 1911 the synagogue was reported as being in "a satisfactory financial state."[33] As a reflection of this, the community was able to secure the employment of the Reverend Isaac Katz of London as minister and teacher to replace the departed Falk. Katz, though, lasted barely a year, and by the beginning of 1913 the Reverend D. Hoppenstein, formerly of Edinburgh, was now minister in Ayr. He urged the community to set up a *Chevrah Torah* (Torah Study Group). Hoppenstein, however, was in place for only twelve months, during which time he presided over a bar mitzvah before leaving to become a school headmaster in Glasgow in 1914, most likely due to better pay.[34] During this period the synagogue moved around as more suitable and/or larger premises were located to accommodate the growing congregation; at one point it was located at 45, Kyle Street but moved to 184, High Street by 1916.[35]

During this time, Ayr was active in fulfilling its charitable obligations under Jewish law. In 1913 the Ayr *Mogen Dovid* (Star of David) Society was formed, although the precise nature of its activities is unknown. During the First World War, Ayr was active in fundraising for relief of Jewish victims of war in Russia, as well as for the Jewish Hospital and Orphanage. An example of their donations was listed in the *Jewish Chronicle* in 1917: Mr. M. Livingstone, Ayr, 2s. 6d.; Mr. and Mrs. E. T. Naftalin and family, Ayr, 23s. 6d, £1 19s.[36] The last name stands out here, for Ephraim Tobias Naftalin, originally from Lithuania but now living at 31, Park Circus, Ayr, had amassed a fortune sufficient enough that not only was he a noted charitable donor—his various and regular gifts being recorded in the pages of the *Jewish Chronicle*—but he also was able to advertise for a Jewish governess in 1918: "Wanted: refined young lady Hebrew teacher, two children, and help mother with light household duties."[37]

A Unique Location

While Ayr suffered the difficulties of all small and provincial communities in securing the lasting services of a minister/teacher/*shochet*, it benefited from its unique location. By 1914, the Reverend D. Hoppenstein had left Ayr to become a headmaster in Glasgow. In his place, the congregation began advertising for a single *shochet* and teacher with "light duties," on a salary of 30s per week (Apply H. Freeman, 184 High Street).[38] The successful candidate was the Reverend J. Chazan; but as with Aberdeen, the minister in Ayr was not well paid, and so he applied and received a subvention from the Jewish Provincial Ministers' Fund in 1915.[39] Evidently he did not stay long because the following year J. Levy, the Honorary President of the Ayr Hebrew Congregation, wrote to the Chief Rabbi, requesting the services of a single man to act as teacher and *shochet* at a salary of 25/ per week. This search, unfortunately, had been unsuccessful, as the community was unable to obtain a reader and teacher "for many years" (to the effect that children were receiving little Jewish religious instruction). In the absence of such a person, a minister, described as "a poor man," visited from Glasgow every weekend to teach the children, but he did so out of his own pocket. A request to the Provincial Ministers' Fund gained £5 for his services.[40]

It seems that the community had difficulty securing a permanent minister, but Ayr's status as a holiday destination came to the rescue. From July 1914, notices had begun to appear in the *Jewish Chronicle* advertising a holiday residence in a private house ("Furnished rooms to let with use sitting-room; respectable locality..."). Jews from Glasgow and Edinburgh, like their non-Jewish counterparts, often spent their holidays on the Ayrshire coast, either in Ayr or in one of its neighbouring towns, such as Troon and Saltcoats. One such person was the Reverend J. Furst of Edinburgh, who was reported in the *Jewish Chronicle* as spending his vacation with his family in Ayr. During his holiday he preached in the *shul*.[41] Obviously, as this example clearly shows, those Orthodox Jews who holidayed in Ayr still wanted to fully observe their Jewish practice. In 1918, on the recommendation of A. Shonfield, and J.P. and R. Green of Glasgow, and with the approval of the members of the Ayr Congregation, it was decided to hold services during the summer season to which visitors to Ayr and the surrounding districts were welcome. The services were held in the Grand Masonic Hall. Two weeks later the *Jewish Chronicle* reported that the "services recently inaugurated by the residents and visitors at Ayr are being conducted by the Reverend D. Hoppenstein," who was presumably, like his colleague the Reverend Furst from Edinburgh, also spending his vacation in Ayr.[42] It became clear that these arrangements were only temporary, because in 1919 the congregation was advertising for a *shochet*-teacher (but preferably a married man this time) able to translate into English on a weekly salary of £3 and perquisites.[43]

Eventually another solution providentially presented itself. In 1923 the first of many kosher and strictly Orthodox boarding houses, "Mount Olive," located at 6, Alloway Place, Ayr, was opened. It showcased all its mod cons: "High-class Strictly Orthodox board Residence. Facing sea; every home comfort; electric light; separate tables. Personal supervision. 5 minutes from station. Non-residents may join us at meals." It even claimed to be the "Oldest Established Orthodox House in Scotland," and by 1927 "[r]ecommended as the finest house in the country" with an "[a]bsolutely unrivalled position." Two years later it was calling itself "the finest Boarding Establishment in the British Isles."[44] The proprietor was Mrs. Millicent Katz of Langside, Glasgow. From 1921, services were held in Ayr, right through the season and including the festivals, such as Passover, led by Mrs. Katz's husband, the Reverend Marcus Katz, formerly the minister of Queen's Park, Glasgow, for the previous sixteen years. On retirement, he moved to Ayr with his wife and, for the next three years, he acted in an honorary capacity as minister of the local community. The residents of, and visitors to, Ayr were fortunate, for not only had they secured the services of a minister *gratis*, but Katz (born in Lemberg in 1870) was also a gentleman of considerable attainment, having studied philosophy, Hebrew literature and astronomy, as well as serving as the headmaster of the Queen's Park Hebrew School. As a mark of this, Katz was held in deep respect and affection, and he and his wife were presented with candelabra by grateful visitors. Business must have been good for them, too, as the guest house was "luxuriously redecorated" with tennis courts the following year.[45] Katz led the services that were held at the Liberal Club Chambers on 69, Sandgate Street until more permanent quarters could be obtained.[46] From its 1924 edition onwards, the *Jewish Year Book* listed the Liberal Club as the synagogue's "temporary premises."

This was still only a temporary solution, as the community was still advertising for a *chazan*, teacher, and *shochet*, on a salary of £4 per week and perquisites.[47] The situation was exacerbated by the death in 1924 of the Reverend Katz, whose obituary was published in the *Jewish Chronicle*. Nevertheless, services continued to be held every Friday evening and Saturday morning in the Liberal Club Chambers. These were led by the Reverend M. Foman of Glasgow, who was staying at Ayr for his holiday, and who offered to officiate on the forthcoming Shabbat. Possibly due to an expanding congregation, services on the High Festivals were moved in 1922 to the Masonic Hall in Nilecourt, and applications for seats were advertised in the *Jewish Chronicle*.

The only surviving description we have of the "Ayr Orthodox Synagogue" is the following from a *Jewish Chronicle* correspondent: "wooden tablets of the Law ... leaving out the Second Commandment and having the tenth twice over." Such was his surprise at this arrangement that he went on to ask: "Is this unique? Where can more of such be seen?"[48] Yet, the community still did not have a permanent minister and was again advertising for a *chazan*, teacher, and *shochet* in 1924.⁴⁹ In 1926 the community abandoned the aforementioned temporary arrangements when suitable and more permanent premises at 40, High Street, Ayr, were found for a synagogue and classroom, both of which were donated to the congregation by Mr. Harris Freeman. The congregation announced, "Visitors to Ayr and district are invited to attend the services, which will be held regularly."⁵⁰

A Scottish Catskills

Reading the advertisements in the *Jewish Chronicle*, it appears that the popularity of Ayr and nearby seaside resorts was steadily increasing, leading to the proliferation of guesthouses. By 1925, further guesthouses had opened up in Ayr. In addition to the Mount Olive Boarding House was the Burnock at 13, Racecourse Road, run by Mrs. S.J. Easterman. Likewise, other kosher boarding houses had opened on the Ayrshire coast at Rothesay and Troon (the latter, "Beachwood," run by Mrs. Max Sugare of London, promoted itself as another "High-Class strictly Orthodox").⁵¹ These boarding houses seemed to function as a Scottish version of the Jewish hotels in the American resort of the Catskills, in that many relationships were formed. Ayr's attraction as a Jewish holiday destination thus had another related benefit: a high number of eligible and potential marriage partners drawn from outside the town itself, resulting in many engagements, marriages and births for those who chose to remain in Ayr. Between 1907 and 1926, marriages announced in the *Jewish Chronicle* between Jews from Ayr and places such as Manchester, Pietersburg, Glasgow, Dublin, and Johannesburg took place. In this way, Ayr was distinguishable from the other small communities, most of which had a small and, over time, ever-decreasing pool of potential partners.

One of the most famous Jews to take advantage of Ayr's coastal location, and who also met his wife there, was Oscar Slater. In 1909, Oscar Joseph Slater (Leachziner), a Silesian Jew who had emigrated to and settled in Glasgow, had been accused and found guilty of the murder of eighty-two-year-old Marion Gilchrist, for which he was sentenced to death by hanging. The day before his execution was due to be carried out his sentence was reduced to penal servitude for life. He served eighteen and a half years at Peterhead prison in Aberdeenshire. Following pressure, led by Sir Arthur Conan Doyle, his conviction was quashed on the grounds of misdirection, and Slater was released in 1928. Upon his release from prison, Slater stayed at the Mount Olive Boarding House in Ayr and decided to settle permanently in Ayrshire, where he lived until his death in 1948. He accepted £6,000 from the government as an *ex gratia* payment for his wrongful conviction. Slater met and married Lena Shand, a Jew of German origin, in 1936; however, both were interned as aliens in 1940. Slater's wish to become a British citizen was never fulfilled, as his application was due to be granted only a few weeks after his death.

During the period between 1931 and 1939, the community in Ayr grew. This was primarily the result of Ayr's status as a holiday destination for Jews from the West of Scotland, particularly Glasgow. Adverts for Jewish boarding houses, such as Westfield House, were using slogans such as "Come to Ayr for a Healthy Holiday" to attract Jewish guests.[52] By this point it took less than an hour to reach Ayr by train from Glasgow, and a regular bus service was departing every fifteen minutes, making it a very attractive destination for many. In Ayr, and to a lesser extent Prestwick, Troon, Saltcoats, Largs, Helensburgh, and even Brodick on Arran, the resident Jewish community was continuously reinforced by holiday makers and wealthy seasonal residents from Glasgow. They were attracted by kosher boarding houses and hotels such as Stern's Promenade Hotel in Saltcoats and Westfield House, and the newly-opened Invercloy Hotel in Ayr. Many visitors from Glasgow also took day trips to Ayr. The *Jewish Chronicle* reported on a trip of one hundred elderly Jews, under the auspices of the "Old Folks Annual Outing Fund," organized by the Jewish ex-Service Men's Branch of the British Legion, who enjoyed a dinner and tea at the Mount Olive Jewish boarding house. Similarly, more than three hundred children from the Glasgow Talmud Torah and its Hillington and Buchan Street branches were taken for a day's touting to Ayr. Included in the party were the children from the Gertrude Jacobson Orphanage. The children from the Garnethill Refugee Hotel were also taken for a day's visit to Rothesay and Ettrick Bay.[53]

It was clear that Ayr benefited from its close proximity to Glasgow, enjoying very close relations with that city. Not only was there a constant flow of visitors and holidaymakers, but Ayr could rely on the far larger metropolis, particularly in Jewish terms, to provide it with essential Jewish services lacking in Ayr. For example, because, unlike Aberdeen and Inverness, Glasgow was easy to reach from Ayr, the town never had a need for its own dedicated Jewish cemetery, and burials were carried out in Glasgow. Reuben Spilg, whose mother lived in Ayr during the Second World War, recalled that he had to arrange for a "special wagon to be put on one of the trains from Ayr to Glasgow."[54] Indeed, to all intents and purposes, Ayr looked to Glasgow rather than London, with which it had little contact other than being represented at the Board of Deputies.

During the festivals, special synagogue services were organized in private homes and hotels. However, in attracting Jewish customers, the West Coast establishments suffered increasing competition from England. In response, they offered increasing attractions, such as special reduced rates, ping pong tournaments and dancing. Among the guests were Glasgow communal leaders and wealthy business people, including Maurice Bloch. Other visitors came from further away, such as the Gold Brothers of Aberdeen, and Isaac Sclar and Alex Ronder from Dunfermline. By 1933 there were sufficient numbers of temporary residents in Ayr to seek officials to lead the High Festival services. Services had previously been held in Westfield House, but now they moved back to the Liberal Club. Organization was apparently in the hands of Mr. R. Naftalin, 31, Park Circus, Ayr. In 1937 Rosh Hashanah services were held in the Masonic Halls, which were attended by one hundred and twenty congregants, including visitors, and Yom Kippur services in Westfield House, led by Mr. S. Wolfson, J.P.[55] These last were followed by a meeting to discuss the practicality of establishing a permanent congregation in Ayr. The post of minister was offered in 1938 to the Reverend Hyman (Hymie) Davies (who would stay in that post until 1948), and during that year there were also *Succot* services at Maryville Boarding House, courtesy of Mr. and Mrs. Warrens.

Embourgeoisiement

Between the wars, the community of Ayr underwent a process of embourgeoisiement. The children of those who then appeared to be the most affluent members of the community at that time, Harris Freeman and Ephraim Naftalin, both began to pass into the professions. In 1926, Cecil Freeman passed the final examination of the Corporation of Accountants and was admitted to the FCRA; however, he went on to join the family furniture business started by his parents. In 1933, Esther, the only daughter of Ephraim and Mrs. Naftalin, graduated with the degree of MA from the University of Glasgow. In 1938, Dr. J. M. Naftalin was appointed lecturer in biochemistry at Bradford Technical College.[56] Born in Ayr in 1909, Harold Levy, the grandson of the Reverend D. Hoppenstein, studied mathematics at Glasgow University but went on to become an acknowledged expert in Hebrew, publishing the book *Hebrew for All*. His teachers included his grandfather, the Reverend Hoppenstein, the Reverend D. Jacobs, and Dr. Nathan Morris. He taught at the Talmud Torah, Hebrew College, Queen's Park Senior Secondary School, and at adult classes in Glasgow before becoming the Inspector of the Central Council for Jewish Religious Education in 1951. It was in this capacity that he would return to Ayr, but only as a visitor to inspect the Hebrew classes there.[57]

Apart from the proprietors of boarding houses and hotels, Jews in Ayr were involved in a variety of professions. H. Freeman and Sons, located at 24–38, Carrick Street were "House Agents" involved in letting furnished houses.[58] Freeman certainly appeared to be taking advantage of the holiday traffic from Glasgow by letting out a few houses in Ayr. The fact that by 1930 he had houses in both Ayr and Princes Square in Glasgow indicated his business was profitable. Maurice Gold owned Hay's House Furnishers, based at 250, High Street. Incidentally, his brothers, Eli and Fred, had a similar business in Aberdeen. In addition to the proprietors of the various kosher boarding houses and hotels, many of Ayr's Jews owned shops selling items such as gifts and jewelry (Markson), leather and handicrafts (Mina Green), costume jewelry (Ernie Blint), jewelry (Carrie Lopato), furniture (Frank Terret, Harris Freeman), and fashion (Charlie Steen, Lillian Russell). There were also other professions: Lewis Wolfson was a pharmacist; Ian Faith was an optician; and Max Wiseman and sons, a spectacle manufacturer, had factories in Mauchline, Ayrshire, as well as in Strathleven and Ballochmyle, one of which was the largest in Scotland.

Concomitant with the increasing size and affluence of the community was a growth in its communal activity. At a meeting of the Jewish Education Area Committee for Scotland in 1926, Ayr was discussed, and the application for a grant from the Jewish War Memorial was considered. Mr. J. Levine, M.A., undertook to visit Ayr on behalf of the Committee in order to bring about the cooperation of the parents and the local congregation in securing the services of a competent Hebrew teacher. It is unclear what happened next, particularly given the high rate of turnover of the ministers and teachers, as we have seen, but in 1938 Herbert M. Adler, Director of Jewish Education, inspected the Ayr Hebrew School, although his observations and conclusions are unknown. The following year the *Jewish Chronicle* rather cryptically announced, "Consideration was given to the arrangements necessary for the Jewish children in Ayr."[59]

Charitable activities were much in evidence. Over the years 1937 and 1938, sums were collected for the Glasgow Board of Guardians and Talmud Torah, and the United Appeal for Jews in Poland.[60] In a "novel scheme for refugee relief," the Westfield, Invercloy, and Aryeh hotels and boarding houses jointly organized and collected £16 10/- for the German Jewish Refugee Fund through a "travelling dinner and dance" arranged by Mr. and Mrs. Gold and Miss Ida Warrens. The Jewish National Fund (J.N.F.) extended its activities to the West of Scotland, including Ayr. A branch was established in Ayr in 1938. The commission had been set up, and charity boxes were placed in Ayr, from which money had already been received. As the result of a collection in aid of charities, Ayr raised over £34, which was divided between the Glasgow Jewish Board of Guardians and the Talmud Torah Hebrew School. A social function in aid of the Gertrude Jacobson Orphanage was held at the Invercloy Boarding House, arranged by the orphanage Auxiliary. In response to an appeal, the Glasgow Talmud Torah and the Board of Guardians received £24 and £19 9s respectively, donated by the Ayr Congregation. Finally, women Zionists from Ayr were reported as participating in a Zionist fundraising drive.[61]

A Safe Haven

If prior to 1939 Ayr owed its good fortune to its location as a prime holiday destination for the Jews of Glasgow, then that location served it equally well during the Second World War, as those same Jews were either evacuated there or chose to move there because it was a safer environment. At the start of the war in 1939, the Jewish population in Ayr rose quickly with the arrival of Jewish families from Glasgow who sought a safe haven on the coast. Indeed, the civilian community in Ayr in general expanded greatly as a result of families taking up residence there in preference to cities more vulnerable to bombing. The *Jewish Year Book* reports a figure of sixty, but this most likely refers to synagogue members and not Jewish residents. In contrast, there were now reports in both the *Jewish Chronicle* and *Jewish Echo* of about a hundred Jewish families in Ayr. These figures most likely did not take into account the high number of Jewish service personnel who were stationed in Ayr, particularly in connection with the air force base at nearby Prestwick, which became the Americans' main air force headquarters in Europe. This expansion meant that the wartime was a boom period for Ayr's resident Jewish community, as it undoubtedly benefited from the arrival of their wealthier, more numerous and influential coreligionists from Glasgow.

The first tangible benefit was the more widespread and systematic provision of religious education for the children. Under the headline "GLASGOW FAMILIES EVACUATE," the *Jewish Chronicle* devoted a significant portion to discussing "Education Facilities at Ayr." Following a meeting convened by the Special Emergency Committee from Glasgow with the Jewish residents of Ayr in the Masonic Halls, it was decided that classes should be opened immediately. Two teachers from Glasgow, together with a local teacher, were placed in charge of the classes, which were divided into three sections—beginners, intermediate, and advanced. The Ayr Hebrew Congregation provided a grant of twenty guineas towards the expense of accommodating teachers.[62] As a result of these attempts to organize Jewish education in Ayr, classes took place on Saturdays (11:30–1:00) and Sundays (10:30–1:00). Forty children in Ayr, including six from Troon, were enrolled and learned the following subjects: history, religion, Hebrew, bible and *Siddur*.[63] Classes were also being held in Annan.[64]

Later, in 1941, the Ayr Hebrew classes were examined by Bernard Glasser, Convener of the Glasgow Talmud Torah. He told the Ayr Education Committee, "Twice weekly was not sufficient for Hebrew tuition in view of the fact that in Ayr there was now quite a community," and that four days of education were needed. The Glasgow Talmud Torah would send teachers. He was "cordially" thanked for his examination of the children, as well as his advice.[65] Later that year Glasser "expressed his delight with the remarkably good progress the children had made since his last visit."[66] The number of evacuated children in Troon had now increased to twenty-seven, whose education was provided by twice-weekly classes run by the Glasgow Talmud Torah. Similarly, there were twenty-six children in Largs and a center in Lockerbie.[67] As the need was so great, by 1944 the community had appointed a headmaster for the children in Ayr and Troon, and the job was given to the Reverend Newman, alongside the minister the Reverend Davies. Both were on equal salaries of £1 1s per week. By this point, classes were held every day of the week in Ayr, with the exception of Friday (Monday, 4:30–6:00; Tuesdays, 4–5 and 5–6; Wednesday, 4–5:30, 5:30–7; Thursday, 4–5, 5–6; Saturday, 4; sun 10–11:30, 11.30–12:30) and twice a week in Troon (Sunday and Tuesday, 3–4:30, 4:30–6).[67]

Many of these children were living in hostels specially set up to house them. Hostels were established in Castle Douglas, Kirkcudbrightshire (designed to accommodate over one hundred boys and girls), Skelmorlie, Ayrshire (sixty pupils and four teachers), and in Ayr, Troon, and Largs. In total, over three hundred children were dispersed over a wide area. (Incidentally, aged evacuees from the South of England were also relocated to Ayrshire.)[68]

One of those evacuated included Herbert Kay from Bratislava in Czechoslovakia. He arrived in London via the *kindertransport* before being sent to Scotland. As the war broke out only a few weeks later, he was evacuated to Kirkmichael, Ayrshire, where he was taken in by John and Agnes Muir.

Benita Golombok from Glasgow was also evacuated to Troon at the outbreak of the Second World War, together with her elder sister and parents, as well as a group of children from her school. Her parents rented a small house there for the duration of the war, as it was near enough for her father to commute to his work (in the fur trade) in Glasgow—about one hour's travel. They lived there until 1947 when they returned to Glasgow. She recalled that there were no more than six to eight Jewish families living in Troon during the war years—not enough to form a *minyan*. For the festivals, therefore, they visited relatives in Glasgow, and kosher meat was also obtained from there. As mentioned above, she remembered a religious studies teacher who came through from Ayr. The only other Jewish people in the area were Jewish soldiers who came on Shabbat or Yom Tov from the various bases in the area. "Life was really very nice in spite of the war as it was a delightful seaside town and anti-Semitism was not a problem, just occasional remarks which were easily dealt with."[69]

A Thriving Community

A second benefit was a thriving social scene. A local Debating Society met in 1939 for the first time in the (Jewish-owned) Invercloy Hotel.[70] A large crowd was recorded as attending the debate on "Communism—A Solution to Anti-Semitism" (incidentally, the motion was defeated). The following month, Dr. Friedlander addressed the society on the subject "Is Judaism Worth Preserving?" The Debating Society engaged in regular biweekly events which, judging by the reports in the Jewish press, were lively and varied. Apart from its debates, it held such events as a Hat Night and a "Living Newspaper," during which participants read out articles they had written. A Jewish Literary Society followed in 1940. In 1943 a Bridge Club was set up and later renamed as the Ayr Wingate Social Club, incorporating the Bridge and Discussion Group Sections, which met on a weekly and monthly basis respectively.[71] Meetings for the Jewish Board of Guardians, the J.N.F., the Ayr Victory Campaign, the Palestine Victory Campaign, and Keren Hayesod were held. They were followed by other youth and social organizations, such as a Jewish Youth Social Club, which held a tennis tournament in 1942

Special organizations to entertain Jewish servicemen were set up in Ayr. In January of 1941 a Hospitality Committee was formed by the Ayr Community, and an invitation was issued to any Jewish members of the Forces to visit any of the Jewish boarding houses in Ayr, where they were accorded a warm welcome. The committee also actively sought donations towards its Hospitality Fund, and members of the community were asked to subscribe generously to this fund in order that the servicemen may continue to be entertained in the Jewish boarding houses. In February of that year, Rabbi Dr. L.I. Rabinowitz, Jewish Chaplain to the Forces, conducted a special service at the Invercloy Hotel for Jewish service personnel in the area. Sir Maurice Bloch J.P., Hon. Air Commodore of the Air Defence Cadet Corps, and the Reverend Davies also attended the service, after which the servicemen were treated to tea, supper, and a dance. Our aforementioned Cyril Harris recalled:

> The Jewish personnel used to visit us regularly; my mother, despite wartime rationing, showed them hospitality, and as my father was a chess champion they loved to challenge him to a game. They all seemed incredibly friendly; and kept bringing us presents from the PX, the store for servicemen, at Prestwick Aerodrome. My elder sister and brother and I were among the very few children to enjoy a constant supply of sweets throughout the war.[72]

A related but un-stated advantage to this hospitality was that it increased the potential of a suitable engagement. One such example was the young woman who met her husband when his submarine docked in Scotland and he was billeted in Ayr with her parents, as they were the local Jewish family.[73]

Charitable endeavors showed a remarkable rise. As a mark of this, a committee for Queen's Park Refugee Relief set up in Ayr because "they expected to derive a good revenue" from that source.[74] A "substantial sum" had been recently raised in Ayr for the Gateshead Talmudical College, following a visit by its principal, Rabbi Landinsky.[75] Likewise, £35 was collected in 1940 for the Glasgow Talmud Torah in Ayr, while only £20 had been gathered from the far bigger community in Glasgow (which, at its height, totaled some 15,000—compared to Ayr's 150!)[76] In a short report in the *Jewish Chronicle* entitled "AYR EXCEEDS U.P.A. TARGET," Ayr was praised for exceeding its target of £2,500 for the U.P.A (the actual sum raised was £2,506).[77] Following an appeal by Sir Maurice Bloch on behalf of the Central British

Fund at a meeting at the Invercloy Hotel, more than £2,000 was raised, which brought the total for Ayr to £5,000 by 1943. Similarly, a Keren Hayesod war appeal raised £1000.[78] The size and frequency of these sums was in no doubt due to the size and wealth of the community, which had been particularly boosted by the recent arrivals from Glasgow. But they were also attributable to the tireless efforts of the Ayr community. In 1941, for example, a *Jewish Echo* report declared, "Ayr Jewry does its bit," commenting on how the growing community does not rest.[79] As a mark of this activity, and also the increasingly middle-class status of Ayr's Jews, as they were now freed from their duties in the economic sphere, separate organizations for Jewish women in Ayr sprang up. These included a Sewing and Knitting Work Party for the Red Cross and the Women Voluntary Services (WVS), as well as a Ladies' Zionist Committee, a W.I.Z.O. committee, a Ladies' Committee for the Glasgow Talmud Torah, the Glasgow Hebrew Ladies' Benevolent Society and an Ayr Board of Guardians Auxiliary. In addition, a number of the younger women had taken up nursing.

How the Ayr community thrived was also shown in a report in 1941 about a Board of Deputies Appeal meeting with Professor Brodetsky, held at the Westfield Hotel. Maurice Bloch presided and said that this was similar to an appeal in Glasgow. Ayr was asked to contribute £1,000, while £5,000 was asked of Glasgow (a community one hundred times bigger).[80] Noteworthy was a report made during the same year on communal activity. Ayr was a growing community in many directions. It was helping the Red Cross, but recent afternoon meetings were less well attended. Jewish soldiers stationed in the area were regularly entertained. A Hospitality Committee had served more than three-hundred-and-seventy-five meals for soldiers stationed in Ayr. Friday night services were held at the Invercloy Hotel for soldiers, officiated by the Reverend Davies, who also served as the civilian chaplain to the forces and spent many evenings entertaining the troops with his singing. A Junior Section Hospitality Committee organized many functions to raise money, such as whist drives and social evenings. Mrs. Millie Abrahams had a special government permit to visit soldiers in hospitals in and around Ayr.

Ayr's Jewish residents also did their part in National Service, serving in the war. Norman Markson, the son of Mr. and Mrs. Philip Markson, Hawkhill Avenue, Ayr, was listed as missing in Thailand since 1941. In January 1942, Lieutenant Henri Stoedarum, 21st Army Tank Brigade, Royal Armoured Corps, was killed in action, while Lieutenant H. Roch, Royal Artillery, was taken prisoner at Tobruk in 1942 and returned to Glasgow in July 1945.[81] Paul Sunderland was killed in Italy in 1943.

The wartime period also gives valuable insight into the religious life of Ayr's Jewish community. This is, in part, a consequence of the additional reporting the community received in the *Jewish Chronicle* and *Jewish Echo* as a result of the quantity and quality of its new (albeit temporary) residents. It is also the result of the survival of the minutes of the congregation from this time. In 1941 a new synagogue, "serving some thirty Jewish families," numbering one hundred and twenty people, was consecrated at 54a, Sandgate.[82] It is notable that this occurred four years before Aberdeen's new *shul* was opened, further demonstrating the affluence and number of Jewish residents in Ayr. Located on the site of a former church mission hall, it was able to seat all one hundred and twenty people. The *Jewish Echo* reported that it presented "a bright and inviting appearance."[83] A *sefer Torah*, which Harris Freeman had bought forty-five years earlier in 1894, was placed in the Ark of the new *shul*. In addition, memorial windows, donated by the members of the congregation, were promised and installed at a later date.

On the day of the consecration, the synagogue was filled to capacity. Afterwards the guests attended a reception at the Invercloy Hotel, where Edward Cohen, the treasurer of the congregation, stated how proud he was to think that when Jews were being persecuted in so many countries that they had been able to open a *shul*. He carried on, saying, "The new synagogue, though small in size, was as complete in every way as any of the largest synagogues anywhere."[84] Harris Freeman praised the "spirit of co-operation among the members," and claimed, in a somewhat far-fetched fashion, that internal dissension did not exist in the Ayr Community; he also saw no reason why it should not grow from strength to strength and become a potent factor in Scottish Jewry.[85] The community also advertised for a caretaker in the *Ayrshire Post* in 1942, and the first wedding to take place in the new building was that of the minister, the

List of Donors, Ayr. *Jewish Echo*, January 12, 1940.

———— PATRONISE ————
THE ADVERTISER
WHO ADVERTISES IN THE
'JEWISH ECHO'

W V S
AYR JEWISH BRANCH

List of Donations

	£	s	d
Mrs L. Abrahams	0	10	6
Mrs H. Freeman	0	10	6
Mrs S. Braverman	0	10	0
Mrs J. Morrison	0	10	0
Mrs P. Morrison	0	10	0
Mrs H. Coutts	0	10	0
Mrs H. Green	0	10	0
Mrs M. Dover	0	10	0
Mrs A. Goldberg	0	10	0
Mrs M. Dover	0	10	0
Mrs I. Green	0	10	0
Mrs J. Kamofsky	0	10	0
Mrs H. Levitus	0	10	0
Mr S. Wolfson	0	10	0
Mrs M. Latter	0	5	6
Mrs B. Lipton	0	5	0
Mrs S. Levine	0	5	0
Mrs M. Black	0	5	0
Mrs A. Berman	0	5	0
Mrs H. Davidson	0	5	0
Mrs P. Merrens	0	5	0
Mrs J. Wolfe	0	5	0
Mrs Greenhill (Leeds)	0	5	0
Mrs B. Levitt	0	5	0
Mrs H. Langman	0	5	0
Mrs J. Levy	0	5	0
Mrs B. Rose	0	5	0
A Friend	0	5	0
Mrs A. Naftalin	0	5	0
Mrs B. Binnie	0	5	0
Mrs B. D. Cowan	0	5	0
Mrs J. J. Millar	0	5	0
Mrs Wolifson	0	5	0
Mrs I. Goldberg	0	5	0
Mrs H. Gerber	0	5	0
Mrs L. Langman	0	5	0
Mrs G. Paris	0	5	0
Mrs H. Michaelson	0	5	0
Mrs Sagman	0	5	0
Mrs A. Green	0	5	0
Mrs W. Wolfson	0	5	0
Mrs H. Morrison	0	5	0
Mrs A. Davidson	0	4	0
Mrs Levison	0	2	6
Mrs Appleson	0	2	6
Mrs M. Steen	0	2	6
Mrs M. Green	0	2	6
Mrs M. Abrahams	0	2	6
Mrs S. Warrens	0	2	6
Mrs I. Bernstein	0	2	6
Mrs J. Freeman	0	2	6
Mrs C. Speculand	0	2	6
Mrs J. Millar	0	2	6
Mrs Markson	0	2	6
Mrs Elvie	0	2	6
Mr I. Faith	0	2	6
Mrs H. Collins	0	2	6
Mrs Raskin	0	2	6
Mrs B. Abrahams	0	2	6
Mrs Roche	0	2	6
Mrs F. Terret	0	2	6
Mrs C. Cohen	0	2	6
Mrs R. Cohen	0	2	6
Miss D. Waldman	0	2	6
Mrs A. Wolfson	0	1	0
Mrs Adler	0	1	0

Reverend Davies, to Bessie Wolfson from Glasgow. Such was the import of the occasion that the *Jewish Echo* reported on it, observing how the bridegroom's parents had travelled from Wales to be present. The reception was held at the Invercloy, and the leaders of the Glasgow Jewish community, including Joseph Sachs, were in attendance.[86] The Reverend Davies presented a *chupah* (wedding canopy) to the *shul* to mark the occasion.[87]

However, despite Harris Freeman's claim that internal conflict was not present in Ayr, the surviving minutes of the congregation from that period give a very different story. Since kosher poultry was being distributed inequitably and inadequately among non-members—at the expense of the members of the congregation—some consternation among the latter was caused until the issue was resolved. At one point in April 1942 an altercation was reported in the minutes, with one member even walking out of the meeting! It was also clear that not all of the practicing and identifying Jews in Ayr (let alone those who did neither) were members of the congregation. In fact, it was reported during 1942 that, owing to its sufficient size, rival *minyanim* had been formed and were meeting at the Invercloy and Laurelle. The *shul*'s committee therefore recommended that "strong steps be taken to bring these under the control of the Congregation."[88]

A report in the *Jewish Echo* in 1943 also shed further light on religious practice in Ayr. The secretary, Ellis Wolfe, reported that there had been a "considerable growth in scope and influence." Many difficult problems had been solved, the main one being *shechita* and the distribution of kosher poultry supplied by Howie the butcher, under the supervision of the Reverend Davies, and the *shochet*, "not only to members of the congregation, but also to all Jewish families resident in Ayr," under the supervision of the Glasgow Beth Din and Rabbi B. Atlas. Festival services were held in the synagogue and conducted by the Reverend Davies, assisted by Mr. I. Zwebner; but owing to the size of the congregation, overflow services took place in the Masonic Halls, with Rabbi Berman and Reverend Barnett, "as the membership continued to be in excess of the seating capacity of the Synagogue."[89] This latter point was surely a first in the history of any small community. Since February 1942 the congregation was affiliated with the Glasgow Jewish Representative Council.[90] In addition to services and religious education, the usual occasions of births, engagements, marriages, and other festive occasions took place. One of those is worth mentioning here because it was a rare occasion when two Ayr residents found each other: Myer Woolfson and Judith Easterman.[91] As indicated above, kosher poultry was available throughout the war but had been the source of some consternation. Kosher milk for Passover was obtained and distributed.[92]

The influx of Jewish residents was undoubtedly a boom time for business. New Jewish-owned boarding houses were opened; in addition to the long-standing Westfield House, newer establishments included Glenpark House,

```
ARYEH HOUSE  21 MILLER ROAD  AYR
       Under Personal Supervision ——— Mrs F. WOLIFSON
   Modern, Comfortable, Excellent Cuisine, H. & C. Water in all Bedrooms
       Strictly Kosher ——— Non Residents Catered For, ——— Week-ends
   Near Sea and Station        Write for ⸺ ⸺. or 'Phone AYR 119111
```

```
HOTEL 'LAURELLE'  20 Seafield Dr AYR
              (ON THE FRONT)
   Modern Orthodox Boarding Establishment. Hot and Cold
   water in all Rooms.
   Bookings & Inquiries now invited        Telephone—AYR 85211.
```

Advertisements for Kosher boarding houses in Ayr, 1941.

Aryeh House, Laurelle and the Invercloy Hotel in Ayr and Netherbank, Largs. Many of those who relocated to Ayr from Glasgow stayed in these establishments, which also entertained and accommodated those Jewish service personnel who were the recipients of Ayr's Hospitality Fund. The *Jewish Echo* reported that over the first six months of 1941, 895 meals had been served in Jewish boarding houses to Jewish members of the Forces.[93] Such hospitality helped to keep these establishments viable because, as the war progressed, there was increased competition from establishments in northwest England, including Blackpool, but also Bournemouth.

One of those who grew up in Ayr during this period was Cyril Harris. Born in Glasgow in 1936, Cyril was evacuated to Annan in Dumfrieshire as a young boy before spending the rest of the Second World War in Ayr. Although he was only in Ayr for a short time, the small community made an impact. In his autobiography, *For Heaven's Sake*, he described the community of his early childhood in Scotland:

> The Ayr Hebrew Congregation, of which my father was the proud chairman—I was introduced to shul politics as an infant—was very close-knit and intimate, and the hundred or so Jewish souls of the seaside town really seemed to care about each other. Perhaps it was the war which brought everyone closer together but I believed every community was as warm as that, and it was one of the reasons I decide early on to become a congregational rabbi.[94]

He eventually became the Chief Rabbi of South Africa, and later in life often spoke about how lovely it was to live in a small village Jewish community.[95]

Of those others who relocated to Ayr, another has left us with a more detailed memoir of his time there. Reuben Spilg, formerly of Falkirk, moved his mother to a house in the Seafield district of Ayr to remove her from the danger zone. Meanwhile, Reuben stayed in Glasgow and spent the weekends in Ayr. "Life in Ayr," he recalled, in what was probably a typical experience for the Jewish refugees from Glasgow, "was very different from the rest of the week in Glasgow, where you knew all the time that there was a war on." He added, "Life in Ayr at the weekend was a wonderful tonic after the rest of the week in troubled Glasgow. As far as I know, only one Nazi bomb was dropped on Ayr during the war and it fell in the sea!"[96]

After the War

Following the growth of the community, in 1946 Ayr had a Jewish congregation with a synagogue, annually elected office bearers, seat holders and regular services. The Hebrew classes had thirty-three pupils.[97] There was also a local Jewish Discussion Group, but it met less regularly than before. The congregation was relatively numerous and wealthy, mainly because of the continued presence of well-to-do business people from Glasgow, who made substantial contributions to Zionist and other fundraising causes. Women continued to play an important part through W.I.Z.O. and the Ayr Jewish Ladies' Guild. Although the latter organization was described as "small in numbers," its contributions in proportion to its size were some of the largest in the country.[98]

By 1949 the number of Jews living permanently or seasonally in Ayr started to drop, with the death of members of the congregation and evidence of people leaving the town, although no exact figures are available. The community was able to continue, unlike similar-sized communities, as we shall see, because holidaying guests helped to augment the declining numbers of those able to attend. The Reverend Davies had left to become minister at the Hull Western Synagogue, to be replaced by the Reverend David Landy, who departed soon after to become minister at Coventry. His replacement, the Reverend Sam Knopp, formed a local Jewish Youth Society which met in people's homes for a while on a weekly basis (for example during the period March-May 1951), but this society, as well as the Discussion Group, had to be revived constantly. In 1950 the congregation no longer advertised seat-letting in the synagogue, but the *Jewish Year Book* listed the Jewish population as one hundred and sixty, and listed the following organizations in Ayr: Hebrew Congregation (54a, Sandgate), Jewish Discussion Group, and Jewish Ladies' Guild. Three years later the Ayr Hebrew Congregation Building Fund, "for the purpose of acquiring premises for religious, educational, and social activities," was inaugurated, indicating that there were problems with the maintenance of the

Sandgate synagogue.[99] *The Third Statistical Account of Scotland* noted that there were also Jewish families living in Prestwick and Troon.[100]

One of those living in Ayr at that time was the Rosenstein family. In 1950, after returning to Glasgow (having spent the war years in Troon), Benita Golombok's parents decided to move to Ayr, by which point there was still an organized community (albeit somewhat smaller). Benita recalled no more than fifty Jewish residents. She remembered the "nice little Shul which at first was located above a furniture shop owned by a member of the community. It was beautifully fitted out and regular Shabbat and Yomtov services were held, and if one needed a *minyan* for a *Yartzeit* it was no problem."[101] The Golomboks were active in the Jewish community. Benita was involved in the Ayr Youth Society, while her father, Woolf, was chairman of the Discussion Group. In 1955 the Golomboks bought and reopened the Invercloy, where Benita was married in 1957.

A young *Chazan*/religious leader/teacher was employed by the community, and there were also a few men capable of running the services (which were run on orthodox/traditional lines). The men and women sat apart, but there was no *mechitza* or separation between them. Many of the members were traditional and wanted to remain attached to the larger communities and shuls for the sake of their children's Jewish education, so many returned to Glasgow after the war. There was no *shochet*, so kosher meat was brought from Glasgow, which also took care of the *chevra kadisha* and burials. There were various Jewish-owned businesses—furniture, a pharmacy, an optician, a bingo hall (Abraham Ross), a high-class dress shop, a high-class fur shop, and various other shops, including a gift shop/antique dealer. There was also an agricultural student, an Israeli student of naval architecture, a children's psychiatrist, and one industrial chemist. Many of the men commuted to Glasgow daily to their various jobs.[102]

Decline in Popularity

Until the mid-1950s Ayr, and to a lesser extent other West Coast towns such as Prestwick, Troon, and Saltcoats (and, further north, Largs, Gourock, and, to an even lesser extent, Helenburgh), remained holiday destinations for Glasgow Jews, and were places to which some of them retired. However, the growing competition from, and accessibility to, English and Irish resorts and destinations abroad (including Israel—by 1950 Hellenic Airlines were offering flights from nearby Prestwick Airport to Tel Aviv, via London) made the Scottish towns less attractive. By that point the only surviving establishment was the Invercloy Hotel, which outlasted all of the other Jewish-run hotels and boarding houses in Ayr. At this point the community could still afford a minister, the Reverend Sam Knopp.

In 1956, reflecting its changing circumstances, the congregation discussed moving the *shul* to alternative premises—the Invercloy—which would be renovated for sacramental purposes.[103] By the beginning of the following year the congregation had purchased and redesigned the hotel, which thereafter became the focus of the community. The *shul*, communal center, and *cheder* were transferred there. At the same time, the hotel was rented out to a Jewish tenant who ran the hotel side of the business. This was a shrewd move because those guest residents at the hotel helped to encourage regular *minyanim*, such that services continued to be held; indeed, for this reason, the congregation ensured that the Invercloy continued to be advertised in the *Jewish Echo*. At the same time, the minutes of the congregation indicate "the apathy of the members towards attendance at the Sabbath morning services, and it was felt that gradual deterioration of religious observance would take place, unless steps were taken to remedy this problem."[104] The optimism of the war years had declined, to be replaced by stark new realities. The chairman of the congregation, Albert Steen, "pressed the point that members must attend services if the Congregation wishes to remain an active part of the community."[105] The Reverend Knopp had left, so, as a consequence, the committee agreed to approach the Glasgow Beth Din to arrange for visits from a minister on a monthly basis.

By this point, thirty families remained, numbering sixty-eight members, according to the *Jewish Year Book*. Some of these families lived beyond Ayr, such as Mr. and Mrs. Hymie Barman and family, and Mrs. T. Appleton and family, who were residents of Dumfries. There were also a number of societies which provided social activities. The Wingate Social Club continued to hold its bridge and discussion evenings; the Ladies Guild held dances and other functions to support charities, particularly ones in Israel; and the Zionist Society raised generous funds, numbering in the thousands, for Israel and arranged talks on Zionist subjects.[106] According to the *Scottish Jewish Year Book*, this continued until 1958. A report by the Board of Deputies on Ayr in October 1959 stated that regular services were conducted by laymen, children were taught by a teacher from Glasgow, but that the congregation was no longer able to keep a full-time minister because of a decrease in its population. It put the Jewish population at seventy, while the *Jewish Year Book* recorded sixty-eight and the *Jewish Chronicle* stated there were thirty-five families in Ayr.[107]

Scanning the pages of the *Jewish Echo* and *Jewish Chronicle*, it becomes apparent that, from around the mid–1960s, the Ayr Hebrew Congregation was almost defunct in its activity. Compared to earlier years, services, annual general meetings, and other social, charitable and fundraising events, began to peter out from 1960, and little appears from that date on, other than memorial notices. The Debating Society as well as the Discussion Group had to be revived constantly, but their work seems to have ceased by the 1960s. The minutes of the congregation noted "a lack of religious zeal in the Congregation," so it was decided to hold the Friday night services later in the evening (8:30 p.m.) in order to boost attendance.[108] Whether this had the desired result is not known. Scanning the pages of the *Jewish Echo* presents a bleak picture of Ayr, as the items relating to the community tended to be announcements and notices of deaths, memorials, and businesses for sale. One of the more shocking of these was the report of the death of seventy-year-old Rachel Ross in her bungalow in 1969.

Abraham Ross, a bingo-hall owner, lived with his wife Rachel in a bungalow at 2, Blackburn Place, near the sea. Abraham, born in Glasgow in 1902, was one of five children who lived in Govan and then the Gorbals. After leaving school, he joined his father in the rag and scrap metal trade. He then emigrated to Canada and the United States, but, in 1933, returned to join his father's business once again. There he met and married Rachel Freedman, his second wife. In 1941, when the bombing of Glasgow began, they moved to rented rooms in Ayr. Eleven years later they bought their house in Blackburn Place, and Abe commuted to Glasgow on a daily basis. Ross was described as "soft-spoken, shrewd, extremely conservative," while Rachel was very intelligent, left-wing, anti–Apartheid, and critical of the Royal family. Her views, in Abraham's words, "didn't make her popular with all our friends in Ayr." In 1961, Abraham launched a new business venture that was to become highly successful when he purchased a cinema in Paisley and converted it into a bingo hall at a time when the game was becoming an increasingly popular pastime. Occasionally, Abraham brought the takings home from the bingo hall at a time and kept them in a safe in the cloakroom cupboard. The safe always contained a great deal of money anyway. Rumors of this spread, and in 1969 two men broke into the Ross's house and tied up and assaulted the couple in order to get Abraham to reveal the whereabouts of the safe and to open it. Unfortunately, Rachel died as a result of her injuries, but Abraham survived the ordeal and continued to live in the house, indeed sleeping in the very bedroom where they were attacked. Patrick Meehan was wrongfully convicted of Rachel Ross's murder, and his solicitor, Joseph Beltrami, considered it a miscarriage of justice that ranked with that of the Oscar Slater case.[109]

The Closing of the Invercloy

During this decade many of the older members of the community began to pass away and were not replaced by incoming Jews because Ayr provided little opportunity for mass employment. Only two reports in the *Jewish Echo* mentioned any new arrivals in Ayr during the 1960s: Mr. and Mrs. Philip Freeman and their two daughters, Jacqueline (18) and Carol (13), who moved from England in 1966–67 when Philip was offered the job of managing Marks & Spencer; and Dr. Eliezer Gelfer, a general practitioner who had retired to

Ayr from Glasgow. Services continued, although how often they were held is not clear. They were led by Dr. Gelfer, who was also a *chazan*, but he died in 1972. Judging by the adverts for the various establishments in Ayr, holidaymakers still visited the town. However, they were not able to stem the slow decline of the community in the face of the deaths of its longest-standing members. As the visitors to Ayr declined, and as the resident community either moved or passed away, so the synagogue became in increasing danger of closing. The *Jewish Chronicle* of 11 October, 1974, announced:

HEBREW CONGREGATION TO LET INVERCLOY HOTEL, AYR
THE ONLY JEWISH (KOSHER) HOTEL IN SCOTLAND, AYR

> Established nearly 40 years. Excellently situated in own grounds near beach, and containing the local synagogue. Applications, invited from suitable persons with capital for necessary expenditure, should be addressed to: The Chairman, C. Freeman, 59 Auchendoon Crescent, Ayr.[110]

The final communal notice relating to Ayr that appeared in the *Jewish Echo* came in 1975. Cecil Freeman, for many years the leader of the Ayr congregation, wrote in a letter to the newspaper that he had attended a Shabbat morning service in Ayr synagogue in connection with a Jewish Students Northern Region weekend seminar held at the Invercloy Hotel. He praised the impeccable decorum, and while he felt that it had been very good to see young people, he stated that he could not escape the "saddening thought that this might well be the last service to be held in the Ayr synagogue, which was first established at the end of the last century, since there are now insufficient members in Ayr to form a *minyan*, and no new tenant can be found for the hotel."[111] The last tenants were Mrs. Solomons and Mr. Freed.

The hotel was sold for £31,500 in May 1975 to a rival hotelier. The synagogue was closed down, and its contents and appurtenances were transferred to the Newton Mearns Synagogue in Glasgow. In a somewhat ironic fashion (as it was his father Harris who had helped found the congregation in the first place), Cecil Freeman took a leading role in the *shul*'s disbandment. The synagogue was replaced with the Ayr Jewish Community Charitable Trust—incidentally, an idea that had been first mooted back in 1959 but for some reason didn't occur until a decade and a half later—the purpose of which was to distribute the proceeds from the sale of the congregation's assets to good causes, such as funding scholarships at Israeli universities, as it did in 1984.[112] Incidentally, Dr. and Mrs. Naftalin endowed an award in biology at Ayr Academy.[113] It was agreed that "Ayr Hebrew Congregation would not be wound up, or dissolved, but would continue, although with limited functions in the present circumstances."[114] At that point, according to the *Jewish Year Book*, the Jewish population was forty Jews, and that number continued to live and worship there, most likely in private homes or at relatives' houses in Glasgow, until 1985, when Ayr ceased to be listed. It was at that point that the community was disbanded, according to the *Jewish Chronicle*.¹¹⁵ By 1982, even Cecil Freeman himself had moved to Newton Mearns, a wealthy suburb of Glasgow. The following year the trustees of the Ayr Jewish community donated £8,000 to the Haifa Technion.¹¹⁶ The last communication from Ayr to the *Jewish Echo* before that newspaper was closed down in 1992 came one year earlier, in November, when Jeremy Cohen wrote about an Israeli peace conference. In March of that same year (1991) the *Jewish Chronicle* announced the engagement of Ian, son of Laura Tomlins of Ayr.¹¹⁷

Conclusion

Part of the reason for Ayr's decline is identical to the reason for its rise: its location and status as a holiday destination. The fortunes of Ayr's Jewish community rose and fell with its ability to attract Jewish tourists, as well as providing a safe haven during wartime. Following the end of the war the evacuees melted away, and, together with its declining capacity to pull in the visitors, Ayr's Jewish community declined. The West Coast of Scotland may well have continued to attract large volumes of visitors, but these tended to seek out self-catering accommodation in remoter locations, such as converted Scottish crofts, rather than Orthodox and kosher boarding houses in Ayr.¹¹⁸ Of course, this was not the Jewish community's fault, but it did not help that many found resorts like Ayr, Dunoon, and Rothesay cramped, rainy, and shabby.¹¹⁹ Unlike in Aberdeen or, as we shall see, Dundee, there were few other reasons to attract Jews on anything other than a short-term basis, as Ayr provided little permanent employment opportunities, such as a university (until 2007, when the University of the West of Scotland was created).

3

Dundee

Moving south down the northeast coast we arrive in Dundee, a port city on the Tay estuary. Famous for jute mills, jam, and journalism, it was settled by many Jewish immigrants from Europe's Baltic and eastern continental lands. For a while it was the largest Jewish community in Scotland outside of Glasgow and Edinburgh. The first links between Dundee and Jews date back to the seventeenth century. William Davidson, a Dundee merchant, moved to Amsterdam in 1640 and built up a network of Jewish agents, intelligencers and partners with whom he invested heavily.[1] Further connections were established in the course of the eighteenth century during the organization of the flax-buying and linen-selling markets.[2] As Henry McGrady Bell put it, "A growing market in cheap linens and packing cloths would certainly have attracted them [Jews] there in the eighteenth century, and they were very likely big buyers in the Dundee markets."[3] According to Kenneth Collins, however, the first connection of Jews with Dundee was in the study of medicine. Jews had been studying medicine under St. Andrews' auspices as early as 1834. They did not have to move there to qualify for the degree, as it was accepted practice that these degrees could be awarded *in absentia*. Louis Ashenheim was the first Jew to graduate, in 1839, followed by Alexander Zeigler in 1845, Maurice Davis in 1852, Leonard Emanuel in 1859, and Simon Belinfante in 1862. None of these individuals moved to the Dundee area, except to qualify by examination, as their studies had been conducted elsewhere, usually London or Edinburgh. Once qualified, they went elsewhere, often abroad: Ashenheim settled in Jamaica, Davis went to London, Emanuel served in the Indian Army, and Belinfante went to Australia.[4]

The German Jews of Dundee

The origins of the Dundee Jewish community date from the early 1840s. For a time it was the largest Jewish community outside of Glasgow and Edinburgh, although there are no precise figures for how many Jews came during this period. Unlike the other small Jewish communities in Scotland, which were primarily Eastern European, specifically from Imperial Russia, Dundee was initially settled by German-Jewish immigrants in the first half of the eighteenth century. They were part of a more general German immigration into Britain, which was distinctive from earlier arrivals in that they were middle-class and "respectable." Many of them were merchants and clerks with a history of large-scale mercantile businesses. They were attracted to Britain because of its unparalleled trading and industrial prominence, especially in textiles.[5]

Commerce (in particular, textiles) attracted Jews to Dundee. From about 1840 onwards, Jewish textile agents from Germany moved into Dundee for the purchase of jute, cheap linens, and packing cloths. With the backing of established merchant houses in Germany, they opened warehouses and offices in Dundee to purchase goods for export to family and business associates on the Continent.[6] Although they were German Jews, their ancestors probably came down the Baltic coast from Russia. By the 1850s, Jewish firms in Hamburg were sending representatives to Dundee, where offices were set up. These Jews soon became direct agents and then independent merchants.[7] Prominent Jewish merchants included Isaac Julius Weinberg, Messrs. Lipman and Hamel, Herman Cohen and Co., Hermann A. Hirsch, Holdheim and Wagner, F. Rosenstern and Co., Julius Salomon, Otto Friedheim, William Schlochauer, Daniel J. Jaffe, Victor Chose, Sampson and Unna, Arnold Cohen, Hassberger and Dreschfield, and Albert Wulf and Co.[8] These Jews formed the nucleus of the Jewish community in Dundee.

These German Jews were particularly influential in the jute business, resulting from the predominance of several German Jewish firms, such as Chose, Weinberg, and Polack, who were instrumental in Dundee's shift from flax to jute in the nineteenth century.[9] They introduced new financial methods and innovative marketing techniques, as well as organizing contacts abroad in places as far away as South America and the Near East. As a result of the boom in jute created by the Civil War and the building of the Midwestern railroads in the United States, these jute merchants prospered. Their wealth was increased even more when the Prussian army began to buy jute as it prepared for war with France, as well as the subsequent Franco–Prussian and Boer Wars, all of which combined to generate growth in the jute trade and triggered periods of high demand and vigorous profits.[10]

However, these German-Jewish immigrants were, according to C.C. Aronsfeld, likely to be "more German (if anything) than Jewish. Certainly few practised the old religion."[11] They "found no Jewish life when they came," quickly integrated, and many completely assimilated.[12] Like their compatriots and co-religionists that went to Glasgow, few of them identified with Judaism.[13] Others may simply have been deracinated in the first place. And a number even converted to Christianity—for instance, Victor Fraenkl (1841–1909). This lack of interest in observance perhaps explains the conspicuous lack of a synagogue until the late 1870s, some thirty years after the first German Jews started to arrive at the port. And even when it was formed, they were often aloof from it.[14] Even though there was a high probability that many of Dundee's German Jews were Reform, since it was originally a German movement, it seems they were either simply not interested in religion or did not have enough numbers to form a *shul*—unlike what had been done by similar well-to-do, assimilationist-minded German textile merchants in Bradford in 1873 (or in Manchester, Hull, and the United States, where Reform communities were established in the mid-nineteenth century).[15] The one person who was interested enough to found a synagogue in the mid-nineteenth century (as he did in Belfast) was Daniel Jaffe, but he had left Dundee by 1851, only having arrived in 1845.

Yet, at the same time, the absence of a *shul* probably allowed the German Jews to swiftly acculturate into Dundee life. Their relative laxity in religious observance explains in part their acceptance by non–Jews in Dundee, as the lack of distinctive religious behavior did not set them apart; indeed, as I have already mentioned, some German Jews were all too willing to adopt the predominant Christian forms of worship. It can also be partially explained by the tolerant atmosphere towards Jews in Scotland in general at that time. As a consequence, the German Jews became extremely well integrated into the commercial, civic and cultural life of the wider community. They were prosperous and hence part of the comfortable middle class. As their businesses flourished they became widely recognized and centrally involved in the daily life of the city, setting a pattern that would be copied by Jews through the nineteenth and twentieth centuries. Their influence extended to music, painting and other arts, and they were particularly active in local charitable organizations, contributing greatly to the general life of the city.[16]

Nevertheless, many of the German Jews did try to sustain some level of a distinctive religious identity. Julius Weinberg, for example, maintained his Jewish responsibilities and was heavily involved in various philanthropic causes, such as the Russian Relief Fund and the Synagogue Building Fund. He was also commended for his assistance to the poorer members of the community. By 1875, enough Jews, like Weinberg, interested in observing some degree of Judaism had arrived in Dundee for a correspondent to write to the *Jewish Chronicle*, calling attention to the increasing number of Jews residing in Dundee and suggesting that an effort be made to form a congregation there.[17] Informal services took place for the first time in 1878 when services were held at the private house of Mr. L. Fredinni, Hilltown.[18] The event was deemed worthy of a report in the *Dundee Courier* under the title "Jewish Services in Dundee," which stated, "Though we are but few in number, I do not think it will be uninteresting to learn that the sons of Abraham, scattered as they are, still continue, whenever opportunity offers, to uphold the religion of their ancestors, and to perpetuate the name of the God of Israel."[19]

The desire to move into more permanent premises soon led to the formal establishment of a synagogue in 1878, and with it the official formation of the Dundee Hebrew Congregation. Given the location of the initial and informal services—Hilltown—a deprived working-class area dominated by slums and tenements, those who attended were most likely poorer Eastern European Jews who had started to arrive in Dundee. Since the premises were a private house, they weren't suitable to house a congregation. Consequently, a synagogue was opened at 123, Murraygate that same year. Demand was high, reported the *Dundee Courier,* under the heading, "Opening of a Jewish Synagogue in Dundee," as "Services were held at nine in the morning, and again at eleven, at which large congregations assembled."[20] As was typical for a community of its size—twenty-two seat holders—it was no more than a couple of rented rooms near the town center.[21] The *Dundee Directory* for 1878–79 lists the building as being occupied by Jason Rattray & Co., linen merchant; Matthew Blackie, commercial merchant; David Gellatly, merchant; Isabella Gillon, dressmaker; John M. Noble, clerk; and William Wilkie, confectioner.

There has previously been some confusion as to the exact date of the formation of the synagogue. A number of sources, such as the *Jewish Year Book,* state 1874, but there is no further corroborating evidence.[22] The *Dundee Courier* in 1920 put the date of the formation of the congregation at 1884![23] Such a discrepancy is not helped by the fact that no list of office bearers was published, or that the records of the congregation have been lost. However, the report cited in the preceding paragraph in the *Dundee Courier* clearly states that services were held *for the first time* only in 1878. Furthermore, had there been a synagogue in 1874, why did one Jewish resident write to *The Jewish Chronicle* to complain about the lack of one? The *Dundee Directories* for these years shed no light on this matter, neither mentioning a synagogue nor even listing the Mr. L Fredinni of Hilltown cited above. In addition, in 1904 an appeal by the community stated that the congregation *had existed for only 26 years.*[24] Thus, it seems conclusive that 1878 and not 1874 was the year of the founding of the Dundee Hebrew Congregation.

The Invasion from the East

According to the 1881 census, the Dundee German community had reached a recorded peak of 81 German-born residents, including Christians and Jews. From the 1880s onwards the nature of the Jewish community in Dundee changed as Jews began to arrive in greater numbers from Russia (and more arrived again in 1904–05 as a result of persecution and poverty in Russia and Poland).[25] They took advantage of the introduction of cheap travel via steamship and railway to come in search of economic opportunities and to escape the conditions in their home countries. Although many Jews simply passed through on their way to the United States and other points in Britain, many others also stayed, drawn via internal migration because of the promise of port commerce and other business opportunities, altering the economic and religious tone of the community.[26]

These Russian Jews received a sympathetic welcome, and Christians and Jews alike were concerned with their plight. In 1891 a meeting was held in the town hall, presided over by the Lord Provost, to further the Russian Relief Fund (which was established in 1892), at which a large number of "leading Christians" were described as being present. Speeches denouncing the persecution of Jews in Russia were made, as well as speeches extolling Jewish philanthropy. More than £1,000 was raised, predominantly from Christians.[27] The Reverend Simeon Singer commented that, on a per capita basis, the amount raised in Dundee exceeded that of other parts of the country.[28] Ewan MacDonald believes that this indicates a widespread acceptance of Jews and Judaism among the upper classes during the 1890s.[29] At the same time, however, it must be stated that there was still a segment of Dundee's Christian population that saw Jews as a target for its missionary activities. Since 1845, a Dundee Female Jewish Association was established to work towards the promotion of "the conversion of the Jews." Interestingly, however, their work seems to have taken place almost entirely abroad, and their reports make no mention of such activity in Dundee itself.[30] This is most likely explained by the recognition of the Jewish Mission Committee of the Church of Scotland, bluntly known as the Committee for the Conversion of the Jews, "that their poor are well cared for by their own rabbis and the better-off people."[31]

The friction that the arrival of the Russian Jews did cause, however, was *within* the Jewish community itself. These Eastern European newcomers stood in "marked contrast" to their German-Jewish coreligionists. While the already-settled German Jews were determined to be "more of the better-off class,"[32] namely middle class, educated, acculturated, cultured, extremely well integrated into the commercial, civic and cultural life of the wider community, and assimilated religiously (if even Jewish in practice at all), the Eastern European Jews were Yiddish-speaking, often poor, living in the Hilltown district of Dundee. Such Jews owned market stalls in Dundee's Green Market and city arcade, tea rooms, lodging houses, general stores, and pawn and material shops.[33] They were described as being "shy and aloof," and "had been brought up in a much more secluded orthodox culture."[34] ("But," as one local remembered, "as they got to understand us they were gradually assimilated or at least tolerated".)

There was some fear that the newcomers might reflect badly upon, and undermine the position of, the earlier arrivals that had already assimilated into Dundee society. Despite some sympathy for their plight, the pre-existing upper-crust German Jews did not take kindly to the influx of their co-religionists from further east, whom they regarded as ill-educated and superstitious *ostjuden*. The ill feeling was probably reciprocated, as the newcomers would certainly have regarded the Germans as snobbish, assimilated, irreligious and too *English*. As a consequence, the two groups of Jews kept themselves apart, leading to two distinctive sub-communities, each with its own synagogue: the "German" and the "Litvak" (which, in this context, would have included the Ukrainian and Belorussian, as well as the Polish and Lithuanian immigrants).[35] Initially, the "Litvak" newcomers met at a site at 7, Ward Road. The *shul* consisted of no more than rented rooms within a block of warehouses and offices, an address shared with the Dundee Burns Club; merchants E. W. Bell and Co. and James Speakman; William Stewart, a boot maker; Miss Lightfoot, a teacher; and the artists James G. H. Spindler and Mary Marshall.[36] (The Jewish architectural historian Sharman Kadish states that it was a house built in the 1880s.[37]) The rival synagogues reflected differences in liturgical style, as well as practice, and, although there is no evidence that the existing *shul* was Reform, its ways probably did not make the Orthodox newcomers feel sufficiently at home. Confusingly, however, the Ward Road synagogue is the only Hebrew congregation recorded in the *Dundee Directory* for 1889-90 leading one to wonder if the Murraygate community still existed by that point, or whether it had been decimated and absorbed into Ward Road.

Significantly, the main divisions in the Dundee community at that time were neither between Jews and their gentile neighbors nor between the German and Eastern European Jews, who might have well come from different worlds, but between the two younger "Litvak" communities. The Litvak sub-community itself divided into two rival congregations: the aforementioned Ward Road site and another one at the private home of S. Fridman, a glass merchant living at 8, Bank Street (a building he shared with John Bruce & Son, architects; Mrs. Crostan; David Grant, fruiterer; Jane Rattray, tobacconist; and the Young Women's Christian Association meeting rooms). The exact dates of the establishment of these two smaller *shuls* are unknown, but certainly they were both in existence by 1882 when the numbers of new immigrants from Eastern Europe were high enough to sustain them.[38]

The Ward Road congregation split over personal differences, and a breakaway, rival congregation was founded in Bank Street. Since this was the home of S. Fridman and his brother Lewis, a wholesale picture frame manufacturer, they were the chief protagonists in the rift. Thereafter a series of personal frictions and differences between the key personalities of each congregation kept the Ward Road and Bank Street synagogues apart. Nonetheless, despite these personal differences, the two communities could probably have coexisted but for their pressing religious requirements: a trained Jewish butcher (*shochet*) was required to slaughter animals in accordance with Jewish law in order to render them kosher, an important requirement for these Eastern European Jews who strictly adhered to Orthodox practice. All of the differences and enmities came to a head over the issue of acquiring a *shochet*, erupting into a major dispute that not only involved the rival congregations in Dundee, but also spread as far as Edinburgh and London.

The crisis arose in 1883 when both of the Eastern European congregations (Ward Road and Bank Street, respectively) simultaneously contacted the Chief Rabbi to request the services of a *shochet*, apparently having been without one for some time. In the absence of one, they had been receiving kosher meat from Glasgow, which was delivered by train. Given the Scottish climate, this was a largely satisfactory—if somewhat inconvenient—arrangement in winter, but at warmer times of the year the meat tended to spoil. Each synagogue corresponded with the Chief Rabbi separately, requesting he send a *shochet*. Eventually, in response to their requests, the Chief Rabbi sent one Hirsch Levi to Dundee. The Chief Rabbi sent Levi, it seems, with the intention of him being hired by the Bank Street congregation, but he was poached and joined Ward Road, during which time he slaughtered meat and poultry for both members and non-subscribers to the congregation who were charged sixpence for every chicken or bird slaughtered and for every pound of beef.[39] Eventually, however, Levi fell out with the Ward Road congregation and defected to the "opposition" *shul* in Bank Street. Meanwhile, both sides corresponded with the Chief Rabbi, largely to no avail (probably on account of the distance between London and Dundee). Ultimately, the case ended in court.[40]

A compromise was achieved and the two communities were reconciled, forming a single congregation which worshipped together thereafter. The synagogue was, according to the *Dundee Directory*, located at 50, Barrack Street. Since it was an address shared with gardener James Sime and photographer Thomas Muir, it seems it may have been another private home.[41] One year later, however, it was listed as being back at Ward Road![42] The Chief Rabbi was so delighted that these remote members of his community had finally behaved in such a mature way that he insisted on attending the *shul*'s dedication in 1892, and preached an uplifting sermon extolling them and pronouncing his admiration for the fellowship of the congregation.[43] As befitting a London-based organ, the *Jewish Chronicle* even suggested, in a somewhat exaggerated fashion, that the Chief Rabbi's visit was the factor that had effected the union of the Jews of Dundee.[44] Ironically, the lack of extant documentation means that the actual response of the Chief Rabbi is unknown. Although the spat was short-lived, it was notable inasmuch that such divisions as occurred in Dundee were not a feature of the other small communities, as the communities tended to be far more ethnically and religiously homogenous. The incident was also a very revealing portrait of how the Dundee community functioned in the late nineteenth century, and furthermore of the relationship of this provincial community to the metropolitan center of Jewish life in Britain, with which it pleaded (unsuccessfully) for intercession, as well as the internal dynamics of a community which was not only stratified by wealth, class and national origin, but also in terms of religious rivalries.

Greater Orthodoxy

As the Eastern European Jews came to dominate the Dundee congregation, a shift to greater Orthodox practice was in evidence. This reflected the demographic change in the Jewish community. By 1892, most of the fifty Jewish families living there hailed from Russia, Poland and, to a lesser extent, Lithuania. Only one or two families of wealthy Jewish merchants of German origin engaged in the jute trade survived, but they were tending towards assimilation.[45] Consequently, a Hebrew School was established in 1893, with the minister and *shochet*, the Reverend Simon Wulf Rosenzweig, as its head. By 1896–97 the school had thirty scholars, until 1902 when the figure dropped to twelve. During his pastoral tour of Scotland in 1896, the Chief Rabbi examined the children of Dundee and pronounced the results as "highly satisfactory," and expressed his approval of "the advanced state of progress made by the children." The Chief Rabbi was also happy with the state of religious observance in Dundee because, unlike in Aberdeen, he did not exhort the congregation to keep the Sabbath more strictly than some of them were in the habit of doing.[46]

In 1894 Dundee's minister, the Reverend S. Rosenzweig, together with the president of the congregation, J.H. Cohen, made arrangements for the supply of kosher Scottish beef to the London market. Adverts for the meat were carried in the *Jewish Chronicle* shortly thereafter.[47] The market for kosher meat in Dundee was limited, and the extra slaughtering was a welcome perquisite to what was an already small ministerial salary. However, not long after the introduction of the Jewish method of slaughter in Dundee, the local press contained correspondence relating to it. As a result of the publicity, the Markets Committee attended the slaughter house and reported on the practice favorably, deciding to take no further action (as had happened in Aberdeen), as the branch was convinced that nothing was at all wrong with kosher slaughter.[48]

There were other signs of this greater religiousness. A Jewish burial society for the preparation of the dead was formed in 1888 by the Flax Shipping Brothers. A Hebrew Burial Fund, the objective of which was to defray the expenses of those unable to pay, was set up the following year. Its income averaged £12 per year, and it assisted three individuals in 1895; but since there was no dedicated Jewish burial ground in Dundee, they were most likely buried in Edinburgh or Glasgow.[49] The community was then able to purchase a sixty-plot section of the public Dundee Eastern Cemetery on Arbroath Road at the lowest rate, owing to the smallness of the funds at its disposal. It functioned as the community's official burial ground since ten-month-old Isabella Nathan was buried there in 1889. As the need grew, further ground was purchased, and one-hundred-and-fifty-four burials were recorded between 1889 and 2005.[50] Vaults in Balgay Park were added later, but these seemed to have been used only by a single family of German Jews.[51]

The crowning moment of this increased faith was the opening of a new *shul* in 1895. While the *Jewish Chronicle* reported that the synagogue was located at 132, Murraygate, the *Dundee Directory* for 1895–96 stated it was at 138; by the following year it had changed its mind and agreed with the *Jewish Chronicle*, even listing its secretary as Nathan Cree.[52] The new premises were described as "commodious and comfortable," and "suitably furnished and tastefully decorated." It could seat more than one hundred worshippers and contained a Vestry Room large enough to entertain members of the congregation.[53] Confusingly, however, the *Dundee Directory* also listed the British & Foreign Metaline Co.; D. Stewart & Co., iron merchants; and John Robinson, clothier, at the same address.

At this point, the community numbered fifty individuals, according to the *Jewish Year Book*, of which only twenty-five were seat holders.[54] The larger size of the synagogue, therefore, reflected some optimism about the future growth of the community, but also the growing comfortableness and integration of the Eastern Europeans into Dundee life. Yet, the community's economic status was still mixed—from wealthy German Jewish businessmen at one end, such as Weinberg, to poor Eastern European Jews who relied on philanthropy and communal charity at the other. As an indication of this, but also of the Orthodox Jewish imperative to provide charitable assistance, a Benefit and Benevolent Loan Society was set up in 1896 to grant short-term interest-free loans to poorer members to assist in establishing and extending their businesses. It disbursed £10–£14 to its claimants in its first year.[55] In this way, the richer members of the community not only helped their less fortunate co-religionists, but such start-up capital also gave its recipients a crucial competitive edge over their non–Jewish rivals. Thus, *The Scotsman* later reported that the Jewish poor of Dundee "are well cared for by their own rabbis and the better-off people."[56]

By 1899, the synagogue's finances were described as "prosperous."[57] Some of these funds went into supporting Zionist schemes. Around 1902, a (Zionist) Shekel Group was formed, with seven members.[58] Nine shares were purchased, at the cost of one pound each, in the Jewish Colonial Trust. By this point, the community was located at 62, Murraygate. Since the *Dundee Directory* also listed the British & Foreign Metaline Co.; D. Stewart & Co., iron merchants; William J. Fraser, printer; and John Robinson, clothier, at the same address, it seems that the numbering of the building, rather than its location, had changed. Indeed, there is no entry for 132, Murraygate whatsoever by that point. The congregation had secured a new minister, the Reverend Gabrial Zacutta (next to his entry in the *Dundee Directory* were the words "Hebrew Church").[59] Zacutta was born in Russia c.1872 before emigrating to England. He was recorded in the 1901 census as living in Liverpool, where he was naturalized in 1900.[60]

In 1902 a set of rules for the congregation was drawn up. The gap between

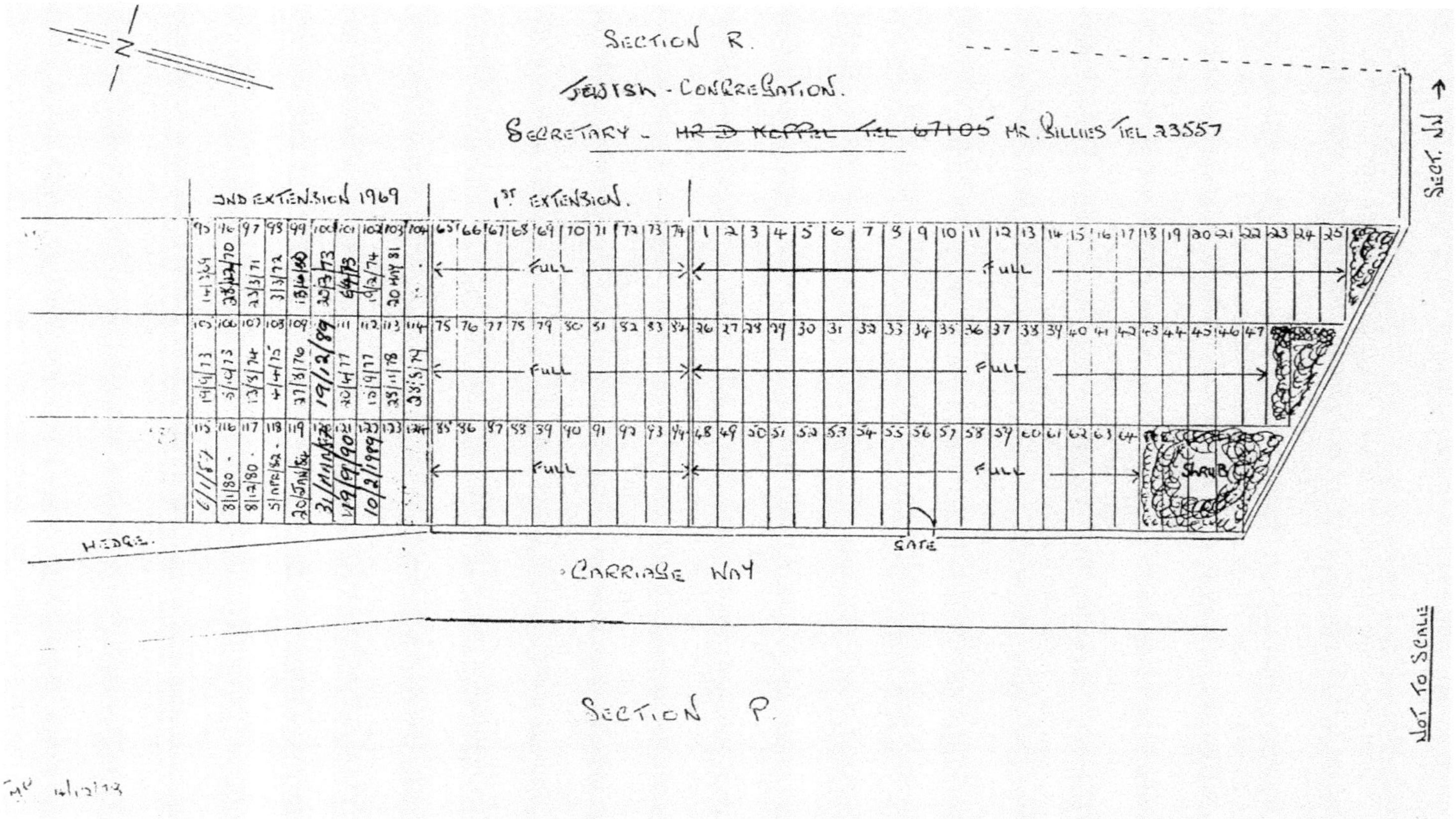
SECTION R.
JEWISH - CONGREGATION.
SECRETARY - MR D KEPPEL TEL 67105 MR. GILLIES TEL 23557
2ND EXTENSION 1969
1ST EXTENSION.
FULL
SHRUB
HEDGE.
GATE
CARRIAGE WAY
SECTION P.
SECT. JJ
NOT TO SCALE

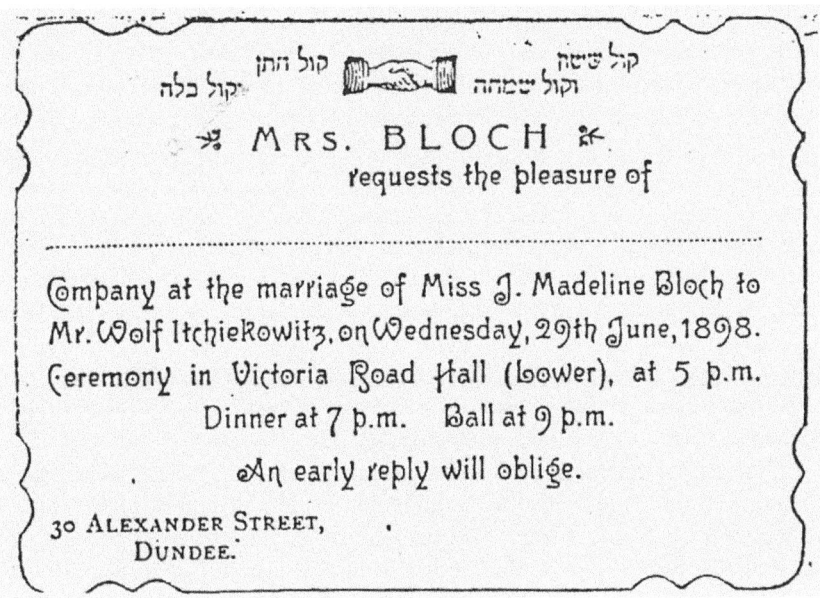

Wedding Invite, Dundee, 1898. (Courtesy of the Scottish Jewish Archives Centre.)

the establishment of a *shul* in 1878 and the writing of its constitution is inexplicably strange. Perhaps the impermanency of the *shul's* tenancy at various locations, combined with the brief split into two congregations, prevented such an occurrence. Thus, it was possibly only with the establishment of a more permanent home that the congregants felt able to develop a set of rules. But still, this does not explain the gap of seven years between the opening of the *shul* in 1895 and the advent of its constitution in 1902. In any case, the document makes interesting reading and provides insight into the Dundee Jewish community at the turn of the twentieth century.

Not only was it clear that the *shul* was a hierarchical organization, but also that it exercised an almost complete monopoly over Jewish life in Dundee. In addition to renting a seat in the synagogue, only seat-holders were entitled to religious requirements for Orthodox Jewish life as provided by the *shul*—namely, kosher meat, the killing of poultry, the teaching of the children, and burial rights. The *shochet*, who was contracted by the *shul*, had to attend all services, at which time he was required to preach and read; conduct marriage, circumcision, burial and tombstone-setting ceremonies; oversee and teach in the Hebrew School for two hours every day (with the exception of Fridays and festivals); and butchering. Such multi-tasking, which was not well-recompensed, as we have seen, was fairly typical of provincial British communities

Opposite page: Plan of Jewish Section, Dundee Cemetery

at this time. It was also clear that there were Jews residing in Dundee who were not members of the *shul* but requested to use it in order to hold a memorial service for departed relatives (*Yahrzeit*), and that, furthermore, such services were often held in private homes at which *shul* members attended (much to the annoyance of the synagogue authorities). The dual requirements that non-members pay for such services in the *shul* and the fining of members who attended them at the private homes of non-members demonstrated a clear attempt of the *shul* to control those areas outside of its immediate jurisdiction.[61] Furthermore, a letter to the *Jewish Chronicle* from one disgruntled member of the community in 1905 illustrates how the synagogue attempted to keep its members in order: "Kindly grant me a small space to inquire of your numerous readers in provincial towns whether in any small congregation the practice exists of stopping the supply of kosher meat to a member who has fallen in arrears with his contribution or offerings."[62]

The earlier optimism had been vindicated, and the community had grown to one-hundred-and-forty-two individuals by 1905.[63] Many of these new arrivals were escaping poverty and persecution in their homelands. Some of those, Wolf Rothman and his family, for instance, found "a small but energetic Jewish community."[64] As a consequence, alternative premises were sought and a Building Fund was established to build or acquire a synagogue and a school room (to which Winston Churchill, then the Member of Parliament [MP] for Dundee, contributed a sum of money).[65] It took six years for the community to locate a suitable building, during which time the congregation used alternative venues; the marriage certificate of Samuel Chodorovsky to Fanny Rothfield in August 1907, for example, lists 62, Murraygate as the site of the synagogue. That of Solomon Bell to Hannah Rothfield is listed as taking place at 124 Seagate.[66] The new location of the *shul* was a house and stores (Sharman Kadish calls it a "converted warehouse"[67]) at 15 and 15a, Meadow Street, previously occupied by coal dealer George Spalding and the St. Andrew's UF Mission Hall. It was acquired at the cost of £520, at which point the community numbered one-hundred-and-fifty. Yet, the synagogue did not open for another nine years (in 1920) due to the financially weak state of the congregation, which could afford to purchase the building but could not meet the expense of altering it for sacramental purposes, needing a further £350.[68] Indeed, it took the community fourteen years to collect the new building fund, but they were still forced to approach the Chief Rabbi and the London Jewish community for additional financial help.[69]

This financial situation, which was described as "one of the most difficult periods in the history of the congregation,"[70] was attributable to an economic downturn in the 1920s. Dundee suffered from the global recession, changing market conditions (with falling demand for jute products), a relatively outdated technological base, comparatively high costs of production, and a lack of new inward investment.[71] The result was the decline of the economic predominance of the German Jews, combined with their declining numbers. Before 1914 they had already started to lose ground, and the First World War damaged their position to such an extent that they never recovered from it. A general weakening in the market, combined with vigorous domestic and foreign competition, caused them to move to other businesses. By the 1930s the jute industry was in depression.[72] No new blood was introduced, as sons chose not to follow in their fathers' footsteps in the textile trade and many left Dundee, possibly as a result of the anti–German feeling prompted by the war, during which German-owned shops were looted and Germans were interned.[73] Others most likely served and died in the war, such as Weinberg's son, who was an officer in the 4th Battalion of the Black Watch and was killed in action at the first battle of Ypres.[74]

This trend was exacerbated by later developments that accounted for the decline in Dundee Jewry's numbers: after a high of one-hundred-and-fifty-two in 1913, the figure dropped to one-hundred-and-forty-two the following year, and one-hundred-and-twenty the year after that. By 1920 the number of Jews was one-hundred. The new Yiddish-speaking arrivals of the 1880s had completely overwhelmed and displaced those who had already settled. Perhaps as a reflection of these changes, the community had a rapid turnover of ministers between 1906 and 1920, employing seven different people during that period: the Reverend A. Eilder or Eilden, Marks Glaser, Mr. Michaelson, Solomon King, J.M. Kahan, the Reverend Leib A. Falk, and Aaron Miller. The Reverend Falk had left Russia, where he was born, and arrived in Inverness in 1908 to take up the vacant position there, but moved to Dundee in 1913, as it was a bigger and hence richer community. In 1915 he married a local Dundee girl, Fanny Rosen of Forebank Terrace, providing one of the few endogamous marriages between Jewish residents of that city. The ceremony, performed by the Reverend J.L. Hillkovitz of Glasgow, was reported in *The Scotsman*, helping to raise the profile of the community.[75]

Changing Times

By the end of the First World War the community was on the rise. As a mark of this revived situation, the new synagogue finally opened in 1920. Rather than simply renting a room, the community had purchased a two-storey building tucked away in a small alley, and hired the architectural services of Bruce, Son & Morton to redesign it specifically for sacramental purposes. In contrast, Aberdeen's Jewish community was only able to open a comparable *shul* in 1945, some twenty-five years later, indicating the more established and affluent nature of the congregation in Dundee. The new synagogue building housed a school room and committee room, which was used for meetings and parties, on the ground floor, and a sanctuary on the second.

As required by Orthodox practice, the *shul* was divided into separate sections—one for men, which could accommodate one-hundred-and-twenty-six, and a ladies gallery, which seated fifty-six.[76] It was the first permanent place of worship in the history of the congregation, as well as the first time that the building was not shared with other people or businesses. The opening ceremony was performed by Maurice Bloch and Rabbi Salis Daiches, after which a reception was held at the Forester's Hall. Bloch, who was born in 1882, had grown up in Dundee before moving to Glasgow as a young man in 1910. With his brother Joseph, he created Bloch Brothers (Distillers) Ltd. The business grew rapidly, especially following the export of whisky to America during Prohibition.[77] He went on to become, in the words of Ben Braber, "an outstanding businessman, philanthropist, Unionist politician and communal leader," and received a knighthood.[78] When Bloch died in 1964 he was called the "uncrowned king" of Glasgow Jewry.[79] The whole event was reported by the *Dundee Courier*.[80] A new minister, Reverend Solomon Bressloff, from Russia, had also been employed in 1920, and he performed the consecration ceremony. However, he had left by 1922, to be replaced by the Reverend M. Franks, who stayed until 1937, only to be followed by the Reverend M. Isaacs, who lasted until 1944/45.

The synagogue's finances were also in a healthy state, showing a balance of £103.[81] By 1924, the congregation reported having had "a record financial year."[82] There were two further markers of the community's stable footing. The first was the graduation of Dundee-born David Jacob in 1922. He read medicine at St. Andrews and, unusually, returned to Dundee to practice, where he was also active in the Jewish community.[83] The second was its ability to elect a Jewish MP for Dundee. Michael Marcus from Edinburgh, who was aged thirty-three at the time of his election, served in this capacity during the years 1929–1931, during which time he was the Parliamentary Private Secretary to Under Secretary of State for Scotland. He often spoke in Parliament on issues that were of particular interest to Jews, not something that all Jewish Members of Parliament, did by any means.[84] The election of Marcus demonstrated just how well Jews had become integrated not just in Dundee in particular, but in Scotland in general. It also showed that Dundee had accepted the Jews in their midst and had no problem electing a Jew as their representative.

The existing community was boosted further by an influx of relatively high levels of American Jewish medical students who arrived in Scotland from 1927 onwards. The imposition of a *numerus clausus*—a deliberately restrictive quota on Jewish students—in American medical schools, in particular those attached to the Ivy League universities, explains this sudden arrival of students from the United States. The peak year was 1933 when twenty-nine American students entered St. Andrews and took their clinical course in Dundee, as they were unable to complete their studies at New York University because of the Depression. The Principal of St. Andrews, Sir James Irvine, actively encouraged Jewish Americans to attend his university when he learned of the difficulties they faced.[85] Other students came from South Africa—for example, Louis Freed of Johannesburg, who was studying medicine at the University of St. Andrews.

The first students who came over made some effort to make contact with the local Jewish community, as their numbers were small and they did not yet have a self-contained society of their own. They received an enthusiastic welcome by the community, especially those with eligible daughters, and were offered mealtime hospitality, especially on Shabbat and the holydays. For example, the president of the congregation, Nathan Cree, kept an open house for them on such occasions.[86] However, often from non-observant backgrounds themselves, the American Jewish students displayed a disregard for Orthodox Jewish practices, which upset their Jewish landladies. Nevertheless, such meetings occasionally led to marriage. In 1933, for example, Jack Morton Greenberg of Brooklyn, New York, married the Cree's youngest daughter Miriam.[87] Marie Kahan likewise met her husband when he came from America to study medicine at the University of St. Andrews.[88] As time went on, though, the Americans became more self-enclosed and interacted less with the local Jewish communities. They met regularly and informally, usually at lunchtimes and weekends. Only a few of them took Jewish digs. One exception was Belle Shedowitz, who recalled being "ordered" to stay with a Jewish family in Dundee; and Herbert Goldberg recalled some students trying to act "British" while avoiding the other Americans. Overall, the students made no discernable boost to the recorded figures of the community, which remained stable, probably because they didn't affiliate with the synagogue and so were not necessarily counted.[89] A survey conducted by Geoffrey D.M. Block in 1936–37, however, found that out of a population of 663 students at St. Andrews, none were Jewish![90] Yet, William D. Rubinstein believes that "this figure is an underestimate" because Block's results relied upon data "provided by the Secretaries of the Inter-University Jewish Federation," and so any student who did not belong to that organization was most likely excluded.[91]

By the end of the 1930s, the German-Jewish influence briefly resurfaced only to decline again even further. Of the one-thousand Jewish refugees who fled Germany for Scotland, a mere thirty-eight came to Dundee, boosting the community's size from one-hundred in 1938 to one-hundred-and-seventeen in 1939/1940. This amounted to approximately thirty Jewish families. Like their predecessors, these Jews tended to be assimilated, educated, wealthy, and middle-class. Although they came from countries influenced by the Reform movement, no Reform synagogue was set up in Dundee, most likely because their numbers were too small, and the immigrants were integrated into the existing religious structures. However, in 1939, when the city was declared a "protected area," they were declared "aliens" and forced to move to Glasgow, explaining the limited rise of the population numbers.[92]

The Second World War was an active period for the Dundee community, much of which was war-related. Twenty-six Jews from Dundee fought in the war, and one was killed: twenty-two-year-old Louis Koppel, a gunner with the 53rd (the Worcester Yeomanry) Anti-Tank Regiment, Royal Artillery, who was killed on 12 May, 1940, and buried in Dundee.[93] Others served on the home front, such as Sam Herman, who was a sergeant in a service unit which fought fires at the height of the blitz. In fact, despite the difficult and prevailing wartime conditions, the community seemed to thrive. The Plebeians, a table tennis club with social activities for about forty Jews and non–Jews, was formed by Dr. David Jacob, who was also the honorary president of the Dundee District Table Tennis Association.[94] Services continued as usual, although from 1939 (until 1961), services took place on the High Holy Days, but during the year only on a Friday evening, as it was not possible to get a *minyan* on Saturday morning.[95]

Dundee's numbers reached an all-time high of one-hundred-and-seventeen when they were boosted by evacuees and Jewish servicemen stationed in the area.[96] One of those was Captain Julius Green from Dunfermline, who was ordered to join the 152 (Highland) Field Ambulance of the 51st Highland Division at Dundee, which was billeted in the Caird Hall in the town center. He was stationed there for six weeks.[97] On Boxing Day in 1940, for example, a large troop of Polish Jewish soldiers were addressed by Rabbi Melcer, chaplain to Polish forces, after which they were entertained at a local café by the Dundee community.[98] A record balance sheet was submitted in 1943, demonstrating that the congregation was on a sound financial footing.[99] The community was also involved in various relief and fund-raising efforts, such as the Emergency Education Committee (set up to provide Hebrew Classes for evacuees), the Central Council for Jewish Refugees, the Dundee Royal Infirmary, Stalingrad Hospital Fund, Aid-to-China Fund, the British Red Cross, the Chief Rabbi's European Relief Appeal, the German Refugees Fund, Save the Children, and the United Palestine Appeal. Various functions, such as dances and concerts, were held to raise money for these and other causes, as well as to entertain the visiting troops. In 1939, for example, a committee was formed to aid Austrian and German refugees, and funds were raised during a well-attended dance in Kidd's Room and ladies' whist drives.[100]

Post-War Stability

The community's good fortunes continued during the years immediately after the war. By 1945, and for the next five years, Dundee's Jews numbered thirty-five families.[101] They mostly owned shops, factories, or warehouses in areas such as clothing, furniture, antiques, and sacking. Other occupations held by Dundee's Jews included electrician, bookmaker, hairdresser, upholsterer, greengrocer, pharmacist, and doctor.[102] As they became more affluent, they moved to the wealthier parts of Dundee, such as the suburb of Broughty Ferry, and their children began to enter university and graduate in areas such as medicine, law, and teaching. Marie Kahan, for example, graduated from Harris Academy and joined the *Dundee Courier Journal* in their bindery operations before opening a small portrait studio in Dundee.[103] The influx and expansion of new post-war light engineering industries into Dundee must have also helped. Goods such as cash registers, batteries, watches, toys, and sound equipment were produced, as American firms moved into the area, attracted by the large pool of cheap female labor. Timex, for example, established a large factory to manufacture clocks and watches.[104]

The community was on a stable enough financial footing in 1945 to hire another permanent and resident minister, *shochet*, and teacher, the Reverend Morris Segal of Dunfermline, on a salary of £6 per week with additional perquisites. He stayed in his post until 1963, when he retired. In the years leading to the establishment of the state of Israel, the community made a relatively large contribution to Jewish and general charity, and to Zionist fundraising; in fact, its contribution was proportionally larger than those of the larger communities in Glasgow and Edinburgh. The role of women, for example, through W.I.Z.O., Ladies' Guild or Ladies Holy Vestment Society seems to have been crucial. In 1962 it was reported that Mrs. H. Gillis was elected as a member of the Council of the Dundee Hebrew Congregation—a first report of this kind, which may symbolize the rising importance of women in Jewish communal work. Fundraising also provided opportunities for social contact, such as whist drives in people's homes. There was also a Jewish Society. A branch of the Orthodox-Zionist *Bnei Akivah* youth group was set up in 1956, and it had a successful year, with regular meetings and outings, all of which were well attended.[105] The formation of such a group and its reported activities in 1956–1960 is remarkable in this context and may also help show the presence of young families with children, as well as the renewed attention for Jewish education and group activities for the younger members of the community.

An article in the *Jewish Chronicle*, "An Outpost of British Jewry," from 1958 gave a revealing portrait of the community at that time. The community numbered twenty-two families or ninety individuals, and was described as "well-knit." Among those described in the article were four doctors, a pharmacist, a schoolteacher, several students (including some from Israel), and two lecturers. There were no living relatives of the older Austro-Hungarian generation who had immigrated to Dundee in the mid-nineteenth century.[106] The German-Jewish influence in Dundee had all but disappeared.[107] W.I.Z.O. meetings were held annually.[108] A J.N.F. group had been set up and grew in strength annually. It raised funds through monthly whist drives, which, since the community was so small, were patronized by non–Jewish friends. Fortnightly teas were held in the members' homes, and each hostess donated a small gift, which helped augment the funds considerably. Obviously, these also functioned as communal occasions, and it was reported that "the ladies enjoy the social atmosphere."[109]

As for the inculcation of Jewish values, a report in the *Jewish Echo* revealed that the Jewish children were "well up to standard in reading, writing and General Hebrew."[110] Students from nearby St. Andrews attended High Holy Day services in Dundee, and Jewish lodgings were arranged to enable them to stay and observe the High Holy Days there.[111] Although by the following year the community was described as "small and declining,"[112] this did not prevent or deter the Jewish students of neighboring St. Andrews from inaugurating a Jewish Society in Dundee in 1959.[113] A testament to the success of Jewish education in Dundee during this period appeared in a 2006 book, whose dedication by one of its editors reads: "To the now almost vanished Dundee Jewish community, where as a teenager I first learnt the meaning of collective Jewish responsibility, at least to assemble a minyan for Yom Kippur prayer."[114]

Overall, for most of this period Jews enjoyed good relations with the host communities. In general, unlike most other European countries, Scotland has had a good record of tolerance towards Jews, and a lack of anti–Semitism. This was especially true outside of Glasgow and Edinburgh. Anti-Semitic activity in Dundee was virtually unknown. Certainly, as far as can be ascertained, Jewish immigrants, fared better than their Irish counterparts.[115] As we have seen, in the past Dundee absorbed its early German Jewish immigrants who rose to high positions in the city's cultural, civic and industrial life. The city was likewise sympathetic to the Eastern European Jews who came in greater numbers in the 1880s, as it was to those fleeing Nazism in the 1930s. Thereafter, the experience was summed up by the following quote from one of the Jewish residents: "Christians ... Jews it didn't make any difference they all got, got on very well together."[116] The only sour notes during this period occurred in 1893 when the introduction of new tailoring techniques by a Jewish firm of tailors known as "Freeman," who had transferred from Glasgow, aroused fierce opposition from local tailors,[117] and in 1960 when two men stuck up an anti–Jewish poster on a Dundee shop window with Union Jack on it and the words "Jewish H.P. get out."[118]

By 1960 the community was in decline, falling to eighty-nine individuals.[119] Two years later it was down to eighty.[120] Each loss of a member resulted in decreased annual income. As a result, the optimism of earlier years had all but disappeared. When Julius Jung of the Office of Small Communities visited in 1962, he reported, "There was agreement among the large attendance that disintegration was setting in; some felt because the Reverend Segal, now an elderly man, had no hold of any kind over the members, particularly those of the more English type."[121] The congregation's annual report of 1963 resounded instead with a real sense of the community's limitations, noting that it was a "tiny community" with only twenty-three paying members.[122] The following year Segal retired, never to be replaced, although he carried out his butchering and teaching services on a temporary basis one day a week for several years thereafter. The community struggled to find a replacement, in part because its limited income—£600 per annum—was not attractive enough even to appeal to a single, young man in light of the better salaries offered by larger communities. At that time, £700 was considered a very moderate sum for such a position, but little could be done about it; as members left Dundee, the community's income was decreased dramatically, creating an inability to hire. Furthermore, few such qualified individuals wanted to leave London's large and active Jewish community for what was perceived to be a Jewish backwater.

In contrast, the students' society presented a picture of buoyancy.[123] Indeed, the community and the students' society seemed to be heading in opposite directions—as the former declined, the latter thrived. By 1968 the *Jewish Chronicle* wrote, "Over the years Dundee's communal batteries have run down—even the ladies guild ... has virtually ceased to exist." Services were held once a week on Friday nights and on the festivals, led by Salo Gillespie, a retired Royal Artilleryman who had moved to Dundee from Glasgow. He continued in this role until 1981 when internal communal politics and ill health led him to retire. As a result of his extensive experience of burying Jewish solders during the Second World War, he was also able to conduct Jewish burial services. But Dundee still had no resident minister, *chazan* or *shochet*, having failed to replace Segal. In comparison, the student society was described as "a bonnie thrustful infant which has quickly made its mark on the Jewish student map." It had thirty members (twenty at Dundee and ten at St. Andrews).[124] As a mark of these trends, just about all of the *Jewish Chronicle*'s coverage of Dundee was devoted to the students and not the community (even if they did hold joint events and cooperated closely).

Given these opposing trajectories, the congregation wisely made the decision to take greater advantage of the incoming student reinforcements in its midst as an opportunity for revitalization. Without the influx of students in this period it is clear that the Dundee community might not have survived. Closer cooperation between the community and the students enabled it to continue during these years, and the presence of two universities so close to Dundee is an explanatory factor in the congregation's survival after the Second World War when others failed. These students were not necessarily members of local families and often came from outside Dundee. In addition to the second generation of shopkeepers that made up the community, the universities had attracted several academics, as well as medical practitioners and specialists from England, Scotland, Israel and America.

A New *Shul* for Dundee

In 1973 the Meadow Street synagogue was closed. This was not, however, due to the decline of the congregation. Rather, the *shul* had been compulsorily purchased, closed, and demolished in 1973 by the local council as part of its plans for regenerating the city center. According to Paul Spicker, the current president of Dundee Hebrew Congregation, "Despite the dislocation, services continued to be held in temporary premises, while the Congregation met to discuss the plans for the new building and future activities."[125] In the interim, in the absence of a *shul* building, improvisation became the key word, as manifested by the use of Lecture Hall Number Two of Dundee University to hold the Yom Kippur services in 1973.[126] Albert Jacob recalled that rooms were borrowed from the chaplaincy center or rented from a local hotel in the University for holding the High Holy Day services. The Scrolls of the Law were portable, and the congregation had a converted wardrobe with a wooden Decalogue placed on top as its Ark.[127] During this period the community was also able to host the renowned bible scholar Dr. Geza Vermes when he was invited by the University of Dundee to deliver the Margaret Harris series of lectures in 1977. A reception was organized, so many members of the community had the opportunity to meet him.

In the meantime, the council was obligated to replace the *shul* with similar amenities out of its own pocket as compensation, which it did with a purpose-built synagogue. Dundee thus became the only small community in Scotland, outside of Edinburgh and Glasgow, which had its own specifically designed synagogue building, but, as one observer put it, "is little used."[128] Due to their limited size and wealth, the other Scottish-Jewish congregations had to wait a long time before they could afford their own building, typically renting rooms for a number of years and then acquiring a structure that could be converted into use as a *shul*. Even then, none of them could afford to erect their own building from scratch. Since ten families remained, it is very clear, then, that without the Council's input, such a synagogue could not have been constructed from the available funds.[129]

In 1978 the new synagogue opened at 9, St. Mary's Place during the anniversary year of the founding of the congregation. As we have seen in the past, such an event usually indicated a growth in size and prosperity of the community. However, this was not the case at this point in the history of Dundee's Jewish community, which now numbered eighty-four people. The new Dundee synagogue was housed in an attractive building based on an Iranian design by local architect Ian Imlach, but also incorporating traditional Ashkenazi features. Its "whitewashed concrete, with stylish use of blue ceramic tiling and pebble stones in the minimalist interior which features a double Ark, the only one in Britain," is a rare example of synagogue architectural experimentation in post-war Britain that, as Sharman Kadish points out, is typically dominated by "the single-story suburban brick box."[130] Divided into two areas—a sanctuary and a communal area (for social functions, Hebrew classes, and so on)—it houses approximately two hundred square feet and can hold up to seventy people. As in the original synagogue, the ladies gallery is situated behind the main area of worship.

The physical structure of the synagogue is interesting in its own right and warrants a longer discussion; suffice it to say here that its design is certainly contradictory in its physical expression. While its interior design is certainly experimental for the United Kingdom, especially given that Sephardic immigration to Dundee in general, and Iranian Jewish immigration in particular, was non-existent, outwardly it essentially resembles the single-story suburban brick boxes that Kadish derides in her article. Furthermore, while the interior is characterized by light, the synagogue has no obvious signifiers of its Jewishness on the outside other than a Star of David on its gate. There is no sign, for example, denoting its presence. Other unusual features, given Dundee's Ashkenazi context, are also based on the Sephardi design used by the architect. The curtain to the Ark is in front of its gates, hailing from a period when Spanish and Portuguese Jews fleeing the Inquisition had to hide their Jewishness, unlike in Askhkenazi synagogues where the curtain is *behind* the gates. Furthermore, the *bimah* possesses a tiled and flat reading desk, clearly designed for the Torah scroll encased in a wooden box and read in the vertical position used by the Sephardim. However, since the Ashkenazi congregation in Dundee possessed scrolls which were unrolled and laid out flat, the reading desk was unfit for its purpose. Apparently, an argument broke out between opposing factions in the congregation over this issue until a compromise was reached: a sloping wooden lectern was placed to enable the scrolls to rest. One final and unusual feature is the design of the tablets of the Law above the Ark: as the first commandment is divided into two clauses, it gives the appearance that there are, in fact, eleven commandments![131]

The Declining Years

The period 1980–1990 saw a rapid and steep decline in Dundee's community from eighty-four to twelve. The reasons for this drop shall be examined later on, suffice it to say here that, as we shall see, the communal activities of the congregation were to be overshadowed by the reporting of other events. Nonetheless, the community continued to be active, holding regular services in the synagogue until 1988. Brothers Davie and Wolfie Koppell played an active role, as did Jack and Milly Miller, and Sam and Esther Hermann. The ladies in particular worked hard, providing hospitality for the outreach programs, while Wolfie Koppell excelled at organizing popular fund-raising beetle drives. The community also contributed to multicultural education and

Dundee Synagogue, interior. (Photograph by Nathan Abrams.)

outreach programs, holding sessions at least once, and often twice, a week. As part of this program, the community held a civic service one Friday evening which was attended by the city's two Members of Parliaments, Lord Provost, and Town Councilors, as well as trade union officials and representatives from the Community Relations Council and the churches.[132] During this period there were also two bar mitzvahs, and in 1989 the community witnessed the occasion of the last Jewish wedding to take place at the synagogue, and the first to take place in eleven years. The synagogue was described as "literally filled to overflowing."[133] Although it marked a rise in Dundee's fortunes, the couple subsequently left the city, as did the father of the bride, Albert Jacob, a mainstay of the community, who packed up and moved to Israel. The Dundee Jewish Society was reactivated in 1985, and the community pledged its support and cooperation, and by 1989 was holding fortnightly meetings.[134] Six years later it was reported that the students had "succeeded in re-opening Dundee Synagogue."[135]

By 2000, the community was mainly formed of academics or medical staff connected to one of the three universities in the area. The community was also boosted by Israelis who visited Dundee on an almost annual basis, many for refresher courses at the National Cash Register factory. Since these courses began in spring, many of the students and their families contacted the congregation about arrangements for Pesach. They were all offered hospitality, and some, like Gad Holzman of Jerusalem, as well as temporary university staff (such as Yuval and Ruti Steinitz, also of Jerusalem), took part in community activities during their stay in the city.[136] One of the more unusual Israelis to move to Dundee in this period was professional player Jean Talasnikov, who played for Dundee United during 1999–2000. His presence at community events, however, has not been mentioned, as one would expect.

The community has limped on since. Local Jewish businessman Harold Gillis kept the synagogue open single-handedly for many years, but following his death in 2001 it was felt that it should be closed. Paul Spicker, a lecturer at Dundee University, took over as de facto head of the community. At this point the number of Jews in Dundee, Angus, and Fife was

Dundee Synagogue, exterior. (Photograph by Nathan Abrams).

two-hundred-and-twenty-nine, according to the 2001 Census. The students frequently used the synagogue for regular study sessions, joint meetings between Dundee and St. Andrews, the occasional party, a communal Pesach Seder, and *minyan*.[137] But by this point, the congregation was in financial crisis; it was so small that it was no longer viable in its own right. Only a donation towards the running costs from the Glasgow Jewish Representative Council enabled it to hold New Year services, which twenty people attended, including two students.[138] It continues to the present, numbering twenty-two, according to the *Jewish Year Book*, although Spicker states the real number is no more than ten. Apart from ad hoc events organized by the Scottish Council of Jewish Communities, it meets in theory monthly, but in practice every two months. Only two of the original Jewish families that made up the community in the early parts of the community's history remain, and Jewish families are spread out in places such as St. Andrews, Newport, and Coupar.[139] In a parallel to the past, the fortunes of the students were diametrically opposed to that of the community, and St. Andrews' Jewish Society is currently the fastest growing in the United Kingdom, with one-hundred-and-fifteen members in 2006, including a few Jewish students at Dundee and Abertay. Yet, this has not arrested the decline of the Dundee community, as, unlike in the past, it has little or no contact with the local community besides the odd communication at festivals alongside an invite to the *shul*. If any of the students wish to go anywhere for services over Shabbat or festivals, they tend to either go to Edinburgh or Glasgow.[140]

However, the community has refused to die out, unlike, as we shall see, those of Ayr, Falkirk, Greenock, and Inverness. Part of the reason for this must surely be the continued existence of the synagogue, at which events can be organized. Another explanation is the increasing urbanization of Scottish society in the post-war period, such that Dundee, Scotland's fourth largest city, grew by six thousand between 1931 and 1961.[141] The city also reinvented itself to some extent, moving from de-industrialized to a biomedical, energy, and high technology center. In fact, 2006 saw a mini-revival, with thirty-two people attending the Rosh Hashanah services, ten of whom were students from St. Andrews, a figure not reached for thirty years. The community was formed of a combination of native Dundonians, other British Jews, and individuals from Canada, America, Israel, France, and South Africa.[142] In 2008 a double bar mitzvah celebration was held at the synagogue, at which forty-two people were present.[143]

Decline

The reasons for Dundee's decline can be explained by the factors that have affected all the small communities in the United Kingdom beyond London and Manchester: death and an aging population. Mobility was a particularly important factor. The search for a better economic climate elsewhere was important. Individuals often moved to Glasgow, London, and abroad. Adverse developments that caused the local economy to stagnate, such as Dundee's post-war economic decline, accelerated this trend. Retirement also took people away. Although Dundee had two universities on offer (and later a third in the University of Abertay), further and higher education took students elsewhere.[144] Those who found the Dundee environment un-conducive to a sufficiently or intensively Jewish lifestyle (particularly those valuing Orthodox religious practice), or those with simply the desire for some normality in Jewish terms, would leave. Families with young children, for example, would consider relocating to a location with a more developed Jewish infrastructure, particularly in terms of Hebrew/Jewish education.

Marriage was another factor in a community's decline. The desire to "marry in" was a particularly strong causal reason. Although there were enough Jews in Dundee to provide opportunities for matches, and this did happen, the pool of eligible singles was not large enough to allow such matches to be taken for granted; rarely did the engagements section of the *Jewish Chronicle* and *Jewish Echo* announce marriages between two native Dundonians (although one such occasion was the engagement of Anne Hirschfield and Arnold Drake in April 1950).[145] More often than not, one would read examples such as the marriage in 1942 of Millicent, elder daughter of Mr. and Mrs. H. Fineberg of Dundee, to Jack Miller from London; or of this rather unusual headline in 1965: "Dundee's got what Manchester likes," which reported that Nadia (23) and Sonia (18), the eldest daughters of Mr. and Mrs. Joseph Koppel, of 3, Briarwood Terrace, Dundee, both announced engagements to Manchester men.[146] Furthermore, young people who grew up together in small communities found the resulting intimacy a barrier to marriage. The bias among male Jews for younger women complicated the issue even further. That four Rosen children in Dundee (Morrice, Blema, Nellie, and Dora) died single perhaps indicates the difficulty of endogamous marriage there.[147] The result was that young Jews would go elsewhere to find their marriage partners. In some cases, entire families relocated to larger communities once their children reached dating age.

Although visitors to the city, such as students and service personnel, had the potential to help maintain endogamy, this did not necessarily occur in Dundee itself. Scanning the engagement and marriage sections of the *Jewish Chronicle* seems to bear this point out, as only one partner in most of the unions that did take place tended to be from Dundee. Furthermore, the young women who wed men from outside Dundee were more likely to move to the hometowns of their husbands. Two examples are representative here: Esther Fineberg of Dundee, who was engaged to Benjamin Nordan, officer in the Merchant Navy, Amsterdam, and Captain Geoffrey Eisen of Hampstead, who married Muriel Hyman of Dundee.[148] And, as we have seen, it was certainly the case that American students in Dundee dated Jewish girls, with some culminating in marriage; for example, the aforementioned marriage of Jack Greenberg of Brooklyn to Miriam Cree in 1933.[149] Furthermore, since American Jewish students often attracted many non-Jewish friends, mixing easily and freely in non-Jewish society, including areas which Scottish Jews would have found hard to enter, some non-Jewish girls even converted to Judaism, married and led typically Jewish lives. However, often these marriages resulted in many of these brides following their husbands back to their homes in other parts of Scotland, England, and the United States. For example, the Greenbergs left Dundee so that Jack could set up a medical practice in Northolt. Likewise, when Marie Kahan's boyfriend left Dundee to return to America when he graduated in 1934, she eventually followed him.[150] Such marriages thus drained the community further.[151]

The numbers of incomers were not high enough to arrest these declining trends. Certainly, student numbers were never that great; at its peak in 1973 the student society contained forty members.[152] In 1968, the number was only thirty. These numbers enabled the community to survive rather than grow significantly. As the *Jewish Chronicle* put it, "This student link could well be a lifeline for the community, for Dundee is unlikely ever to attract Jews in large numbers. The continued and increasing presence of Jewish youth at the academic centres on both sides of the Tay should be an insurance not only for survival but for future dynamic."¹⁵³ Unfortunately, the latter part of the final sentence did not prove to be the case, as students didn't play an active role in the community. Furthermore, only young families with children of marrying age would be able to stem the loss of the younger generation, but many of those were dissuaded from staying for the reasons outlined above. This included newcomers, who often left soon after they arrived.

Finally, intermarriage, although impossible to quantify with any precision, was certainly a factor in the decline of the Dundee Jewish community. The scarcity of Jewish marriage partners there often led to the selection of non-Jewish mates. Intermarriage sometimes resulted in conversion, but only rarely, and only once was such a case recorded in Dundee.¹⁵⁴ Often, however, Jews who married out retained some sort of Jewish identity—attending services, for example—but the reality was that if the mother was Christian, then the children were likely to be raised as such.

Anti-Zionism and Anti-Semitism

There is one final reason for the decline in Dundee's population. By the 1960s, problems with the non-Jewish population arose. The major source of the troubles was anti-Israel and anti-Zionist activity in Dundee, a city which attracted many Arab and Muslim students. Since there were only a handful of Jewish students only in Dundee, they felt overwhelmed by the greater numbers of Arab and Muslim students. Matters were not helped by the support and sympathy shown towards the Arab cause, which, far from consisting of isolated incidents, developed into a pattern. In 1969, Munther Qualaj of Fatah addressed the Dundee University Socialist Society against a backdrop of anti-Israeli posters, including leaflets stating, "Hate Israel." The perception of Benjamin Vincent, the secretary of the Dundee Jewish Society, was very telling. He described Qualaj's speech as "a vehicle for pure hate and emotional invective against Zionist Jews and Israel. Here was the impassioned demagogue, the confirmed fanatic—there would be no reasoned argument, no soothing logic on this night." The reaction of those present compounded his assessment. "Unfortunately his mood beautifully suited the 300-strong audience crammed into the Students' Union." Furthermore, "the chairman of the meeting was totally biased," and the "partisan" audience was "solidly behind the speaker," as pro-Israel comments "fell on deaf ears."¹⁵⁵ Debby Taylor, a Jewish resident of Dundee, recalled the occasion: "Words cannot explain how much hatred was in the atmosphere towards the Jewish students at Dundee University. The air was thick with anti-Semitism. It was a good reason to avoid studying at Dundee."¹⁵⁶ The Glasgow Jewish Representative Council perceived the meeting as the launching of an Arab anti-Israel campaign in Scotland.¹⁵⁷

A march was held in April 1970 when eight Arab students staged a protest in Perth and demonstrated against Israel and Zionism.[158] Yet more anti–Zionist activity was reported in 1976.[159] The following year, a six-point anti–Israel motion declaring that Zionism was racist passed at Dundee University's student union general meeting. Students who attempted to speak against the motion were physically threatened. A representative of the Jewish student society described the events as "extremely worrying."[160] At neighboring St. Andrews, "direct undisguised anti–Semitism" was reported, and "virulently antisemitic material was pushed under a student's door."[161] In 1979 a group of Jewish students at Dundee were assailed with Palestine Liberation Organization (PLO) slogans and obscenities, and PLO supporters forced the abandonment of a meeting in the Dundee University Union at which Israel Embassy information attaché Mr. Jacob Rosen was scheduled to speak.[162]

A "small core of neo-Nazis" in Dundee frequently caused trouble in the 1970s and 1980s.[163] In 1979, the south wall of the synagogue was spray painted, although a city council report concluded, "The nature of the graffito indicated that this was an everyday act of vandalism, without political overtones."[164] The twin trends of anti–Semitic and anti–Zionist activity did not overlap until March 1981, when the first recorded anti–Semitic incident took place. Up until this point, specifically anti–Semitic activity was virtually unknown in Dundee, although it seems that the pattern of anti–Zionist and anti–Israel activity to some extent prepared the ground for it. In 1966, *The Jewish Chronicle* reported that Nazi movements may be operating branches in Dundee.[165] Eleven years later, the National Front announced its intention to fight East Dundee in the coming General Election.[166] Predictably, the new synagogue was the focus of attack. Swastikas, British Movement symbols, and other anti–Semitic graffiti were daubed on its walls, as well as on those of the home of David Jacob. The pretext was a protest by the Jewish community against the twinning of Dundee with the West Bank town of Nablus, and the display of the PLO flag in council chambers.[167] The Dundee community—augmented by Jews who came from all over Scotland to express their solidarity—had turned out in strength to oppose and condemn the twinning, which it perceived was being used as a vehicle to promote the PLO, a terrorist organization devoted to the destruction of the state of Israel and using terror against civilians. The flying of its flag only seemed to confirm those suspicions. The local neo-Nazi groups obviously saw the climate surrounding the twinning and subsequent demonstration as an opportunity to express their anti–Semitic sentiments, and there was no evidence to suggest that Arab or Muslim students were responsible.[168] The local and national Jewish community was deeply upset by both the twinning and subsequent anti–Semitism, and this was manifested by the reporting of these events, which made the front pages of the *Jewish Chronicle*, in contrast to that paper's normal practice of burying its reports on the provincial communities deep inside the paper.

The attitude of the councilors responsible for the twinning deepened the Jewish community's sense of outrage. Ignoring the community's pleas to have the twinning arrangement reversed, they took a trip to Nablus, and on their return promised to "spread the word" about the PLO in Britain. Councilor Colin Rennie stated, "It is the Israelis who are the terrorists. But under the leadership of the Palestine Liberation Organisation, victory is assured. We will be your voice in Scotland, the United Kingdom, and in the rest of Europe."[169] As if to compound the insults, Bassam Shakaa, the Mayor of Nablus, visited Dundee at the council's invitation, and then almost a year later, Nabil Ramlawi, the PLO's representative in London, was discreetly invited to a Burns Supper.[170] They then pooh-poohed the community's fears by denying any link between the twinning and the anti–Semitic activity. Lord Provost, Councillor James Gowans, claimed, "There is no antisemitism in Scotland"; while Ernie Ross, MP for Dundee West, argued it was "not an isolated incident" and had hit all parts of the city.[171] Furthermore, and without irony, Albert and Debby Jacob were told there had been no anti–Semitism until "you lot" had started kicking up a fuss over the twinning.[172]

The friction between the city council and the Jewish community did not die down thereafter. In fact, if anything, it increased as the 1982 war in Lebanon precipitated a wave of condemnation of Israeli policy by Labour's grassroots members.[173] The Dundee Labour Party, driven by George Galloway, was an especially active supporter of the Arab and Palestinian causes in Britain, marking the shift of the focus of anti–Zionist activity from the campus to city politics. Galloway, described as the "guiding spirit" behind the twinning, was a self-confessed "figure in the demonology" of the friends of Israel "lobby," and at the forefront of pro-Palestinian activism in Dundee. He had been involved in Middle Eastern affairs since his student days. In 1977 he visited Beirut, at the invitation of the British Anti-Zionist Organisation, where he met members of Black September and the Popular Front for the Liberation of Palestine. In 1981 he was instrumental in persuading the Scottish Labour Party to recognize the PLO. Together with Ernie Ross, he founded the Trade Union Friends of Palestine (TUFP) and became its secretary. Following the twinning controversy, he proposed a motion twinning the Student Representative Council at Glasgow University with that of Bir Zeit University in the West Bank.[174] For his part, Ross was a member of the steering committee of the Trade Union Friends of Palestine and joined the Advancement of Arab-British Understanding. He later organized a pro-Arab lobby of Parliament and attended a meeting of the pro-Palestinian NGOs at the UN office in Geneva.[175] Other members of the TUFP included Dundee district councilors Tom McDonald and Colin Rennie.[176]

A series of further activities deepened the tension. The Dundee Labour Party forged links with Palestinian activists studying at Dundee University, such as Yousef Allen, who later became the British representative of the Palestinian Trade Union Federation. It also organized public meetings that were addressed by PLO representatives. The Lord Provost and other councilors adopted a crudely anti–Zionist position, alleging "the mass media is in the hands of the Zionists."[177] They referred to Ariel Sharon and Menachem Begin as "fascists," and accused the Israeli Army of "genocide." Following the invasion of Lebanon, the council unanimously adopted a resolution condemning Israel for its actions and its occupation of the West Bank and Gaza.[178] Furthermore, Orfan al Arab, of the League of Arab States, was invited to address the council.[179] An article equating Zionism with racism then appeared in the *Dundee Standard*, the monthly journal published by the Dundee Labour Party grouping.[180] Members of the Dundee District Council and the local trades council then snubbed a delegation from the Histadrut.[181] At a pro-PLO meeting held in Aberdeen, Paula Sneyder of the *Dundee Standard* spoke.[182] The Dundee branch of the National Union of Journalists tabled the only anti–Israel motions at its annual delegate meeting in 1983 (which, incidentally, was held in Dundee) and 1984.[183]

The Jewish community clearly felt tense, and the events reverberated not only in Dundee and Britain but across the world, too. Philip Kleinman of *The Jewish Chronicle* described Dundee as "the beating heart of anti–Zionism in this country."[184] The president of the Board of Deputies, Greville Janner, described the situation as "a watershed," one threatening to "endanger the calm communal relations which have existed in Dundee for more than 100 years."[185] The insensitivity shown by the councilors produced a great deal of ill will, particularly as a majority of Dundee's citizens opposed what was revealed to be an involuntary twinning on their part. Eventually, the issue of Nablus faded into the background, and although the local Labour party remained unequivocally pro-Palestinian in outlook, its anti–Israel bias became less strident. The Jewish community and the council agreed to differ on the Palestinian-Israeli issue, and their relations became warm, but for many the damage had already been done and the cordial relations were too little too late.[186]

It did not help that the Dundee Labour Party's pro-Palestinian activism was simultaneously accompanied by further neo-Nazi anti–Semitic activity. Following the Sabra and Shatila massacres in Beirut, increased activity by the National Socialist Action Party, which had been seen recruiting youngsters, with some success, outside schools in Dundee, was reported. There was further vandalism of the synagogue. The words "six million" had been daubed on a step, and swastikas and the letters "SS" sprayed onto the windows. One window was cracked and broken.[187] In 1984 a poster campaign against the synagogue was also initiated. Then, in early 1986, the car of the Dundee representative on the Board of Deputies of British Jews was vandalized on several occasions. Windows of the synagogue were smashed on two further occasions.[188] Dundee had seemingly become a focus for anti–Jewish activity, a perception further reinforced when a representative of the PLO and two West Bank mayors were invited to attend the Liberal Party conference in 1985. The Scottish Society for the Prevention of Cruelty to Animals also proposed to hold a meeting to discuss "ritual slaughter."[189] Meanwhile, the PLO flag still flew above the city chambers—to the considerable discomfort of the Jewish community.

As a result of these incidents, the community nearly halved by 1985, dropping to forty-five from eighty in 1984. By 1988 the community had fallen to a quarter of that figure again.[190] Yet, despite the small size of Dundee's community (twelve individuals out of a population of one-hundred-and-eighty-thousand), anti–Semitic activity continued unabated. The far-right British National Party (BNP) and National Front were active in Dundee, and the unsuccessful attempt of the former to hold a rally there in May 1990 resulted in an upsurge of violence. A group broke into the synagogue and smashed open the ark in which the scrolls were kept.[191] The synagogue was again daubed with swastikas, as well as the words "BNP" and "Jacob must die," most likely an attack on the community's most prominent representative, Albert Jacob, who was subject to a hate campaign, having received personal death threats, poison pen letters, and hoax bomb threats. The attacks culminated in a gang of youths breaking into the accommodation of a group of holidaying Chasidic families and attacking them while shouting anti–Semitic abuse.[192] Jewish graves were also vandalized, and the word "slaughter" was daubed on one tombstone.[193]

Another incident did not occur until 2001, when the synagogue was vandalized yet again with swastikas and the words "Combat 18."[194] Paul Spicker, now de facto head of the community, was the target of personal racial abuse, something he had not witnessed before moving there.[195] As before, the response of the local MPs was not only deemed less than sympathetic, but as a possible cause of the graffiti. Ernie Ross, for instance, was reported to have suggested that the recent screening on television of a drama about the Nuremberg Trials of Nazi leaders following the Second World War was designed to elicit sympathy for Israel during the ongoing Middle East crisis.[196]

Conclusion

Even though anti–Semitic and anti–Zionist activity has since died down in Dundee, the mud has stuck, and with its reputation for fostering such goings-on, the city has possibly found it hard to attract Jews. The tiny size of the Dundee Jewish community and its lack of infrastructure only serve to exacerbate the problem. Even today, the city still has a standing recruitment center for Islamic fundamentalists, as its history of pro-Palestinian activism and high numbers of students from Muslim and Arab countries have made it attractive to politically motivated students.[197] Nonetheless, as we have seen, the community continues to survive, and thrive even.

4

Dunfermline

Dunfermline was one of the most short-lived of all the communities. Its congregation was formed in 1908, although Jews had begun to arrive some twenty-eight years earlier, and it was formally wound up by 1950, even though Jews continue to live there today. Thus, it only officially existed for a mere thirty-six years. Nonetheless, as shall be seen, for such a small community it produced a number of high-profile and successful individuals—far out of proportion to its tiny statistics.

The town of Dunfermline in Fife, east central Scotland, lies three miles inland on the Firth of Forth, and sixteen miles away from Edinburgh, which is to the southeast. Given its location, the burgh of Dunfermline served as a link between Sterling and the towns of the east coast of Fife. It lay in the rich farmlands of Fife, and according to Robert Gourlay and Ann Evans, "in one of the most important industrial areas of Scotland."[1] In the eighteenth century it developed coal mining and fine loom weaving as two of its principal industries. By 1801, the year of the first official government census, its population had reached 5,484.[2] Seventy years later—ten years before the first Jews were registered in the town—this number had trebled to 23,116. During the late nineteenth century, linen had emerged as the predominant industry in the town, if not Scotland. There were also collieries, lime works, iron foundries, breweries, dye works, a flax-spinning mill, bleach-works, and power and hand-loom factories. During the twentieth century, Dunfermline developed into a center for the manufacture of table linen and terylene, as well as silk, coal, and engineering. The naval base of Rosyth became part of the city in 1911.[3]

The New Jews

Perhaps the earliest mention of Jews in Dunfermline is in 1880. Isidore Lyons, a jeweler born in Poland, married Hannah Markson in Dunfermline in that year, and, in the Census of 1881, is shown living with his wife "Ann" at 72, Netherton Street. In addition, two Jewish travelers named Samuel Cronson (27) and Iacbod Rubeins (42), both of Russian origin, were lodging at 21,

1880. MARRIAGES in the District of Dumfries in the County of Dumfries. (Page 37.)

No.	When, Where, and How Married.	Signatures of Parties. Rank or Profession, whether Single or Widowed, and Relationship (if any)	Age.	Usual Residence.	Name, Surname, and Rank or Profession of Father. Name, and Maiden Surname of Mother.	If a regular Marriage, Signatures of officiating Minister and Witnesses. If irregular, Date of Conviction, Decree of Declarator, or Sheriff's Warrant.	When & Where Registered, and Signature of Registrar.
73	1880. on the Twenty Ninth day of May at East Lithenhorn Mount Dumfriesshire After Publication according to the Forms of the Church of Scotland	(Signed) Landon Lyons Weaver (Bachelor) Hannah Markinson her x mark Name of Hannah Hunt	24 17	Thornhill Dumfriesshire High Street Dumfriesshire	Louis Bennet Lyons Farmer (Deceased) M. I. Corrow (Signed) Isaac Markinson Smith Arthur Markinson (Deceased)	(Signed) L. Henderson Ch. Minister (Signed) I. Henderson Witness M. I. Markinson Witness	1880. May 31st At Dumfries Sept B. Isaac Hall Registrar.
74	1880. on the Twenty Eighth day of May at Westhaunt Mount Dumfriesshire After according to the Forms of the United Presbyterian Church	(Signed) Alexander Galloway Bachelor (Bachelor) (Signed) Christiana Pratt Domestic Servant (Spinster)	30 30	Laurelie Dumfriesshire Woodhouse Westbetting Dumfriesshire	Thomas Galloway Contractor (Deceased) John Galloway M. L. Chisamn (Deceased) Hugo Pratt Bucargyman Martha Pratt M. L. Melwith (Deceased)	(Signed) David Russell U. P. Anagrach Ch. P. Church (Signed) John Wilson Witness Isaac Austin Witness	1880. June 1st At Dumfries Sept B. Isaac Hall Registrar.

Isaac Hall Registrar.

Carnegie Street.[4] The *Dunfermline Directory* for 1896–7 also listed Morris Cohan, hawker, at 3, Goldrum Street.

By 1901, the number of Polish and Russian-born citizens in Dunfermline had increased. Israel Bernstein (15), a Russian Jew, lived at 6, Reform Street; while Israel Newman, a jeweler from Russia resided at 19, Reform Street with his wife Sarah, also born in Russia, and their daughter Annie, born in Glasgow. Bernard Dorfar or Dorkar, a hawker from Russia, was living at 11, Carnegie Street. The Dorfman family lived at 80, James Street; they consisted of Max, a jeweler from Russia (who naturalized in 1914),[5] his wife Lena, also from Russia, and their four children, Isaac, Sarah, Edith, and Annie. Max's mother-in-law, Anne Berg, who was also Russian, lived with them. Max Hunter, another jeweler from Russia, lived at 84, Woodhead Street. At 13, Gardiner Street was George and Maggie Suider, both from Poland. The Bernstein family lived at 21, Rose Crescent and included John (23), a jeweler from Russia, and his wife Soffie (21), also Russian. Their son, Morris, was the first recorded Jew to be born in Dunfermline. Louis Braverman (25), another Russian subject and a tobacconist, lived at 54, Morrison Street with his English wife Betsy (22) and brother Samuel (15). Jacob Braverman (27), a waterproof coat maker from Russia but naturalized as British, lived with his Russian wife (also naturalized) Jeanie (23) and their daughter Bettie (ten months).

Finally, Abraham Braverman (27), an ice cream merchant from Russia, lived with his Russian wife Jeanie (27) and his sister Mary (12), also born in Russia. Another family that had arrived in Dunfermline from Latvia in 1901 was the Ruddicks. Jacob Radek, from Lithuania, was a left-wing student whose political affiliations made him go "on the run." His wife was a farmer's daughter from the village of Simbursk, near Riga. Soon after they married they sailed to Scotland and decided to settle in "the country as their Glaswegian relatives sarcastically referred to Dunfermline."[6]

The following year Phillip Levy came to Cowdenbeath from Edinburgh. Phillip was originally from Memel in Lithuania but left during the late nineteenth century and sailed on one of the timber boats that journeyed from the Baltic to the port at Leith. Initially, Phillip worked as a travelling jewelry salesman, but he prospered and built a shop at 200, High Street. According to Martin Eastwood, Phillip Lucas returned to Edinburgh in 1906 or thereabouts and became very wealthy in property.[7] However, the *Fife Trades Directory* for 1914 lists Philip S. Levy & Co., cabinetmaker, at the High Street, Cowdenbeath. At that time there were also several other Jewish businesses in the town. M. Sclar had a pawnbrokers and drapery shop at 580, High Street, while J. Levine was a draper and furniture dealer at 74, High Street. A Robert Stein, joiner, was also listed at Park Street.[8]

Opposite page: **Certificate of Marriages in the District of Dunfermline, 1880.**

Initially, the Jews of Dunfermline were, with very few exceptions, of the poorest class. As the above information demonstrates, they were concentrated in a very limited range of the typical immigrant occupations found in the provinces in the late nineteenth century: jewelers, travelers, and hawkers. The exception here is George Suider, whose occupation was listed as "miner," which could cause one to doubt that he was, in fact, Jewish, as Jewish miners were a rare occurrence in Scotland. Yet, Jewish miners were not unknown outside of Scotland, as there were examples of such in Wales, and Dunfermline was situated in a coal mining region of Scotland. As the above addresses demonstrate, most of the Jews were clustered around a few streets concentrated in the less salubrious, densely populated, poor, working-class areas in the center and north of the town, in roads very close to the now defunct Dunfermline Upper Railway station. It was a slum area, and most of the Jews lived in tenement-style houses.

Dunfermline provided a sympathetic reception for such Jews. As early as 1848, the mayor and town council of Dunfermline, along with those of Castle Douglas and Alnwick, had agreed to petition for the removal of Jewish disabilities.[9] There were even non-Jewish subscribers to the *Jewish Chronicle*. In 1852 the paper was being received by Captains James and Lewis Maitland, of Maitland, Rossie House and Rankeillour House, Cupar Fife, respectively, as well as John Learmouth, Fernie Castle, Cupar Fife, and the public reading rooms in Cupar Fife, St. Andrews, Perth, Arbroath, Dundee, Montrose, Kinross, Dunfermline, and Kirkcaldy. The *Jewish Chronicle* commented at the time, "Our liberal Christian friend who has transmitted the above order, and who never loses an opportunity of forwarding the interest of the *Jewish Chronicle*, informs us that captains James and Lewis Maitland are the nephews of the late Sir Frederick Maitland, the commander of the Bellerophon, in which the late Napoleon Bonaparte took refuge after the battle of Waterloo, and that Fernie Castle is one of McDuff's ancient residences."[10]

An Eccentric Choice

Although there were a few Jewish families in Dunfermline, it was considered an "eccentric choice" for Jewish settlement.[11] So why did Jews move there? The main reasons accounting for the Jewish presence in Dunfermline in the late nineteenth century were commercial opportunities and economic competitiveness. As Kenneth Collins has said, "Dunfermline grew as a result of internal migration within Scotland with Jews looking for locations from which trade could be conducted with less competition than could be found in the larger centres."[12] Jews, emigrating from Eastern Europe as part of the mass migration from 1880 onwards to escape persecution in Russia or conscription into the Tsarist Army, as well as looking to better themselves economically, would not have arrived directly in Dunfermline. Rather, their port of disembarkation would have been Leith. Dunfermline was close enough to Edinburgh, however, that these Jewish immigrants could use the Scottish capital as a base for travelling out into the Scottish countryside to sell their wares, typically cheap jewelry, clothing, lace, and picture frames, before returning home for the Sabbath. These could be obtained on easy credit terms from warehouses, often without a deposit.[13]

Some of those peddlers settled in Dunfermline, others followed, and a community was eventually created. Many of these peddlers would not, initially, have been able to speak English, which caused them to cluster so that they could be with people who understood their language, and, crucially, Jewish beliefs and practices. Alternatively, a start-up loan could be obtained from one of the Jewish free-loan societies, like that established in Dundee.[14] Typically, once enough capital had been accumulated, then the Jewish peddler would invest in permanent premises. Jacob Ruddick, for example, was given a letter of introduction to a factory in nearby Inverkeithing which produced wood pulp for newspaper. What came of it is unclear, but he later bought a property in Dunfermline—a shop in Bruce Street.[15] The Brown family started out as peddlers, hawking goods around the stately homes of Fife before setting up businesses in sliver, jewelry, and furniture.[16] According to Kenneth Collins, "Peddling inevitably declined as the Scottish retail system improved, and those still involved as pedlars became a more forlorn and impoverished group, economic failures that were unable to make the transition into retailing as the more successful had done."[17]

In his autobiography *Two Worlds*, David Daiches, the son of the de facto chief rabbi of Scotland, Salis Daiches, recalled those travelling Jewish salesmen who would leave Edinburgh by train every day to peddle their wares in Fife:

> They were the "trebblers," in their own Scots-Yiddish idiom; they had come as young men from Lithuania or Poland seeking freedom and opportunity but somehow had never got on as they had planned. Those with more push and enterprise had moved westward to Glasgow and often on from there to America; a few had managed to build up flourishing businesses in Edinburgh; but the trebblers were the failures, who spent their days carrying their battered suitcases from door to door in the little grey towns of Fife, to return home in the evening with a pound or so gained to a shabby but comfortable flat in one of the more run-down districts of Edinburgh.[18]

They could be seen on weekdays on the Dundee train, completely filling a compartment, with their phylacteries strapped to their arms and forehead, chanting the morning prayers.[19] They spoke a mixture of Yiddish and English, but with a Scottish accent, producing what Lloyd P. Gartner has called "an interesting but transitory linguistic hybrid."[20] An example goes thus "Aye mon, ich hob' getrebbelt mit de five o'clock train."[21] Furthermore, peddling persisted later in the outlying regions than it did in the metropolis. In Scotland, in particular, the proportion of peddlers to Jewish residents was even higher than in other provincial communities, especially around Edinburgh and Glasgow. This is probably the case in the even remoter communities under study here, but there are, as yet, no precise statistics to support this contention.[22]

Dunfermline Hebrew Congregation

Enough Jews had arrived by 1908 that Dunfermline Hebrew Congregation was founded.[23] The *Dunfermline Directory* for 1909 lists both a John Herchberg at 39, Pittencrieff Street, and a John Hersberg at 30a, Chalmers Street. The latter address was his business premises where he was listed as an "ice cream maker," a very unusual profession for a Jew—his Jewish-sounding name standing out from the Italian ones beside him in the directory listing. John Bernstein, a pawnbroker, was listed as working at 13, Bruce St. and living at 8, East Port Street. By 1910 he had branched out and was also listed at 36, Bruce Street as a boot and shoe maker. (Incidentally, by 1914 he had acquired a third property, at 9, Bruce Street, and was also listed in the trades directory as an auctioneer.) And our aforementioned Max Dorfman now had a jewelry shop at 13, High Street and was living at Canmore Street.[24] These individuals formed the nucleus of the Jewish community in Dunfermline and, as we shall see, became the first officials of the synagogue. The *Jewish Year Book* lists the first officers of the congregation as J. Hirschberg, president; J. Bernstein, Treasurer; and S. Levi, Secretary.

Strangely, however, like with the synagogue in Ayr, this was not reported in the *Jewish Chronicle* until the names of the *Chatan Torah* and *Chatan Bereshit* for 1908 were announced as Mr. H. Bloch and Mr. J. Hersberg, respectively.[25] Soon after, a Social Literary and Debating Society was inaugurated, at which the Reverend S. Michelson-Herschell gave an address, and Hebrew Classes were started.[26] The *Jewish Chronicle* then records the usual occurrences for a community. On 19 September, 1912, at Linwood-villas, Meadwell-road, Dunfermline, Mrs. William J. Hodes (née Annie Weiner from Dublin) gave birth to a son. On 23 March, 1913, Katie Berman of Cathcart, Glasgow, married Israel Miller, of Dunfermline, in Glasgow. The community set up committees to organize fundraising and contributed to a number of charities with the proceeds, including the Fund for the Relief of Jewish Victims of the War in Russia, and the Appeal for Poland and Eastern Europe. Its chief donors at that point included: Mr. W. Hodes, Mr. H.A. Bloch, Mrs. Joseph Myers, Mr. A. Ronder, Mr. D. Gilinsky, Mr. M. Isaacs, and Ernie Hodesh. 1918 there were thirty Jewish families in Dunfermline. Owing to its size, by the following year the community was sending a representative, Joseph Cohen, to meetings of the Board of Deputies.[27]

Coincidentally, during the First World War, two of the three Spilg boys from Falkirk were both found in Dunfermline. George Spilg worked in a photographic shop. He earned his living by what was known as "mug-faking"— taking a sample enlargement of a photograph around the country districts and trying to persuade housewives to have existing photographs enlarged. It wasn't well paid; typically he earned £2 per week, rising to £3 if sales were good. However, sometimes he'd return with a picture developed, enlarged, and framed, but the housewife who had ordered it would turn it down. In May 1914, aged seventeen, Reuben Spilg joined the Glasgow Highlanders. After several weeks in Glasgow, he was transferred to Dunfermline, where he was billeted in the Carnegie Baths. In November his battalion was sent to France on active service, but as Reuben was too young, officially, to go to the Front, he was left behind in Dunfermline.[28]

By 1919 the synagogue was based at 38, Coulton Street, having moved from an earlier site on New Row. In a letter to the Chief Rabbi, Mr. William I. Hodes, the Honorary Treasurer and Secretary of the Congregation, wrote that Dunfermline is "a very small and poor community. We are only about eight or nine paying members and fourteen children."[29] Two months later his successor stated that there were now twelve families, with fifteen to sixteen children "who have no religious instruction whatsoever."[30] By 1920 the synagogue had moved to what would become its permanent location until it closed in 1944-5, Pittencrief Street, at the heart of where the Jewish community was then clustered.[31] Emmanuel (Mendel) Greenberg, the youngest son of Mr. and Mrs. Nathan Greenberg, 38, Constin Street, Dunfermline, celebrated his bar mitzvah at the new premises in October of that year.[32]

Edith Ruddick's autobiography provides a description of the synagogue. It was "a small stone hall lined in yellow pine up an open wynd."[33] It was built, or used, as a meeting house for Seventh Day Adventists or Jehovah's Witnesses. It had a ladies gallery and an outside toilet.[34] It is likely that, as with other areas in Scotland (and indeed elsewhere), the synagogue catered to Jews who lived in nearby places but which did not have organized communities.[35] One such example was the Jesner family, who lived in Lochgelly, and Dunfermline was surely the nearest local network that they had.[36]

Despite its small size and lack of wealth, the community was nonetheless able to afford the services of a minister, but at the cost of "a substantial levy from each family."[37] At some point the Reverend Morris Balanow filled that position, as well as carrying out the roles of *shochet* and teacher. He stayed long enough for his son, Sholem, to be born, but moved to London soon after his boy's birth. Little is known about the Reverend Balanow, but his son also trained in London to be a minister and was eventually appointed to the Netherlee and Clarkston Synagogue in 1959. He subsequently became Registrar of the Glasgow Beth Din and Supervisor of the Glasgow Board of *Shechitah*.

By 1924 the community had secured a full-time replacement that, unusually for the minister of such a small community, stayed in that role until the synagogue closed in 1944. That appointee was the Reverend Morris Symon Segal, who originally came from Lithuania, via Russia, in 1906, aged eighteen. He had served as a minister in Leven and as a *shochet*, reader, and teacher in Edinburgh under the supervision of Rabbi Salis Daiches, where he was naturalized on 24 October, 1914.[38] In 1924 he married Millie Sclar in Edinburgh and subsequently had two children, Philip (born in 1925) and Doris. By all accounts, Segal was expected to undertake a variety of tasks for which he was not well paid. In 1936 and 1937 he received the sums of £26 from the Provincial Jewish Ministers Fund as a subvention to his salary.[39] This multitasking was vividly remembered by a child from another community at which Segal served, following his appointment in Dundee, but which must have also taken place not only in Dunfermline but in the other small communities, too:

> As our congregation was very small the same man was rabbi, cantor, teacher, ritual slaughterer and I suppose that he circumcised the baby boys too. Sometimes in the middle of a Hebrew lesson he would be interrupted by a man bringing two squawking hens. The rabbi would excuse himself, go round to the back yard, we'd sit in frozen horror as the squawks rose to a crescendo then there would be an abrupt silence, and the lesson would continue.[40]

Edith Ruddick recalled a similar scene, but in her own home: "He took out a knife with a yellowish handle from his jacket and held it in his teeth whilst he tucked the bird under his arm, he held it back by the head, plucked a few feathers from its neck, cut its throat and then held it over the washtub to let the blood run away."[41]

"We observed our religion pretty strictly," observed Edith Ruddick, despite the obvious difficulties in doing so, given the small size of the community (roughly eight to ten families after the First World War).[42] The Ruddicks "struggled to keep Saturday holy and free from every day work."[43] The community organized Jewish education for its children. The synagogue was used for "inculcating Jewish religion into the few children who were born in Dunfermline."[44] They were taught Biblical Hebrew ("unsuccessfully," in Edith Ruddick's case) and the kosher dietary laws.[45] In 1936 the classes were visited by Herbert M. Adler, Director of Jewish Education. He was highly satisfied with the children's progress. Their teacher was the local minister, the Reverend Segal. Their education must have been rather good, as one of those pupils, Irene Hodes, of 11, St. Lawrence Street, Dunfermline, was gifted enough to win a prize in a national competition organized by the *Jewish Chronicle* in 1933.[46] There was also a Dunfermline Lady Zionists group, which in 1933 was addressed by Rabbi Daiches after he had spoken to the Dunfermline Civic Club about National Minorities. Other activities included fundraising for the United Appeal for Jews in Poland and the J.N.F. through card evenings and a bazaar, which were reported to have been social and financial successes. The Reverend Segal was listed as the J.N.F. Commissioner in the *Jewish Year*

Book from 1928 until 1940. Kosher meat was available from a special department in the Dunfermline Co-Operative Society.[47] During Passover all the congregants used to place an order with the kosher grocer in Edinburgh, and the goods would be delivered the week prior to the festival. Synagogue services were held at the High Holy days, and there was always a *minyan*.[48]

Growing Professionalization

By 1937 there were at least nine Jewish families in Dunfermline. They included Isaac Sclar and his brother David Clare, both electrical engineers, and their respective wives—Doris (née Shulman) and Miriam, but known as Milly (née Ruddick); Mr. Brodsky, of Russian origin; Mr. and Mrs. Warrens, who left Dunfermline around 1939 to open the popular Maryville boarding house in Ayr; Mr. and Mrs. Isaac Bernstein, who had a large furniture store in Chalmers Street; Jacob Ruddick, who had a draper's business in Pittencrieff Street and lived in a flat above the shop; Julius Gladstone, a commercial traveler, and his wife Fanny; Israel Miller, a commercial traveler who specialized in picture frames, and his wife Katie (née Berman); William Hodes, a shopkeeper specializing in antique, modern and good second-hand furniture at 7, High Street;[49] Mr. Jay Green, a dentist with a practice near Pilmuir Street, and his wife and son, Julius, who also became a dentist; Harry Green, who owned a draper's shop, and his wife; and Alex Ronder, a pharmacist.[50]

From this list it is clear that the Jews of Dunfermline were well represented in the immigrant Jewish trades (travelling, drapery, furniture and shopkeeping). Yet, the electrical engineers and dentists demonstrated increasing acculturation and embourgeoisiement. Even those who remained in retail occupations saw their lifestyles improve. Jacob Ruddick, for example, now had three shops (a ladies' outfitters, a gents' outfitters, and a clock, watch, and jewelry shop). Their improved position was reflected in moving from the poorer Pittencrieff Street to a nicer house overlooking Pittencrieff Glen.[51] Their initially frugal lifestyle was enhanced by the ability to hire a maid and washerwoman.

This trend was extended as their children, by and large, entered the professions: Philip Clare followed his father and uncle into the "family business" to become an electrical engineer; Jack Clare trained as a social worker; Isaac Ruddick became a violinist, and his sister Edith an actress who taught acting techniques at a Glasgow Academy. From 1966 to 1970 Edith also appeared in episodes of *Dr. Finlay's Casebook*, as well as the movie *Local Hero* (1983), starring Burt Lancaster. Max Hodes worked for the *Daily Express* after serving in the Air Force during the Second World War; and Julius Green graduated to become a dentist after his stint in the army. All but two of this generation

(Fanny, or Fay, and Leah Ruddick) left Dunfermline to settle elsewhere in the United Kingdom and abroad.

On the eve of the Second World War, a report from the Board of Deputies described Dunfermline as "too small to be given in the JEWISH YEAR BOOK"![52] Yet, that same year the congregation was listed as having thirty seat holders (fifteen men and fifteen women). As if in response, in 1941 the *Jewish Echo* contained a report on the Jewish community of Dunfermline from Flora Sclar, 12, Park Avenue, Dunfermline, in which she stated: "We are but a handful of Yiddishe people here—seven families in all—yet ... we have a shool [sic] and manage to uphold Jewish traditions and everything pertaining to Judaism."[53]

As the religious leader of the community, the Reverend Segal was very active during the Second World War. His home became a magnet for the Jewish service personnel who were stationed in the area. Indeed, he would go to the local barracks to round up any Jewish men in uniform who would be given leave to attend services on Saturday mornings. Edith Ruddick remembered, "During war times, of course, there were always Jewish soldiers that came."[54] It was only during the war that Shabbat services were possible. The Reverend Segal also continued to teach the local children, and Rabbi Daiches inspected the Hebrew Classes in 1942 and declared his satisfaction with their progress. Segal also found time to qualify as a *mohel* in London, as well as acting as an air raid warden. He also raised money for the Red Cross by organizing a local "Penny-a-week Red Cross Fund." The Reverend Segal started the fund at 33, Shamrock Street, where he then lived. He knocked on every door and asked if the household would be willing to donate a small sum every week when a collector called. The takings during the first week were approximately £3. Flushed with success, he approached the next street and so on. On average, £150 per month was collected, with the total amount being raised reaching into the thousands of pounds. The Reverend Segal's nextdoor neighbor in Shamrock Street worked at the local bank, and so acted as the fund's treasurer.[55] After 1943 all of the money raised was donated to help Fife prisoners of war.[56] "It was a tremendous boost to them and made a great difference," councilor James Simpson stated. "He [Segal] was quite a remarkable chap."[57] Segal's energies set the pattern for the congregation, and local Red Cross working parties were formed by the women of Dunfermline.[58]

Jews from Dunfermline also fought in the war. Born in Carlisle, Julius Green was brought up in Dunfermline. He joined the Medical Unit of the Edinburgh University Officer Training Corps. During the Second World War he served in 152 (Highland) Field Ambulance of the 51st Highland Division but was captured at St. Valéry in France in 1940. He was passed through a succession of German Prisoner of War camps, ending up in Colditz Castle. As a dental officer with the rank of captain, he moved around a great deal, which gave him the idea of sending coded messages about troop movements and the like via letters home to his family, then living at 53, Malcolm Street.

The information was then forwarded to MI9 British intelligence, which responded with letters in kind. It included material supplied to Green by recaptured escapers about local German railway, troop and shipping movements, and anything else gleaned while on the "outside." Green also advised on what materials useful for escape could be smuggled into Colditz via parcels from home, as well as offering advice on what officers should carry with them in battle in case they were captured and sent to Colditz—hidden compasses, for example—that would be useful for escapes. Green's other important act was to expose the English Nazi stooge in the prison, Purdy, who was prosecuted for treason after the war. He was mentioned in dispatches for brave conduct. In order to avoid being executed, Green managed to hide his Jewishness by ditching his identity discs, which gave his religion, and posing as a Presbyterian. However, in his own words:

> This harmless little deception seemed to satisfy everyone, including the Germans, until one day I received a letter from a female relative, of whom I am very fond. The dear old soul, in the course of her innocent prattle calculated to cheer up the poor boy languishing in Nazi hands, mentioned that she had met so and so the synagogue a few weeks previously. She added for good measure that she was going away for the Passover.

Of course, the Germans were "fascinated," so they sent him for examination. Fortunately, the British Medical Officer "decided to report that I had been provided with the identification in which they were interested in later life, and not in early infancy."[59] Following his release, Julius returned to Scotland and was engaged to Anne Miller of Glasgow in 1945.[60] After the war, he wrote a best-selling book about his experiences entitled *From Colditz in Code*.[61]

The only Jewish burial to take place in Dunfermline of which we are aware was also during the war. Born in Wysock, Poland, in 1924, Harold Irving Chizy of Montreal, Quebec, a Sick Berth Attendant in the Royal Canadian Navy Voluntary Reserve, was killed in action onboard H.M.C.S. Nabob, a Canadian-manned aircraft carrier which was torpedoed off North Cape, Norway, in August 1944. He died aged twenty. The *Canadian Press* of 3 July, 1945, reported the tragedy, and on 11 November reported the funeral service:

> On a sunny autumn afternoon in a little wooded cemetery along the north bank of the Firth and Forth ... 10 Canadians and four British were buried following a mass funeral. They had sailed together, fought together and they had died together.... Protestant, Roman Catholic and Jew were administered the rites of their respective faiths before three volleys rang out over their graves.[62]

He was buried in Douglas Bank Cemetery in Dunfermline.[63]

Dunfermline's Jewish Decline

After the war the synagogue moved from its Pittencrieff location to Athol Place.[64] In 1945 the Reverend Segal left to take up a similar position in the far larger community of Dundee, where he remained until his retirement. The *Jewish Year Book* listed the figures for the period 1945–1950 (with the exception of 1946) as thirty "seat holders" (fifteen men and fifteen women). In its 1951 edition, the number was twenty five. Unfortunately, despite its wartime activity, the community proved too small to sustain a synagogue, and it was formally wound up by 1950.

A comparison between the trades listed in the *Fife Trades Directory* for 1929 and 1947–8 are revealing. In 1929 the directory presents a picture of economic health. It lists the following businesses in Dunfermline: H. Sclar, boot stores, Bruce Street; J. Green, dentist, 5, Douglas Street; I. Bernstein, draper, 24, Chalmers Street; J Ruddick, drapers, 51 Chalmers Street; W. Hodes, furniture warehouse, 7, High Street; H. Sclar, 58 Bruce Street, furniture warehouse, also boot maker and general dealer; and S. Warrens, 9, Bruce Street, broker. In contrast, by 1947–48, only Green, Ruddick, and Sclar remained, while Hodes, Warrens, and Bernstein had disappeared from the Fife directories. Only one new business was added in that period: Grant & Co., furniture dealers, at 130, High Street, but this was not owned by a Dunfermline Jewish resident, so it didn't increase the population. This decline may well be due to the general economic climate in Dunfermline. The linen industry suffered severely from wartime economies—fewer servants to starch napkins and tablecloths for the rich—and after the war, less formal eating habits, foreign competition, and the demise of the floating grand hotels that were the transatlantic liners reduced the demand for what was now considered a luxury item. While Jews were not directly affected in terms of employment, the higher unemployment as a result would have impacted on the ability to consume the sort of services that Jews in Dunfermline typically provided.[65]

The decline in Jewish-owned businesses is attributable to the desire to move where there was some sort of Jewish infrastructure. Once the synagogue had closed, several families either moved west or southwards to join the larger Jewish communities in Glasgow and Edinburgh, respectively. As evidence of this, nothing relating to the community was announced in the *Jewish Chronicle* after the announcement of the marriage of Louis Pakman of Southport to Kathleen Green, of 53, Malcolm Street, Dunfermline, in October 1948.[66] Ironically, as the Jewish community was shrinking, the general population in Dunfermline was growing. In fact, between 1931 and 1961, Dunfermline's expansion by 12,100 was the largest increase in size among all the Scottish burghs.[67]

Nonetheless, Jews continued to live in Dunfermline and the surrounding areas after the synagogue had closed. In 1951 the *Jewish Year Book* listed twenty-five individuals. As further evidence of Jewish settlement, the valuation rolls for the 1950s contain a list of Jewish-owned properties in the town center. These included Leah Ruddick, 3, Pittencrieff Street; Isaac Bernstein, 28, Viewfield Terrace; John Levinson, 5, Douglas Street; Catherine Watson, 40, East Port (a number of locals stated that she was Jewish, although married to a local non-Jew, explaining her surname); Edith Heasman, 13, Bridge Street; Mrs. Dorothea Nowak, 61, Buffies Brae; and George Green, 9, Pittencrieff Street. Another business not included in the rolls was a chain of shops called Grant's Furniture and TV, located at the top of the New Row in Dunfermline and on the Main street in Cowdenbeath, both owned by Harold Oppenheimer, who lived in Edinburgh and had another shop on the North Bridge there, as well as in Nairn.[68] In the 1950s and 1960s, Mr. and Mrs. S. Hyman lived in Alva, Clackmannanshire, some seventeen miles from Dunfermline. Their son Clive celebrated his bar mitzvah in 1961, although where is not known. Furthermore, while the *Jewish Chronicle* may have ceased to report on Dunfermline, several items did appear in the *Jewish Echo*. In 1958, the successful passing of their final examinations by C. and I. Caplan at the Dunfermline College of Physical Education warranted a mention, as did the birth of the son of Mr. and Mrs. H. Berkley (née Marlene Stein), 4, Paton Street, in 1960. The final communal notice of such a nature was the birth of Jeffrey Bernstein in Dunfermline, the first grandchild of Mr. and Mrs. Bernstein, 28, Viewfield Terrace, in 1965.[69]

The Sclar and Lovatt families also still lived in Dunfermline in 1951. The most prominent member of these families was Isaac Sclar. His parents, Philip and Fanny, emigrated from Russia in the late nineteenth century, first settling in Leeds and then the small mining village of Cowdenbeath in Fife, where Philip had a drapers and furniture store. After moving to Dunfermline, Philip died young and left Fanny with a large family of eight children: Milly (who married Morris Segal), Ellen (never married), Isaac, Dora (married Robert Lovatt from Dublin), David (married Milly Ruddick), Rachel (never married), Leah (who died during the influenza epidemic), and Flora (never married). Ellen and Flora had a three-storey furniture shop at the corner of the New Row and the High Street, where Dora had a boutique dress shop (the first of its kind in Dunfermline). Rachel was a housewife, and David (who took the surname Clare) worked with his brother Isaac.[70] Isaac was born around 1900 and began working as an apprentice for the Fife Coal Company. From these humble beginnings he carved out a successful career in the electrical contracting industry. He joined James Watt & Company in Dunfermline in 1918. In 1928 he was made a partner in James Scott (Electrical Holdings) Limited. In 1932 he was unanimously elected as President of the Dundee Sub-Centre of the Institute of Electrical Engineers for 1932–1933, and also served as a member of the Glasgow committee of the same body. He was also president of the Edinburgh Electrical Society. He was one of the few Jews working in the technical side of the electrical engineering industry.[71]

In 1946 Isaac Sclar became managing director and chairman of James Scott, which he developed into a leading business in its field, with subsidiaries overseas, including one in Israel. During the Second World War, in collaboration with Lieutenant A. Feldmann, an officer in the Polish armed forces,

Sclar designed a tiny wireless transmitter, less than six ounces in weight, intended for strapping to the body, preferably the wrist, when an alert sounds. Should the wearer be buried in a bombed building, a slight pressure in the device sends out a signal which can be picked up by a modified form of the ordinary portable battery wireless set and thus direct the rescuers. A larger edition of the device can be installed in an air-raid shelter. A public test in Dunfermline showed the potential of the apparatus. Sclar was awarded an Order of the British Empire (although the *Jewish Echo* stated that it was the lesser honor, the Commander of the British Empire) in 1973, and he retired in 1975.[72]

Sclar was at the same time actively involved in the town's Jewish affairs; from 1920, for twenty-five years, he served as secretary and treasurer of the Dunfermline Hebrew Congregation. In 1931 he married Doris Shulman from Glasgow, and they lived in Transy Grove, Dunfermline. Three years later they had a daughter. Sclar eventually moved to Glasgow, where he became a prominent communal leader, involved in building the new Giffnock and Newlands synagogue. Sclar supported many Jewish and non–Jewish religious and educational institutions. The Doris and Isaac Sclar Charitable Trust donated to the Royal Academy, among other causes. He was responsible for endowing several research scholarships, both at Scottish and Israeli universities, in medical electronics and opthalmics. He endowed two research scholarships (worth £1,000 each) in his name at the University of Strathclyde. Awarded annually by the Boards of Trustees on the recommendation of the chairman of the appropriate department, the holder of one scholarship is required to undertake research at the University or at another approved institution in the field of electronics, or in the application of electronics to medicine, or in the field of electrical engineering, or in the humanities, in that order of preference. The holder of the second scholarship is required to undertake a program of research at the University or at another approved institution in the field of pharmacy or bioengineering. Isaac Sclar died in January 1988, aged eighty-eight.[73]

The Jewish community in the 1960s numbered approximately twenty-five individuals. In 1964 the *Jewish Chronicle* noted that "a few Jewish families" continued to live there.[74] In 1968, the well-known firm of clothing manufacturers in Dunfermline appointed Nathan Goldberg as a director. However, Goldberg stayed in London, where he lived, even though he was responsible for directing the activities of the Dunfermline business. By 1970, Goldberg's, a department store, was opened at 15, New Row, but by 1970 it had relocated to larger premises in Kirkcaldy. Another store opened around 1973 in St. Margaret Street. When it closed down in 1990 it was remembered as the town's longest established department store. Moving into the present, a small number of Jews continue to live in the West Fife area today, including at least one Jewish family in Rosyth that still practices Passover.[75] The last Jewish inhabitant of Dunfermline was most likely Fay (Fanny) Ruddick, who died in 1977.[76]

Epitaph

As in Dundee, the synagogue building has long since been demolished, and the area has now been redeveloped into a new housing estate and community center. However, in June 2005, in a unique gesture among the small Jewish communities in Scotland outside Edinburgh and Glasgow, the Town Council decided that its former Jewish community should not be allowed to vanish without trace, and remembered and honored it with the unveiling of a commemorative plaque. The inscription on the plaque reads as follows:

Commemorative Plaque, Dunfermline. (Photograph by Nathan Abrams.)

FORMER SITE OF THE JEWISH SYNAGOGUE

> The original Jewish community in this area had their synagogue on this site. Many arrived in Dunfermline around 1900 from Eastern Europe and soon became prominent in the retail trade. Some such as the Sclars, Bernsteins and Ruddicks became well known local families. The Reverend Morris Segal followed the Reverend Balanow as the minister for Dunfermline's Jewish community and served them from the mid-1920s until the closure of Dunfermline's Synagogue in 1944. Several families then moved westward to join the larger Jewish Community in Glasgow.

In only the second time in Scottish History, the unveiling of the plaque was coupled with the naming of a new street ("Segal Place") after a Jew: the Reverend Segal.

Relatives of the Reverend Segal, representatives of the Scottish Council of Jewish Communities, the Edinburgh Jewish community and of the Scottish Jewish Archives Centre joined the Provost, Councilors, and members of the local Dunfermline community to remember the small but active Jewish community that once lived and worked in the town, and to honor its leaders. The ceremony was followed by a kosher reception in the city chambers, which one participant commented was probably the first time a *brachah* (religious benediction/blessing) had ever been said there! The following year, in January 2006, Scottish National Holocaust Memorial Day was held in Kirkcaldy, Fife, approximately fifteen miles outside Dunfermline.

5
Falkirk

Falkirk is situated near the western end of the Firth of Forth, between Edinburgh and Glasgow. It was an affluent town that was steadily growing in both wealth and population by the 1870s. John Stewart noted, "The burgh became in the nineteenth century one of the units of the industrial area of central Scotland." From 1871 onwards, the town witnessed an "influx of population ... consequent on the growth of the iron industry, which then became the staple one of the district."[1] By 1894 the population of this "busy town" was approximately 20,000. By 1911, it was 33,574, and it rose to 36,566 in 1929.[2] As Stewart notes, "The prosperity of the town, as shown by its increased valuation, was the course of the great increase in population."[3]

Such a town would have been attractive to Jewish immigrants. Its rural environment was surely an improvement on the Glasgow slums from which many came and it provided "locations from which trade could be conducted with less competition that could be found in the larger centers."[4] Thus, like the other small Jewish communities in Scotland, it "grew as a result of internal migration within Scotland."[5] Indeed, Falkirk probably owed the rump of its Jewish community to its position on the Edinburgh-Glasgow train line.[6]

Resulting from its role as a center for communications, Falkirk became the principal regional service center between Edinburgh and Glasgow, and thus became economically attractive to Jewish retailers from Edinburgh and Glasgow. Yet, when compared to all of the other small Jewish communities in Scotland, Falkirk was a late arrival on the scene, a synagogue not being established until well into the twentieth century. It was also the most short-lived of all the Scottish Jewish communities outside of Edinburgh and Glasgow, having declined at some point after the Second World War.

The First Arrivals

In his history of the origins and growth of Falkirk, John Stewart notes a banker called H. Salmon living in the town in 1838. It is not known if he was Jewish; while the date suggests he was not, the name and profession may suggest that he was. What we do know for certain, however, is that Jews began to arrive in Falkirk in the second half of the nineteenth century. According to the 1871 census, brothers Simon (23) and Henry Cohen (21) of Poland were photographers living at 11, the Back Row, Falkirk. The Back Row (which has since changed its name to Manor Street) "contained many second-hand shops selling clothes, watches, tools and a thousand and one items," according to Lewis Lawson. "It had lodging houses frequented by tramps, beggars, strolling street-singers and musicians." He added that during the nineteenth century "it was not a recommendation to come from the Back Row."[7] In addition to the Cohen brothers, a "Mr. Slack" of Falkirk subscribed and donated 15s to "Penny Dinners for Jewish Children" in 1875, as did a "Mr. Stalk," who gave 11s 6d in 1876.[8] It is possible that Slack and Stalk was the same person, that the *Jewish Chronicle* contained a misprint, or that neither was Jewish.

Others began to arrive as part of the great migration of Jews from Eastern Europe to the United Kingdom from 1880 onwards. The census of 1881 records an Isal Galdberg (21) and Mier Galdberg (18), both unmarried men from Russia lodging at Baxter's Wynd, whose occupations were listed as "hawkers." It was not atypical for Jews to travel from Falkirk to the mining communities of Stirlingshire, just as they did from Glasgow to Ayrshire, and from Edinburgh to Fife.[9] Furthermore, a series of individuals were naturalized during the period 1889 to 1912, such as David Cohen from Russia, who was already a resident in Falkirk when he was naturalized in 1889.[10] Likewise, so was Lewis Meyer Cohen, also from Russia, when he naturalized in 1900.[11] Eight years later, Abraham Lewis Garbarski (known as Abraham Lewis), from Russia, settled in Falkirk,[12] to be followed by Francis Hassmann[13] from Germany in 1911, and Abraham Bulbin from Russia in 1912.[14] Four years later, Max Spilg from Russia, resident in Falkirk, was naturalized in 1916.[15] Furthermore, a receipt held by the Falkirk Council Archives, dated 16 November, 1897, indicates that B. Turiansky had been resident in Falkirk for some time. It describes his occupation as "Jeweller, Watchmaker and House Furnisher," selling "A large Selection of Diamond Rings, Brooches, Earrings, Scarf-pins, Silver plate, Cutlery, etc. Watches and Jewellery Cleaned and Repaired—Charges Moderate. Pianos, Organs, and all kinds of Musical Instruments kept in Stock." The receipt lists Turiansky's primary business address as Newmarket Street, Falkirk, with another branch at 123, Dalkeith Road, Edinburgh.[16]

Not all of those who came to Falkirk settled, however. As a young boy of twelve in 1896, Manny (Emmanuel) Shinwell was sent by his father to the mining districts around Glasgow, where he had many customers. Every Friday or Saturday, Manny was sent with a parcel of suits to, and to collect payment from, places like Cambulsang, Bellshill, Falkirk, Stirling, and California, a small village near Falkirk, before returning to Glasgow.[17]

Another Jew living in Falkirk at that time was Louis Saltman. Louis' father, Isaac, was a waterproof manufacturer who had married Jane Goldstone (variously named as Jean or Jeanie, and latterly Dora), the daughter of a Manchester publican. Isaac and Jane left Manchester for Edinburgh, where Louis was born in 1889. Louis earned his living as a shop assistant, and he was attracted to another, non-Jewish shop assistant, Mary Ann Rutherford, the daughter of a local butcher. They fell in love and married in Leith by what is known in Scots law as an "irregular marriage"—a declaration made before the Sheriff substitute—but is considered to be valid nevertheless. Given that Mary was not Jewish, the Saltman family would have frowned upon such a union and hence did not participate in the ceremony. Not only was the marriage "irregular," it certainly wasn't a Jewish ceremony, but also it was most likely a "shotgun" wedding, as their first child, Annie, was born in Falkirk seven months to the day after the wedding. "I have visions of Louis being pursued by his future-father-in law with a bloodstained cleaver," Avrom Saltman wrote. After his marriage, Louis set up as a fruiterer, and the business prospered. Subsequently, Louis and Mary Ann lived happily together until her death in 1953, during which time they had another son, Jack, born in 1922. At the age of 18, Annie got married in Glasgow, also "irregularly." Like her mother, she married a Jew, Louis Mirsky of Glasgow, described as a student of medicine.[18]

The list of children enrolled in Falkirk Schools between 1903 and 1926 provides a snapshot of the community during that early period. Abraham Bulbin was a traveler living at 9 Melville Street, with three children, Leah, Rebecca, and Henry. David Bulbin lived at the same address with his father, Edwin. Morris Rosenberg lived at 28, Fir Street, as did Samuel Kaplan from New York and his three daughters, Pauline, Rose, and Helen. David Cohen lived at 17, Canfield Street. Harris ("Harry") Kaplan, a peddling draper, lived at 25, Glebe Street with his daughters, Rebecca, Leah, and Morna. Gershon Spilg lived at the same address with his wife Sarah (née Hellman) and their children, Isaac (George), Wolf or Woolf (William), and Reuben. Dora Sandberg lived with her son Roland at Garrison Chambers; Abraham Lewis with his daughter Fanny at the Williams Building; and Gershon's eldest son, Max, lived with his children, Rosa, Hillel, and Laura, in Melrose Place. Isaac Camenski was resident in the same street with his four children, Louis, Harry, Matilda, and Fanny. Max Camenski lived with his daughters Fanny, Dora, and Leah at 172, High Street. Lionel Turiansky, Samuel Horowitz, and Lily Benson were listed, as was Simon Rosenberg, a general dealer at Lesley 2, Pleasance Square, with his sons David, Hyman, and Benjamin. Alice Carnovsky lived with her father Morris in Kerse Lane. Wolf Cemblar [sic], traveller, lived at 4, Melrose Place with his sons Lewis and Hyman. Joshua A. Sadler had two daughters, Hilda and Dorothea. Louis Taylor, a shopkeeper, lived at 4, Firs Street with his son Harold. Finally, Morris Levenson, shoemaker, lived with his daughters Jacky and Leah at 25, Glebe Street (although they had left for Glasgow by 1926). As can be seen, the community clustered

Group Photo, Coronation Gallery, 76 High Street, Falkirk. (Provenance unknown.)

into a very few streets in Falkirk and were concentrated in a very few of the typical immigrant trades.

When Was the Community Established?

There seems to be some confusion as to when the congregation was actually founded. The JCR-UK website states 1926,[19] elsewhere the date 1917 is given, most likely based on the *Jewish Year Book*, which includes Falkirk Hebrew Congregation for the first time in its edition of that year, suggesting that the synagogue was in existence the previous year at least. (Incidentally, in its 1945–46 edition, the *Jewish Year Book* states that the Jewish community of Falkirk "dates from about 1826," a date which can't be taken seriously, as it is far too early in terms of Jewish immigration into Scotland.) In terms of precisely dating the foundation of the community, it does not help that the records of the congregation have been lost. However, items in the *Jewish Chronicle* suggest that the community was established by 1913. In that year Falkirk warranted sending a deputy, Dr. L. Turiansky, to the Board of Deputies.[20] This was most likely Louis Turiansky, who graduated in medicine from the University of Edinburgh in 1903, eventually settling in London's East End; Turiansky, according to Kenneth Collins, was a noted "student of the Talmud."[21] In October of that same year, the *Jewish Chronicle* listed the *Chatan Torah* and *Chatan Bereshit* for "Falkirk Synagogue" as Mr. Wolf Cimbler and Mr. M.S. Spilg, respectively.[22] Thus, according to the *Jewish Chronicle*, we can date the existence of the congregation to 1913 at the earliest. Reuben Spilg, however, remembers that the community was able to hire his father as a minister and *shochet* in 1904, so a congregation must have been in existence as early as then.[23] Collins states that it was established in 1905.[24]

Gershon Spilg and Family

The community's first minister was Gershon Spilg, who was born in Russia around 1840. He emigrated from Lithuania in 1885 to the Gorbals where he was listed in the 1901 census as living with his wife Sarah (39) and their children Max (29), Isaac (5), and Jeroham or Jerucham (3). Max was married to Sophia (30), and had four children, Eli (7), Elizabeth (5), Rosie (3), and Leah (1). When Jeroham, born 15 May, 1897, was six or seven years old, two men came from Falkirk to offer his father a job. They explained that there were sixteen Jewish families in Falkirk and they desperately needed a minister and *schochet*. They offered him twenty-five shillings per week and a halfpenny for every hen he killed. His youngest son, Jeroham/Jerucham, known as Reuben or "Ruby," recalled: "This would be about 1904 and, though the pound was worth a lot more then, it still wasn't much of a salary." Although he was in his sixties, "it was better than my father could get in Glasgow and so he accepted the appointment and we moved from the Gorbals to Falkirk."[25]

Spilg was a very poor man. His modest income, including the three shillings which was the average weekly payment for the slaughtering of hens, wasn't sufficient to maintain his family, so he supplemented his salary by peddling drapery goods in Polmont and Redding, using his contacts in Glasgow, mainly Goldberg's. He would send his youngest son to Glasgow to pay off the credit and to collect new merchandise for selling, including blue-striped overalls, blue jumpers, heavy flannelette shirts, ladies underwear and combinations. Somewhat unusually, Spilg also augmented his income by compiling chess problems for the local newspaper, as he was one of the champions of the Falkirk Chess Club.[26] Reuben remembered, nevertheless, "We were very poor. I remember setting my heart on buying a pair of brown boots out of Greenlees which cost four shillings."[27] Aged about seven, he went out to work at the Steeple on the High Street on Saturday nights, selling newspapers. He also began hanging out at Grahamston Station, selling timetables and offering to carry parcels and baggage for people arriving by train. He earned 3d for selling six dozen newspapers, of which he spent a half-penny on chips, another half-penny on hot peas, and a final half-penny on the 1910 version of the one-armed bandit, the Pickwick machine. That left $1^1/_2$d left over to apply towards a holiday or those boots he so cherished. However, he recalled, "Whenever I was about half-way to my target, my mother needed the money more than I did to keep the family. I never did get those boots." Instead, he walked barefoot all the way to the Tryst, and his brother George had patches on his trousers.[28] "I knew the family were just existing and no more."[29]

Spilg was very observant and strict. The family ate strictly kosher food at home, albeit on a budget. "Every Friday night in Falkirk our little house was shiningly clean. There was a white tablecloth on the table and the candles were burning. We had prayers before the meal and grace after the meal and in between we sang religious songs. Perhaps there wasn't much food on the table but there was a festive atmosphere."[30] The boys changed their underwear especially for the occasion and on Saturday morning put on their best clothes, even though they had patches on them. "My father put his religion above everything else," Reuben recollected.[31] He wouldn't even allow his eldest son to attend a bursary examination for Falkirk High School because it was on a Saturday morning. No matter how much time he invested in selling drapery goods around the villages or compiling the chess problems, his main energies were focused on his teaching and religious services. A small hall of the Falkirk High Street (perhaps Burns Court) was rented, and there were synagogue services every Friday night and Saturday morning from nine until noon. Hebrew Classes for the children, taught by Spilg, were held four nights a week and on Sunday mornings.[32]

Reuben Spilg's biography is invaluable, as it provides the fullest account of and insight into the sort of life that a minister in a small Scottish Jewish community led during the early nineteenth century. It also demonstrates the sort of rags-to-riches story that was common among many of the Jews in the small and isolated Scottish Jewish communities. Spilg began life as a poverty-stricken child in Falkirk. Although his father was the minister to the congregation, the family was so poor that Reuben had to walk barefoot as he sold newspapers and other items. He then went to the Central School in Meeks Road, never forgetting the day he received six strokes from the headmaster, Mr. Allison. "What a tyrant he was." He then went to Victoria School, enjoying "very happy years" under the headmaster Jimmy Johnston and teacher Jimmy Croal, who was something of a local celebrity because he played in Falkirk's Scottish Cup-winning soccer team and won several international honors representing Scotland. This early interest in soccer led Spilg to become, many years later, a director of the now-defunct Third Lanark team, and he worked closely with Cathkin bosses such as George Young and Bob Shankly.[33] After leaving school, Spilg became a printer's "devil" with Inglis in the Howgate, but his apprenticeship was ended when he demanded too much time off for the Jewish holidays. By that point, in 1911, his parents had decided to leave Falkirk for Glasgow, fear of the temptations of intermarriage being the principal reason. As their boys were growing up, they "wanted to see us in a place where we could meet other Jewish people."[34]

Spilg joined the Glasgow Highlanders in 1914 at the age of seventeen. In

1919, Spilg left the Army with a £40 gratuity, and after working for just three months in a jeweler's shop, which went bankrupt, he decided to "go it alone" and started door-to-door selling. "I worked from a room and kitchen to Govanhill and sold absolutely anything my customers asked for, from shoes and suits to lengths of purple velvet." In 1924 he paid £50 for the key to a warehouse in Great Clyde Street, took over a small shop for £150 in Eglinton Street, and just "growed and growed." His business grew to four stores in Glasgow, as well as others in Edinburgh, Paisley, Ayr, and Kirckcaldy. Eventually Spilg became one of Glasgow's top businessmen and a millionaire as the founder and managing director of Stirling's (Glasgow) Ltd. a giant warehouse firm that incorporated the former Stevens and Glen warehouses, employing 1,400 employees, and with an annual turnover of £6m. Spilg changed his name to Robert Spence in 1940 when the Nazis threatened Britain. In 1945 he married, and they lived in a comfortable suburb of Pollokshields in Glasgow. His son gained a B.A. degree from Strathclyde.[35]

Religious Needs

Little is known about the synagogue. We do not, for example, have a single precise address for its location, as one was never listed in the *Jewish Year Book*. According to Jackie Taylor, the first *shul* was probably located in Sword's Wynd, a street which contained several inns and halls, as well as the meeting places of the Baptists, Church of Christ, and members of the Evangelical Union. It stayed there, she said, until 1925.[36] However, correspondence and other documents indicate multiple addresses given for it in 1917: Howgate, Lorne's Hall, and the High Street.[37] There are, at present, only two surviving descriptions of the synagogue. The first, from Thomas Tate, states that initially it was in a hut or a wooden building in Howgate.[38] Unfortunately, the site no longer exists, as it was torn down and replaced with a shopping complex as part of the city center regeneration of Falkirk. An historical photograph of the street shows a mixture of housing and businesses, such as the Inglis Printing Works, although no wooden structure is visible.[39] Lewis Lawson points out, however, that the Howgate "for long was notorious for its dirt and squalor and for being one of the most unhealthy parts of the town."[40] Another description, although for which location remains uncertain, was provided by Nat Dolan: "The 'Synagogue' consisted of a large room in the Town center rented only during Rosh Hanukah and Yom Kippur. It was furnished only with some chairs and benches with the female section curtained off."[41] His use of quotation marks to denote the word "Synagogue" is telling, implying that it wasn't much of one at all! It seems that the synagogue moved around a great deal. From 1925 to 1946, according to Jackie Taylor, the *shul* moved to the High Street.[42] According to Lewis Lawson, further west along the High Street, a "Jewish synagogue stood in Burns Court," but, frustratingly, he provides no further details in terms of the date or the sources of his information.[43]

The community also attempted to provide for its other religious needs. There was some sort of religious instruction for the children, and the teaching must have been of a sufficient quality because David Bulbin of Falkirk was commended in a *Jewish Chronicle* competition in 1914.[44] The Reverend Spilg had been replaced by the Reverend S. Gerber, but he left by 1913 to join the congregation in Inverness.[45] The Reverend B. Finkelstein from Russia was the next person to fill the vacant ministerial post, but he, too, left in 1915 to become minister of the Langside Hebrew Congregation in Glasgow, to be followed by the Reverend J. Chazan, who performed a *brit milah* (circumcision) on J. Cohen in 1916. A collection was made at the ceremony for the "Fund for the Relief of the Jewish Victims of the War in Russia," to which the following contributed: J. Chazan, 5s; A. Bulbin, 6s 6d; L. Bloch (Treas.), 5s; J. Aitken, 3s 6d; J. Cohen, 4s; J. Joseph, 4s. It was the first time that the "Falkirk Hebrew Congregation" was mentioned in the *Jewish Chronicle*. Other collections for the same fund were made in the same year.[45] By October 1916, however, the Reverend Chazan had left, and the community was advertising for a *shochet* and teacher.[46]

The successful applicant was Abraham Samet, who was born in Lodz (then in Russia) on 7 April, 1878. He acted as minister, *shochet*, and teacher. Soon after his appointment on 29 May, 1917, however, Samet was called up for military service. Samet applied for exemption under the Military Service Act, which caught the attention of the *Jewish Chronicle*. Reporting on "Russian Jews and Military Service," under the subheading, "THE CASE OF A MINISTER AT FALKIRK," the newspaper stated:

> At a sitting of the Appeal Tribunal for the County of Stirling, held last Friday at Falkirk, several appeals were heard from Russian subjects including an application by the Hebrew Congregation at Falkirk for the redemption of their minister, who acted as teacher to about forty children in the districts of Falkirk, Stirling and Bonnybridge. He also slaughtered the cattle and sealed the meat. A letter was submitted from the Chief Rabbi, stating that the gentleman in question had been a minister before the date of the Convention, and was therefore entitled to exemption. The appeal was refused, but two months were given in order that the case might be taken before the Central Court.[47]

Following his court appearance, on 19 December, 1917, Samet presented himself at the Russian Vice-Consulate in Glasgow in order to gain official Russian confirmation that he was a Russian subject (as he did not hold a Russian passport), in order to avoid conscription.[48] It would have been a major imposition on the small community of Falkirk to gain and then lose a minister so soon after his appointment. Fortunately, Samet's appeal was successful, and he obtained deferment from military service after it was demonstrated that his appointment predated his conscription.[50] Given that so many of the ministers of the Jewish communities in Scotland were foreign born, as we have seen, this problem must surely have been endemic among those of military age. Similar reports, however, were not received from the other small communities.

Between the Wars

Following the end of the First World War, the community was rather active in terms of Jewish practice. It had a new minister, the Reverend Samuel Kibel. Mr. and Mrs. (née Florence Rome) Lewis Taylor had a son in 1919, and presumably, although this is not mentioned in the *Jewish Chronicle*, the Reverend Kibel performed the circumcision. The Reverend Kibel was also described as the "celebrant" at a wedding celebration in Falkirk that same year. The community, despite its small size, continued to collect and donate money to charity. At the aforementioned wedding, the sum of five guineas for the Talmud Torah in Edinburgh was raised, as was £5 3s 6d. for Jews in Poland and Eastern Europe. The community also continued to be represented on the Board of Deputies in London. By 1933, a Jewish Youth Body had been set up.[51] Abraham Bulbin purchased one share at the cost of one pound, in the Zionist funding scheme the Jewish Colonial Trust.[52]

Over the years, Shabbat morning services were held monthly rather than weekly, and the times of the Friday night worship varied according to demand. A clear example of this in Falkirk came when "the man who conducted the service was also the porter at Falkirk High Station, and so the *minyan* had to be timed to coincide with the train timetable. He was collected at station as soon as the Edinburgh train had left, taken to the *minyan*, and then back to the station in time to meet the Glasgow train."[53]

Falkirk also managed to provide for the education of its children. The Reverend Kibel was also the Headmaster of its Hebrew Classes. The *cheder* was subsidized by the Central Education Committee of the Jewish War Memorial, which gave a grant of £26 to Falkirk in 1923. It is not known if this grant was a one-off payment, but later reports hint that it was an annual award when classes were in progress. In 1930, for example, the Central Committee for Jewish Education agreed to renew its grant to Falkirk, subject to the appointment of a new teacher approved by the director. In return for its money, the classes were also inspected by these central authorities on an annual basis. The Director of Jewish Education, Herbert M. Adler, visited in 1936, to be followed by the minister of the Garnethill Synagogue in Glasgow, Dr. I. K. Cosgrove, in 1937. During the following year they both inspected the "Falkirk Hebrew Religion Classes" again, as did Adler in 1938.[54] The only surviving report is from 1936, when Adler wrote that the classes at Falkirk were "now being conducted in one central place, that being a condition of the grant by the Central Committee, and the children were being properly taught."⁵⁵ The implication of Adler's observation was that the Hebrew Classes had lacked a central location for some time, possibly being conducted at a variety of locations as a result of there not being single suitable premises for both the synagogue and schoolroom. Alternatively, different classes might have been conducted simultaneously. The other inference one can make from Adler's report is that, in spite of its best efforts, the level of education for the children of Falkirk was not always satisfactory. The reason for this, as Adler reported, was the succession of short-term ministers and teachers that typically affected all small, provincial communities; as he said, the children of Falkirk "had not had continuity of teaching."⁵⁶

This report is reinforced by the recollections of Nat Dolan, who grew up in Falkirk. He recalled that "Jewish education was virtually non-existent. From time to time a young scholar from some Yeshiva would be recruited to try to 'educate' the handful of young boys but their efforts were futile as a complete lack of discipline resulted in complete chaos."⁵⁷ Instead, Nat travelled to Glasgow every Sunday for about a year to learn his bar mitzvah portion and to learn to read Hebrew. Following the efforts of the Reverend Cosgrove, however, Hebrew classes were planned on Sundays and Thursdays, from 2 p.m. until 4 p.m. in the Central Halls.⁵⁸ A Mr. Zwebner of Glasgow was employed to visit the classes once a week in 1938, and Adler requested that the Committee resume its grant of £36 per annum, which was approved. Through its subventions and regular inspections, therefore, the larger metropolitan communities of London and Glasgow helped sustain a smaller and poorer community such as Falkirk.

A letter printed in the *Jewish Chronicle* in 1938 gives a fascinating insight into the communal life of Falkirk between the wars. Mr. Isaac Benjamin, of 12, Grahams Road, Falkirk, wrote in to complain about the "disregard of the Sabbath":

> May I protest against the increasing practice of Jews participating in tournament bridge playing on Sabbaths. They would earn higher respect from their Gentile friends if those Jews selected to represent their respective countries or cities were to refuse to play on the Sabbath. On a recent Saturday, no fewer than twelve members of our faith participated in a bridge tourney at Harrogate.⁵⁹

The letter was probably prompted by the failure of the congregation to obtain a *minyan* for the preceding Shabbat, suggesting that religious observance was not of primary importance to the Jews of Falkirk at that time. As evidence of this, Nat Dolan recalled that the "majority of people were not orthodox, especially second generations, and were more concerned with assimilation—blending in with the local community."⁶⁰ Indeed, the above letter demonstrated that the Jewish community was well-integrated into local life, and that the abandonment of a strict Orthodox lifestyle was a means of achieving that.

Yet a *minyan* was always available, albeit only for the occasional *Yarzheit*. When such services were held, they were conducted by the senior member of the community, but, as Nat Dolan remembered, they "were not Orthodox by any means." Other communal facilities were sorely lacking. As we have seen with the remoter community of Aberdeen, kosher food, in particular meat and poultry, was purchased from kosher butchers in Glasgow on a weekly basis and put on the train or bus to be collected at the other end by those households unable to collect their food personally. Alternatively, businessmen often drove into Glasgow as part of their work and picked up meat and other supplies on their way home. Initially, most of the food was strictly kosher, but as time went by, the laws of *kashrut* became less respected — most likely as a result of the difficulties of obtaining it, combined with a declining interest in Orthodox observance among those Jews born in Falkirk. Ultimately, services in Falkirk were abandoned, with most of the community travelling to Glasgow to participate. Likewise, no Jewish burials took place in Falkirk, as there was no dedicated cemetery. Given the town's proximity and equidistance from both Glasgow and Edinburgh, burials most likely took place in either of those two cities. Due to the small size of the community, Nat recalled, no one was either available or willing to carry out communal duties, nor were there any formal Zionist or other charitable activities (although families made regular donations to the typical Jewish charities).[61] However, in 1938 arrangements were made to ensure that every Jewish household in Falkirk had a J.N.F. collection box.[62] And it was noted in 1940 that "good sums had been raised."[63]

Jews in Falkirk were restricted to a limited number of occupations. They mainly ran their own businesses and shops. Scanning the available directories for Falkirk and the surrounding districts from 1913 until 1967, we find the following trades listed: jewelry, decorating, drapery, "general dealing," furniture and house furnishing, boot and shoe making and selling, and gents outfitting. Primarily, the community was involved in some sort of retail, although one of the more unusual professions was Stanley Bloch's photography studio. And, judging by the addresses given for the congregation in the *Jewish Echo*, the various trade directories, and the different addresses for the synagogue (Comely Place, Gartgows Road, High Street, Pleasance Square, Glebe Street, Baxter's Wynd, and Arnothill Gardens), the Jews clustered in the center of Falkirk, near to the Grahamston railway station.

After the War

As with Reuben Spilg in the First World War, during the Second World War a few male members of the community became servicemen. One of those included Lieutenant H. Rosenberg, a member of the Royal Army Medical Corps, who was taken prisoner by the Germans in 1940.[64] At the end of the war, according to the *Jewish Year Book*, there were a total of sixty-two Jews living in Falkirk, a figure unchanged since 1939. The High Street synagogue closed and moved to Glebe Street for only one year (1946–1947). Given that the Levenson, Spilg, and Kaplan families had all previously lived at the same address on Glebe Street, it is likely that this address was a private home.[65] A report in the *Jewish Chronicle* mentioned the Falkirk "congregation" in March 1950 when it donated a *sefer Torah* to Israel.[66] Possibly the paper was referring to the several, and sometimes related, Jewish families that continued living in the town at addresses that were close together. The Riffkins may have disappeared from Falkirk, but the Bloch, Cembler, Etkind, Marks, Normand, and Taylor families remained to form the community, albeit with no formal congregation. Their numbers, however, were reduced, as their children tended to meet and eventually marry Jews from outside Falkirk and then leave the town to live with their partners. Myra Sinclair married Harry Bradman from London; Harold Taylor was engaged to Joyce Creme from Blackpool; and Nat Normand married Josephine Solomon from Leeds. However, not all of them left: Stanley Bloch became engaged to Margaret Dent of London, and they subsequently married and remained in Falkirk, as did Normand and Taylor. According to a report in the *Jewish Echo*, Margaret was still living there in 1978.[67] While the Bradmans had a son in Falkirk in 1947, it is not certain that they continued to live in the town.[68] Furthermore, older members of the community began to pass away. Millie Bloch died in 1959, and her husband Lazarus endowed a bed in the Old Age Home in Glasgow in memory of her.[69] In October of the following year Jack Normand also died.[70]

Nonetheless, the *Jewish Chronicle* continued to note the existence of "a few Jewish families" in Falkirk in 1964.[71] These included the Bloch family (Stanley, Neil and Ralph), Harry Cembler, Max and Morris Marks, Harris Riffkin, and Harold and Lewis Taylor. Jack Normand may have died, but his business remained open until 1967 at least.[72] Paul Morron, a leading figure in the Glasgow Jewish Student Society and a senior vice-president of the Inter-University Jewish Federation, was a law graduate employed as a social worker by Falkirk Town Council in 1971; and, as mentioned earlier, Margaret Bloch still lived in Falkirk.[73] Prayers were carried out on a regular basis until around 1980, the same year that Riffkin's shop closed, suggesting that the end of prayers was connected.

Farther afield from Falkirk there was a sprinkling of individuals and families who may or may not have attended their synagogue there. Between 1921 and 1924, a convalescent home, possibly for Jews with tuberculosis, was opened in Binniehall House, near Slamannan, about seven miles from Falkirk.[74] In 1946, Mr. and Mrs. Hyman moved to Alva in Clackmannanshire, where he was a town and county councilor. They had three children before moving to Glasgow in 1966. Dr. and Mrs. Harold Sherry lived at 14, Wilson Terrace, Stoneyburn, by Bathgate, West Lothian, approximately fifteen miles from Falkirk. He is included here simply because of proximity, although it is not known whether he participated in the Falkirk congregation. Harold had been educated in Glasgow, and practiced in Birmingham and Leeds, before taking up a post as a general practitioner in West Lothian, which was a mining area, where, according to his obituary, he attended "to the injured down the mine."[75] Initially for six months, his period of service was extended to twenty-five years. He was much loved; when he wanted to move to Glasgow for the religious education of his children, "the offer was made to build a synagogue in the district to retain his services."[76] Coatbridge was the residence of Solomon Hill, his wife, and six children. In addition, Harry Crivan was teacher, vice-principal and later principal of the town's technical college, although he commuted from Glasgow, where he lived. Relatives of Leah Rubin lived in Airdrie, and Kelso was the residence of Rochelle and Raymond Mason and their family.

Epilogue

Despite declining numbers, Jews remained in the town. In 1984, for example, the marriage of Robert, the only son of Annie and Bobbie Buchanan of Falkirk, was announced.[77] Given his name, though, one wonders if he was, in fact, non–Jewish and marrying a Jewish girl. In 1999 the *Jewish Chronicle* reported, "Falkirk hosts its first siyum." The communities of Edinburgh and Glasgow *Daf Hayomi* held a joint *siyum*—commemoration of the completion of the book of the Talmud—by meeting half way between the two cities in the Falkirk home of Jackie and Raymond Taylor. "It was the first time in living memory that a *siyum* had been held in Falkirk."[78] In the year 2000 there were still two Jewish families in Falkirk, and by the time of this writing in 2008, the Taylor's Furniture Store, at 69, Manor Street, remained open for business.[79]

6

Greenock

Dispelling a Few Myths

The town of Greenock, with a population of about 45,000, is situated on the south bank of the river Clyde near the western coast of Scotland, approximately thirty miles west of Glasgow. Since 1826, Greenock was the principal British port for all transactions with America.[1] As a consequence, a myth has grown up that Jews settled in Greenock because of, in the words of Kenneth Collins, "its position on the trans-shipment route."[2] It was said that Greenock was the port of embarkation for those Jews who, having arrived in Scotland from Eastern Europe, desired to continue their journey to either Ireland or across the Atlantic to the United States of America. They would journey by train from Leith across Scotland to Greenock, where they would embark.[3] As Sharman Kadish has pointed out, "For most, it was a transient stopover, on the steamship route from the Baltic to New York."[4] Mark Smith has written, "Around the turn of the century, Jews poured into Greenock in their thousands. Great steamships loaded with Jewish refugees pulled up the River Clyde alongside the giant clippers, fishing boats and tugs. In those days, Greenock was one of the busiest ports in Britain."[5]

Some, it has been argued, decided not to carry on and chose to stay in the port, where they settled. Smith, for example, wrote, "Many were penniless or too tired to go further. Still others who had paid full fare to America were hoodwinked by captains who told them Greenock was New York."[6] Smith's own great-grandmother recalled why she hadn't gone to America: "Because the boat stopped at Greenock. They told me to get off, so I got off."[7] Similarly, Ethel Hofman records that her grandparents, Jacob and Esther Segal, "disembarked in Greenock," adding, "the Glasgow seaport," suggesting that there might be some confusion on her part as to the exact location of their landing.[8] Collins also repeats the story of Jews tricked into believing that Scotland was New York.[9] Smith continues to paint a picture of Greenock in the late nineteenth century. He relates:

> Jewish boarding houses were established and kosher soup kitchens were set up at dockside to cater to the thousands of homeless Jews. Some remained only long enough to catch the next ship out. Others stayed on and were later helped to Amer-

ica with the aid of the Jewish community. Others travelled inland to Glasgow or south to London, Manchester, Leeds and other places.[10]

Yet, there is no evidence for any of these assertions. As Nicholas J. Evans, while working on the Scottish Emigration Database, discovered, primarily only native Scots left from the port of Greenock. He found that a mere two-hundred-and-forty-five Jews sailed from Greenock to New York between 1892 and 1924.[11] When compared to the fifty thousand who left from Glasgow, this number is virtually insignificant, and hence does not account for the formation of a Jewish community in Greenock. It seems, therefore, that Smith is particularly guilty of propagating certain myths. There were never thousands of Jews in Greenock (maybe sixty families at most at the turn of the century). The story of being deceived by unscrupulous agents or captains is a common one told among immigrant Jewish families, but one for which there is no actual evidence. I suspect it is used as a cover story for those who were simply sick of traveling on what must have been a horrendous journey. Furthermore, Smith's article implies that Jews disembarked at Greenock ("a third of all passenger ships that crossed the Atlantic from the Baltic ports to New York stopped off there"[12]), which certainly never happened, as ships traveling from Eastern Europe would not have sailed to the West coast of Scotland!

Similarly, there is no evidence of any lodging houses in Greenock, although there were many in Ayr, as we have seen. If a lodging house had been run in Greenock by a Jew then it was most likely for non–Jewish clientele. The dockside catering was for very few Jews. Even fewer were homeless. While there was a shelter in Glasgow, there was none in Greenock.[13] This also explains why the Jewish community in Greenock was so small; if Jews had left Greenock *en masse*, then surely a larger presence in the port would have been recorded, as in the other major Scottish ports (namely, Dundee and Edinburgh). The reason that Jews were attracted to Greenock was because of its relative proximity to Glasgow—it provided a base for their commercial activities on a more competitive basis than in the overcrowded Jewish areas in Glasgow.

The First Arrivals

Possibly the first Jew to move to Greenock was Joseph Hyndman, a baker at 74, Vennel, listed in *Slater's Directory* in 1846. Solomon Alexander, born in Aberdeen in 1858, at some point in his lifetime practised as a medical herbalist in Greenock until he died in 1897.[13] The bulk of Jewish immigration to Greenock, however, did not begin until the late nineteenth century. In 1874 a legal case involving two German Jews was reported in *The Greenock Telegraph*[14]

GERMAN JEWS IN COURT

At the Justice of Peace Court to-day a rather amusing debt case was heard. Mr. Josiah Saquy, a German Jew and auctioneer, sued Mr. Isaac Lyons, another German Jew, for two sums of 35s, the first for wages and the second for wrongful dismissal. It came out in evidence that the partner had been offered his weekly wage of 35s in coppers, and had declined to take it saying that he wanted his money in sliver, and gold like a gentleman. (Laughter.) Defender said that he had been offered his wages, and that he had been in drink and had sworn all sorts of foreign oaths (Laughter.)

Decree for £3 5s was given for the defender.[15]

The unusual presence of German Jews in the town suggests that they were based in Glasgow and travelled to Greenock, or lived in Greenock, having moved there from another city or country altogether. The Home Office Naturalization Certificates reveal that there was a significant German presence in Greenock, for between 1895 and 1913 no less than ten German and Austrian citizens were naturalized.[16] One of the reasons for this German presence in Greenock, contemporaneous with the German immigration into Dundee, was its sugar-refining industry, which had existed in continental Europe many years before its introduction into Great Britain. Consequently, German names were not unfamiliar in Greenock during the first half of the nineteenth century. We do not know, however, if any of them were Jewish.[17]

Several Jewish families were listed in the census by 1881. These included Jacob Coul (22) and Houston Jacobs (23) from Poland, a tailor and tailor's wife, respectively, both lodging at 8, Cross Shore Street. The Levy family was also living at the same address: Pinkus (25), Maria (22), and their son Jacob (1). Pinkus was a picture frame maker from Russia. His wife, quite unusually, was born in England. They were joined by Israel Levy (33) from Russia, listed as a "visitor" and glazier who was most likely a relative. Israel Goodman (32), a tailor from Poland, was living with his wife Rebecca (28) and their children, Michael (10), Rebecca (10), Ancel (7), Annie (4), Polly (2), and Levi (one month), at 34, Ann Street. Michael, Rebecca, and Ancel were all listed as "scholars." Abraham Jacobs (37) from Poland was a "master tailor," employing fourteen men and two women. He lived at 5, William Street with his wife Cecelia (39) and his children: Philip (20) and Morris (17), tailors, Betsy (14), Wolf (12), David (10), Solomon (8), Israel (3), and Sarah (two months). In addition to the trades listed above, other occupations found in Greenock from that time onwards included clothiers, stationers, tobacconists, boot and shoe sellers, shoemakers, hairdressers, drapers, general dealers, travelers, aerated water manufacturers, confectioners, and plumbers.[18]

By 1883, the *Jewish Chronicle* noted that "Jews were to be found now" in Greenock.[19] They included John Barnett of 42, Roeburgh Street, and Isabella Stepman, who were married at the Glasgow New Hebrew Congregation (most likely owing to the lack of a synagogue in Greenock).[20] Two years later, in 1885,

Samuel Abrahams, a tailor and clothier living at 14, Dalrymple Street, was listed in the *Greenock Street Directory*. In 1893 he was mentioned in the *Jewish Chronicle* when he gave £1 1s to the Glasgow Jewish Board of Guardians.[21] The 1891 census recorded the Freedman family at 21, Lyle Street, consisting of Abraham (38), a tailor from Poland, Milly (27), a tailor's wife (also from Poland), and their children Mark (14), born in Leeds, Isaac (12), Aaron (10), Rebecca (8), and Annie (1). The last four children were all born in Glasgow, indicating that the Freedmans had moved from there to Greenock. In 1894 the Kaminsky family from Latvia had arrived. Gershon Spilg and his wife Sarah moved from Glasgow to Greenock in 1895; where their son George was born the following year (although by 1897 they had returned to Glasgow). As Spilg was a minister and *shochet*, he may have gone there to lead the religious services. In 1898, Velvel Itzikovitz arrived from Lithuania. The story told by the family (although, like many similar immigrant tales, it may be apocryphal) is that the Scottish immigration officer had trouble with the name Itzikovitz. Since Velvel was Wolfe, he gave him the surname Wolfe. Velvel then anglicized his name to Walter. Thus was born Walter Wolfe. When his brother, Joseph Itzikovitz, came a year later, in 1899, he called himself Joseph Wolfe.

A Congregation Is Established

Services were first held in Greenock in 1894. The *Jewish Chronicle* reported:

> The six Jewish families in Greenock succeeded in holding a *minyan* during the recent festivals. The services were held in a small hall on the New Year and the Day of Atonement and during Tabernacles in a room lent by Mr. Abrahams. Mr. Spilk [perhaps this is a misspelling of Spilg?] of Glasgow officiated. Mr. Jackson was *Chatan Torah* and Mr. Blint *Chatan Bereshit*.[22]

In light of this, the usual date given for the foundation of the congregation is 1894, although there is no further corroborating evidence for such a development. As with Ayr, Dundee, Dunfermline, and Falkirk, it does not help that the records of the congregation have been lost. In their absence, there are a variety of sources which all cite the same date, most likely because they are all quoting and/or repeating the same information. The JCR-UK website, for example, states "possibly 1894." It then goes on to claim that in 1895 there were twelve "seatholders," citing the *Jewish Year Book 1896* as its source.[23] However, there is no entry in the *Jewish Year Book* of that date for Greenock whatsoever! In *Second City Jewry*, Kenneth Collins, somewhat strangely, cites the date 1891.[24]

The location of the services is also a mystery, other than the report's mention of a "small hall." However, the extant sources all seem to agree that it was 27, Cathcart Street. For example, Sharman Kadish states, "A synagogue was opened in 1894 and a cemetery next door on Cathcart Street."[25] The JCR-UK website is a bit more cautious (which is surprising, given the erroneous information it cited above): "Believed at 27 Cathcart Street, Greenock."[26] Mark Smith also gives the year as 1894, adding, "In that same year, Greenock Synagogue was built," implying that there was some sort of purpose-built physical structure, which, given the poverty and small size of such a community, would never have happened without a major financial injection from the outside community.[27]

Thereafter, there were certainly some Jewish-related occurrences in Greenock around that time, but none with the weight of the establishment of a *shul* and cemetery. For example, Israel Zangwill lectured at the Scottish Society of Literature and Art at Greenock, but this does not seem to be a specifically Jewish event.[28] And in 1899, the following advert for kosher Passover sugar appeared:

Kosher Sugar for Passover
By permission of the Ecclesiastical Authorities and the Chief Rabbi, Dr. Adler
MESSRS. A. LEVY & SONS,
59, Commercial Street,
London, E.,
WHOLESALE GROCERS AND MERCHANTS,
Have much pleasure in informing the Jewish public that they have been appointed
Sole Agents for London & Provinces
FOR PASSOVER SUGAR
Manufactured by the
GLEBE SUGAR REFINING Co., Greenock,
Under the Special Supervision of the
Revs. J. Bridge and A. Caster, of Glasgow.[29]

The Greenock connection here is incidental, the town being merely the location of the sugar refining mill, with no evidence pointing to a congregation organized around a synagogue.

The first mention of the Greenock Hebrew Congregation in the *Jewish Year Book* came in the 1902 edition (thus the date of establishment was likely to be 1901). The following are listed: reader, H. Dorfman; president, Peter Jacobs; vice-president, Abraham Freedman; and honorary secretary, Emanuel Edwards. Unhelpfully, there is no mention of a synagogue or any address given. In terms of the Jewish press, any specifically Jewish communal activity in Greenock does not appear until 1905 when an editorial in the *Jewish Chronicle* noted the existence of a small community in Greenock and recommended that it share an "educated minister" with the larger, but still small, community of Edinburgh.[30] In December of that same year a service was held in the Terrace Road Hall, unusually on a Sunday, conducted by the Reverend Israel Tiemianka, who also delivered a sermon. Afterwards, a Mr. J. Hastie showed a series of "limelight views" illustrating notable events in Jewish history.[31] The *Jewish Year Book* begins to list the figures of Greenock's congregation in its

1906 edition, meaning that its figures were gathered in 1905. It put the number at thirty "members" (a figure which remained unchanged until its 1909 edition). Going purely on this evidence, then, Greenock did not start a congregation until 1901 at the earliest. Furthermore, it was in 1906 that an address for the synagogue was first given: "27, Carthcart Street."

Thereafter, the community engaged in notable activities. On 3 January, 1906, Abraham (also known as "Abrom" and "Abram") Levy (also known as "Pinkus") of 5, Cathcart Street, married Teresa (or Theresa) Tytz at Shepherd's Hall, Cathcart Street.[32] Abraham was listed as a "Clothier's Traveller," and Theresa as a "Tailoress." The marriage was witnessed by Moses Morris (a traveler) and Emanuel Edwards, and the celebrant was the Reverend Tiemianka.[33]

In March 1906 a public meeting on Zionism was held in Greenock.[34] Smith describes it as "a demonstrating supporting Palestine ... in the streets of Greenock."[35] This sounds highly unlikely and a most surprising occurrence for such a small Jewish community, as Jews tended to keep a low profile, and no such similar event was recorded elsewhere in Scotland in our isolated congregations. Four of Greenock's Jews (E. Blumberg, Rebecca Cown, Benjamin Abram, and Dora Abrams) did purchase shares in the Jewish Colonial Trust, however.[36] A *B'nei Zion* society was established, and the following were elected: the Reverend Israel Tiemianka, honorary president; Mr. Isaac Hyman, president; Mr. E. Blumberg, vice-president; Mr. Joseph Wolfe, treasurer; and Mr. M. Etzman, secretary.[37] And at the end of the year a special Chanukah service for the children of the community was held at the Orange Hall and officiated by the Reverend Tiemianka. Hebrew classes had been set up, as the children were able to sing the Chanukah songs (aided by Miss Jackson at the organ).[38] The repetition of the name of the Reverend Tiemianka here and in the previous paragraph suggests that he had been hired as the community's minister and teacher. This is confirmed by the 1906 entry in the *Jewish Year Book* which lists him as the "Minister and Honorary Secretary."

In 1906, Henri Temianka was born into a fairly well-off Polish immigrant diamond-dealing family. At the age of six his father gave him his first violin lessons. He then went off to study music in Berlin and Paris. He made his debut in New York in 1928 before returning to Scotland, where he was the leader of the Scottish Orchestra from 1937 to 1938. In 1946 he founded the Paganini Quartet, which played for twenty years. In 1960 he returned to the United States, founded the California Chamber Orchestra, and held a number of teaching professorships. He was by then known as a virtuoso violinist, a great teacher, a fine writer, and an all-round musician. He played under conductors such as George Szell, Pierre Monteaux, and Otto Kliemperer, and with violinists Isaac Stern, David Oistrakh, Henryk Szeryng, and Yehudi Menuhin. At the age of eighty he gave master classes in England and

No. 253   **Office of the Chief Rabbi,**
                     22, FINSBURY SQUARE, LONDON, E.C.

AUTHORISATION FOR THE CELEBRATION OF MARRIAGE
(Subject to compliance with the provisions of the Marriage Acts of Parliament).

Date of Marriage ... [Hebrew] 566 6 / January 3rd 1906

Bridegroom ... [Hebrew] / Abraham Levi

Address ... 5 ___ Street. Greenock

Brothers (if any) ... [Hebrew]

Bride ... [Hebrew] / Teresa ___

Address ... As above

Synagogue ... Greenock   Hour 3 p.m.

Place of Celebration ... Shepherds Hall. Greenock

Name of Celebrant ... Minister J. ___

                                  CHIEF RABBI.

                 Date December 7th 566 6

To the Secretary of the Greenock Synagogue.

*** This Form should at once be handed to the Secretary of the Synagogue.

Authorization for the Celebration of Marriage, Greenock, 1906

Shanghai, and was a judge at Beijing's first international violin competition. He died at age eighty-five in 1992.[39]

Henri was a most unusual individual, atypical for a native-born Jew in a small Scottish Jewish community at that time. Apart from his choice of career, his family would have stood out in Greenock in the early part of the century for not being poor (like most of their immigrant co-religionists) and also for being involved in the diamond trade, an unusual profession to be found in a small Scottish Jewish community at that time. The family must not have felt entirely comfortable in such a small and poor community, for not long after Henri was born they had moved to the Netherlands.[40]

By 1907 the community was large enough to merit a visit from the Chief Rabbi and his son. He met with members of the Jewish community in Greenock and delivered a sermon; a service was led by the Revered Tiemianka in the Shepherds' Hall. His visit was considered to be so important that members of the Town Council were invited, and it was reported in both the *Jewish Chronicle* and the local newspaper, the *Greenock Telegraph and Clyde Shipping Gazette*. These reports provide a fascinating insight into the community at that time. In the course of his sermon, the Chief Rabbi pleaded for better observance of the Sabbath, implying that standards of orthodoxy were perhaps lax at the time. He also asked that the Jews of Greenock "do their utmost to further moral and spiritual welfare of their children." From the hall, the party proceeded to the schoolrooms, where the Chief Rabbi and his son examined the children in Hebrew and expressed their satisfaction with their progress. Prizes were also distributed. Intriguingly, the *Jewish Chronicle* reports that the Chief Rabbi "settled some difference which had arisen in connection with communal matters."[41] Frustratingly, though, no further detail about the matter was provided, and the lack of records for the community means that it remains a mystery.[42]

Although the congregation itself might not have been in harmony, relations between the Jewish community and their non–Jewish neighbors were on good terms. The Reverend Tiemianka thanked the Town Council on behalf of the congregation for "the kindness and goodwill shown towards them in the past," and expressed the hope that "the spirit of love and brotherhood would continue amongst all classes without distinction of creed or race." He was pleased to see "the good relations between the Jews of this town and the Christians, and hoped that every prosperity would attend Greenock in the future." The very presence of non–Jews, including town officials, pointed to the level of tolerance Jews in Greenock experienced at that time.[43]

As was typical of smaller Jewish communities, the congregation moved around a great deal. As indicated from the events described above, between 1905 and 1912 we find multiple locations given for the synagogue, services, and classes in Greenock. They are: Terrace Road Hall (1905); 27, Cathcart Street (1906); Orange Hall (1906); Shepherds' Hall (1907); and 6, Trafalgar Street (1912—listed in the 1913 edition of the *Jewish Year Book*). This suggests that the community made use either of private homes (Cathcart Street and Trafalgar Street) or public spaces (the various halls). The venue used for the visit of the Chief Rabbi is particularly interesting, as the report stated, "[F]rom the hall the party proceeded to the schoolrooms," suggesting that the community did have some sort of base (until 1909 at least). There is one further explanation here: that the *Jewish Year Book* erroneously stated the address of the community's correspondent as being the site of the synagogue, and that its location did not actually change. Without the records of the congregation, however, there is no way of verifying this. At the very least, it can be said with

Jewish Section, Bow Road Cemetery, Greenock. (Photograph courtesy of William Sutherland.)

some certainty that when compared to a community like Aberdeen, which has used only two buildings for its *shul* since 1893 (to this day), the relative stability of the latter is highlighted.

Greenock's Burial Ground

Greenock also had a dedicated Jewish burial ground as part of a larger public cemetery. According to Alexandra Kirkpatrick and David Wolfe, there are headstones with inscriptions in Hebrew in the Old Greenock Cemetery on Inverkip Street.[44] Further confusing matters, Harvey Kaplan, director of the Scottish Jewish Archives Centre, has stated, "Greenock Hebrew Congregation buried sixteen members in the cemetery in Bow Road between 1908 and 1945."[45] However, Harold Pollins' inspection of the cemetery indicated a number half that size—he counted eight gravestones—and that the dates held by the Scottish Jewish Archives Centre and those inscribed on the headstones did not always match.[46] Mark Smith counted the same number.[47] Sharman Kadish also states that the Jewish cemetery was in the Bow Road public cemetery, but she counted "a total of seven Jewish tombstones in a row, the earliest dated 1911 and the most recent 1945."[48] In fact, there is such a discrepancy between Pollins, Kadish, and Kaplan's information that one wonders if they are, in fact, referring to the same cemetery! The inconsistency in the number of people buried is attributable to the fact that not all of them had headstones.

Left: Gravestone of Hanna Ferguson, Bow Road Cemetery, Greenock. (Photograph courtesy of William Sutherland.) *Right:* Gravestone of Samuel Abrams, Bow Road Cemetery, Greenock. (Photograph courtesy of William Sutherland.)

One of those that did, however, and who was definitely buried in Bow Road, was Samuel Abrams, who died on 18 September, 1911, at 51, Rue End Street, Greenock, leaving behind his wife Miriam. His tombstone was consecrated in "the Hebrew portion of Greenock Cemetery" in 1914, demonstrating that the Jewish cemetery was a separate section of a larger, public cemetery, as in Aberdeen, Dundee, and Inverness.[49] The first burial was of Emanuel Cominskie (most likely Kaminisky), who died stillborn in 1908. The last burial was that of Anna Ferguson of 1, Mearns Street in 1945. Thereafter, Greenock's Jews were buried in Glasgow.

According to Pollins, three others buried in the cemetery were the Freedman brothers. As two of them had married non-Jews, they were not commemorated on their father Abraham's gravestone. The son whose name that *was* inscribed was Private Joseph Freedman (born in Greenock in 1902), who had served in the Argyll and Sutherland Highlanders. His brother Ben had served in the Black Watch, and just before the war ended was gassed; he had been wounded twice before.[50] Other Jews from Greenock were buried in cemeteries in Glasgow due to its relative proximity, particularly after the Second World War.[51] One such example was Samuel's widow, Miriam, who was interred in the Riddrie Cemetery in Glasgow in 1921, thus begging the question of why they weren't buried together, as one might expect.[52]

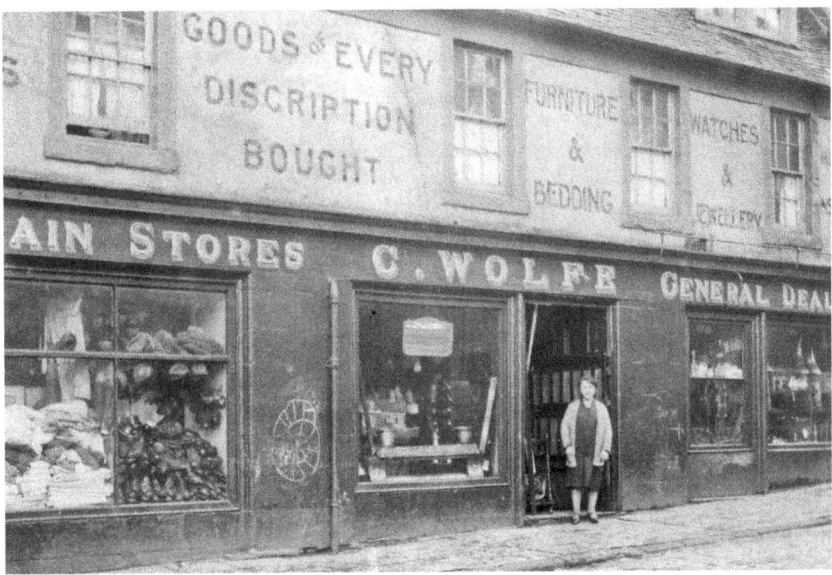

Celia Wolfe in front of her store, Greenock. (Photograph courtesy of L. Alexander Wolfe.)

Relative Stability

By 1913 the community had twenty members, according to the *Jewish Year Book*. These included both immigrants from Russia, such as Harris Banks, Ruben Fagerson (known as Ruben Ferguson), Edward Blumberg, Abraham Freedman, and Joseph Wolfe and his family, as well as native-born Jews.[53] The following year, in 1914, a "Joseph Lopes" from Italy was a resident in the town when he naturalized. While his name implies that he was Jewish, the arrival of an Italian (and, therefore, most likely Sephardi) Jew was a rare occurrence in Scotland in the early twentieth century, as the overwhelming majority of Jewish immigrants were of Ashkenazi descent.[54] The Wolfe family members were émigrés from Lithuania who had arrived in Greenock but settled in Glasgow, where their son David was born in 1912. Joseph was listed as a "tailor's presser" in the 1901 census. A few years later the family moved back to Greenock, where, with an additional son, Sidney, they grew up in a one-room tenement house in the Potteries. The father, Joseph, was a peddler, and the mother, Celia, had a shop for second-hand goods. Incidentally, Emmanuel (Manny) Shinwell, a future Jewish M.P. from Glasgow, visited Greenock as part of his job to organize the Clydeside seamen when he was vice-chairman of the Glasgow Trades Council in 1911.[55]

After a period of relative stability, the synagogue reverted back to 27, Cathcart Street from its 6, Trafalgar Street location in 1913, where it stayed until 1924 (when the *Jewish Year Book* stops listing it from its 1925 edition onwards). As the Reverend Tiemianka had left Greenock in 1908 to become an assistant teacher to the Hebrew classes at the Queen's Park Hebrew Congregation, a new minister was also employed: Reverend A. Apolin. He did not stay long; by the following year he had been replaced by the Reverend M. Morris.[56]

Kenneth Collins sates, "[B]y 1920 there was a cemetery and a synagogue at 27 Cathcart Street."[57] The first mention in the *Jewish Chronicle* of the synagogue being in Cathcart Street came in 1917.[58] According to former Greenock resident Thomas Tate, the synagogue was in a room above some shops at number 27.[59] However, as a result of the German wartime bombing, there is no longer any evidence of a *shul* or of its accompanying cemetery.[60] Furthermore, Harold Pollins argues that since Cathcart Street was in an important commercial area, a Jewish cemetery there was most unlikely.[61] He continues to state that old photographs of Greenock show Cathcart Street to have been a completely built-up street with apparently no room for a cemetery. Rent payments for that street over a number of years contained no mention of a cemetery or *shul* either.[62] This led Pollins to wonder "if there was a synagogue in Greenock or whether people just used private houses for services."[63]

During the First World War the usual activities that one would expect to see in a Jewish congregation took place. Jack Edwards celebrated his bar mitzvah in 1915, at which a collection for "distressed Polish Jews" was taken, raising £2. Robert Shenken was engaged to Fannie Fletcher of Glasgow. Two *brit milot* took place, at which further charitable collections took place. In 1917, over consecutive months from June to October, services were held for Jewish military personnel. These were often led by the soldiers themselves, in addition to the minister, the Reverend L. Wolfe. George Spilg served in France during the First World War, where he was awarded the Military Medal with Bar. After the war he moved to Glasgow and helped found the Glasgow Jewish Ex-Service Men's Association, which later became the Glasgow Jewish branch of the British Legion. He managed the local Jewish Institute, as well as being secretary of the Glasgow Jewish War Services Committee.[64] A particularly poignant note from the wartime period was the "Lost Relatives and Friends" notice in the *Jewish Chronicle* from Miss Izickson, a refugee from Kovno, who was enquiring after B. D. Isaacs from Greenock.[65] By the end of the war the figure cited for the community in the *Jewish Year Book* was nineteen.

The Interwar Period

Between the wars, the Greenock community continued along much the same lines. In 1921 a Zionist meeting was held—the first for eighteen years—

at the Temperance Institute. David Adams presided and Mr. S. Lipton, secretary of the Keren Hayesod, delivered an address. He referred to the part which had been played in Jewish history by the small Jewish communities, and appealed to the Jewish residents of Greenock to take a share in the work of Keren Hayesod. As a result of this appeal, which was supported by Mr. B. Mintz, chairman of the Glasgow Committee, and Mr. Sunderland, of Glasgow, about £150 was raised, and it was decided that the other members of the community should be approached and a regular system of collections arranged.[66] In that same year, Miriam Abrams died, while her son, Benjamin, celebrated his marriage to Rachel Levi of Leeds, and her youngest daughter, Dora, was engaged to Alec Silverstein of Clydebank. Two years later Dora gave birth to a son. At the *brit milah* of the son of Mr. Goldman the sum of £7 11s. 6d. was collected. The money was distributed to both Jewish and non-Jewish charities, such as the Greenock Hospital. Sarah Temple, of 16, Bearhope Street, passed (first class) the Primary examination for piano at the London College of Music, showing the increasing affluence of the community in being able to provide such lessons for their children. In 1923, despite the small size of the community, the Jewish Missions Committee took note of the community in Greenock.[67] At this point there were a maximum of sixty Jews in Greenock, but still not enough men willing to form a *minyan*. In order to insure the existence of a *minyan*, relatives were press-ganged into coming from nearby Glasgow. During the 1920s, for example, three young cousins of one member of the congregation were drafted in from Glasgow to make up the numbers.[68] At one stage or another, services were held on Yom Kippur and Rosh Hashanah at 15, 17, or 23 West Blackhall Street.

During the years 1928–1930, a series of reports in the *Jewish Echo* confirm Pollins' suspicions. Under the headline, "Greenock Hebrew Congregation," the newspaper stated:

> As has been customary in recent years, the Jewish residents in Greenock again established their temporary Shool at the house of Mr. J. Wolfe, who with Mrs. Wolfe, worked hard to ensure comfort for everyone. The congregation is deeply grateful to Mr. Morris for the manner in which he fulfilled the arduous duties of Chazan, conducting all the services himself. Mr Ferguson was the usual enthusiastic and capable Parness. The whole conduct of the Little Shool was dignified and strictly orthodox. After the services, the happy fraternising in which the residents and a few Glasgow friends joined, was indeed a token that this is a season of goodwill between fellow Jews.[69]

Meanwhile, the sugar mill at Greenock continued to supply Passover sugar.[70]

Leaving the Town

Jews began to leave Greenock from the 1930s onwards, according to Kenneth Collins, although he provides no explanation for this exodus. One of those who departed was Sydney Friedman, the owner of the King's Theatre, who moved with his family to London in 1930. His brother, Reggie, remained in Greenock and managed it for him in his absence.[71] By 1931 the Jewish population of Greenock, as well as nearby Gourock, was already very small. While in previous years, for example 1928, 1929, and 1930, it had been possible for the *Jewish Echo* to report on High Festival services, these reports ceased after 1930. Children of the Greenock families often found partners from Glasgow and other large cities. In 1932, for example, Julie Kaminsky, the second daughter of Mr. and Mrs. Manuel Kaminsky, 43, Regent Street, Greenock, got engaged to Bert Banks from Glasgow. Her sisters, Gertrude and Lillian, were also engaged to Glasgow men. The Kaminsky sisters then left Greenock to live with their husbands. As this case demonstrates, children of local residents frequently moved from the smaller towns to Glasgow or other cities where they had found partners. Further evidence of this trend is provided by the diffusion of the Abrams family, who, by 1926, were living in Glasgow; Houston, Texas; Edinburgh, and Leeds.[72] Such dispersal of the second generation of Greenock Jews eventually contributed to the decline of the community. Death also took its toll. Nat Morris died in 1934, as did his father Moses in 1936.

Another reason for the decline of Greenock may have been Scotland's interwar unemployment. The shipbuilding industry on the Clyde, being based on export, was extremely vulnerable and began to decline. Unemployment in the shipbuilding industry was over seventy percent in 1932, and more than thirty percent in 1937. Greenock itself registered twelve thousand people out of work in 1932 alone.[73] Although no Jews that we know of were employed in the shipbuilding industry, this high unemployment and depression of the 1930s would have led to decreased demand for the sort of goods and services that the Jews of Greenock sold and supplied until the increasing acculturation of their children led them into the professions. Furthermore, this trend was exacerbated by the decline in population witnessed in Greenock (and nearby Gourock, where some Jews were located) from 1921 onwards.[74]

By 1933, there were only five Jewish families in Greenock, according to the *Jewish Chronicle*. The trade directories, helpfully scoured by Harold Pollins, for that decade include Lillian Kaminsky, hairdresser, 21, Cathcart Street, and Manuel Kaminsky, draper and outfitter, 40, Cathcart Street (both living at 47, Brougham Street); and the Morris family (Moses, Rachel, and Nat and David). Unusually for a Jewish businessman, David sold gramophones and records at 49, Rue-end Street. Unhelpfully, no figures are given in the *Jewish Year Books* for those years. Nonetheless, Greenock was still big enough to be represented on the Scottish Council of Youth Organisations.[75] Yet, two years later there were seven families listed, indicating some unexplained growth![76] A report in the *Jewish Chronicle* noted ruefully that "a few years ago there was a thriving community."[77]

Good Status

Despite its small size, the Jewish community boasted a relatively good status in Greenock, as it underwent acculturation and integration into the wider community. As a sign of this, Mr. Abrahams was the Chief Clerk of H.M. Customs and Excise in Greenock from 1938 to 1946. His son, Sidney, was educated at Greenock Academy and then Glasgow University. Sidney graduated from the University of Glasgow in 1946 with first-class honors in chemistry, and was awarded a Ph.D in 1949. In that same year he was appointed to the University of Minnesota, under the sponsorship of the US Office of Naval Research, where he took charge of a small scientific team of research workers.[78]

Furthermore, another of Greenock's Jewish residents, David Adams, was returned for one of the wards at the 1930 Municipal Elections in Greenock. He was re-elected in 1933. Two years later he was the dean of the Guild of the Greenock Corporation and was unanimously appointed as one of the bailies to the town of Greenock, the only Jew in Scotland to hold that position. He was also the convener of the Parks Committee, trustee of the Harbour Trust and a member of the Public Library Committee. Adams was honorary secretary of the Greenock Hebrew Congregation before he moved to Glasgow, where he became well known for his participation in Jewish communal affairs. He was a founding member of the Langside Synagogue, eventually becoming its president, as well as a prominent Zionist (he presided over the Zionist meeting in 1921).[79] The *Jewish Echo* reported that it was a "matter of pride for the Jewish fraternity of Greenock" that one of them has been so honored.[80] Adams was still in office in 1947 when he was presented to the King and Queen on their royal tour of Scotland.[81] Adams' meteoric career suggests that Jews in Greenock met little or no problems in taking up public positions or representative posts in other organizations. Similar appointments, as we have seen, occurred in the other small towns and cities, such as Michael Marcus in Dundee, Isaac Sclar in Dunfermline, and Manny Shinwell, MP for Hamilton.

Dissolution or Not?

According to Collins, "The community was dissolved by 1936."[82] Yet, Mr. and Mrs. Arthur Matthews were still living at 40, Robertson Street in Greenock when their only son, Harold Lionel, died aged nine in that same year.[83] The following year the J.N.F. extended its activities to Greenock, where there were "small numbers of Jewish families."[84] The Kaminsky sisters, Gertrude and Lillian, were engaged in 1937 and 1939, respectively, as was Rose Brown in 1941.[85] While all three women married men from outside

Greenock, their parents remained in the town. Another Jewish inhabitant of Greenock was Reggie Friedman, who was still managing the King's Theatre. When he was enlisted in the Army and serving in Madagascar and East Africa, Rachel (Rea) Ferguson managed the theater for him. When Reggie and Rea left, it was taken over by Billy Friedman, who still lived in Greenock with his wife Rosa and son David until 1955, when the cinema was sold.[86] Furthermore, the *Jewish Year Book* only ceased listing the congregation and its contact details in its 1940 edition. Nevertheless, a *siddur* (daily prayer book) held in the Scottish Jewish Archives Centre was presented to the "Greenock Hebrew Congregation" in 1942, suggesting that the congregation was still in existence.

Indeed, there were services in Greenock during the Second World War, as a result of an influx of Jewish military personnel. Greenock became one of the main staging posts for the transatlantic shipping convoys.[87] It was thus a port of embarkation for troopships, and many servicemen and women boarded there. As we shall see, many of the wounded crew and others from arriving ships were unloaded and treated in Greenock. While the vast majority would not have been free to make contact with the local population before embarking (or even when disembarking, upon return from overseas), many did, as demonstrated by notices in the *Jewish Chronicle*. The Reverend S. Hoocker, Jewish Chaplain to the Armed Forces, held regular monthly services at Greenock, Stranraer, Dumfries, Lockerbie, Helensburgh, Hamilton and Lanark in 1942. Services were also held on alternate Sabbaths at 41, Union Street, Greenock, the home of Trooper Michael Rosenhead, in 1942, at which servicemen and civilians were present.[88]

The war also saw a temporary increase in Jewish residents in Greenock when the *Athenia* was torpedoed in 1941. Since the ship was hit in the Irish Sea, near to Greenock, the survivors were brought to the port, of whom six were Jewish. As everyone who could take a survivor in had already done so, the local prison's facilities were used. A local woman working at the prison at that time recalled:

> But there were three orthodox Jews and three ordinary Jews and the orthodox Jews did not like the other three Jews, and they had an awful carry on. They were terrible—we had to get special mugs from the state for them. And they kept them and nobody touch[ed] these things but themselves. And the other three they just mucked in with everybody else and they were very pleased to get there. They weren't very long there—maybe about four or five days when the Rabbi came down from Glasgow. He had heard about them. Mind you they were doctors—there was three of them doctors and they were very high positions they had. They were escaping from Germany to America and they were on the *Athenia*!
>
> I remember him coming down and he said, He spoke so—he was an awful nice man, the Rabbi and he said he was trying to make the chance of another boat to take these six people away to America if they wanted to go. So he did do that and they went away.
>
> But one young girl—she was a nice girl, Maria, we called her, of course they were Austrian but they all spoke English perfectly. She said—we didn't know what the

rest were going to do—but Maria was going out to be married to her young man out there. And she said she hoped everything was alright as he would be worried when he knows that the *Athenia* has been down because he knew that was the boat she was coming on. However, they all went away and they weren't very long away when we got a letter from Maria thanking us on behalf of the six people who stayed with us thanking us for our kindness.[89]

After the War

"Gradually," according to Mark Smith, "by the 1940s, the Jewish population began to dwindle," as Jews left Greenock to move to Glasgow, London, America, and Israel.[90] He adds, though, that religious services continued in the "homes of the pious."[91] Etta Kaminksy remained in the town at 47, Brougham Street, as her hairdressing business was listed in the Greenock directories until at least 1970. In 1950 a report in the *Jewish Chronicle* still referred to the Greenock "congregation" when it donated a *sefer Torah* to Israel.[92] By that point, the town had less than a handful of Jewish families, who met in private homes. These included the Kaminsky family in Brougham Street—until the youngest daughter, Hilda, married Sam Spiner from Glasgow and moved there in 1948, and her parents, Manuel (Mendel) and Etta, died in 1952 and 1962, respectively.

Clothier Isaac Wolfe was also living in Greenock with his wife, Minnie Atkin. Minnie, who was born in the East End of London and educated at King's College, had moved to Greenock immediately after the war following an appointment as the burgh's Assistant Medical Officer of Health. Her salary was £556 plus war bonus. At that time illnesses and diseases, such as rickets, whooping cough, diphtheria, tuberculosis, scabies, gastroenteritis and malnutrition, were commonplace. She was a highly respected member of the community, becoming deputy medical officer in 1971, during which time she commissioned the £12m Inverclyde Royal Hospital, which opened in 1979. "Despite her diminutive stature," her obituary stated, "her energy and enthusiasm were infectious and ensured the cooperation of her colleagues, whatever their discipline."[93] Although she retired in 1980 and moved to Gourock, she continued to oversee the smooth running of the hospital and even began studying Hebrew. When she died in 2000 she was the last Jewish person in the area, her husband, Isaac, having died a year earlier.[94]

In 1965 David Wolfe was appointed as treasurer of Greenock Town Council. David was born in Cartside Street in Glasgow on 20 November, 1912, but, as mentioned above, a few years later the family had settled in Greenock. From humble origins—they lived in a one-room house—David went to Greenock High School, where he learned to play the violin. With an improvement in their economic situation the family moved to either 15 or 23, Blackhall Street, where services were held in the family home on the Jewish high holy days, New Year, and Yom Kippur. David then attended Glasgow University, where he began studying medicine, although he eventually qualified as an optician. He spent the war years in the Navy in the Clyde River Patrol. In 1951 he met Frieda, the youngest daughter of Cantor Meyer Fomin of South Portland Street Synagogue in Glasgow, and they married, setting up home in Glasgow, where they had two children: Leonard and Cherry. David continued working in his optician's practice at 1, West Blackhall Street and then 4, Cathcart Street, both in Greenock. He still possessed the two Torah scrolls belonging to the community, which he donated to South Portland Street Synagogue.

Eventually David went into politics. He was described by his son Lenny (Leonard) as "a dyed in the wool socialist." At the same time, "He felt a great debt to the town of Greenock because it was here that his father tasted his first breaths of freedom, when he came from Lithuania." A friend suggested to David that he translate this emotion into practicality, which he did by first acting as the election agent for MP Dick Mabon. He then was elected to the Greenock Town Council, serving from 1959 to 1965 as a councillor, and from 1965 to 1968 as the deputy provost (treasurer) representing the fifth ward. At the end of the 1950s and the beginning of the 1960s David brought Christmas lighting to Greenock by persuading the council to buy Glasgow's lights from the previous year! In April 1961 he authored and published the "Wolfe Plan," which was a vision to build an ocean terminal for Greenock and Scotland. It received widespread publicity throughout the Scottish press, and was endorsed by a number of prominent individuals, such as General Sir Gordon Macmillan and the Earl of Muirshiel. For one reason or another it was never implemented; however, a modified version of David's plan *was* adopted.[95] David also set up the "Good Companions," a small group of people who distributed provisions to needy pensioners at Christmas; in 1968, for example, he organized a raffle to raise money for the widow of a Greenock man who had been killed in storm.[96]

David was also active in Jewish affairs. A *sefer Torah* was kept in his home throughout the year, and when discussing religion he felt that his was "true Judaism keeping the spirit of the religion alive in remote regions without the help of a big community."[97] In later life he became prominent in the Jewish community in Glasgow, and around 1966 was chairman of the Glasgow Zionist organization.[98] He also set up the Glasgow Aliyah group. His son recalled that he had a tremendous sense of humor. This was illustrated when David and his wife Frieda attended the Queen's birthday party in Holyrood Palace during the 1960s. When it was their turn to be introduced to the Queen and Prince Phillip, the Duke of Edinburgh looked at David and asked, "How's business?" David replied, "I'll change with you." Needless to say, many in the Jewish community felt that Phillip's question was an anti–Semitic slight, but David was only able to see the humor in it. His other great loves in life were the Scottish hills and the poetry of Burns, and he was proud to belong to the Mother Club in Greenock. He would recite the Selkirk Grace and the first stanzas of "Tam O'Shanter" and "Ode to a Mouse"—by heart—up until his ninety-second year at the Burns' suppers his son hosted in Jerusalem for his benefit and which continue to this day. In 1973 David retired, and he died, aged ninety-three, in 2006.

Beyond Greenock

The pages of the *Jewish Echo* indicate that there was a sprinkling of individuals and families that lived, relatively speaking, in nearby towns and villages. The Freedman and Levy families lived for a while in Gourock on the Clyde, to which they may have retired. Dr. Alec (Alex) Binnie worked in Paisley. Binnie was also active in local politics. He was elected as a town councilor, became convener of the Environmental Health Committee, and was appointed as senior magistrate of the Burgh of Paisley and later as police judge for Renfrew District. As he was a member of the Garnethill Hebrew Congregation in Glasgow, he may well have lived in Glasgow or at least travelled there for services. Mr. and Mrs. F. Goldberg lived in Dumbarton. Hugo Joseph, his wife Mary, and his stepdaughter resided in Blanefield, while Mr. and Mrs. Hans Reininger lived in Bothwell. East Kilbride was the residence of Dr. and Mrs. S.D. Coleman and their daughter; Dr. Harold J. Fields and his family; and Mrs. M. McKendrick. Anthony Karpf and his wife Ruth had a jewelry and china shop, which was one of the first in the new Olympia precinct in East Kilbride. Karpf, who had been born in Poland and settled in Scotland following the Second World War after serving in the British army, worked in the East Kilbride/Hamilton area for forty-three years. In 1974, Dr. Maurice Miller, a Glasgow town councilor and, since 1964, MP for Glasgow Kelvingrove, won the new constituency of East Kilbride for Labour. Since some of these places are nearer to Glasgow, some of these families (like Alec Binnie), may well have attended services there but have been included here for convenience.

Epilogue

The last communal note for Greenock's Jewish community in the *Jewish Echo* came in 1966 when the birth of Lewis, the son of Adrienne (née Todd) and Cecil M. Rifkind, 2, Lyle Road, was announced.[99] Thereafter, we have little record of the community's activities, suggesting that it had completely died out. It is not presently known if any Jews live there today.

7

Inverness, the Highlands, and Islands

In March 1830 Ezekiel Caspar Auerbach, a thirty-five-year-old hawker of stationery and other articles from Warsaw, Poland, was baptized and received into membership in the Inverness Gaelic Church. Such was the popular interest that well before the service commenced, "The Gaelic Church was crowded to excess, the doors and passages being completely blocked with persons anxious to witness a scene so novel in this part of the country."[1] This is the first mention of a Jew in connection with Inverness. There was no suggestion, however, that Auerbach was part of a Jewish community in that town, as there were no signs of a community in the Highlands at all for most of the nineteenth century. But, in view of Inverness's status as a port, it is not surprising to discover that individual Jews like Auerbach had made their way to the town; indeed, Auerbach was a merchant who had come to Britain two years earlier after suffering a downturn in his business. It is even likely that other Jews had followed Auerbach's trail to Inverness, given its status as an important port by the the mid-nineteenth century, with over one-hundred-and-fifty vessels, owned by local people, trading with, among other places, the Netherlands and the Baltic ports, all places where contact could have been made with Jewish people. In fact, from as far back as the sixteenth century there were trade links between Inverness and Germany. Some of these links seem to have been very cordial, extending beyond the formalities of commerce, (in c.1803, for example, a German named Klein left a bequest for the benefit of poor Inverness families).[2] Other than Auerbach, the odd individual traveler and tradesman made their way to the town. Itinerant Jewish peddlers operated in the Highlands, and one such traveler was a Mr. E. Barnett, a cattle trader.[3]

They were received with the greatest interest and warmest sympathy.[4] John Ross notes: "From at least the mid-seventeenth century and the arrival in the Highlands of the Directory of Public Worship, Westminster Confession of Faith and the Larger and Shorter Catechisms there existed in the Highlands a sympathetic interest in the Jewish people."[5] On 15 April, 1830, Robert Grant, Liberal MP for Inverness, introduced into the House of Commons the

Jewish Emancipation Bill, the first of a series of bills to open the gates of the legislative bodies to Jews in the United Kingdom. The first bill was memorable for its ardent appeal for justice for the Jews, addressed to the commons. Grant brought in subsequent bills in 1833 and 1834. Each time, the bills passed the commons but were rejected in the Lords. In February 1848, the *Inverness Courier* reported that a public meeting was held in Forres in support of the removal of Jewish disabilities as a result of the election of Baron Rothschild for the City of London.[6] A petition appeared in the *Courier* following the meeting, which stated:

> That your petitioners profess the religion of Christ, which enjoins upon them, as one of the principal duties, to do unto others as they would that others would do unto them. That to exclude from any civil rights any of their fellow subjects, who conduct themselves as good members of society and contribute their fair portion to the burdens of the state, merely because they worship their God in that mode in which they have been educated and consider to be right, is not to treat others as we would that others should treat us, and is therefore unchristian as well as unjust.[7]

Similarly, the moderator and presbytery of Tain were also reported as having petitioned parliament on the admission of Jews into the commons.[8] In December 1853 the Reverend Mr. Ramsey delivered a lecture on "The Restoration of the Jews to Their Own Land" in the Temperance Hall, Wick.[9] Finally, at the annual congress of the Incorporated Association of Scotland in 1910, held in Elgin, the association's president praised the Jews' superior code of sanitation as laid out in the Torah.[10] Despite its lack of Jews, pro-Jewish feeling was high in Inverness. However, this sentiment was not always directed toward the Jews' best interests, and, according to John Ross, "From the early decades of the nineteenth century it found its main channel of expression in strong support of the Jewish mission established by the Church of Scotland in 1838 and continued with even greater enthusiasm by the Free Church of Scotland after 1843."[11] This was manifested in the various reported appeals and collections made in Inverness and the surrounding areas for the conversion of Jews. Between 1841 and 1855, various sermons, activities and donations to that end were reported in Wick, Dingwall, Inverness, Kirkhill, and Unst.[12]

The New Arrivals

Thereafter, individual Jews and their families made their way to Inverness but did not stay for long. One such example was Abraham Mendlson and his wife Rose (née Clarkson), who emigrated from Poland to Edinburgh, from where they moved to Inverness in the 1860s. We know this because their children, "Isac," Sarah and Flora (Florie), were born in Inverness on 17 April,

1866, 18 January, 1868, and 24 May, 1869, respectively. Abraham Mendlson was listed variously as a "hawker of pictures," "picture framer," and "picture dealer." For reasons we do not know, however, the Mendelsons had left by 1870.

At least two Jewish families, as well as some Jewish travelers, were living in Inverness by 1881, according to the census of that year. They were listed as Lawrence Cohen, aged sixteen, a "Commercial Traveller" living at 4, Inglis St.; Goodman Lewenthal (25), a General Merchant from Russia, living at 16, Glebe Street; the Morris family, consisting of John, a general dealer (34) from Warsaw, Poland, and his wife Bertha, aged 25, from Riga, Courland, and their children Perulina (3), Annie (2), and Abraham (11), all born in Inverness and living at 108, Church Street; and the Stenberg/Sternberg family, living at 1, Gilbert Street: Levy, 35, from Poland, General Merchant, his wife Emilia (25) from Russia, and their children Helen (7), Bertha (4), Annie (3), and Isaac (1). Since only Isaac was born in Inverness, the Stenberg/Sternberg family must have only arrived in 1880. The addresses of these families and individuals reveal that they lived in a limited commercial part of the town with easy access to the harbor. Based on these numbers, the *Jewish Chronicle* reported in 1883 that Jews were living as far north as Inverness (and Greenock) but supplied no further details.[13]

As with the other communities, the main immigration into Inverness took place in the last quarter of the nineteenth century, most likely during the 1880s and 1890s in particular. It likewise consisted of Ashkenazi Jews either fleeing persecution in Russia and Poland, and/or seeking economic betterment. Around 1895, Jonas and Milcah Rosenbloom, who were married in Brody, Austria, in 1884, moved to Crown Street, Inverness, where he was a jeweler. The *Jewish Chronicle* in 1911 lists Jonah as "I. Rosenbloom."[14]

On 28 February, 1930, at the Jewish Synagogue (address unclear, but it appears to end in "Yard"), Hilda Rosenbloom (born 24 December, 1904) married Michael Jackson (a kosher poultry seller) from Glasgow. Towards the end of that year they had moved back to Glasgow, where they gave birth to a daughter, Mildred. Given his training, Michael could have been based in Glasgow but come up to Inverness to *shecht* periodically for the community. Milcah Rosenbloom died in Inverness in 1924, aged sixty; and John Rosenbloom died in Tradeston, Glasgow, in 1939, aged seventy-six.[15]

Michael Wezel (although at that time it might have been spelled Wiesel or Wizel or Vizel) from Romania, and his son, went to Inverness in 1902 or 1903 from Romania in response to an advertisement stating that male Jews were needed in order to form a *minyan*. It seems unlikely that this was the only reason they went there, but it becomes plausible when viewed together with the existence of a small Jewish nucleus and the lure of economic opportunity.[16] Other Polish and Russian émigrés included Moses Morris, Lewenthal Friedman, Moses Merrens (naturalized in 1905),[17] Joseph Coats (naturalized in 1906),[18] Isaac Finkelstein (also naturalized in 1906),[19] Charles J. Taub (who was a frequent correspondent to the *Jewish Chronicle*), C.S. Taube, Moses Golumb (naturalized in 1912), and L. Mitchell.

The 1901 census lists a number of Jewish individuals in Inverness. They include Harris Isenman (38) of 205, Glebe Terrace; John (34) and Milly (Milcah) Rosenbloom, 227, Stephen's Brae; and Louis (21) and Lotty Hirschberg at 59, Rose Street. At that time the community was clustered around a few streets in the city center, such as Baron Taylor's Lane, Castle Street, Seaforth Mansions, Falcon Square, Inglis Street, Young Street, Charles Street, Crown Drive, and Stephen's Brae.

A New Place of Worship

The numbers of Jews in Inverness had grown to such an extent by 1905 that "the want of a place of worship ha[d] been felt for a long time," reported the *Jewish Chronicle*.[20] The previous year, fifteen families in Inverness, according to a letter written to the Chief Rabbi, were reported. As with all the other small Scottish communities, they desired to have a *shul*, reader, *shochet*, and *mohel*.[21] As there were now enough Jews in Inverness to form a congregation—about eighteen families in 1905—a meeting was called by Moses Merrins, the former president of the Glasgow South Side synagogue, with this aim in mind. As a result, a suitable hall in the center of Inverness was located, and the following Sunday the synagogue was opened in the hall, at which a consecration service was held. It was reported that many Christians were also present, and, "They all expressed their pleasure that the Jews in their midst had now a regular meeting-place, and had become a more consolidated body than heretofore."[22] Mr. I. Isenman opened the new *shul*, and Mr. Charles J. Taub performed the consecration ceremony and delivered a sermon. It was resolved that the synagogue should be placed under the jurisdiction of the Chief Rabbi, to whose health was drunk. Isenman presented all the furniture used in the synagogue.[23] Merrens was elected president. The Inverness Hebrew Congregation was now in existence.

Little is known about the synagogue. We do not, for example, have a single precise address for its location, as one was never listed in the *Jewish Year Book*. At times the names of Inglis Street and Falcon Square are given in correspondence, but these might have been business or private addresses rather than the synagogue chambers itself. Various correspondents have recollected that it was situated at the bottom end of Academy Street next to the Empire Theatre, on Eastgate, and on Falcon Square. It is possible that it was at all of these locations at one time or another. However, a copy of a 1909 invoice for work carried out for "the Jewish Synagogue" by L.D. Mathesons, a registered plumber, indicates that it was located in the Crown Hall, Washington Court, behind Inverness Railway Station. It stayed there until at least 1917 (according to a letter from Isaac Finkelstein to the Chief Rabbi, dated 20 August, 1917). Since the building housing the synagogue has long since been knocked down, we have little knowledge of its physical layout, but it was described as being up two flights of steps. Although we have no exact information on how services were conducted at the synagogue, since the community's records have been lost, we can guess that it was Orthodox (in line with the experiences of the other small Scottish communities).

Religious Infrastructure

Alongside the synagogue, the Jewish community took steps towards establishing the required religious infrastructure as it sought to preserve its Jewish heritage and traditions. A committee was set up to run the congregation; Moses Merrens was its first president and Charles Taub the treasurer. In a significant departure from the other small communities in Scotland, the Inverness Hebrew Congregation appealed for a *mikvah* (special bath), most likely motivated by its remoteness from all of the other sites of significant Jewish settlement in Scotland. The community had even gone so far as to make an arrangement with the local Swimming Bath Co. for a space on which to build one. However, there is no evidence, either documented or extant, that this actually happened. The Reverend S. Arkush was contracted to conduct services on the holyday of Passover and to provide his services as a teacher.[24] Arkush was born in Kalisch, Poland, in 1875, where he studied for five years before coming to Britain in 1903.[25] The Reverend Arkush also performed a circumcision in 1907.[26] And in 1909, according to the *Jewish Year Book*, there were one "male birth," two marriages, and four deaths in the Inverness Jewish community.

The congregation also arranged with the town council the following year to acquire a piece of ground in the town's public cemetery at Tomnahurich to be used for Jewish burials. The need for a dedicated Jewish cemetery was great, given the religious requirement to be buried separately from gentiles. The lack of one had been felt for a number of years, as earlier interments always took place in Glasgow, over two hundred miles away. For example, Betsy Clouts was born on 23 March, 1892 at 74, Academy Street, but died fourteen days later and was buried in Janefield Cemetery, Glasgow. The recent death of a young immigrant named Hyman Cooper, aged twelve, who had only just arrived from his home in Russia motivated the congregation to take this step, and his body was the first to be buried in the new ground.[27] The council placed a railing around the Jewish burial ground, which contained twenty-two plots, to demarcate it from the rest of the public cemetery. On the advice of the Chief Rabbi, the congregation made appeals to the larger Jewish community for money to fund these religious necessities.

Jewish Burial Ground, Tomnahurich Cemetery, Inverness. (Photograph by Nathan Abrams.)

Those buried in the cemetery did not just come from the town of Inverness. Others came from the surrounding area, such as Buckie, Nairn, Dingwall, and Forres. One of the more unusual burials was that of Mrs. Chano Silver in 1911, whose death shook the small community of Inverness. Her husband, immigrant Russian jewelry traveler Isaac Lazarus Silver, was indicted on the charge of having assaulted his wife in their house in Glebe Street, cutting her throat with a razor and murdering her. Silver, who himself was wounded in the neck by a razor cut, pleaded not guilty on the grounds of insanity, or in such an unsound state of mind as to make him irresponsible for his actions.[28] After a trial in Aberdeen, the jury deliberated for twenty-five minutes and returned a unanimous verdict that Silver was guilty of culpable homicide.[29] He was sentenced to fifteen years imprisonment.[30] The funeral for Chano was conducted by the minister of the community, the Reverend Samuel Markin, and she was buried in Tomnahurich cemetery.[31]

Because of its small size and consequent low payment abilities (a problem dogging all small and provincial communities), the Inverness Hebrew Congregation was never able to obtain the services of a full-time, permanent rabbi. In search of better pay and bigger communities, the ministers (who also acted as butchers, readers, and teachers) frequently departed after several years of service. The Reverend Arkush left Inverness to take over as minister to the water proofers of the Dalry Synagogue, Edinburgh, before being appointed as teacher, minister, *chazan*, and *mohel* to the Queen's Park Hebrew Congregation.[32] Eventually he became a resident of Cardiff, where he and his daughter, Esther, were naturalized in 1923.[33]

Arkush was replaced by the Reverend Leib A. Falk, who himself had been minister in Ayr. While in Inverness, Falk inaugurated the pioneering and progressive *ivrit b'ivrit* (literally, Hebrew in Hebrew) method in Jewish education, by which Hebrew was taught as a modern language. It was considered to be the best form of Hebrew instruction and was typically found in the innovative schools established by Zionists; so to find it in Inverness was quite rare and unique.³⁴ Furthermore, it seemed to be going down well with the children there.³⁵ However, he did not stay long enough to assess the results, for by 1913, Falk had left to take up a position in Dundee, and the community advertised for a "Shochet and teacher, [who] must be able to translate in English, married man preferred; salary: 26s-50s per week."³⁶ The successful applicant turned out to be the Reverend S. Gerber, who stayed until 1916 when he resigned to be elected the minister of Waterford.³⁷ Before he left, he wrote a very sad letter, in Yiddish, to the Chief Rabbi that illustrates with some poignancy the sort of life such a minister led in this period.

Inverness 17/11/15
4 Crown Avenue
In honour of the great rabbi our master Rabbi Dr Hertz

Honourable Sir, it is already eight years that I am in this country a cantor and slaughterer. The first place was Falkirk. Now I am in Inverness.

Alas I must now give up my position because I am very sick. The doctor has pronounced me incurable and wants to send me away to a home for the incurable. But I cannot go and end my last days among gentiles, I therefore turn to you, Honourable Sir, to ask if you can try to see to get me into a home. I have nobody to turn to. I am now all alone in the world. A single man. My trouble is with the lungs. And if nobody will take pity on me I will God Forbid fall away in the street. Because I am going under from day to day.

Sh. Gerber³⁸

Gerber's vacant slot was filled by the Reverend Isaiah Ticktin. The case of Ticktin is illuminating in its description of the problems facing ministers in such small and remote communities. Ticktin held the position of reader, *shochet*, and teacher in Inverness since July 1916. He had previously held the same position at Boston, Lincolnshire. As a foreign-born male, Ticktin required permission to reside in Inverness, a restricted area during wartime. This was a problem during the First World War because, as "friendly aliens," foreign-born ministers in the small communities were liable to either be viewed as a threat in sensitive military areas like Inverness or Aberdeen, or drafted for military service. This problem only disappeared when, as the twentieth century progressed, ministers began to become British-born. If Aberdeen is the model, then this started to occur between the wars.

By all accounts, Ticktin did not earn a good salary. By 1919, £2 10 per week was a typical wage for such a position in Inverness.³⁹ He resided at 13, Grieg Street and, as minister to the congregation, he received a much needed subvention of £5 for instruction of the children of the community. In 1918, however, four members of the congregation left, leading to a reduction of his salary, which, as a result, became too small to support him, so he began looking for alternative employment elsewhere.⁴⁰ In October 1918 he wrote a two-page letter in Hebrew (most likely because it was better than his English) to the Chief Rabbi. It was a heartfelt plea for his livelihood. Even though he was the Hebrew teacher and slaughterer in Inverness, he had read an advertisement in the *Jewish Chronicle* that Inverness was looking for another teacher and slaughterer! He pleaded with the *Beth Din* to assure him that his position was kept secure until he found another. He also mentioned a reduction in salary that left him and his family in dire straits. It seemed that someone in Inverness had been plotting against him![41]

Ticktin eventually left Inverness and took up a similar position in Bangor. An interesting letter sent by Isidore Wartski, president of the Bangor Hebrew Congregation, to the Reverend Feldman, c.1920, provides a fascinating insight into Ticktin's character as perceived by Wartski and others. Wartski wrote, "I have now had an opportunity of forming an opinion of Ticktin and have come to the conclusion that there is nothing but chronic laziness and dirt ... the matter with him. He is 'bone' lazy and any idea of confusing this—except as a cause—with mental deficiency is pure evasion on his part."[42] He then continued to list a catalogue of complaints, including failure to punctually slaughter the meat, as well as turning up for Shabbat services unkempt and still with bed-feathers in his uncombed hair.[43] It is hard to ascertain the accuracy of Wartski's complaints, but it is certainly indicative of the contempt in which such small community ministers could be held by their congregations, and likewise the quality of the minister that such a community could attract.

This succession of such ministers in Inverness created the problem of intermittency of provision of religious necessities. No doubt there were gaps between the employment of an outgoing and incoming minister. Those who suffered most would have been the children. Hebrew classes were set up for the children by 1906. Initially, the standard must have been quite high, for Jacob Taub, aged thirteen, received an "honourable mention" in a Hebrew writing competition organized by the *Jewish Chronicle* that year.[44] By that time the children of the Hebrew classes were examined annually, and when the then Chief Rabbi Dr. Herman Adler conducted a tour of Scotland, which took in the small communities of Aberdeen, Inverness, and Greenock in 1907, he personally examined them.[45] However, the succession of teachers on short-term contracts, with its resulting lack of continuity, must have had a negative impact on the children's education in the long run. At a dinner held by the Glasgow Committee of the War Memorial in 1921, Mr. Lionel de Rothschild, M.P., commented that in Aberdeen and Inverness, "Many Jewish children at the present time were receiving little or no Jewish education ... this painful fact was deplorably evident."[46]

Despite its small size, the community maintained its charitable obligations as required by Jewish law. Throughout the First World War, the community as a whole, as well as individuals like Finkelstein, made a series of donations to various refugee and victims-of-war funds. This continued well into the 1950s, as the small community contributed in excess of its small size.

At one point the community contributed more than £1,000 to the Central British Fund, which then constituted a record for *any* appeal made in Scotland, demonstrating both the Inverness community's generosity and how wealthy it had become, given that its average size at its height was twelve families.[47] Alongside *tzedakah*, Zionism was a feature of Jewish communal life in Inverness. In 1912 a Dorshei Zion Society (Hebrew for "Seekers of Zion") was set up, and a share club of the Jewish Colonial Bank was established.[48] At the celebration of Isaac Taube's bar mitzvah that same year, a collection was made for a tree in the Herzl Forest in his name.[49] In 1918 a donation was made to the Zionist Preparation Fund.[50] Despite its distance from the center of British Jewish life in London, the congregation maintained its ties with the metropolis by communicating with the Chief Rabbi, electing a deputy to the Board of Deputies, and subscribing to the *Jewish Chronicle*.

Why Inverness?

What brought these few Jews to Inverness? As with the other small Jewish communities, according to Kenneth Collins, Inverness "grew as a result of internal migration within Scotland with Jews looking for locations from which trade could be conducted with less competition that could be found in the larger centers."[51] Since medieval times, Inverness had been a principal center for trade in the Highlands. It also established itself early as a port and center for shipbuilding.[52] Inverness, therefore, provided opportunities for travelling Jewish salesmen to peddle their wares. One of those included Isaac Finkelstein, whose fortunes provide an illustrative account of a Jewish family in this area. Isaac married in Glasgow on 30 August, 1899 at the Oxford Street Synagogue in the Gorbals district of Glasgow. He was twenty-two and gave his occupation as "Jeweller Traveller." His wife Fanny (née Josephart) was nineteen and listed as a dressmaker. They both gave their address as 280 Rutherglen Road, Glasgow. Isaac's parents were Soloman Finkelstein (a draper) and Sarah Finkelstein (née Lekotzski). Fanny's parents were Israel Josephart (a butcher) and Leah Josephart (née Buttermond). At some point, Isaac and Fanny moved to Inverness and settled in a small rented terrace house at number 14, Charles Street. Isaac started out life as a peddler selling his wares on the station concourse of the railway station in Inverness, as well as at the nearby Cameron Barracks in Fort George.[53] As business grew, he moved to more permanent and suitable premises, renting a shop at 18, New Market in the Victorian covered market in 1903, where he set up "the Railway Watch & Clock Company"—a jewelry, optician's, and clock/watch repair shop. Isaac stayed there until he sold the shop on his retirement. The interior of the shop is still unchanged, and its famous exterior, with Art Nouveau windows and ornate Victorian decorated half-moon glass fascia above the window and entrance, are still visible today.

7—Inverness, the Highlands, and Islands

Isaac Finkelstein's shop. (Courtesy of William Morrison.)

Isaac's success enabled him to become very well integrated into the cultural and civic life of Inverness. He donated large sums of money to charity, becoming prominent and well-respected. In 1951, for example, he gave £525 to the Glasgow Jewish Institute's building fund.[54] Isaac in particular was very active in Jewish communal affairs in both Inverness and Glasgow. He was also a Freemason and at one time the Grand Master of the Ardesier Lodge, a means by which he could build bridges with the non–Jewish community. His business interests diversified, and he bought two houses in Charles Street in 1915–16, one of which he rented out. In 1934, Isaac even claimed to have spotted the Loch Ness Monster at Lochend! He described it "as dark in colour with a long neck rearing out of the water. It poised for a few minutes as if treading water. Ultimately it dived & disappeared."[55] Fanny resided in Edinburgh at 3, Wilton Road, Edinburgh, and died there in 1949. Isaac stayed in Inverness and re-married six months after Fanny's death to Leah Silver, a secretary from Glasgow. They lived in the Caledonian Hotel, owning the *sefer Torah*, which, at one stage, belonged to the small community. Isaac died in 1963.[56]

The Finkelsteins had three children. Their respective biographies illustrate the difficulties of maintaining Jewish identity among the second generation in such a remote community as Inverness. Morris/Maurice was born in 1905, Lily in 1907, and then Daisy in 1911. They were all registered at 14, Charles Street. As Isaac Finkelstein's business was a success, he was able to move his family in 1922 to 32, Crown Drive, a larger detached house in the

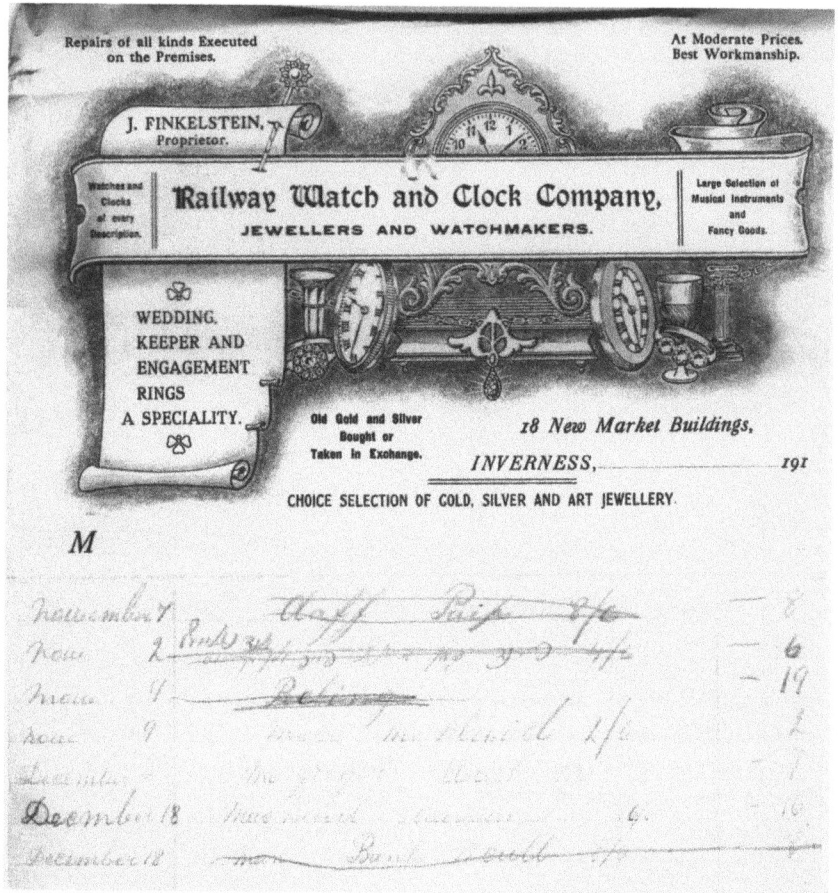

Receipt from the Railway Watch & Clock Company. (Courtesy of William Morrison.)

same area and still within walking distance of the town center. He was also able to afford the fees to pay for his three children to be educated at the Inverness Academy, and the *Jewish Chronicle* regularly reported their achievements. Although Jewish families like the Finkelsteins sought to preserve their Jewish heritage and traditions, they were geared toward integrating with the larger society, a process which was helped by having the children attend secular schools, a choice forced upon them as there were not enough Jewish residents in Inverness to sustain a Jewish educational establishment.

Maurice graduated to read medicine at Edinburgh University and qualified as a doctor. By 1931 he was working as assistant to Professor Mackie in the Bacteriological Research Department of Edinburgh University before being awarded the prestigious Rockefeller Fellowship to travel to America.[57] Ultimately, Maurice emigrated to South Africa and became a consultant pathologist in Cape Town. He married and had five children, but changed his name to Finlayson before emigrating; this was probably due to the anti-Semitism prevalent at that time. Meanwhile, Daisy and Lily both gained distinctions in pianoforte and elocution at the Inverness Music Festival in 1923, and in the following year Lily passed her examination in piano.[58] Lily and Daisy were then sent to a Jewish boarding school in Leicester, probably because of the lack of a Jewish educational establishment in Inverness, and also the consequent unlikeness of them meeting suitable Jewish partners. Eventually, Lily went to London to study music at the Royal Academy of Music, and Daisy followed her. They both married non-Jewish partners and were disowned by their parents.

Isaac Finkelstein. (Photograph courtesy of William Morrison.)

The other prominent family in Inverness in the 1930s was the Morrises. Lewis Morris was known as the "Harris Tweed King" in the highlands and islands, where he travelled to sell his wares. By 1927 he owned a ladies wear shop, "Morris' Bargain Stores," at 2, Church Street.[59] By 1929 he was described as a "costumier."[60] This is known because the fire brigade was called to put out a fire at his premises. The fire was under control within a short time. His wife Bessie, known professionally as Madame Goldrich, sold ladies coats and gowns at various venues in Inverness, such as the Royal Hotel, 23, and 28, High Street, during the mid-to-late 1920s.[61] By 1933, Lewis and Bessie were able to afford permanent premises and rented numbers 8–10, Union Street, which opened as the Fashion Salon. Through the rest of the decade and continuing into the 1940s the shop became very popular with the ladies of Inverness. This was, in part, because it was refurbished in an Art Deco style, which attracted customers to it simply because it was the only shop in the town decorated that way. Lewis was well known at the Royal Hotel next door to his shop and was eventually elected as a councilor for Inverness. The Morrises had four sons, David, Raymond, Ivor, and Kenneth, as well as one daughter, Doris. As with the Finkelstein family, the sons left Inverness, settling in the United States, where they were very successful. Ivor became a judge and currently resides in Burlingame, California. David also lives in California (San Francisco), and is a National Guard colonel, deputy sheriff and ex-CIA agent. When Bessie Morris went over to visit her son she was invited to dine with then-president Lyndon B. Johnson.[62]

Other Jewish families and businesses flourished in Inverness, displaying a diversity of occupations. Jonas Rosenbloom was listed as a "fancy goods dealer" at 4, 6, and 10, the New Market in 1911. This is presumably the same Rosenbloom (although here "John") that was listed in the 1901 census as living with his wife Milly at 227, Stephens Brae. Eliezer Hirschberg from Glasgow (but born in Latvia) peddled fancy goods before opening a jewelry shop in the covered market diagonally opposite Isaac Finkelstein's premises. Moses Golumb was a tailor presser. Louis Clouts was a boot and shoe merchant. Greenwold was a turf accountant on Stephens Brae. Louis Gavin had a Jeweler's and Watch and Clock Maker's shop on the High Street[63]; in 1921 he was advertising alarm clocks in the *Inverness Courier* at 6/8d. each.[64] The Lisman (originally Leishman) family had a fish shop in the covered market. One of the more colorful figures of the community was Mark Cymbalist, who operated a bespoke tailoring business at 38, Waterloo Place, where he lived. He had two sons, Norris and David, and the latter is still a tailor in Inverness. Mark Cymbalist was a member of the Communist Party in the 1960s, when he was in his sixties, helping to run Marxist education classes. He also assisted on the campaign that resulted in Mabel Skinner being elected as a Communist Party councilor in the Merkinch area of Inverness. He was described as a very knowledgeable and intellectual man who had been a conscientious objector in the war. His son, Norris, was also politically active; as a Communist in the RAF he was sentenced to ten years imprisonment for his part in a "mutiny" which took place in 1946.[65] Cymbalist (as he was known) also ran poster campaigns against the Vietnam War, some of which were posted in all weathers on rock faces along the A9. He would regularly discuss for hours on end the state of countries all over the world, for the condition of humanity worldwide was his concern.[66]

Despite some families and individuals who stood out, in general the Jewish community kept a low profile. According to Sheila McKay, of the Inverness Local History Forum, "There were some Jewish families in the town, mainly in the confectionary business or with small restaurants, but there wouldn't have been a lot of them. Anybody coming into Inverness at that time would have been well noticed and commented on."[67] One of the reasons for this low profile, and a condition commonly afflicting the smaller communities, was a sense of vulnerability owing to the Inverness Jewish community's small size. For example, the *Inverness Courier* reported in 1930 that "members of the Jewish faith in Inverness were asked by the Chief Rabbi to hold a memorial service for the late Earl Balfour. They were unable to do so as a *minyan*

Top: Rendering of the exterior of the Fashion Salon, Inverness. (Courtesy of Hector MacDonald.) *Bottom:* The Morris Family, Inverness.

couldn't be convened, as Inverness had less than the required ten adult males over the age of thirteen."[68] Seven years later, in 1937, the *Jewish Echo* contained a report entitled "Duty Calls," sent in by Lewis Morris. In it, Morris described an incident on a Sunday when a traveler from Glasgow arrived at night in Inverness and called him to ask whether it was possible to make up a *minyan* because he was an *ovel* (mourner). As there were only two families in Inverness, with three members in both households, Morris drove around calling at all hotels and boarding houses in the area. Three hours later, and by sheer luck—as Morris arrived at one boarding house a car had just pulled up containing a Jewish traveler from Edinburgh whom he was able to commandeer—he was able to collect eight Jews, forming the *minyan*. In three cars they drove to Morris' house and performed the service, which finished at 11:55 at night! The report ended by stating that it was the first occasion that a *minyan* has been performed in Inverness that late at night for forty-one years.[69]

Another reason for this low profile might have been the outbreak of fascism in Europe in the early thirties and the knock-on effects this might have had at home. At a public meeting in 1934 at the Dr. Black Memorial Hall in Inverness, Reverend James Black expressed the view that if the Jews were taken into the Christian Church then all the problems and exclusions that were the main causes of the troubles in Europe would be settled. Two hundred people attended the opening of the Inverness conference on Jewish Missions that same year.[70] Then William Joyce (later Nazi propagandist Lord Haw Haw) spoke in support of Mosley's BUF in 1935 in the Inverness Town House. The following year the BUF launched a propaganda campaign throughout the northeast of Scotland, with meetings in Inverness.[71] Yet, at the same time, there was still much sympathy for Jews in evidence. In 1933, the *Inverness Courier* reported, "The Church of Scotland Presbytery met on Tuesday, when the Reverend William Norton, Nairn, made a trenchant criticism of Hitler's treatment of Jews. Many eminent men have been driven from their jobs and deprived of places in Universities, Civil Service and Hospitals. There is no justification for this treatment."[72] Three years later, in 1939, the Inverness Church of Scotland Presbytery appealed at its monthly meeting for help for the Jewish refugees.[73]

The Second World War

The information about the community in the years prior to the outbreak of the Second World War is conflicting. The *Jewish Chronicle* reported in 1938, "The Congregation in Inverness has been defunct for some years."[74] The story mentioned earlier points to this being the case, except when numbers were boosted by seasonal influxes of holidaying Jews (thus making a *minyan* possible). Yet, in 1939, and in contradiction to the aforementioned story he sent in to the newspaper, Morris wrote to the *Jewish Chronicle*, stating that there were only three Jewish families in Inverness. He continued to say:

> Until recently, we had our own Synagogue, and we have a small Jewish cemetery at Tomnahurich. During the last few months two of our members have died. Up to now we have been very fortunate in getting a Minyan every Sunday for Kaddish.

These families get kosher meat every week from Glasgow, and they are all regular readers of the *Jewish Chronicle*. A copy of the paper has been provided every week in the lounge of the Caledonian Hotel, Inverness, for the past seventeen years, ordered by Mr. I. Finkelstein. The paper is enjoyed by Jewish and non-Jewish travellers.[75]

Elsewhere it was stated that before the war there was a very small synagogue that just had a *minyan*. Further muddying the waters is the *Jewish Year Book*, which lists the communal figures for the years 1938 and 1939 as 108! Either this is a misprint or the figure included a new wave of arrivals.

The outbreak of the Second World War did, in fact, witness an influx of Jewish service personnel to the region. Jews were stationed at Fort George and other bases in Inverness shire. The large number of Jewish servicemen stationed in the area boosted synagogue attendance, and regular services with as many as sixty people were held at the Morris house. There was no resident rabbi, and services were taken by whichever Jewish Forces chaplain was in the Cameron Barracks or Fort George at the time. These included the Senior Jewish Chaplain to the Armed Forces, Rabbi Israel Brodie, who would go on to serve as the Chief Rabbi from 1948 until 1965, as well as a number of other ministers. The Morris and Finkelstein families also entertained the troops in the evenings throughout the war years. Both Isaac Finkelstein and Mrs. Morris received gold medals from Rabbi Brodie for their services in appreciation of the welcome they had given and in their hosting, entertaining, befriending and advising the numerous Jewish servicemen.[76]

The community was also boosted by a tiny number of refugees arriving before, during and after the Second World War. Two Jewish refugees living at the Czech Refugee Camp in Inverness, Culloden House—Mr. Hans Beriach and Miss Lotte Oschinski—were married. As there was no synagogue or minister, the local Jewish families (the Gavins, Morrises and Finkelsteins) made the arrangements, and the ceremony took place at the Gavin house, with the Reverend T. Vainstein travelling two hundred miles from Glasgow to conduct the ceremony. Many non–Jews were among the guests.[77] The *Jewish Echo* noted the "generous hospitality of the Scottish people in general and the kindness of the Inverness Jews towards the refugees in particular."[78] Another refugee that came to Inverness after the war was Ernest Elijs Jacobs, who came to Scotland in 1948 from a displaced persons camp in Southern Germany, recruited as a tunnel miner for the Fannich Hydro Electric scheme. He was then just nineteen years of age, a rare survivor of the Jewish community of Riga, Latvia. He had no active participation with the small Jewish community in Inverness during the 1960s and 1970s, however, when he lived there, working as the manager of the Craigmonie Hotel.[79] Another refugee who settled in Inverness was Zygmunt Glass. After having escaped from Warsaw in 1939, he served with the Polish Forces, eventually working in the timber trade in the town until his death in 1973.[80] It is possible that the generation of hydro-electricity in the Highlands drew further Jewish migrants and immigrants that we don't yet know about.

From 1945 onwards, following the end of the war and the concomitant withdrawal of the Jewish servicemen who had helped to keep the tiny community going during the years 1939–45, the Inverness Hebrew Congregation witnessed a slow decline. Towards the end of the war the community was formed of five families, totaling twenty individuals. By 1945, this number had dropped to sixteen remaining Jews, making it the smallest community in Scotland, as well as the most northerly community in the entire United Kingdom.[81] One year later there were only twelve families left.[82] It is possible that there were more Jews in the area but they decided to join a much stronger and healthier congregation, such as Aberdeen's, which had just opened a new synagogue in June 1945. A G. Rosengarten of Inverness, for example, was listed as living in Huntly, but he celebrated his son's bar mitzvah in the Aberdeen synagogue, to which he gave £21 for its building fund. In 1953 the community lost another member when the local newspaper reported that Meyer Rosenbloom, a jeweler, aged fifty-three, was found dead in his locked shop in the Market Arcade.[83] At the same time, Nathaniel Sherick, a newcomer from London, settled in nearby Forres. By the years 1955–57, Inverness had only ten Jewish residents and no synagogue or societies.[84] Five Jewish families were left in Inverness, with two children, in 1962, but the number had dropped to four families by 1964.[85] By that point, Jewish children were sent to London to be educated, and a minister would visit occasionally from Glasgow. The *sifri Torah*, which were stored at the Morris residence, were donated to an organization in Israel.[86] Lewis Morris sounded a depressing note when to he wrote to Julius Jung, "There is no Jewish social life here, and as for ourselves no doubt we will be returning to London where I was born. Am here nearly thirty-five years, and had had enough of it."[87]

Furthermore, the core founding members of the community began to pass away. Isaac Finkelstein died in September 1963; Maria and Louis Gavin both died by 1964; and Bessie Goldrich (Morris) died in 1967. The remaining remnants of the community included Mrs. Finkelstein, Mr. and Mrs. Glass, Miss Gavin, and the Morris family.[88] One bright note during this dark period was the occasion of a Jewish marriage in 1968, presided over by Rabbi Weinberg from Edinburgh.[89] But this did little to reverse the decline. By 1970 the population was listed as twelve,[90] or four to six families by 1973.[91] Zygmunt Glass died in 1973. Although it was quipped that there was "no need to court Jewish voters there," in August 1975,[92] Jews remained in Inverness, and, until 1981, they were visited annually by Rabbi Weinberg.[93] The last visit by Weinberg mentioned in the *Jewish Chronicle* was in 1981, when he arranged for the erection of a memorial stone for Jerzy George Glass, brother of Zygmunt, who had died that year.[94] Less than a handful of Jews still live there today. Given its remoteness, particularly in comparison to the other small communities of Ayr, Dunfermline, Falkirk, and Greenock, it seems quite amazing that Inverness's community survived for so long.

Why Did the Community Decline?

Why did the community decline? According to Salis Daiches, the de facto Chief Rabbi of Scotland, "The reason why cities like Perth, Inverness, Aberdeen do not attract Jewish settlers is to be found in the economic conditions prevailing in these cities, the lack of suitable industries, and the distance that separates Northern Scotland from the Jewish centers in England and the Continental countries."[95] Certainly, the lack of available marriage partners was a factor. Rarely, if ever, did the engagements section of the *Jewish Chronicle* announce marriages between two native Inverness Jews, indicating the difficulty of endogamous marriage there. Indeed, the *Jewish Chronicle* listed the following marriages involving Jews from Inverness:

1. Mr. J. Henry Dove, M.B., CH.BM F.R.C.S. (ED.) and Miss Sandelson. The engagement is announced between J. Henry, elder son of Mr. and Mrs. C. E. Dove, of Seaforth Mansions, Inverness, and Rosée Dorothy, youngest daughter of Rabbi Sandelson.[96]
2. Annie, only daughter of Mr. and Mrs. M. Golumb, Einasthan House, Broadstone-park, Inverness, to Sidney Yaffy, Glasgow.[97]
3. Rose Gavin of Inverness married David Bradman from London in London (and their son was born in Inverness on 10 November, 1944).[98]
4. Miriam, the daughter of Leopold and Mrs. Golden of Inverness, married Arthur Speculand of Glasgow.[99]
5. Doris Sonia Morris of Inverness engaged to Ellis Robinson of San Francisco and married on 24 June, 1951 in San Francisco.[100]

In all but one of the above instances, Jewish women from Inverness married Jewish men from elsewhere (Glasgow, London and San Francisco). We know that they are Jewish as it is doubtful that a mixed marriage would have been announced in the *Jewish Chronicle*. Although joyous occasions for the families, such marriages served to drain the community, as the newlyweds rarely settled in Inverness. Consequently, there was not a younger Inverness-born third generation to boost the community. In fact, the last recorded Jewish birth in Inverness was in 1958, so there was not a new generation to replace those who either left or died.

Furthermore, these five marriages occurred over the years 1921 to 1951, demonstrating that the pool of eligible Jewish singles was not deep enough in Inverness. There were also simply not enough Jewish visitors to the town. The result was that young Jews would go, or be sent, elsewhere to find their marriage partners. A clear example of this were the Finkelstein daughters, who were sent to be educated in Leicester but then married non–Jews nevertheless. The smallness of Inverness' community also meant that matches between Jews and non–Jews were increasingly likely, as when Norman Seller, a non–Jew, fell in love with Leah Rosenbloom in 1919. Louis Gavin wrote to the Chief Rabbi, clearly distressed, "We tried our best to separate them but unfortunately did not succeed, they got married by the Sheriff by Special License to make their separation impossible." Although married, they did not yet live together, but her parents were described as "brokenhearted" [sic] nevertheless. From the parents' point of view, however, there was a happy ending: Seller subsequently converted to Judaism in 1919 and even underwent circumcision.[101]

Beyond Inverness

Beyond Inverness, Jews spread out to points further north and west on the mainland, as well as to the different Scottish islands. Richard Kearton observed in 1898:

> The Western Isles form a happy hunting-ground for a number of Jew pedlars, and one of these found his way to St. Kilda on the steamer which came to take us off. No sooner had this man opened his bundle of gaudy wares than lie was surrounded by an excited crowd of women and children, who began to handle and examine everything he had. I saw the minister's servant-girl seize a brilliantly-coloured petticoat, and rushing up to her reverend master thrust it in his face with childish glee and begged him to buy it for her.[102]

One such traveler was Julius Quint (originally Kvint) from Danzig. Born in 1868, he came under the influence of a Christian Mission and converted to Christianity in 1893. His family disowned him, but he sailed to Scotland and later arrived on Shetland with his wife, Jessie Maxted, and his children. For some time he also lived on Unst. He was a travelling peddler selling towels, bedspreads, pillowcases, men's trousers and drawers from a large sailor's bag which he carried on his back as he walked from district to district. In an attaché case he kept boot laces, razor blades, tie pin brooches and necklaces. He became a familiar figure on the West Side of Shetland in the 1920s, and died in March 1938 at Trolligarth, Walls, where he is buried in the Parish Church Cemetery.[103]

Another Jewish salesman who reached the more distant parts of Scotland was Isaac Mor An Iudhach (Big Isaac the Jew), as he was known on the Gaelic-speaking Stornoway, Lewis, in the late nineteenth century. He owned a jewelers or watchmakers shop, but not much more is known about him.[104] It is possible that Big Isaac the Jew was Isaac Bernestein of Stornoway, who sued M. Stave in July 1897. Under the headline "Jews in Court," the *Highland News* reported that Bernestein claimed that he was engaged by Mr. Stave on a monthly basis as an interpreter at 125s per month but was dismissed suddenly with no wages. The defendant gave his oath in the usual form, but the other three Jews who were examined preferred to be sworn with head covered and hand resting on Old Testament scriptures. The judgment was found in Bernestein's favor.[105] An interesting item from this case is the fact that three Jews are listed as living in Stornoway at that time. It is possible that one of those was Kravitch (Kratvitz), who, in January 1917, appeared before the Stornoway Sheriff Court for an unpaid gambling debt.[106] Kravitch had a jeweler's shop at the end of Cromwell Street, Stornoway, according to the *1931 Stornoway Street Directory*.[107] A Polish Jew was known to be living, or peddling, on Skye in 1879 because the *Inverness Courier* reported how "John Stewart & his wife have been apprehended & are in prison awaiting trial for stealing two gold rings & a watch from a Polish Jew."[108] Elizabeth Caldwell Hirschman and Donald N. Yates further claim that Skye cemeteries contain the graves of Jews of Sephardic ancestry whose names derived from Hebrew antiquity or tribal or given names.[109]

Other individuals are recorded as living on some of these islands. In 1932 Eva Birnbaum and Lionel Greenwald, sister-in-law and brother-in-law of Wolf Brook, who died in Lanark but probably lived in Glasgow, gave their address as Lerwick, Shetland. The following year, according to the *Jewish Echo*, Rabbi Salis Daiches wrote in *The Scots Magazine* on "Scotland and the Jews," and included a plea that persecuted Jews from Germany be allowed to settle in the remoter parts of Scotland. "There is no doubt that the Highlands and Islands would greatly benefit if a few thousand Jews would take up their abode there." Nothing seemed to come of this plan, but in 1938 the crofters on the Glendale Estate, Isle of Skye, offered land to Jewish Czech refugees to settle and cultivate.[110] In 1936 the *Jewish Echo* reported "An Act of Courtesy" when a man named Levy, who had resided for many years in Lerwick, died, leaving no dependants, and the local authorities used £8 found in his home for his burial in the local cemetery. Mr. S. Lichtenberg from Glasgow, who frequently visited Shetland on business, got in touch with Lord Provost Olason because he thought it not right for a Jew to be buried in non–Jewish burial ground, and they applied to the Home Office for a permit to transfer the body to a Jewish cemetery.

We do not know where any of these individuals came from, but most likely they came following in the footsteps of fishermen or seamen, as Stornoway was then a busy and prosperous fishing town and seaport. In 1900 there were around nine hundred boats leaving Stornoway to fish for herring—with thousands of fishermen—while others fished for white fish. The port was very busy, and Stornoway kippers were exported around the globe (thousands of barrels of white fish were also sent to Europe). Foreign ships called for these cargos. Approximately twelve thousand men were employed in the fishing industry in the Western Isles. Boats from the Western Isles traded to the

Baltic and Europe for hundreds of years. The islanders also fished on the East Coast of Scotland and down into English waters. A good living could be made catering to local and visiting fishermen, seamen, and crofters. They may have come from one of the Baltic coastal countries, Germany or even England.

Other Jews who ended up in Stornoway unfortunately did not decide to go there. On 28 June, 1904, the Scandinavian-American emigrant liner *SS Norge* of Copenhagen foundered on the reef off Rockall. The ship was loaded with 765 passengers and seventy-one crew members, many of whom were European emigrants bound for the United States. The ship was wrecked and sank, with the loss of six-hundred-and-thirty-five lives—"the worst shipping accident that took place during the whole period of mass Jewish emigration from Eastern Europe between 1881 and 1914," according to Sharman Kadish.[111] The survivors were landed in Stornoway and housed, hospitalized, and treated there. They included Jache Ginsberg and daughter Shmuel Lioginsky, Isidor Bass, Aaron Chatzkelewitz, Berl Gerstein, Aaron Kotkin, Hersch Lew, Yosel Liben, Leib Rosenman, Chaim Rasowksy, Avrom Scharf, Aaron Shulmeister, Myer Schalich, Baruch Sirotkin, Leib Tschernobrov, Sarah Posansky and her two children (Abraham and Dora), and Chaie Wexler and her children Moisha (five), Israel (four) and Meir (two), all of whom were Jews. Those who were not so fortunate and whose bodies were recovered were buried at Sandwick Cemetery, Stornoway. They included Max Posansky (7) and Rebecca Posansky (11) of Sloman, Russia; and Salman Reismann (eleven months) and Sara Reismann (5) of Shofsky, Russia. The death of the two Reismman children meant that their mother Rivke had lost two of her children.[112] Their graves are marked by a single pointed headstone, "somewhat inappropriately accompanied by a verse from the New Testament book of Revelations."[113]

Other Jews buried on the islands included Jewish service personnel; a tombstone engraved with a Star of David in the cemetery on Lamlash, Isle of Arran, marks the grave of a Jewish army officer who died there in 1941. Intriguingly, *The Scotsman* mentioned Jews "on the shores of the Island of Arran" in 1921 but provided no further details.[114] Royal Canadian Air Force Pilot Officer Moses Lewis Usher of Montreal, Quebec, was reported killed in action overseas on 31 March, 1942, aged twenty-five. He was interred in Lerwick Cemetery in the Shetlands, the first Jew to be buried in the islands. The RAF placed a special aircraft at the disposal of Chaplain H.I. Alexander to enable him to reach the Shetlands to perform the burial.[115] Twenty-two-year-old Polish-born Sergeant Moses Charton of the Royal Canadian Air Force, from Verdun, Quebec, was killed while serving as an observer overseas on 6 October, 1942. He was buried in the Kinloss Abbey Burial Ground, and his gravestone is marked with a Star of David.[116] And Pilot Officer Mortimer Regenstreif (or Regenstrief) of the Royal Canadian Air Force was reported killed in action on 16 August, 1944, aged twenty-two. He was buried in the Soroby Burial Ground, Argyllshire.[117]

Jews also moved to other Highland and island regions. The 1871 census listed Nathan M. Goldberg, age 56, a "china and rag dealer," born in Russia but a naturalized British subject, living at 6, Bridge Street, Wynd, Kirkwall, Orkney, along with his wife Elizabeth (52), born in Eday, Orkney (suggesting that she was not Jewish), and their son Nathan (15), a scholar born in Edinburgh. Two further travelers are also mentioned: Jacob Stern (24) and Solomon Morris (22), both unmarried men from Russia, living at Broad Street, Kirkwall. During the First World War, Reuben Spilg from Glasgow was sent to Kinlochleven in the Highlands because, although he was an enlisted soldier, he was too young to serve at the front. Instead, he worked at a temporary hydroelectricity factory making concrete pipes. Max G. Taylor was a peddling salesman (hawker) who, in 1921, travelled to the Shetland Isles and Kirkwall. There he stayed in a boarding house, where another guest was Louis Bodvisky, whom the locals called "Badwhisky" because they could not remember or pronounce his Polish name. Bodvisky had stayed in Kirkwall for an unknown number of years, selling jewelry, and people forgot he was Jewish. Other Jewish travelers also used this boarding house.[118]

In 1949 and 1951 respectively, I. Florence was living in Thurso, and Mr. and Mrs. Sam Harris and their daughter resided on Bowmore, Islay. In 1977, Ike Gibson moved to Ullapool, where he still runs a guesthouse. Gibson was born into an orthodox Jewish (Polish) family in Hamburg. He came to the United Kingdom with his two older brothers and two older sisters on the *Kindertransport* that arrived at Harwich on 2 August, 1939. He and the younger of his sisters, Esther, stayed with an orthodox family in Finsbury Park, the Kahns, for just three weeks before being evacuated to St. Ives, Cambridgeshire. He and his sister were moved through three different "billets" before ending up with a Miss Wiles, the sister of the St. Ives Billeting Officer and the daughter of the recently deceased pastor of the local Baptist chapel. He came to regard May Wiles as his "mother." She married an Eduard Gibson after the war, and although Esther had by this time moved out to become a nurse, Ike remained with Ted and May Gibson. He was brought up as a strict Baptist, but after the age of sixteen he ceased to go to the chapel and has not maintained any religion since. He had no contact with Jewish people until he became friends with a Jewish colleague after he started a lectureship in genetics at Hatfield Polytechnic in 1966. Finally, Rowena Macdonald, a psychology student at Stirling University, delegate to the Glasgow Jewish Representative Council, and chairman of the Inter-University Jewish Federation Northern Region, was a member of the only Jewish family in Skye, where her parents were farmers.[119]

Londoner Barry Kaye moved to Dunoon in 1986. He had to take a ferry to the nearest synagogue in Glasgow. With the aid of a £500 grant, he set about locating other Jews in the Argyll and Bute regions. Eventually, those Jews scattered about the Highlands and islands organized themselves into the

Argyll and Bute Jewish community. It is not a "congregation" as such, since it has no synagogue. It later renamed itself the Jewish Network of Argyll and the Highlands when Jews from the Mull of Kintyre up to Ullapool and others further east linked up with the group, no longer making Oban the obvious focal point. In 1997 it was listed under "Dunoon" in the *Jewish Year Book* for the first time. The 2001 census recorded forty-five Jews in Argyll and Bute. The Network currently has between fifteen and thirty members, including a couple from Israel, most of whom have little or no formal Jewish background. The Network is presently organized by Frank and Valerie House, who, having lived in Aberdeen, retired to Gairloch in 2002. They celebrate Shabbat each week (although without a community), hold two Seder services, and are able to keep kosher by receiving frozen meat from Manchester.[120] In 2005 they arranged with the Highland Council to secure a Jewish burial plot in the cemetery in Gairloch, demarcated and separated by white painted bricks in the grass.[121] Over the following year, in 2006, Yom Kippur services were held in Findorn, Moray, led by Esther Aronsfeld, an ordained interfaith minister, as well as a Chanukah party in Lochgilphead.[122]

The other place to feature documented Jewish settlement was Lerwick in the Shetland Isles. Harry, Louis, Hyman and Woolf Greenwald (ne Pochapovsky) travelled from Gorodea (a Belarussian shtetl near Minsk) to Scotland in order to escape poverty, as well as "fear, danger and persecution."[123] After having landed in Scotland (the exact location is unclear; although Hofman cites Greenock, this would have been a most unusual route, and the story may have become confused over the years; the most common routes of Jewish immigration to Scotland were from the Baltic ports, or Hamburg to Leith or Hull), the Greenwalds trudged along dirt roads to Aberdeen, attempting to sell jewelry along the way and picking up the occasional lift from wagons going between farms. From Aberdeen they took the ship the *S.S. St. Magus* to Lerwick, where they eventually settled.[124] The Greenwalds continued as jewelry peddlers in the Shetlands, selling to the crofters and fisherman, eventually building up their business to the level where they could acquire a property at 163, Commercial Street. Initially, it began as an ice cream saloon before becoming a jewelry and watch repair shop. Eventually, however, Louis, Hyman and Woolf became tired of their isolation and left Lerwick to be with their "own folk."[125] During that time, Woolf and his wife Sadie (née Ettinger) had had a child, Fanny Rose Greenwald, who died of gastritis in December 1924, only ten days old. She was buried "on a hill in the Lerwick cemetery," perhaps one of the most northerly Jewish graves in the British Isles.[126] By 1934, Harry remained alone and built up the business into a much-loved general store with the slogan "You can get it at Greenwalds." Because Harry wanted a Jewish wife and there were no other Jews on Lerwick, he arranged a marriage to Jean Segal from Glasgow, who relocated to live in Lerwick in an attempt to better herself.

The Greenwalds, like the other Jewish families dotted about the Highlands and islands of Scotland, had to decide how best to live a Jewish life in such a far-flung outpost. And their experience is typical and representative of the other Jewish families in the region. Despite their distance from any other organized Jewish life, the Greenwalds attempted to maintain their Jewish identity. They subscribed to the *Jewish Echo* (Scotland's only Jewish newspaper, published in Glasgow), referring to its calendar for the times for lighting candles on a Friday night. They resolved to bring up their children as Jewish, and despite the obvious difficulties, they instilled a strong and proud sense of Jewish identity into their two children, Ethel and Roy. Ethel wrote, "In spite of our isolation, Ma was determined to retain her Jewishness and pass on its rich heritage and culture to her children. From the moment I could talk, I knew I was Jewish, and that we did some things differently from our neighbors."[127]

Inevitably, this required compromises. The Greenwalds started off ordering kosher meat from Glasgow, but when the first batch arrived at the end of a long hot sea journey "crawling with maggots," Jean decided, "my children must have meat, whether it's kosher or not. God will forgive me...."[128] Henceforth they bought meat from the local butcher, but not pork or shellfish, and maintained the required separation of milk and meat dishes. They also ordered kosher food from Michael Morrison's delicatessen in Glasgow, such as fifteen boxes of *matzos* on Passover (so that they could share them with their non–Jewish friends and neighbors). There were also paradoxes. While the Greenwalds requested that Ethel be excused from scripture classes in school, the children hung up their stockings on Christmas Eve. Their mother decided, "There's no harm in it. The children know they're Jewish, and a few toys certainly won't make them Christian."[129] Ethel devotes two pages of her memoir of these years to how the family made their annual Christmas cake. At the same time, during *Chanukah* they lit colored candles in the *menorah* and ate traditional *latkes*.

During the Second World War, as with other parts of Scotland, Lerwick's natural harbor became a strategic base for British naval operations, since Norway, under German occupation, was only two-hundred-and-twenty-miles away. Among the thousands of troops based on the islands (which included Orkney, Shetland, the Outer Hebrides, and Caithness) were three hundred Jewish servicemen.[130] Enlisting the help of Rabbi Brodie, the Greenwalds organized Passover Seders for the Jewish soldiers. Hundreds of pounds of matzos, matzo meal and wine were shipped to the Greenwalds via the commanding officer at the Shetland Naval Air Station. With the help of local women and camp cooks, Jean prepared the traditional Passover Seder meals for the troops. The Jewish chaplain J. Israelstam flew from Inverness to officiate. Then aged seven, Ethel asked the four questions. The *Shetland Times* even reported the event under the headline, "Jewish Services Personnel Celebrate Passover."[131] Many of the Jewish troops came to look upon the Greenwald house as their second home, and in recognition of their services a presentation was made in 1945 to the Greenwalds for "their unfailing hospitality to Jewish personnel and their helpfulness in connection with arrangements for Services and socials."[132]

Eventually, Ethel left Lerwick for Glasgow and then America; however, her parents and brother remained. In 1972, Harry died and was buried in Glasgow. Roy converted the two buildings (they had since expanded and bought the vacant shop next door at number 161) the family owned on Commercial Street into a department store. Throughout the 1970s, and until 1981, Rabbi Weinberg visited the Greenwalds.[133] Jean died, but Roy continues to live there, although he no longer owns his department store, having sold it in 1991.

A Diaspora from a Diaspora

The diverse and scattered nature of the Jewish immigration to the Scottish Highlands and islands really demonstrates the remoteness and isolation of some Jewish families and individuals in Scotland. At the same time, however, it shows how they were able to cope and thrive in the face of adversity, and to maintain their Jewish heritage and identity against the odds. Of course, as we have seen, this was not always successful, as manifested by the decline of the Inverness Hebrew Congregation, the closure of the synagogue and the various intermarriages. Nevertheless, Jewish life still exists in the most far-flung regions of the United Kingdom and forms what may be called either a Diaspora from a Diaspora or, alternatively, a Diaspora within a Diaspora.

Conclusion

In the previous chapters I have attempted to provide as comprehensive a picture of the seven Jewish congregations outside of Edinburgh and Glasgow, as well as those Jews and their families scattered the length and breadth of Scotland, as is currently possible from the available records. Here I would like to provide some summary remarks that draw the thematic links between all of them. Clearly there are significant points of comparison and overlap between these seven communities.

Character

As most of the communities grew as a result of the large-scale immigration into Britain during the period 1880-1920, but began to decline in the era following the Second World War, the initial character of the small Jewish communities in Scotland was composed, for the most part, of Jews of foreign birth. With one exception, they were primarily Eastern European—specifically, Russian, Lithuanian, and Polish. Dundee, in contrast, was originally settled by German-Jewish immigrants, although there were a handful of German Jews in Greenock. Later, all of these communities became largely Eastern European but of British birth, with the "exception of an element of elderly foreign immigrants,"[1] until foreign students, primarily from the United States (and to a lesser extent elsewhere, such as South Africa), began moving to Scotland to study in the 1920s and 1930s. Then German Jews, fleeing Nazism, began to arrive from 1936 onwards. Of the approximately one thousand Jewish refugees from Nazi Germany who came to Scotland, a trickle made their way to the small communities outside Glasgow and Edinburgh.[2] None of these communities ever had a strong Sephardic influence—if Sephardim did visit, it was only temporarily as students or scholars.

Trade

What, then, exactly attracted Jews to such small and often remote and isolated communities? Since Jews had primarily been town dwellers in Eastern Europe, and were restricted to certain trades (such as finance, tobacco and clothing), Jewish immigrants to Britain tended to migrate towards urban rather than rural areas (despite the folksy notion, as propagated by the film *Fiddler on the Roof*, that Jews were rustic peasants).[3] Furthermore, they "gravitated towards occupations requiring skills they already possessed, or which could be easily learned, and where language problems could be minimised," or which required little training.[4] Many of the first arrivals in the late nineteenth and early twentieth centuries were commercial travelers—poor peddlers and hawkers—looking for new business opportunities throughout Scotland. Often they were based in one place and travelled to all of the local villages to sell their wares, returning home for the Sabbath. They had come in search of economic opportunities and eventually settled as these new locations provided competitive prospects.[5] The main reasons accounting for remote and isolated Jewish settlement within Scotland in its initial years in the late nineteenth century were commercial. As Glasgow and other large British cities were overrun with Jewish immigrant peddlers, jobs became scarce, so those Jews who pioneered the settlement of remoter locations did so in an attempt to establish themselves economically, particularly if they were bachelors and hence did not have the burden of a family.

Many of these who began as peddlers often bought properties and eventually settled in the remoter communities and set up businesses as shopkeepers. Consequently, the occupational structure of all of the small Jewish communities was quite homogeneous. Once settled, the majority of Jews were self-employed, working at home or in backstreet workshops.[6] Their language and accents would have been a mixture of German or Yiddish, English, and Scottish, if they had even learned the native languages at all. Those Jews who lived in isolated towns and villages throughout Scotland "were involved in either commercial activity, providing professional services or running the local store."[7]

Such Jews mostly became engaged in the retail business as shopkeepers in the following trades: furniture, shoes, fish, clothing, drapery, electrical contracting, jewelry, watch and clock repairs, tailors, stationers, tobacconists, boot and shoe sellers, shoemakers, hairdressers, general dealers, travelers, aerated water manufacturers, confectioners, ophthalmologists, plumbers, cabinet makers, hat making, antiques, market stalls, general stores, tea rooms and lodging houses, decorating, "fancy goods," greengrocery, haberdashery, fur, and fruit. Initially they were, with very few exceptions, of the poorest class. They primarily lived in the less salubrious, densely populated, poor working class areas, often in slums and tenements. The incumbent residents were boosted by seasonal incomers such as those who worked in the herring trade or soldiers billeted on service in the military bases dotted across Scotland. Many Jewish service personnel passed through the many bases stationed all over Scotland over the course of the twentieth century, including Fort George,

Shetland, Stornaway, Dunfermline, Prestwick, Kinloss, and Lozells. Most of the residents enjoyed a modest living, but "not infrequently ... were [probably] tempted to accept payment in kind."[8] The exception here was the pre–First World War German Jews of Dundee who, in contrast to their Eastern European co-religionists, were "more of the better-off class."[9]

This occupational structure remained largely in place until the First World War. Thereafter, although a sprinkling of peddlers remained, they were rapidly becoming the exception, and we see the Jewish communities becoming more prosperous through successful business, leading to a move into the professional classes or a branching out into new ventures, such as cinema exhibition. As Jews became wealthier they moved to the more prosperous parts of their respective towns and cities, and their children began to enter university and graduate in areas such as medicine, dentistry, electrical engineering, law, teaching, and even music and drama. The native-born were joined, from 1927 onwards, by larger numbers of American Jews who began arriving in those towns with universities (Aberdeen and Dundee) when a *numerus clausus* in operation at American medical schools brought an influx of students from the United States.[10] The arrival of the more assimilated, educated, wealthier, and middle-class German Jews fleeing Nazism in the 1930s helped to intensify the embourgeoisiement of the indigenous Jewish communities, and this shift accelerated after the Second World War as the younger generation spread among the professions.

From 1945 onwards, however, we see a decline in the small Scottish Jewish communities, with all but two of them being wound up in the post-war period. The drop in figures is due to a number of factors: an aging population, intermarriage, and emigration, as children moved away to university, in search of employment, and/or a suitable marriage partner, or by families with young children relocating to a location with a more developed Jewish infrastructure. The downturn in the Scottish economy after 1945 especially accelerated this migration away from the small communities towards the central belt, especially Edinburgh and Glasgow, and England, (in particular, London). Furthermore, Scottish communities were unable to adopt the survival strategy that was implemented elsewhere: merging. When the small congregations of North Wales (Bangor, Colwyn Bay, Llandudno, and Rhyl) began to decline, for example, they amalgamated to eventually form one—the Llandudno Hebrew Congregation. However, given the distances involved, the communities in Scotland could not choose this option.

Of the two communities which survive, Aberdeen and Dundee, their respective sizes and universities, hospitals, and other employment opportunities account for their longevity. Aberdeen and Dundee are Scotland's third and fourth largest cities, respectively; Ayr, Dunfermline, Falkirk, Greenock, and Inverness were medium-sized towns. As the twentieth century progressed, other than a scattering of individuals and families, Jews on the whole tended to prefer urban settings.

Although Aberdeen and Dundee did not manage to stem the tide of outward migration, they were able to attract Jews. Medicine had long been a big draw for Jews to Scotland because of the relatively low fees and living expenses, the international reputation of Scotland's universities, and their long tradition of religious tolerance.[11] This trend is set to continue, as the institution of tuition fees pushes English students north of the border; in 2005 it was reported that St. Andrews was the fastest growing student Jewish Society in the United Kingdom, and the University of Aberdeen re-established its defunct Students' Jewish Society the same year. Furthermore, Aberdeen has thrived where Dundee has not because of other factors, such as the energy industry and the discovery and exploitation of oil in the late 1960s and 1970s. At one point, at least three members of Aberdeen's Jewish community were helicopter pilots for British Airways, flying to and from the oil rigs in the North Sea.[12]

Practice

Since many of those who initially settled in the remoter parts of Scotland were from Eastern Europe, Jewish facilities, without exception, were organized upon Orthodox lines. There were no Reform, Liberal, or Conservative congregations in the small Scottish Jewish communities. However, it is not certain that this reflected the actual private practice of the congregation as a whole. Compromise was necessary because there was not the resources to sustain more than one synagogue. Often the communities were amalgams of Jews of every religious attitude, and if it is not to split, then a course that unifies all the participants in a spiritually satisfying way for all concerned had to be found. The need to base everything in a single congregation is a distinctive feature of small community Jewish life. This corresponds with experience elsewhere in the United Kingdom, where small-town Jewish life "was based primarily on the coming of East Europeans [and] it was common in the early twentieth century to find only a single congregation, Orthodox in practice."[13] Although many strived to do so, many other Jews, however, did not always maintain a strictly Orthodox lifestyle and made compromises in their personal observance. They opened their stores on Saturdays, although they may not have actually worked in them, and perhaps did not observe in full the laws of *kashrut*, simply because of the practical difficulties of doing so. Thus the organization of synagogue services, while Orthodox, had to take the needs and desires of its congregants into account.

Religious concerns were central to these communities, despite their small size. As Flora Sclar wrote to the *Jewish Echo* in 1941, "We are but a handful of Yiddishe people here—seven families in all—yet, small a community as we are, we have a school and manage to uphold Jewish traditions and everything pertaining to Judaism."[14] This experience was fairly typical of Scotland's small

Jewish communities. Despite their remoteness, size, and difficulties in doing so, Scotland's small Jewish communities maintained at times a full range of religious, cultural, and social services, as befitting a Jewish congregation. As these communities grew, they were able to achieve self-sufficiency in terms of a Jewish infrastructure. All of these communities had, at one time or another, a synagogue, resident minister, *chazan*, *shochet*, *mohel*, kosher meat suppliers, kosher bakers, Hebrew teachers, and even *shabbes goyim* (non–Jews hired to perform tasks forbidden to Jews on the Shabbat). A non–Jewish local in Dundee recalled that "Ikey Rosen used to get the local lads to put out his gas jets on Friday, the eve of the Jewish Sabbath. Depending on their age, they got either a fag or an apple."[15] However, there is no evidence that any community had access to a dedicated *mikveh* outside of Edinburgh and Glasgow, although Inverness did begin a fundraising appeal to construct one. So while this Jewish infrastructure was not as extensive as elsewhere, it was not nonexistent, as implied by those who feel that less than a hundred Jewish members precludes a full-fledged Orthodox Jewish existence. (Conversely, as the communities declined, their dependency on the larger ones of Glasgow and Edinburgh increased.)

The congregations were Orthodox in practice but independent. This meant that they resembled the United Synagogue but were not affiliated with it, although they did often appeal to the Chief Rabbi for help with securing ministers, raising funds, and generally adjudicating on other religious matters. They also sent representatives to the Board of Deputies. Indeed, the relations of the small Scottish Jewish communities with the center of British life in London are an interesting dimension of this study, although one that will need to be fleshed out in more detail in the future. No doubt due to the distances involved, London seemed remote to these small Scottish Jewish communities, who understandably had more contact with their closer, metropolitan neighbors. Thus, with the help of Jewish organizations and individuals from Glasgow and Edinburgh, Jews in these towns and cities maintained their Jewish identity or were encouraged to do so.

This was certainly the case with Ayr, as we have seen, which enjoyed close relations with Glasgow. However, the attitude of the center has not helped matters. For example, 1907 was the last time that a chief rabbi visited Aberdeen, even though various incumbents have visited Glasgow and Edinburgh. One was not even present for the consecration of the Dee Street synagogue in 1945. This has led to a justifiable perception of a sense of aloofness, if not indifference, on the part of the Chief Rabbinate by some of Aberdeen's congregants. When, in 1992, the Chief Rabbi's Council requested a sum of £120 from the congregation, the president suggested responding with a "No." The president then contacted the Scottish representative on the Chief Rabbi's Council, requesting that it ignore Aberdeen and Dundee in future and not send any more bills, which would be ignored if received.[16] To date, a chief rabbi has still not visited Aberdeen one hundred years later, which communicates the wrong message to the United Kingdom's smaller communities.

Initially, when Jews arrived in a new town they were either too poor or too few to organize formal facilities. Consequently, such Jews met informally in a private house for worship. Nonetheless, as these small Jewish communities grew, they still lacked the necessary population base and resources to support either purpose-built facilities or more than one congregation. As a result, they only supported a single congregation since their inception, usually housed in a rented accommodation, such as a hall (often used for other purposes) or rooms above shops. This was a distinctive feature of remote Jewish life in Scotland (with the exception of Dundee, when, as a result of the regeneration of the city center, the Dundee Council demolished the existing synagogue and built a new one for the community in the 1970s), as was the conspicuous absence of multiple or dissident congregations (again with the exceptions of Dundee and Ayr). Consequently, there was usually only one synagogue available to those who wished to affiliate with an established religious institution. Ayr and Dundee, however, were exceptions. Ayr was able to support rival *minyaim* during the Second World War as a result of an influx of evacuees from Glasgow. And in Dundee the small community divided and, for a while, had as many as *three* congregations (the principle one at 123, Murraygate, and two rival ones at Ward Road and Bank Street, respectively).[17]

It was often a feature of remote Jewish life that synagogue premises changed frequently, reflecting the inadequacy of their locations in terms of size and condition. Nevertheless, once established, the synagogue acted as the hub of Jewish activity in these small communities, whereas in a larger community Jewish life might be much less centralized due to an increased availability of different services and social activities.[18]

Yet it is certain that not all those Jews who came to small communities necessarily became involved in congregational life, and, unfortunately, the available statistics do not allow for a precise analysis of rates of congregational affiliation. Furthermore, it can be said with some certainty that some Jews did not participate at all: they came, married non–Jews, and/or changed their names and disappeared. In Dundee, for example, the German-Jewish immigrants were, according to C.C. Aronsfeld, likely to be "more German (if anything) than Jewish. Certainly few practised the old religion."[19] They "found no Jewish life when they came," quickly integrated, and many completely assimilated.[20] A number even converted to Christianity. Others may simply have been deracinated in the first place, the only visible signs of their Jewishness, if any, would be the Star of David on a necklace or a Menorah on a mantelpiece.

Those services that took place in these small communities were usually, as far as we can tell, conducted along Orthodox lines, but not always by a minister or cantor. In their absence, a lay member of the congregation would take responsibility for leading the services.[21] The communities owned their own Torah scrolls, prayer books, and the other items necessary for running religious services. And, at times, the small communities were able to engage the services of a permanent minister or, even more rarely, a rabbi. The norm, it seems (with the exception of Dundee and Dunfermline, which were both able to engage a permanent rabbi—incidentally, the same person on consecutive contracts), was to employ a series of various short-term visiting ministers who would conduct the High Holy Day festivals and perform other duties.

Often those ministers and rabbis who did enjoy longer-term contracts were required to perform multiple tasks but were not well paid for them. The *Jewish Chronicle* listed these duties as: teaching the children "in approved mediaeval fashion," "slaying bullocks for the material sustenance of his flock," "consorting with butchers in the slaughterhouse" and collecting from members of the congregation "the small weekly pittance that it allows him."[22] Typically they were recent immigrants from abroad, usually Russia, Poland, and Lithuania, and could not speak English. In the two court cases which involved such ministers (Hirsch Levi of Dundee and James Littman of Aberdeen), interpreters were required. Their salaries were "notoriously low," not out of a lack of respect for religious leadership, as Collins rather harshly suggests, but most likely reflecting the small size—and hence poverty—of the small communities, which simply could not afford higher salaries. This low pay "led to the need to augment income by means of teaching or accepting gratuities for the rendering of religious services," or "supplementing it by hawking small-ware in the neighbouring villages." An editorial in the *Jewish Chronicle* was concerned enough with the low quality of provincial ministers in 1905 to propose severing the ministerial from the butchering functions, not least because in the eyes of "their non–Jewish neighbours, their 'minister' is their representative. It is he and his wife who receive the invitations to functions at which the local authorities desire the Jewish congregation to be represented."[23]

As time went on, and since members often came from a wide range of Jewish backgrounds (and some often had no religious tradition at all), unanimity on matters of religious practice, ritual and liturgy were highly unlikely. Remote Jews have had to operate in a spirit of compromise in order to sustain the support of all or most of the local Jewish residents. The practices of the synagogue were, to an extent, molded at least in part by the diversity of the local Jewish population, since religious life revolved around the lone congregation in town.[24] Sticking to a strictly and exclusively Orthodox line would have alienated some potential congregants and hence undermined the already low, and declining, number of attendees.

Minyanim

Because of their small numbers, the major and perennial problem for the small and remote communities was their increasing inability to attract regular *minyanim*. It was not unusual, therefore, for remote communities to meet less frequently, and, as a result, for services to be scheduled to fit around the needs of the community rather than the community fitting purely around the religious requirements. Over the years, Shabbat morning services were held monthly rather than weekly, and the times of the Friday night worship varied according to demand.

Often lacking a stable core of eligible members, small communities pressganged anyone they could into attending. Often non–Jewish partners of Jewish men were approached to persuade their husbands to attend the synagogue, or holidaying guests, Jewish servicemen, and relatives were encouraged to attend. It is possible that being a valued and valuable member of a community which could not count on assuming the attendance of ten men was an incentive to Jews to come to services in such small communities.

Unfortunately, however, old age, death, and dispersal led to the winding up of all but two of these remote and small congregations. As older members became too infirm to attend synagogue or died, and younger members moved away (either abroad or to other parts of the British Isles), the small Jewish communities' synagogues struggled to find ten Jewish males over the age of thirteen. When this happened on a consistently regular basis, the congregations dissolved, as was the case in Ayr, Dunfermline, Falkirk, Greenock, and Inverness. Nonetheless, as we have seen, Jews often remained and worshipped in such places long after the official community had been wound up. Dundee and Aberdeen survive because of their ability to attract a constantly changing stream of university staff, students, and other workers (in the latter case, particularly in the herring and oil industries). This "revolving door" nature of high population turnover has enabled Aberdeen and Dundee to survive consistently for over one hundred and ten years. Another reason is that a remote and small community like Aberdeen has not been deterred simply because it lacked a *minyan*. Services were still held regardless.

Burials

Aberdeen, Dundee, Greenock, and even Inverness had dedicated Jewish burial grounds, usually part of a larger public cemetery; Ayr, Falkirk, Dunfermline and the outlying regions and islands of Scotland did not. It would appear that no *Jewish* burials were made in Ayr, Dunfermline, and Falkirk. Yet there are Jewish graves in other cemeteries elsewhere in Scotland, beyond the formal communities. The most northerly Jewish graves in Britain must be in the Shetland Islands, which include those of at least three Jews. Outside of these communities, it is highly unlikely that if buried *in situ* that these sites were Jewish, and it is unknown if the burials proceeded according to Jewish ritual tradition. Jewish burial societies (*chevra kadisha*) for the preparation of the dead (*taharah*) were set up. These societies did not perhaps adhere to the highest Orthodox standards as practiced in London, but they did the best that could be done in the circumstances.[25]

Kashrut

For most of the communities, kosher meat and poultry was available at one time or another. Typically, the minister acted as *shochet*, for which he charged a small fee to members and a slightly higher one to non-members as a perquisite to his typically meager salary. Alternatively, non-kosher butcher shops had a kosher counter or corner, but some communities received their meat from Glasgow and Edinburgh by train or bus.[26] Although the first slaughter of a bullock in Aberdeen raised some concern with the local branch of the Society for the Protection of Animals, resulting in a legal case in which *shechita* was upheld, thereafter, *shechita* continued as normal in all of the small communities and Aberdeen, for a while even supplying a kosher butcher in London with Scotch beef daily.

In general, for the small Jewish communities in Scotland (and particularly for the remoter ones), *kashrut* was a very difficult problem, particularly in the absence of a resident *shochet*. Kosher meat was purchased from kosher butchers in Glasgow, put on either the train or the bus, and collected at the other end. Fortunately, the cold Scottish weather tended to keep the meat in good condition. Alternatively, businessmen often drove into Glasgow as part of their work and picked up meat and other supplies on their way home. Similar arrangements occurred in Aberdeen and Falkirk. Ayr, however, was unusual in that it not only catered for the provision of kosher meat and poultry, it had several kosher hotels at one time or another; Jews from Glasgow holidayed in Ayr during the summer months, and larger numbers of Jews were evacuated there during the Second World War.

Yet, this method of ordering meat was not always suitable, as it often rotted during the journey, or rats ate it. Furthermore, the higher costs of transportation made the cost of kosher meat prohibitive. The remoter the community, the more complex the provision of kosher meat became. Although it is likely that a strict form of *kashrut* may have been abandoned altogether in some cases, it was not discarded entirely in others; instead, a pragmatic version that adapted to the peculiar circumstances emerged which accepted animals even if not properly slaughtered, but shunned shellfish and the mixing of meat and dairy. At least one example of this is recorded on Lerwick, Shetland, as we have seen.

Bread presented another problem. Under the *kashrut* laws it was preferable to buy bread from a Jewish baker, and such products were available from time to time. In Aberdeen in 1940, for example, a German Jewish refugee was employed by a local bakery producing Continental and Jewish specialties.[27] Where no Jewish baked bread was available, it was perfectly permissible to buy from a non-Jewish baker. However, with no kosher bakeries in the small communities, Jews had to rely on non-Jewish bakers, but the widespread use of lard and other products gave rise to doubts as to the purity of the bread. As a consequence, Jews in small and remote communities often resorted to baking their own bread and *challot*. Since 2005 the certification of Kingsmill, Allinson, Burgen and Sunblest brands has meant that the largest bread producer in the United Kingdom is now kosher and available to Jews all over Scotland.

With the spread of the motor car, the provision of kosher foodstuffs was facilitated, as was the widespread advent of domestic freezers (prior to the 1960s, such appliances were often prohibitively expensive and difficult to obtain). In the twenty-first century the spread of the Internet has made the provision of imperishable items much easier. Now, the acquisition of perishable items, such as kosher meat, is possible in the remoter communities like Aberdeen and Inverness, in addition to the mis- or over-ordering at the supermarkets. This is ad hoc and unpredictable, but when such an event does occur, a message goes around the community and a rush to obtain said scarce supplies of meat ensues. The alternative is a five-hour round trip drive to either Edinburgh or Glasgow. Random items are sometimes available, such as Yarden humus and Palwin's kosher wine, from the supermarket, and online shops such as Titanic's in Manchester now deliver almost everything imaginable, too. *Challot, hamentashen*, and other baked products are often homemade.

If everyday *kashrut* created problems, the High Holy Days, in particular Passover, presented even more. A 2005 survey conducted among Jews in Scotland reported that this was a problem endemic to the whole country: "Almost all respondents, even those in the larger communities of the Central Belt, reported that they have to look beyond their local Jewish community to access particular goods or services. These ranged from Chanukah candles, kosher meat and Passover food to circumcision, burial services, and Jewish education."[28]

As a result of the difficulties, and despite the best of intentions, remote Jews did not and could not always maintain a strictly Orthodox lifestyle, and made compromises in their personal observance.[29] Indeed, living in a small community simply became too impractical for some, and members drifted away to the larger centers of Jewish population in Glasgow, Edinburgh, and points south. In Lerwick, for example, by 1934 all but one of the Greenwalds had left to settle in Glasgow, a trend often matched in small communities as

Jews wanted to settle "in civilization" with their "own folk."[30] It is a factor of British life in general that young adults from small communities either never return permanently from university or move away in search of a job or a suitable partner, fearing intermarriage and assimilation if they stayed. Others simply intermarried.

Yet, the remarkable feature of remote Jewish life is that genuine attempts *were* made to maintain Orthodox practice in the face of such difficulties. In Aberdeen, for example, two boys were circumcised in 1896, aged twelve years and four months, and seven years and five months, rather than the prescribed eight days! Even more interestingly, the minutes record that their mother wasn't even Jewish.[31] Jews opened their stores on Shabbat because business was brisk on Saturdays, and to close the shop would have meant financial ruin, although they may not have actually worked in them. Others forbade writing, sewing and homework on the Sabbath.[32] Many perhaps did not observe *kashrut* to the fullest extent of the laws—simply because of the practical difficulties of doing so—but attempts to keep within the guidelines were made at the very least. Yet, despite the increasing move away from Orthodox practice, unlike in other parts of Britain, and even in Glasgow and Edinburgh (which held its first Liberal bar mitzvah in 2006), there was no concomitant rise of Reform, Liberal, or Conservative Judaism. This might simply be because of the small numbers, but also because the remaining Jews continued to recognize and maintain a level of Orthodox Judaism. Besides, these compromises in personal practice are typical of Jews in Britain in general, and in places where a full-fledged Jewish existence is possible. Congregants may recognize the Orthodox line even if they don't personally practice it themselves.

Education

The provision of Jewish education, like everything else required by a traditional Jewish existence, remained a particular problem for the small Jewish communities. Even the simplest task of acquiring Jewish books was difficult in small and particularly remote communities, as such materials were not easily available or cheap. And, of course, the small, isolated, and remoter communities could not provide the extensive educational opportunities available in larger cities. Nonetheless, attempts to pass on the outlook and practices to a second generation were carried out in the face of these difficulties. All of the communities supported some sort of religious and Hebrew instruction at one time or another, even if the numbers of children requiring instruction remained quite small. As mentioned above, the resident ministers often doubled up as Hebrew teachers for the children, and Hebrew schools were established in all of the communities. These were regularly visited by outside educational authorities such as Chief Rabbi Hermann Adler when he visited Scotland, Herbert

M. Adler, Julius Jung, and Harold Levy in his capacity as the Inspector for the Central Council of Jewish Religious Education in the United Kingdom. Similarly, Rabbi Salis Daiches of the Edinburgh Hebrew Congregation often made it his business to visit the smaller communities outside of the Scottish capital.

In the absence of a minister or others qualified to carry out the teaching duties, Jewish education was provided on an informal basis. The key note was improvisation. Advantage was taken, when possible, of "the casual assistance by competent people, such as university students, summer visitors, High Festival officiators, and so on."[33] In Aberdeen, when doctoral student Emil Fackenheim arrived from Germany in 1939-1940 he was contracted to teach Hebrew classes. Yet, the high turnover of teachers meant that continuity became extremely difficult to achieve, as gaps opened up in the regular provision of Hebrew education. As Harold Levy noted, "Progress must be slow because of the paucity of the hours of tuition and also because absences are frequent."[34] He went on to say: "The pupils of course suffer by living in a really isolated community where services are irregular and Jewish life tenuous. Those whose parents do provide a full Jewish home are the more fortunate. All are fortunate in that their Jewish education is not being entirely neglected."[35]

And where numbers required the more systematic provision of education in, say, Glasgow, this never occurred in the small communities, and educational provision remained ad hoc, inadequate, improvisational in nature and often lacking in quality, provided by those with little formal teacher training. As a consequence of the lack of a structured and consistent Jewish education, "[T]he inability ... to pass on ... attitudes and knowledge meant that the children ... invariably came to adopt a way of life that was far less intensively Jewish than that of their mothers and fathers."[36] The problem was exacerbated and self-perpetuating: Jews who valued Jewish education moved away to provide a Jewish education for their children. The example of Walter Levy's family in Greenock here is representative, as he moved to Glasgow as a small child with his newly-widowed mother, as "she was anxious to secure her children's Jewish education."[37] The result was that those left behind may have been less steeped in Jewish tradition, practice, and law, which in turn led to the decline of small communities as young adults moved away in search of a suitable Jewish partner. As Ian Shein recalled, "Young people seeking further education did not return to the city [of Dundee] and it was extremely difficult to meet young Jewish company."[38]

For those beyond these small urban communities in even remoter locations, such as Lerwick, Jewish education was near-impossible. The nearest Hebrew schools were often too far away. Even if the will and knowledge were present (which wasn't always necessarily the case, surely), parents were often too busy working, shopping, cooking, cleaning, and caring for their families. Yet, it was still possible to implant a strong sense of Jewishness in one's children. In the absence of educational provision in the small communities, families either sent their children away to be educated or relocated to bigger Jewish communities. As the *Jewish Chronicle* reported in 1926, "With the exception of the small Jewish settlements of Inverness and Aberdeen, where were scarcely any Jewish children left to be taught, through the removal of families to larger Jewish centres, all the smaller congregations in Scotland were now provided with Hebrew teachers."[39]

An insight into some of the problems for isolated Jews, which were also relevant for the small Jewish communities, comes from Dianne Wolfson, long-time headmistress of Calderwood Lodge in Glasgow. She was a daughter of Dr. and Mrs. Harold Sherry, Stoneyburn, by Bathgate, in West Lothian. In 1976 the *Jewish Echo* interviewed Dianne on the occasion of her appointment as headmistress at Calderwood Lodge. Although she spoke about the necessity of a Jewish day school in Glasgow, her thoughts also seem related to her own upbringing and early education in a non–Jewish environment: "No matter how well a Jewish child is instructed in most non-denominational schools, much of the creative work, music and atmosphere is geared at particular times to the major non–Jewish festivals.... This produces a conflict of identity."[40] This is not to say that Dianne suffered from an identity crisis, but it highlights what problems isolation could cause. At the same time, however, Valerie House felt, "Being part of small, isolated communities means my Judaism both as a religion and a culture is more important than when in a large community where everything is provided easily."[41]

Zionism, Charity, and Society

Zionism was a feature of small community life. As an expression of this, Jews in some of the small communities purchased shares at the cost of one pound each in the Jewish Colonial Trust. Dundee bought nine, Aberdeen six, Ayr five, Greenock four, and Falkirk one.[42] Zionist groups were in existence from 1905 onwards, including branches of the Jewish Territorial Organisation, J.N.F., *Dorshei Zion*, *B'nei Zion*, *B'nei Akiva*, and W.I.Z.O.

Each of the remote communities maintained Jewish communal social activities linked to their charitable obligations under Jewish law. A wide variety of charities, both in the United Kingdom and abroad, especially pre-state Palestine and Israel (as would be expected), received donations from the communities, however small. In 1910, *The Scotsman* reported that the Jewish poor of Aberdeen and Dundee "are well cared for by their own rabbis and the better-off people."[43] The source of this information was the Committee for the Conversion of the Jews of the General Assembly of the Church of Scotland, which possibly explains its lack of missionary activity among the Jews of Scotland. Often Zionist, social, and charitable events merged. Card evenings were typical. Ladies Guilds were established, and all of the communities supported discussion and youth groups, literary, and Zionist societies and the like at one time or another. Given their size relative to the other communities, Ayr and Dundee were particularly vigorous. The latter, in particular, maintained a Benevolent Society, Burial Society, the Ladies Holy Vestment Society, a J.N.F. Committee, Trades Advisory Council, and W.I.Z.O.[44] In 1956-57 it even established a *Bnei Akivah* group.[45] Where the student population was great enough, university Jewish Societies were also formed, notably in Aberdeen and Dundee. Indeed, as mentioned above, St. Andrews Jewish Society is currently growing at a rapid pace, and Aberdeen reformed its Jewish society in 2005 after it had been defunct for several years. As David Cesarani has pointed out, "These institutions were bedded into the communities which they served; they became the local institutional foci and also the points of reference for a second-generation identity."[46]

Yet, despite their small size and remoteness in some cases, these small communities did not escape the perennial problem of *schnorrers* (beggars; one who habitually takes advantage of the generosity of others; a parasite). Bennett Teff, who lived in Aberdeen, described them as those "mendicants [official and unofficial, individual and on behalf of groups] who had mapped out an itinerary which had covered the whole country, often with Aberdeen as the last port of call. Representatives came from religious schools (*yeshivot*), Zionist organizations, the Hebrew University, old peoples' homes, etc. all armed with the names and addresses of likely victims."[47]

The size as well as the remote and transient nature of these communities meant that they were not always marked by a rigid hierarchy as in other communities, particularly as those who would constitute such a hierarchy had either died or moved away. Typically, it would be fair to say that small Scottish Jewish communal life revolved around a hub of committed individuals or families who tended to dominate, forming the nucleus of the community at any one point. It is they who tried to get a *minyan* together or organize events. In Aberdeen, the Orkins, Shragos, and Shoshans have taken this responsibility at successive times. In 1970, *The Jewish Chronicle* reported, "As with the community, it is the Orkins who are the kingpins where the Jewish students are concerned. It is their hospitable kosher home over the years which has kneaded congregation and students together."[48] In Dundee, Harold Gillis kept the synagogue open single-handedly for many years, until he died and was replaced by Paul Spicker. Without Paul it was felt that the synagogue would have been closed.

Nonetheless, new members could integrate and contribute very quickly, if they wished, as the honors system and hierarchy that might be evident elsewhere was not so engrained in a small and remote community. The result is that such a community could provide a certain amount of flexibility for its members, particularly when it came to matters of faith and personal practice.

Conclusion 181

This fluidity perhaps created a chance for freedom within faith and practice not evident elsewhere, allowing new members to find their niche quickly and contribute as they see fit. Thus, the small size of the community enabled diversity and individuality, and was conducive to individual choice in practice and thought.

Anti-Semitism

So how were Jews looked upon in these predominantly Christian areas? Scotland is often described as one of the few European countries with no historical record of serious anti–Semitism, largely due to the lateness of Jewish settlement in the country and the partiality of the Presbyterian Scots for the Jews as the "People of the Book." It has become almost a cliché that Scotland has never witnessed anti–Semitic persecution of the type seen in every other European country. It has even been suggested that Jews, noting that Scotland's universities "had led the way in relation to education," allowing them to graduate in medicine for a long time before they could do so elsewhere, "may well have regarded this opportunity as an aspect of Scottish egalitarianism." And it was in Aberdeen, as we have seen, that the first Jews in the English-speaking world were allowed to take medical degrees, though there is no evidence as to how widely known this was. The newly arrived Eastern European Ashkenazi Jews of the late-nineteenth century would have had almost no contact with the earlier Sephardic arrivals from Spain and Portugal. As Suzanne Audrey has pointed out, "The majority of Jewish refugees in the 1880s and 1890s were less concerned with the right to read medicine at university than the ability to find a home, earn a living and practice their faith with the minimum of interference."[49]

There is also an argument that Scottish tolerance may be attributable to the affinities between Scottish Protestantism and the Hebrew bible. A parallel can be drawn with the United States, where the Pilgrims and Puritans perceived themselves as a modern-day incarnation of the Children of Israel:

[And] as "the People of the Book," the Jews and their beliefs have a fascination for a country much of whose religion was deep rooted in Scripture. Enough of the old Calvinism remains to prevent the Jew being regarded as an entire stranger, nor does the Jew in Scotland see himself as such.[50]

Similarly, John Toland, an early Enlightenment thinker, referred to a number of "resemblances so easily observable." Alas, he did not elaborate on those reasons, but they were enough that he saw them as "Reasons for Naturalizing the Jews in Great Britain and Ireland, on the Same Foot with All Other Nations."[51] Another example of such attitudes was the Reverend David McDougall, minister of Dalry Church, Edinburgh, and editor of the *Jewish Mis-*

sion Quarterly, who wrote of the similarities between Scottish Christians and Jews:

> Both alike had a love for the Old Testament; both had an ardent and consuming affection for their own land, combined with a capacity for settling in other lands and making money in them; both alike had simplicity of worship, a somewhat similar church government, and a veneration of the Sabbath.[52]

David Daiches recalled that his teachers and school friends in Edinburgh "had the Presbyterian respect for the People of the Book and regarded me with interest and sometimes even with a touch of awe."[53]

Perhaps, too, Jews and Scots share a perception of themselves as marginalized outsiders. As David Katz put it:

> In an age [the late seventeenth century] that prized linguistic precision, the Jews were notoriously difficult to define: they simply did not fit comfortably into any of the existing categories. They were undoubtedly "strangers," in religion, in language, in appearance, and in habits. But so were the Scots...[54]

And it may also be that Scottish sectarianism—the conflict between Protestants and Catholics—has meant that Jews were more likely to be ignored by their gentile neighbors than in less divided societies.[55]

Tom Devine argues that anti-Semitism was absent because most Jews did not compete directly with Scots or others in the labor market. The Jewish immigrants were not seeking menial labor, and, as we have seen, they clustered into a relatively few, self-contained trades. Their traditions of self-help and charity also pre-empted any suggestions that Jews were a drain on public welfare schemes, such as the Poor Law.[56] Whatever the reasons, Jews found Scotland to be a congenial and welcoming home.

Anti-Semitism, although not non-existent (as some might like to claim), both in terms of attitudes and practice, was limited up until very recently. Initially, there was suspicion among the locals when Jews began to arrive, as many had never seen Jews before. In time, however, they integrated well, and had no shame about their Jewish customs and observances. By and large, Jews were tolerated and treated with a respectful curiosity regarding "the sons of Abraham."[57] Neighbors were invited to observe festival celebrations and to taste typical Jewish foods. Many reports from the small communities, particularly at the end of the nineteenth and beginning of the twentieth centuries, report the presence of non–Jews at synagogue services and other events, as well as interfaith activities after the Second World War. Thus, the Jewish communities' relations with their wider non–Jewish communities were largely positive.

As a barometer of how they were treated by their non–Jewish neighbors, Jews were involved in the civic life of the towns and cities in which they settled. Jews met little or no problems in being elected to, and taking up public positions as, councilors, Members of Parliament, and Justices of the Peace, or representative posts in other organizations, such as the Masons. The appointments of Louis Bittiner, David Adams, Minnie Atkin, and David Wolfe in Greenock; Michael Marcus in Dundee; Isaac Sclar Dunfermline; and Lewis Morris in Inverness; as well Manny Shinwell in Hamilton; suggest a wider development in Scotland. Even more notable was the fact that Marcus and Adams were both outspoken Zionists. Neither was the case, as happened in Glasgow, Leeds, and London, that Jews were excluded from social and sporting clubs. Another measure of their integration is that Jews from all of the small communities fought and died in both world wars.

Ominous notes, however, were sounded. Church officials and missionaries in early nineteenth-century Aberdeen had expressed uniformly negative opinions of Jewish religious life and practice. Dr. Alexander Black, Professor of Divinity in Marischal College, was typical. Speaking at a meeting of ministers in Edinburgh in 1842, specifically dealing with the issue of converting Jews, Black called the Jewish oral traditions, that is the Talmud and other Rabbinic literature, "absurd and incoherent," while the writings of Jewish learned men were "not infrequently debased with barbarism." He regarded the synagogue service as irreverent and a "mournful proof of the absence of all religious feeling and of all spiritual knowledge and discernment." Jewish education was also inadequate, according to Black: the *Heder* system lacked reverence and a "perception of meaning," and he bemoaned the Jews' "lamentable ignorance of their own scriptures."[58]

Yet, even the Jewish Mission Committee of the Church of Scotland, bluntly known as the Committee for the Conversion of the Jews, strangely did not bother to target Jews in its own country. In c.1909, the General Assembly of the Scottish Church remitted to this Committee "the question of mission work among the Jews in Scotland"; and it duly inquired into the number of Jews in Scotland and into whether missionary work was being carried out among them. In Aberdeen, it was found that there was none, as it was "understood that their poor are well cared for by their own rabbis and the better-off people."[59]

In 1936 the Reverend Dr. James Black of Edinburgh noticed that discrimination against Jews was "subtly creeping in" to Scotland, having seen shop posters stating, "No Jew need apply."[60] But while the histories of Aberdeen and Inverness show that fascism, as represented by the British Union of Fascists, did have some support in Scotland, this was limited and short-lived; and furthermore, there was no evidence that the signs the Reverend Black saw in Edinburgh were replicated in the smaller communities. Yet, the experience of Dundee's Jews, particularly surrounding issues connected with Israel, does stand out in this respect. An issue only touched upon in this study are the experiences of single families and individuals, simply for lack of evidence, but we do know that they could also encounter anti–Jewishness, such as the 1954 *Jewish Echo* report about an "Anti-Semitic Advertisement" in the *Banffshire Journal and Northern Farmer*.

A 2005 survey conducted among Jews in Scotland suggests that perceptions of anti-Semitism might be on the increase:

> Approximately 15% of respondents said that their friends and neighbours did not know they were Jewish. This is probably not surprising given that over 50% of respondents reported that they had experienced antisemitism.
> Several respondents mentioned that Jewish people often find themselves being identified very closely with Israel and that criticism of the Israeli government and its policy tends to impact negatively on the Scottish Jewish community. One respondent informed us that an internet directory providing information about local services included both anti-Israel and antisemitic comments next to the address and contact details of the local synagogue under the heading of "Jews." He described the directory as "an invitation to come and throw stones at our windows."[61]

The report concluded, "Antisemitism—and the fear of antisemitism—are a significant issue for Jewish people throughout Scotland," leading to "some people's hesitancy to reveal that they are Jewish, in many cases due to a fear of triggering antisemitic incidents."[62] Yet, it is not known how many of these respondents live in small communities, as the survey included Glasgow and Edinburgh. Mark Gardner, of the Community Security Trust, added:

> It is also the case that where a community is relatively small, cases of anti-Semitism may be less likely to be publicised as victims feel isolated and are unwilling to draw further attention to themselves. Nevertheless, anecdotal and statistical evidence does suggest that Scottish Jewish communities are caught in the same global trend as other Diaspora communities around the world, whereby hatred of Israel is serving to raise the levels of anti-Semitic abuse per se.[63]

Law and Crime

An area which warrants further study is the involvement of Jews with the law and crime, either as victims or perpetrators. Often, as we have seen, it is how we know that Jews were located in the more far-flung places. Such a study has been conducted with reference to South Wales before the First World War.[64] As in South Wales, a brief survey of our communities shows that Jews were not typically involved in either violent or sexual crimes (with the exception of Lazarus and Chano Silver in Inverness, and Abraham and Rachel Ross in Ayr). While much has been written about Oscar Slater, this aspect of Scottish Jewish history is somewhat neglected and begs deeper exploration.

The Future

It is hoped that this brief study of Scotland's small Jewish communities, as well as other individuals and families scattered throughout that country, will begin to scratch the surface of a subject hitherto neglected. To return to a

Conclusion   185

theme I raised at the very outset, the term "Anglo-Jewry" has shaped the study of the Jewish communities in Britain by either subsuming the experiences of the non–Anglo communities into the larger English ones, or by precluding their study altogether. As a consequence, there are still further questions to ask, in addition to those raised above. For example, what impact did the Jews of these small communities have on their non–Jewish neighbors and wider communities, and what was the long-lasting effect on the Jewishness of these remote Jews?

How particular patterns of Jewish life in small communities differed from those in larger ones is what this book has aimed to explore. Through these seven case studies, perhaps our notions of Jews in small, remote, and isolated communities can be widened. It is clear that the internal dynamics of a small community differ greatly from those of larger ones, and, in the words of Lee Shai Weissbach, "Small Jewish communities were not simply miniature versions of larger Jewish centers but, rather, alternative types of settlement in many respects."[65] It is also clear that our notion of a "community" has to be fluid and flexible. Given the size of the Scottish landmass and the dispersal of Jewish individuals and families throughout it, congregations often included those who lived some distance from the synagogue and, for this reason, could not attend or participate as much as they desired, but still felt a sense of community and hence wanted to be included in it. There were numerous other Scottish towns and villages, as we have seen, where a single Jewish family or individual lived as Jewish doctor, or shopkeeper, furrier, draper, jeweler, and hairdresser.

It is in the wish that the overwhelming pessimism with which this topic has been treated in the past can be replaced with an optimism that, while many of these small communities have not survived, given the right conditions, not only can they continue to exist but they can thrive, too. It is true that such communities do suffer from persistent problems, as outlined by a 1959 report prepared by the Board of Deputies of British Jews entitled "The Problems of the Smaller Jewish Communities." The "Summary and Conclusions" section listed the following general problems:

- Lack of ministerial and teaching services, finances and sense of communal responsibility.
- Infrequency of services, insufficiency of classes for varied age groups, uncertainty of obtaining officiants for High Festivals, and the maintenance of communal life outside the orbit of the synagogue.
- Apathy: "There are in many small communities, as also in large towns, a number of Jewish families who are not attached to the Synagogue, and who take no part whatever in communal activities. In one or two areas the 'unattached' may constitute 50% of the estimated local Jewish population."
- Financial problems leading to the inability to pay for ministers and teachers. Often, Hebrew education was paid for out of parents' own pockets.
- Services typically held on Friday nights and not Shabbat.[66]

Conclusion

Yet, these "problems" also affect far larger communities, too. This means that a small community should not automatically be militated against. Indeed, Malcolm Weisman, visiting minister to the small communities in the United Kingdom, noted how many of the small communities "often put bigger urban communities to shame by their activity." He continued, "Both religious and cultural ... festivals, both major and minor, are celebrated in tiny communities in a manner which can be as spiritually inspiring as the way they are observed in the larger communities."[67]

Furthermore, while some of the small communities may have disappeared, others are growing or are permanent fixtures. A report conducted by the Scottish Council of Jewish Communities in 2005 actually noted a "demographic stability," in contrast to the larger communities:

> Whilst the trend is for people, particularly young people, to move away from the larger Scottish Jewish communities of East Renfrewshire, Glasgow and Edinburgh to still larger communities in Manchester, London and Israel, the population in the smaller Scottish Jewish communities is much more stable and may even be increasing slightly. The majority of respondents in the smaller communities had lived there for more than 10 years and anticipated that they would still live there in five years time. However, a significant minority of people in the smaller communities had moved to Scotland within the last five years and the majority of these also expected to be living in the same place in five years time.[68]

It also noted that there "may be a small increase in the Jewish population in the more rural and isolated areas of Scotland," and that "Living away from a settled Jewish community does not imply that people do not require access to specifically Jewish goods or services."[69] The Scottish Council of Jewish Communities recognizes these issues and is actively taking steps to remedy them, providing a clear model for other organizations to follow. Even the *Jewish Chronicle* recognized over one hundred years ago that:

> Nor should all the light be concentrated on the metropolis and the provinces left in total darkness. The problems of provincial Jewry are also the problems of Anglo-Jewry.... The welfare of provincial Jewry is the welfare of London Jewry, and, to a still greater extent, the troubles of the small congregations in the country react on the Jewish life of the Metropolis. Unfortunately, hitherto these small congregations have, for the most part, been greatly neglected.... These small communities of fifty or a hundred souls are the outposts of Anglo-Jewry; they represent Judaism and Jewry in the eyes of the country population.[70]

Small and remote Jewish communities are nothing new to Jewish life. As Diana Pinto has pointed out, "Pre–eighteenth-century European Jewry was numerically small, scattered in many communities but nevertheless very much present." She continued:

> There is no reason why small but committed communities cannot survive in the contemporary world, when European Jewish networks can easily provide the necessary "marriage pool" and cultural contacts. Jews, even in tiny homeopathic doses, can create a strong Jewish presence in any society. The "electronic fax Jew" need no

longer feel isolated and lost. It is important to have a Jewish presence in as many places as possible as living proof of a pluralist Jewish identity. World Jewry cannot be completely contained in one nation-state with its own internal and external problems.[71]

The ongoing communities of Aberdeen and Dundee, together with the Jewish Network of Argyll and the Highlands, are living proof of this thesis in Scotland.

Appendix A

Figures for the Size of the Communities Drawn from the Jewish Year Book, 1896–2008

Year	Aberdeen	Ayr	Dundee	Dunfermline	Falkirk	Greenock	Inverness
1896	12*		50				
1897	18*		127				
1898	17*		127				
1899	17*		160				
1900	17*		160				
1901	17*		160				
1902	17*		110				
1903	23*		110				
1904	23*		142				
1905	23*		149				18**
1906	23*		152			30*	18**
1907	23*		152			30*	18**
1908	23*		152			30*	18**
1909	23*		152			30*	18**
1910	25*		152			20	18
1911	25*		152			20	18
1912	20*		152			20	18
1913	20*		152			20	18
1914	20*		142			14	18
1915	20*		120			16	18
1916	20*		120			16	18
1917	20*		120			16	18
1918	18*		120			19	18
1919	18*		120			19	18
1920	18*		100			19	18
1921	18*		100			19	18
1922	18*		100			19	18
1923	18*		100			12	18
1924	18*		100				
1925							
1926							
1927	56		10				108
1928	56		100				180

189

Appendix A

Year	Aberdeen	Ayr	Dundee	Dunfermline	Falkirk	Greenock	Inverness
1929							
1930							
1931							
1932							
1933							
1934							
1935	56		100				108
1936	56		100				108
1937	56		100				108
1938	56		100				108
1939	50	60	117	30*	62	40	16
1940	40	60	117	30*	62	40	16
1941							
1942							
1943							
1944							
1945	50	60	117	30*	62	40	16
1946							
1947	50	60	35**	30*			16
1948	50	160	35**	30*			16
1949	50	160	35**	30*			16
1950	50	160	117	30*			20
1951	50	160	100	25			5**
1952	50	160	100				20**
1953	50	160	100				20**
1954	50	160	89				12
1955	181	68	89				12
1956	175	68	89				12
1957	70	68	89				12
1958							
1959	85	68	89				12
1960	85	68	89				12
1961	85	68	89				12
1962	40	68	84				12
1963	20	68	84				12
1964	20	68	84				12
1965	20	68	84				12
1966	50	68	84				12
1967	50	40	84				12
1968	50	40	84				12
1969	50	40	84				12
1970	50	40	84				
1971	50	40	84				
1972	40	40	84				
1973	40	40	84				
1974	40	40	84				
1975	40	40	84				
1976	40	40	84				
1977	40	40	84				
1978							

Figures for the Size of the Communities

Year	Aberdeen	Ayr	Dundee	Dunfermline	Falkirk	Greenock	Inverness
1979	40	40	84				
1980	40	40	84				
1981	30	40	80				
1982	38	40	80				
1983	39	40	80				
1984	39/40	40	80				
1985	40		45				
1986	40		45				
1987	40		45				
1988	40		12				
1989	40		12				
1990	40		12				
1991	30		22				
1992	30		22				
1993	30		22				
1994	30		22				
1995	30		22				
1996	30		22				
1997	30		22				
1998	30		22				
1999	30		22				
2000	30		22				
2001	30		22				
2002	30		22				
2003	30		22				
2004	30		22				
2005	30		22				
2006	30		22				
2007	30		22				
2008	30		22				
2009	30		22				

* Seat holders
** Families

Appendix B
"A New Letter"

Gershom Scholem, in his *Sabbatai Sevi*, described "A New Letter" as "An instructive example ... [of reports] from the Orient regarding the movement of the lost tribes [which] arrived in England, and quickly spread among chiliast circles where they begat more rumors."[1] The letter, Scholem states, was published by Robert Boulter, who "took a great interest in the imminent redemption of Israel, and printed a number of pamphlets during the early days of the Sabbatian movement."[2] Michael McKeown added, "Rumors that the Jews, and especially the Ten Tribes, were marching toward Jerusalem first became fairly common in England in the autumn of 1665."[3] The initials "R.R." "refer to the compiler in London who collected and edited the various pamphlets and not to the letter writer in Aberdeen."[4] Protestant millenarians showed a great interest in the lost ten tribes, as they saw the conversion of all the descendants of the ancient Israelites as a necessary precondition for the return of the Messiah.[5] Immediately prior to the Whitehall Conference in 1655, called by Oliver Cromwell's government in order to discuss the desirability of Jewish resettlement in England, "the debate over the lost ten tribes was at the peak of its intensity," according to David Katz, and after 1665 "the issue of the lost ten tribes became meshed with the speculations revolving around the activities of the Sabbatai Sevi."[6]

But the letter is highly controversial. Peter Davidson argues that it is a fiction, the product of a London imagination. References to "sails of satin" and "ropes of silk" were a popular motif in folk literature, and had the ship possessed them, it is doubtful that it would even have made it out of port. No such position of the Professor of Tongues and Languages then existed.[7] Rather, suggests Davidson, the letter probably arose from the general English fascination with the Sabbatian movement in the seventeenth century, as exemplified by the concerns of John Dryden's poem "Annus Mirabilis."[8] As Michael McKeown states of the Sabbatai Tsvi in England:

> People of diverse backgrounds and commitments—royalist, republicans, amateur scientists, professional astrologers, Puritan prophets—were ready to entertain news of him with some enthusiasm, and many made a natural and ingenuous connection in their minds between the news of the Sabbatai and the other wonders and judgments which they, among others, anticipated for 1666.[9]

Williamson also notes that the letter's tone was "rather like much seventh-century utopian literature."[10]

The only significance of the Aberdeen location is in its remoteness, making the facts unverifiable to a London audience.

Scholem adds, "There is a *prima facie* case for suspecting Christian writers of having invented some of these reports by way of embellishment of the news of a messianic revival among the Jews."[11] Referring to the *Letter from Aberdeen*, he lists the contemporary and non–Jewish (most likely Protestant) embellishments:

"Liberty of Conscience" was a major issue at the time, and a political slogan with the Protestant sects in England. It was undoubtedly reassuring to be able to attribute the same ideal to the tribes of Israel. The anti–Turkish feeling, too, is not genuinely Jewish. The Jewish masses living under Muslim rule certainly did not harbour excessively warm pro-Turkish sentiments, yet it is evident that the particular note of hostility sound by the letter from Aberdeen carries a different undertone. The utter ruin and extirpation of the Turks—and Turks in this context is usually synonymous with Muslims in general—was a Christian chiliast rather than a Jewish ideal.[12]

He insists, however, that such letters and pamphlets should not be thought complete fabrications:

[R]umours about the lost tribes were afoot even before Christian writers had heard about the Jewish messianic movement. The subject is, in fact, far more complicated. The earliest, albeit vague and hazy, reports that reached some oriental and North African communities had already passed through a "filter" of popular legend, which had removed all concrete ad specific details and added instead a good many imaginary elements. This process was not necessarily due to conscious manipulation or censorship. It would certainly be wrong to represent these reports as emanating from Europe and then awakening an echo in the oriental Jewish communities. The news progressed in the opposite direction. After the first vague reports about tribes in the East had reached Europe toward the end of the summer of 1665, they were taken up and further embellished by Christian writers with millenarian inclinations.[13]

Consequently, for Scholem, the letter (which "contains many points of interest," not least "the explicit reference to earlier reports of the same subject... may be to the letters from Salé and Egypt, or possibly to some earlier printed pamphlets that are lost") is an example of an originally Jewish report which had "acquired a new coloring" as it "passed through Christian hands," for "Those engaged in spreading the news did not fail to embellish it with details of topical interest by way of a contribution to contemporary discussion."[14] Needless to say, further research into this letter and whether it holds any truth of the evidence of the visitation of Jews to Aberdeen in the seventeenth century is required.

Appendix C
Burials in the Jewish Section of Grove Cemetery, Aberdeen*

Name	Born	Died	Age
Reyna Renee Altares, wife of Ramsey		1993	75
David Hyman Barnett	1901	1986	
Gertrude Barnett, wife of James Grey		1955	56
Henry Samuel Barnett, husband of Matilda Myers		1957	
Isaac Barnett, husband of Hannah H.		1932	88
Magdalene Barnett	1908	1963	
Rebecca Barnett, daughter of Isaac		1914	18
Hannah Harris Bernstein, wife of Isaac		1936	73
Caroline Bittiner, widow of Max B.		1921	72
Julius Bittiner		1958	72
Leopold Bittiner		1972	32
Louis Bittiner, husband of Marie		1947	73
Irene Buchner	1923	1994	
Ben Burke, husband of Frances		1993	87
Frances Josephine Burke, wife of Ben		1993	88
Rachael Burton		1950	
Theodore Chanock, son of Mr. J.		1923	18
Lena Cohen, nee Lann, wife of Louis Cohen		1989	
Louis Cohen		2004	91
Ben Collins, husband of Dorothy		1989	87
Frida Cossman-Springer (born Cologne)	1889	1948	
Louis Cowan, husband of Mary		1982	69
Boris Bernard Diamantstein	1882	1969	
Sophie Diamantstein, wife of Bernard	1891	1976	
Emma Gertrude Sarah (Silberberg) Fackenheim		1988	
Dr. Julius Fackenheim	1884	1970	
Meta Fackenheim, nee Schlesinger		1951	
Abraham Fineberg		1911	
Edward Flateau		1942?	18
David Franklin		1938	55
Harry Goldberg			22
Barnett Gordon		1941	
Albert Gordon, husband of Rachel		1981	

*Compiled by Harvey Kaplan, based on a video made by Arnold Rabinowitz, 1995.

Burials in the Jewish Section of Grove Cemetery

Name	Born	Died	Age
Rachel Gerta Gordon, wife of Albert		1982	
Leah Grant		1957	63
Leah Rebecca Grant		1987	
Myer Grant		1960	72
Violet Hajnal, nee Borovic	1903	1968	
David Hall, husband of Catherine Burns		1919	
Annie (Hannah) Harris		1989	81
Morris Harris		1941	
Abe Cowan Jablonsky, husband of Annie Angus (d 1985)		1958	63
Sarah Jablonsky		1971	74
Bernard Jackson		1932	78
Freda Kalson		1985	79
Myer Kalson		1978	81
Abraham Katz, husband of Eleanor Taylor	1910	1971	
Aron Beer Konig	1873	1962	
Bertha Konig	1880	1972	
Bella Wolfe Lann		1958	75
Edith Lann		1990	86?
Israel Lann		1953	75
Bernard Mandell (Mandelcwajg) (Senior Lecturer; b. Lodz)	1912	1972	
Joseph Nathan		1936	
Rabbi Dr. Gustav Pfingst (son of Max Pfingst/Amelie Schott; d. 1942, Europe)	1900	1957	
Rosa (Altmann) Pfingst	1893	1975	
Eileen (?) Ross		1931	
Ruth Elizabeth Ross (b. Adelaide, Australia) (younger daughter of Paul & Gerti Ross)	1942	1980	
Frances Rubenstein, widow of late Morris Harris		1968	
Sarah Silver, wife of Barnett Gordon		1927	64
David & Ellis Silverman (twins)		1917	
Alexander Sliufko			74
Fanny Tublusky, wife of I. Leveson		1914	

Appendix D
Burials in the Jewish Section of Bow Road Cemetery, Greenock

Surname	Given Name	Age	Died
Cominskie	Emanuel	Stillborn	2 April, 1908
Levy		One day	10 June, 1908
Wyse	Pearl	Ten weeks	5 January, 1911
Stone	Alyman	34	18 January, 1911
Abrams	Samuel	73	18 September, 1911
Brown	William	Two weeks	9 October, 1916
Jacobs	Peter	70	17 February, 1919
Shenken	Annie	Six months	27 March, 1922
Vinitskey	Isaac Hyman	44	11 September, 1922
		Stillborn	12 February, 1923
Ferguson	Isabella	2	7 May, 1923
Friedman	Abraham		8 January, 1924
Morris	Matthew	34	17 May, 1934
Morris	Moses		11 August, 1936
Morris	Rachel	70	10 February, 1944
Ferguson	Hanna	65	27 March, 1945

Appendix E
Burials in the Jewish Section of Tomnahurich Cemetery, Inverness*

Surname	Given Name	Age	Died
Cooper	Hyman	12	1906
Wimberg	Nathan		1908
Levie	Joseph	61	1908
Arkush	Jacob	Four days	1908
Finkelstein			1910
Coats	Esther	Thirteen months	1911
Silver	Chano	37	1911
Gavin			1912
Golumb	Edith	Fifteen months	1912
Herschberg			1913
Golumb	Rachel	70	1921
Joseph	Edith	Ten months	1926
Morris	Stillborn		1929
Lisman	John	46	1930
Lipman	Jack Emmanuel	Two days	1931
Fieber	Bella		1942
Lisman	Bella	69	1942
Cymbalist (née Strauss)	Rosa/Rosie	73	1970
Glass	Zygmunt	54	1973
Glass	Jerzy George	59	1981
Sherick	Nathaniel	88	1989
Solomons	Bessie		1997
Gavin	Lilian	84	2002

* The majority of this information comes from a list of burials held by the SJAC as derived by the Inverness City Council. Additional information has been supplied by Rhona Hay.

Appendix F

List of Children Enrolled in Falkirk Schools

1) Pupil:	Leah Bulbin	Rebecca Bulbin	Henry Bulbin
2) School:	Falkirk High (Primary)	Falkirk High (Primary)	Falkirk High
3) Admission #	1015	1016	
4) Admission date:	1/9/1903	1/9/1903	5/9/1904
5) D-O-B:	29/6/1898	17/11/1896	1/10/1891
6) Father's name:	Abraham	Abraham	Abraham
7) Occupation:	Traveller		
8) Address:	9 Melville Street	9 Melville Street	9 Melville Street
9) Other Info:			Class V, May 1905

1) **David Bulbin**	**Morris Rosenberg**	**David Cohen**	**Rose Kaplan**
2) Falkirk High (Primary)	Falkirk High (Primary)	Falkirk High (Primary)	Falkirk High
3)	1422		
4) 27/4/1908	27/4/1908	19/3/1906	1/9/1904
5) 12/6/1902	6/12/1902	27/1/1898	1/4/1892
6) Edwin	Simon	Louis	Samuel
7)			
8) 9 Melville Street	28 Fir Street	17 Canfield Street	28 Fir Street
9)			From New York November 1904

1) **Helen Kaplan**	**Rebecca Rifkin**	**Leah Rifkin**	**Morna Rifkin**
2) Falkirk High	Falkirk High	Falkirk High	Falkirk High
3)		1485	1635
4) 5/9/1904	7/9/1904	6/5/1908	10/4/1912
5) 10/8/1893	22/5/1901	2/9/1903	14/3/1905
6) Samuel	Harry Rifkin	Harry	Harris
7)			Drapery Traveller
8) 28 Fir Street 57 Wallace Street	25 Glebe Street	25 Glebe Street	25 Glebe Street
9) Went to Elementary High			

1) **Isaac Spilg**	**Wolf Spilg**	**Reuben Spilg**	**Pauline Kaplan**
2) Victoria Park	Victoria Park	Victoria Park	Victoria Park
3) 1693	1694	3131	2258
4) 30/5/1904	30/5/1904	11/8/1908	4/9/1905
5) 15/9/1895	11/3/1894	15/5/1897	12/7/1897
6) Gershon	Gershon		Samuel
7)			

List of Children Enrolled in Falkirk Schools

8) 25 Glebe Street   25 Glebe Street
9) Came from Camden Street Glasgow South

28 Firs Street
Went to Falkirk High Jun II

1) Roland Sandberg (?)	Fanny Lewis	Rosa Spilg	Hillel Spilg
2) Victoria Park	Comely Park	Comely Park	Comely Park
3) 3162	1437	1934	
4) 11/8/1908	20/4/1903	31/5/1905	31/5/1905
5) 22/11/1901	3/11/1897	17/8/1898	27/6/1894
6) Dora Sandberg	Abraham	Max	Max
7)			
8) Garrison Chambers	Williams Building	Williamson Street (?)	Melrose Place
9) left 9/10/1915, Reason: Exemption		Last school: Gorbals; left school August 1912	Last School: Gorbals; left CP August 1907 Exemption by Board

1) Laura Spilg	Louis Camenski	Harry Camenski	
2) Comely Park	Comley Park	Comely Park	
3) 1955	3153	3164	
4) 5/6/1905	23/8/1909	23/8/1909	
5) 24/5/1896	17/8/1904	27/8/1899	
6) Max	Isaac	Isaac	
7)			
8) Melrose Place	38 Melrose Place	38 Melrose Place	
9) Came from Gorbals; Left August 1910	Came from Boness Public; Left Dec. 1913; Went to Greenside Glasgow	From Greenside St. Glasgow (?); left August 1913 because of age	

1) Matilda Camenski	Fanny Camenski	Fanny Camenski	Dora Camenski
2) Comely Park	Comely Park	Comely Park	Comely Park
3) 3173	3182	3850	3851
4) 23/8/09	30/8/09	10/1/1912	10/1/1912
5) 22/8/01	2/1/1897	18/8/1900	15/11/1901
6) Isaac	Isaac	Max	Max
7)			
8) 38 Melrose Place	38 Melrose Place	172 High Street	172 High Street
9) Came from Boness; went to Greenside School, Glasgow	Last school: Boness; left January 1911, of age to leave	Came from Boness	Came from Boness

1) Leah Camenski	Lionel Turiansky	David Rosenberg	Samuel Horowitz
2) Comely Park	Falkirk High	Falkirk High	Falkirk High
3) 3852	1652	1629	2263
4) 10/1/1912	11/5/1910	4/10/1912	4/9/1916
5) 25/12/1902		14/3/1905	28/5/1906
6) Max		Simon	
7)		General Dealer	
8) 172 High Street		Lesley Place (Pleasance)	
9) Left 1913, back to Boness	Last school: Pollokshields		

Appendix F

1) **Benjamin Rosenberg**
2) Falkirk High
3) 1810
4) 12/3/1912
5) 10/2/1907
6) Simon
7) Traveller
8) 2 Pleasance Square
9)

Lily Benson
Falkirk High
1463
Around 1908

Alice Carnovsky
Comely Park
3644
15/5/1911
29/12/1905
Morris

Kerse Lane
Came from Northern School; left to go to High School

Lewis Cemblar
Falkirk High
2344
18/4/1917
11/5/1911
Wolf
Traveller
4 Melrose Place

1) **Hyman Rosenberg**
2) Falkirk High
3) 2453
4) September 1918
5) 26/11/1913
6) S. Rosenberg
7) Traveller
8) 2 Pleasance Square
9)

Annie Marks
Falkirk High
2587
20/10/1919
30/3/1913
Max
Jewellery Traveller

Glebe Street

Hyman Cemblar
Falkirk High
3027
1924

Hilda May Sadler
Victoria
613
15/8/1911
19/5/1900
Joshua A Sadler

Mary Court
Left 14/12/1914

1) **Dorothea Sadler**
2) Victoria
3) 1153
4) 12/8/1913
5) 14/12/1901
6) Joshua A Sadler
7)
8) Ingleside Pleasance
9)

Harold Taylor
Victoria
3565
28/4/1924
16/3/1919
Louis
Shopkeeper

49 Firs Street
Went to High School 31/8/1930; exempt from religion education

Jacky Levenson
Comely Park
65
19/2/1923
19/7/1919
Morris
Shoemaker

25 Glebe Street
Moved to Glasgow December 1926

Leah Levenson
Comely Park
7231
25/1/1926
3/9/1920
Morris

25 Glebe Street
Moved to Glasgow 3/12/26

Glossary of Hebrew and Yiddish Terms

Aliyah: lit. "going up." Emigration to Israel.

Bar Mitzvah: ceremony marking the thirteenth birthday, the age at which the Jewish male achieves religious responsibility.

Bat Mitzvah: ceremony marking the twelfth birthday, the age at which the Jewish female achieves religious responsibility.

Beth Din: Jewish court of law.

Bnei Akivah: lit. "sons of Akivah." Orthodox and Zionist Jewish Youth Group.

B'nei Zion: lit. "sons of Zion."

Brachah: religious benediction/blessing.

Brit Milah: Jewish covenantal circumcision.

Challah: special bread eaten on Friday nights, Saturdays, and festival days.

Challot: plural of *challah*.

Chatan Bereshit: lit. "bridegroom of Genesis." Those honored with being called to the reading which commences the Torah.

Chatan Torah: lit. "bridegroom of the Torah." Those honored with being called to the reading which concludes the Torah.

Chazan: cantor or leader of the synagogue prayers.

Cheder/Heder: Hebrew/religious classes.

Chevra kadisha: lit. "holy brotherhood." A Jewish burial society.

Chevrah Torah: lit. "Torah brotherhood." A Torah study group.

Chupah: marriage canopy.

Daf Hayomi: the daily study of a page of the Talmud.

Dorshei Zion: lit. "Seekers of Zion." Zionist Group.

Hamentashen: lit. "Haman's ears" or "Haman's pocketbooks." A pastry traditionally eaten on the Jewish festival of Purim.

Ivrit b'Ivrit: lit. "Hebrew in Hebrew." Method of teaching the Hebrew language by only using the medium of the Hebrew language.

Kashrut: the Jewish dietary laws.

Keren Hayesod: Palestine Foundation Fund.

Kosher: that which conforms to the Jewish dietary laws.

Megillat Esther: the Book of Esther.

Mehitzha: a partition segregating men and women typically found in Orthodox synagogues.

Menorah: nine-branched candelabrum used on the Jewish festival of Chanukah.

Mikveh: special bath primarily used by married women to keep the laws of family purity.

Mikvaot: plural of *mikveh*.

Minyan: the minimum number of ten Jewish males over the age of thirteen required for an Orthodox communal religious service. Although some denominations include women in the count, since all of these communities were Orthodox, *minyan* is only used here to refer to men.

Minyanim: plural of *minyan*.

Mogen Dovid: lit. "Shield of David." Star of David.

Mohel: trained person responsible for carrying out the procedure of Jewish circumcision.

Ohel: lit. "tent." Usually refers to a structure built over a grave.

Ovel: mourner.

Sefer Torah: Torah scroll comprising the five books of Moses read on an annual cycle.

Schnorrer: beggar.

Shabbes Goyim: non–Jewish neighbors asked to perform duties on the Sabbath forbidden to Jews, such as lighting fires.

Shul: synagogue.

Shechita/h: Jewish method of humane slaughter in which the animal's jugular and carotids are cut with a single swift stroke of an extremely sharp knife, severing all blood supply to the brain, producing instant unconsciousness. *Shechita/h* is carried out by a *Shochet*.

Shiur: informal lecture.

Shochet: lit. "butcher." Someone with years of religious and veterinary training which emphasizes the welfare of the animal.

Siddur: lit. "ordered." Jewish daily prayer book.

Sifrei Torah: plural of *sefer Torah*.

Siyum: lit. "completion" or "conclusion." Custom of completing a Talmudic Tractate with a discourse followed by a festive meal.

Sukkot: lit. "booths." Jewish festival commemorating the wandering of the Hebrews in the desert following the exodus from Egypt.

Taharah: the process of preparing a Jewish dead body for burial.

Tzedakah: lit. "righteousness." Charity.

W.I.Z.O.: Women's International Zionist Organization.

Yarzheit: lit. "year time." Anniversary of a death.

Yeshivot: religious schools.

Chapter Notes

Introduction

1. Salis Daiches, "The Jew in Scotland," *Records of the Scottish Church History Society, Vol. III*, ed. W.J. Couper and Robert McKinlay (Edinburgh: The Scottish Church History Society, 1929), p. 196.
2. Cited in Kenneth Collins, *Second City Jewry: The Jews of Glasgow in the Age of Expansion, 1790–1919* (Glasgow: Scottish Jewish Archives, 1990), p. 15.
3. Cecil Roth, *A History of the Jews in England* (Oxford: Clarendon, 1941), p. 92.
4. James Howell, *The Wonderful and Most Deplorable History of the Latter Times of the Jews* (London, 1653), cited in David S. Katz, *Philo-Semitism and the Readmission of the Jews to England, 1603–1655* (Oxford: Clarendon, 1982), p. 191.
5. John Toland, *Reasons for Naturalizing the Jews in Great Britain and Ireland, on the Same Foot with All Other Nations* (London, 1914), cited in David S. Katz, *The Jews in the History of England, 1845–1850* (Oxford: Clarendon, 1996), p. 188.
6. A.M. Hyamson, *A History of the Jews of England* (Oxford: Oxford University Press, 1941), p. 7.
7. Abraham Levy, *The Origins of Scottish Jewry*, reprint of a paper read before the Jewish Historical Society of England, 13 January, 1958, place and date of printing unknown.
8. *The Universal Jewish Encyclopedia*, Vol. 9 (New York: 1948), p. 447.
9. Nathan Abrams and Harvey Kaplan, "Jews in Scotland: Myth and Reality," *History Scotland*, 6:4 (July/August 2006), p. 38.
10. Levy, *The Origins of Scottish Jewry*, p. 1.
11. Patricia Skinner, "Introduction: Jewish in Medieval Britain and Europe," in *The Jews in Medieval Britain: Historical, Literary and Archaeological Perspectives*, ed. Patricia Skinner (Woodbridge: Boydell, 2003), pp. 2–3.
12. Skinner, "Introduction," p. 3.
13. Elizabeth Caldwell Hirschman and Donald N. Yates, *When Scotland Was Jewish: DNA Evidence, Archaeology, Analysis of Migrations and Public and Family Records Show Twelfth Century Semitic Roots* (North Carolina and London: McFarland, 2007), p. 45.
14. Skinner, "Introduction," pp. 2–3.
15. David Ditchburn, *Scotland and Europe: The Medieval Kingdom and Its Contacts with Christendom, 1241–1560* (East Linton: Tuckwell, 2000), p. 34.
16. Harvey Kaplan, "Review of *When Scotland Was Jewish: DNA Evidence, Archaeology, Analysis of Migrations and Public and Family Records Show Twelfth Century Semitic Roots* by Elizabeth Caldwell Hirschman and Donald N. Yates," *Jewish Culture and History* (forthcoming).
17. Henry Maitles, "Attitudes to Jewish Immigration in the West of Scotland to 1905," *Scottish Economic & Social History*, 15 (1995), p. 45.
18. William Cunningham, "Differences of Economic Development in England and Scotland," *Scottish Historical Review*, 13 (1916), p. 170.
19. Sidney Caplan, "Jews in Scotland in Medieval Times," unpublished ms. in author's possession.
20. Hirschman and Yates, *When Scotland Was Jewish*, p. 1.
21. *Ibid.*, p. 50.
22. *Ibid.*, p. 155.
23. Kenneth Collins, *Go and Learn: The International Story of Jews and Medicine in Scotland* (Aberdeen: Aberdeen University Press, 1988), p. 57.
24. Cited in Tali Joan Segal, "The 5th Corner," *Four Corners*, 15 (September 2007).
25. Levy, *The Origins of Scottish Jewry*, p. 1; William Ferguson, *Scotland: 1689 to the Present* (Edinburgh: Oliver & Boyd, 1968), p. 132.
26. Daiches, "The Jew in Scotland," p. 198.
27. Ferguson, *Scotland*, p. 132.
28. *Ibid.*, p. 381.
29. Tom M. Devine, *The Scottish Nation, 1700–2000* (London: Penguin, 1999), p. 518.
30. See, for example, Geoffrey Alderman, *Modern British Jewry, 2nd Edition* (Oxford: Clarendon, 1998); Vivian D. Lipman, *Social*

History of the Jews in England, 1850-1950 (London: Watts & Co., 1954); idem, *A History of the Jews in Britain since 1858* (Leicester: Leicester University Press, 1990); Cecil Roth, *A History of the Jews in England*, 3rd Edition (Oxford: Clarendon, 1964); idem, *The Rise of Provincial Jewry: The Early History of the Jewish Communities in the English Countryside* (London: Jewish Monthly, 1950); Todd M. Endelman, *The Jews of Britain, 1656 to 2000* (Berkeley: University of California Press, 2002); Harold Pollins, *Economic History of the Jews in England* (New Brunswick, NJ, and London: Associated University Presses, 1982).

31. Miri J. Freud-Kandel, *Orthodox Judaism in Britain Since 1913: An Ideology Forsaken* (London and Portland, OR: Vallentine Mitchell, 2006), p. xi.

32. A by no means comprehensive list includes Rosalyn D. Livshin, *The History of the Harrogate Jewish Community* (Leeds: Leeds University Press, 1995); Murray Freedman, *Leeds Jewry: The First Hundred Years* (York: Jewish Historical Society of England, Leeds Branch, 1992); Amanda Bergen, *Leeds Jewry, 1930-1939: The Challenge of Anti-Semitism* (Leeds: Thoresby Society 2000); Ernest Krausz, *Leeds Jewry: Its History and Social Structure* (London: Heffer, 1964); Aubrey Newman, *Birmingham Jewry, Vol. 1, 1749-1914* (Leicester: University of Leicester Press, 1980); Ernest C. Sterne, *Leeds Jewry 1919-1929* (Leeds: Jewish Historical Society of England, 1989); Zoe? Josephs, *Birmingham Jewry, Vol. 2, Further aspects, 1740-1930* (Oldbury: Birmingham Jewish History Research Group, 1984); Bill Williams, *The Making of Manchester Jewry, 1740-1875* (Manchester: Manchester University Press, 1976); Louis Hyman, *The Jews of Ireland from Earliest Times to the Year 1910* (Shannon: Irish University Press, 1972); S. Levy, "Notes on Leicester Jewry," *Transactions of the Jewish Historical Society of England*, 5 (1902-05), pp. 34-42 ; Vivian D. Lipman, *The Jews of Medieval Norwich* (London: Jewish Historical Society of England, 1967); Judith Samuel, *Jews in Bristol: The History of the Jewish Community in Bristol from the Middle Ages to the Present Day* (Bristol: Redcliffe, 1997); Grahame Davies, ed., *The Chosen People: Wales & the Jews* (Bridgend: Seren, 2002); Dermot Keogh, *Jews in Twentieth-Century Ireland: Refugees, Anti-Semitism and the Holocaust* (Cork: Cork University Press, 1998); Ursula R.Q. Henriques, ed., *The Jews of South Wales: Historical Studies* (Cardiff: University of Wales Press, 1993).

33. Pollins, *Economic History of the Jews in England*, pp. 9, 10.

34. Endelman, *The Jews of Britain*, p. 12.

35. Ibid., p. 130.

36. Kenneth Collins, ed., *Aspects of Scottish Jewry* (Glasgow: Glasgow Jewish Representative Council, 1987); idem, *Go and Learn*; idem, *Second City Jewry*; idem, "Maintaining a Jewish Identity in Scotland," in *Scottish Life and Society: The Individual and Community Life, a Compendium of Scottish Ethnology*, Vol. 9, eds. John Beech, Owen Hand, Mark Mulhern, and Jeremy Weston (Edinburgh: John Donald Ltd., 2005), pp. 486-496; idem, *Scotland's Jews: A Guide to the History and Community of the Jews in Scotland*, 2nd Edition (Glasgow: Scottish Council of Jewish Communities, 2008); Charlotte Hutt and Harvey L. Kaplan, *A Scottish Shtetl: Jewish Life in the Gorbals, 1880-1974* (Glasgow: Scottish Jewish Archives Centre, 1974); Henry Maitles, "Jewish Trade Unionists in Glasgow," *Immigrants and Minorities*, 10:3 (1991); idem, "Attitudes to Jewish Immigration in the West of Scotland to 1905"; William Kenefick, "Jewish and Catholic Irish Relations: The Glasgow Waterfront, c.1880-1914," *Jewish Culture and History*, 7:1-2 (Summer/Autumn 2004), pp. 215-234.

37. Avram Taylor, "Breaking Free from 'A Scottish Shetl': The Life, Times and Jewishness of C.P. Taylor," in *Representing the Holocaust: Essays in Honour of Bryan Burns*, ed. Sue Vice (London and Portland, OR: Vallentine Mitchell, 2003), pp. 143-183; idem, "Remembering Spring Through Gorbals Voices: Autobiography and the Memory of a Community," paper presented at the Symposium on Jewish Settlement, Development and Identities in Scotland, 1879-2004, 17 October, 2004; Linda Fleming, "Jewish Women in Glasgow, c1880-1950: Gender, Ethnicity and the Immigrant Experience," unpublished work in progress; Ben Braber, "The Integration of Jewish Immigrants in Glasgow, 1880-1939" (Ph.D. dissertation, University of Glasgow, 1992); idem, "The Trial of Oscar Slater (1909) and Anti-Jewish Prejudices in Edwardian Glasgow," *History*, 88 (2003), pp. 262-279; idem, *Jews in Glasgow, 1879-1939: Immigration and Integration* (London and Portland, OR: Vallentine Mitchell, 2007).

38. Glasgow has tended to be the focus of much of the writing on Scottish Jewry, as evidenced by titles such as Collins, *Second City Jewry*; idem, *Be Well!*; Hutt and Kaplan, *A Scottish Shtetl*; Maitles, "Jewish Trade Unionists in Glasgow"; idem, "Attitudes to Jewish Immigration in the West of Scotland to 1905,"; Suzanne Audrey, "Glasgow Jewry," in her *Multiculturalism in Practice: Irish, Jewish, Italian and Pakistani Migration to Scotland* (Aldershot: Ashgate, 2000), pp. 46-61; Abel Phillips, *A History of the Origins of the First Jewish Community in Scotland-Edinburgh, 1816* (Edinburgh: John Donald Publishers, 1979); Levy, *The Origins of Scottish Jewry*.

39. Kenneth E. Collins, "Growth and Development of Scottish Jewry, 1880-1940," in *As-

pects of Scottish Jewry, ed. Collins, p. 1. See, for example, Abraham Levy, *The Origins of Glasgow Jewry, 1812–1895* (Glasgow: A.J. Macfarlane, 1949); idem, *The Origins of Scottish Jewry*; Collins, *Be Well!*; idem, *Go and Learn*; idem, *Second City Jewry*; Braber, "The Integration of Jewish Immigrants in Glasgow, 1880–1939"; idem, *Jews in Glasgow 1879–1939.*
40. See C.C. Aronsfeld, "German Jews in Dundee," *The Jewish Chronicle*, 20 November, 1953; Ewan A. MacDonald, "Discovering the Jews of Dundee: With Particular Reference to German and Russian Jews" (Unpublished Single Honors Dissertation, University of Dundee, 2005); Katharyne C. Newland, "Immigrant Minorities in Dundee, 1850–1914: The Irish and the Jews" (unpublished undergraduate dissertation, University of Dundee, n.d.). There are also scattered references in Collins, *Go and Learn*; idem, *Aspects of Scottish Jewry*; Lloyd Gartner, *The Jewish Immigrant in England, 1870–1914* (London and Portland, OR: Vallentine Mitchell, 2001); Janice Murray and David Stockdale, *The Miles Tae Dundee: Stories of a City and Its People* (Dundee: Dundee Art Galleries and Museums, 1990); Neil Robertson, ed., *An A-Z of Hilltown: A History of Dundee's First Suburb* (Dundee: Grey Lodge, 1994). For Aberdeen, see my own article "The Jews of Aberdeen: A Revolving Door Community Since 1893 and Its Antecedents," *Northern Scotland*, 27 (2007), pp. 147–68.
41. Collins, *Go and Learn*.
42. As the title of her study suggests, Audrey, for example, only focuses on Jews in Glasgow. Similarly, Tom Devine's chapter on the "New Scots" in his *The Scottish Nation, 1700–2000* is not only typical in its focus on the Jews of Glasgow, but also isn't even aware that communities existed in Aberdeen, Inverness, and Dunfermline in 1914. Martin Gilbert's map of "The Jews of Britain, 1660–1914," in his *The Routledge Atlas of Jewish History, 7th Edition* (London and New York: Routledge, 2006), excludes all the Scottish communities except Edinburgh and Glasgow. Likewise, Maitles' "Attitudes to Jewish Immigration in the West of Scotland to 1905" ignores the communities of Ayr and Greenock established in 1902 and 1894, respectively.
43. Collins, *Go and Learn*, p. 75. Of these, Levy wrote, "There are a few Jewish families scattered throughout Scotland—among the hills and glens of the highlands and in the agricultural and pastoral counties of the lowlands—but they are not in any way organised and have no position in or influence on Scottish Jewry as a whole." Levy, *The Origins of Scottish Jewry*, p. 29.
44. *Jewish Chronicle*, 3 October, 2003.
45. The literature about "small-town Jews" from both an empirical and a conceptual view is small but growing. Particularly notable is the work of Ewa Morawska, such as her *Insecure Prosperity: Small-Town Jews in Industrial America, 1890–1940* (Princeton, NJ: Princeton University Press, 1999), and Lee Shai Weissbach, who has defined such communities as "only those population centers with 100 or more Jewish inhabitants." See his "Unexplored Terrain: The History of Small Jewish Communities in Western Society," *Shofar*, 17 (Fall 1998). However, while the experiences of the communities under study here incorporate elements of small-town life, their isolation and remoteness are large and important factors. Consequently, I have arrived at the formulation of "remote Jews" to distinguish them simply from "small-town Jews."
46. *Jewish Chronicle*, 7 June, 1907.
47. Records of the Aberdeen Hebrew Congregation, 6 May, 1896; *Jewish Chronicle*, 15 May, 1896.
48. Records of the of the Aberdeen Hebrew Congregation, 3 May, 1992.
49. Records of the Aberdeen Hebrew Congregation, 6 September, 1992.
50. A recent example of this is a *Jewish Chronicle* editorial which described the winding down of the Jewish community of Sunderland as "Sad, but inevitable." *Jewish Chronicle*, 24 March, 2006.
51. Lee Shai Weissbach, *Jewish Life in Small-Town America: A History* (New Haven and London: Yale University Press, 2005), p. 28.
52. He goes on to say, "The presumption that at least 100 Jews were needed for the maintenance of an active communal life is borne out, at least in part, by the fact that triple-digit population seemed to be a good predictor for the presence of fundamental communal institutions in the decades before World War II." Weissbach, *Jewish Life in Small-Town America*, p. 29.
53. Collins, "Maintaining a Jewish Identity in Scotland," p. 487.
54. Ursula R.Q. Henriques, "The Jewish Community of Cardiff, 1813–1914," in *The Jews of South Wales*, ed. Henriques, p. 14.
55. An example of this is recorded in the minutes of the Aberdeen Hebrew Congregation when two boys, Saul and Abraham Goodstein, are circumcised, despite having a Jewish father and a Christian mother. Records of the Aberdeen Hebrew Congregation, 26 May, 1896.
56. *Aberdeen Free Press*, 18 March, 1904; 1 April, 1904; 5 April, 1904; 9 April, 1904. See also *Scottish Notes & Queries* (January and February 1905); John Malcolm Bulloch, ed., *The House of Gordon*, Vol. II (New Sporting Club, Aberdeen, 1907), p. xxv.
57. Alexander Gammie, *The Churches of Aberdeen: Historical and Descriptive* (Aberdeen:

Aberdeen Daily Journal Office, 1909), unpaginated.
58. *The Scotsman*, 17 May, 1910.
59. Bennett Teff, *O'er Vales and Hills: Some Reminiscences* (unpublished ms. in author's possession), p. 13.
60. Collins, "Maintaining a Jewish Identity in Scotland," p. 490.

Chapter 1

1. *Jewish Chronicle*, 29 January, 1999.
2. *Jewish Chronicle*, 24 June, 1910.
3. William Skene, *East Neuk Chronicles* (Aberdeen, 1905), pp. 51–2.
4. *Jewish Echo*, 24 July, 1959.
5. Skinner, "Introduction," pp. 2–3.
6. Hirschman and Yates, *When Scotland Was Jewish*, p. 1.
7. Collins, *Go and Learn*, p. 57.
8. Roth, *A History of the Jews in England*, p. 175.
9. Arthur H. Williamson, "'A Pil for Pork-Eaters': Ethnic Identity, Apocalyptic Promises, and the Strange Creation of the Judeo-Scots," in *The Expulsion of the Jews: 1492 and After*, eds. Raymond B Waddington and Arthur H Williamson (New York and London: Garland, 1994), p. 249.
10. *A New Letter from Aberdeen in Scotland, Sent to a Person of Quality Wherein Is a More Full Account of the Proceedings of the Jewes Than Hath Been Hitherto Published*, 26 October, 1665, reprinted by the *Jewish Chronicle*, 6 May, 1938.
11. Constance Oliver Skelton and John Malcolm Bulloch, *Gordons Under Arms: A Biographical Muster Roll of Officers Named Gordon in the Navies and Armies of Britain, Europe, America and in the Jacobite Risings* (Aberdeen: New Spalding Club, 1912), p. 251. I am grateful to Thomas Brochard for making me aware of this.
12. Collins, *Go and Learn*, pp. 34–5; Geoffrey Cantor, *Quakers, Jews, and Science: Religious Responses to Modernity and the Sciences in Britain, 1650–1900* (Oxford: Oxford University Press, 2005), p. 71.
13. Collins, *Go and Learn*, pp. 34–7.
14. Levy, *The Origins of Scottish Jewry*, p. 29.
15. Collins, *Second City Jewry*, p. 16.
16. Collins, *Go and Learn*, p. 48.
17. Skene, *East Neuk Chronicles*, pp. 51–2.
18. *The Scotsman*, 23 April, 1842, and 15 June, 1842. See also *The Diced Cap: The Story of Aberdeen City Police* (published by the Chief Constable on behalf of the Corporation of the City of Aberdeen, 1972). I am grateful to Graham Keith for pointing this item out to me.
19. I am grateful to Petra Laidlaw for making me aware of this information.
20. Collins, *Be Well!*, p. 146.
21. See John Morrison's chapter in Terry Brotherstone and Donald J. Withrington (eds.), *The City and Its Worlds: Aspects of Aberdeen's History Since 1792* (Glasgow: Cruithne Press, 1996), pp. 194–210.
22. *Aberdeen Journal*, 23 August, 1871.
23. *Jewish Chronicle*, 10 June, 1873.
24. Devine, *The Scottish Nation*, p. 518.
25. Home Office: Registered Papers, Supplementary HO 144/295/B1959 Nationality and Naturalization: Zamek, Alexander, from Poland. Resident in Aberdeen. Certificate A5548 issued 17 September, 1887.
26. *The Scotsman*, 12 September, 1893; *The Scotsman*, 17 May, 1910.
27. Kenneth Collins, "The Aberdeen Shechitah Case," *Four Corners*, 17 (April 2008).
28. *The Scotsman*, 12 September, 1893.
29. Collins, "The Aberdeen Shechitah Case."
30. Gammie, *The Churches of Aberdeen*.
31. *Jewish Chronicle*, 19 December, 1913.
32. *Jewish Chronicle*, 13 October, 1893.
33. *Jewish Chronicle*, 15 September, 1893.
34. *Aberdeen Journal*, 9 September, 1893.
35. Daiches, "The Jew in Scotland," pp. 208–9.
36. *The Scotsman*, 17 May, 1910.
37. *Jewish Chronicle*, 3 January, 1902; Harvey Kaplan, "The Jewish Colonial Trust" (unpublished document in author's possession).
38. *The Scotsman*, 4 October, 1893.
39. *Jewish Chronicle*, 20 October, 1893.
40. *Jewish Chronicle*, 9 March, 1894.
41. Collins, "The Aberdeen Shechitah Case."
42. *Ibid.*
43. *Jewish Chronicle*, 29 September, 1893.
44. *Jewish Chronicle*, 20 October, 1893.
45. *Aberdeen Journal*, 6 October, 1893. L. Shrago to Glasgow Jewish Representative Council, 3 December, 1993, Records of Aberdeen Hebrew Congregation.
46. Gammie, *The Churches of Aberdeen*.
47. Home Office: Registered Papers, Supplementary HO 144/14335 Nationality and Naturalization: Ostrow, Itzig (known as Isaac Ostroff), from Russia. Resident in London. Certificate A20100 issued 8 July, 1931.
48. Collins, *Go and Learn*, p. 69.
49. *The Aberdeen Journal*, 12 September, 1893.
50. Records of the Aberdeen Hebrew Congregation, 6 May, 1896.
51. *Jewish Chronicle*, 15 May, 1896.
52. Emanuel "Manny" Steen, cited in *Ellis Island Interviews: In Their Own Words*, ed. Peter Morton Coan (New York: Checkmark Books, 1997), p. 118.
53. *Jewish Chronicle*, 7 June, 1907.
54. I am grateful to Alan Wilson for this information. Stella's husband, Samuel, was also buried in Edinburgh in 1917. Both headstones,

particularly Stella's distinctively shaped pillar, can be viewed at "A Photographic Record of Headstones in the Jewish Section of Newington Cemetery (Formerly Echobank), Edinburgh," http://www.newingtoncmy.fsnet.co.uk/edel shain.htm. Last accessed August 2008.
55. Email to the author, 9 May, 2005.
56. *Jewish Chronicle*, 23 July, 1915, and 24 March, 1916.
57. *The Scotsman*, 12 September, 1893.
58. Henry Maitles, "Blackshirts Across the Border: The British Union of Fascists in Scotland," *Scottish Historical Review*, 82:1 (April 2003), p. 48.
59. Audrey, "Glasgow Jewry," p. 47.
60. Robert E. Tyson, "The Economy of Aberdeen," in *Aberdeen in the Nineteenth Century: The Making of the Modern City*, eds. John S. Smith and David Stevenson (Aberdeen: Aberdeen University Press, 1988), p. 20.
61. R.E.H. Mellor, "Aberdeen—the Great Century," in *Aberdeen in the Nineteenth Century*, eds. Smith and Stevenson, p. 15.
62. Mellor, "Aberdeen," p. 15; David Newlands, "The Regional Economies of Scotland," in *The Transformation of Scotland: The Economy Since 1700*, eds. T.M. Devine, C.H. Lee, and G.C. Peden (Edinburgh: Edinburgh University Press, 2005), p. 163.
63. Audrey, "Glasgow Jewry," p. 47.
64. Pollins, *Economic History of the Jews in England*, p. 178.
65. Teff, *Oe'r Hills and Far Away*, p. 17.
66. *The Scotsman*, 20 June, 1896; *Aberdeen Weekly Journal*, 20 June, 1896.
67. *Scotsman*, 17 May, 1910.
68. J.R. Coull, email to author, 14 July, 2005.
69. Ranald MacInnes, *The Aberdeen Guide* (Edinburgh: Birlinn, 2000), p. 207.
70. Ethel G. Hofman, *Mackerel at Midnight: Growing up Jewish on a Remote Scottish Island* (Philadelphia: Camino Books, 2005), pp. 9–12.
71. J. Albert Hunter, "Julius Quint: Shetland's Wandering Jew," *New Shetlander*, 159 (1987), pp. 24–5.
72. Braber, *Jews in Glasgow*, p. 5.
73. Hal Kwalwasser, "My Mother: An Honorary Ambassador," *Four Corners*, 14 (Summer 2007).
74. W.D. Rubinstein, *A History of the Jews in the English-Speaking World: Great Britain* (London: Macmillan, 1996), p. 226.
75. "Bromberg, Ernest," *Scottish Screen Archive*, http://data.scottishscreen.com/personality/detail.php?id=10004. Last consulted February 2006.
76. Teff, *Oe'r Hills and Far Away*, p. 17.
77. *Jewish Chronicle*, 27 April, 1923.
78. Collins, *Go and Learn*, p. 114.
79. *Ibid.*
80. Geoffrey D.M. Block, "Jewish Students at the Universities of Great Britain and Ireland—Excluding London, 1936–1939," *Sociological Review*, 34 (1942), p.184. See also Rubinstein, *A History of the Jews in the English-Speaking World*, pp. 475–6, n. 24.
81. Rubinstein, *A History of the Jews in the English-Speaking World*, p. 229.
82. Teff, *O'er Vales and Hills*, p. 14.
83. *Ibid.*, p. 18.
84. Walter Kress, *From the Holocaust to the Highlands* (Aberdeen: Cauliay, 2007).
85. Colin Cross, *The Fascists in Britain* (London: Barrie & Rockliff, 1961), p. 108.
86. Liz Kibblewhite and Andy Rigby, *Fascism in Aberdeen: Street Politics in the 1930s* (Aberdeen: Aberdeen People's Press, 1978), p. 23.
87. *Jewish Chronicle*, 23 September, 1938; *Glasgow Herald*, 26 July, 1937; *Aberdeen Press and Journal*, 26 July, 1937; *Glasgow Herald*, 4 October, 1937; *Aberdeen Evening Express*, 4 October, 1937; *Aberdeen Press and Journal*, 7 October, 1937; *Glasgow Herald*, 12 November, 1938; *Aberdeen Press and Journal*, 6 July, 1938.
88. *Jewish Chronicle*, 23 September, 1939; Maitles, "Attitudes to Jewish Immigration in the West of Scotland to 1905," p. 97.
89. Cross, *The Fascists in Britain*, p. 108. He adds on p. 78: "Motherwell branch's claim of 200 members in the spring of 1933 was, if true, a flash in the pan."
90. Kress, *From the Holocaust to the Highlands*, p. 29.
91. *Jewish Chronicle*, 10 March, 1944.
92. Allen Bordoley, email to author, 1 May, 2007.
93. *Jewish Chronicle*, 10 May, 1940.
94. *Jewish Chronicle*, 11 December, 1942.
95. *Jewish Chronicle*, 15 May, 1943.
96. *Jewish Chronicle*, 30 June, 1944.
97. Teff, *O'er Vales and Hills*, p. 20.
98. *Ibid.*, pp. 20–1.
99. *Jewish Echo*, 14 May, 1948.
100. *Jewish Echo*, 13 February, 1953.
101. *Ibid.*
102. *Jewish Chronicle*, 20 August, 1982.
103. *Jewish Echo*, 11 February, 1955
104. *Hashanah: The Scottish Jewish Year Book, 1955–56*.
105. *Jewish Echo*, 12 July, 1957.
106. *Jewish Echo*, 16 November, 1956.
107. *Jewish Echo*, 24 May, 1957.
108. Robin Smith, *The Making of Scotland: A Comprehensive Guide to the Growth of Scotland's Cities, Towns and Villages* (Edinburgh: Canongate, 2001), p. 10.
109. *JYB, 1960, 1961.*
110. Harold Levy, 24 June, 1960, Aberdeen Hebrew Congregation Records.
111. *Four Corners*, 10 (August 2006).
112. *Jewish Echo*, 23 March, 1973.
113. *Jewish Echo*, 18 April, 1980; *Jewish Chronicle*, 29 February, 1980.
114. *Jewish Chronicle*, 4 July, 1980.

115. *Jewish Chronicle*, 26 November, 1982.
116. *Jewish Chronicle*, 8 April, 1983.
117. *Jewish Echo*, 6 May, 1983.
118. Alfred Dunitz, interview with author, 18 March, 2007.
119. *Jewish Chronicle*, 3 June, 1983.
120. *Jewish Chronicle*, 1 May, 1987.
121. *Jewish Chronicle*, 11 May, 1990.
122. *Jewish Chronicle*, 21 October, 1994.
123. *Jewish Chronicle*, 7 March, 1997.
124. *Jewish Chronicle*, 11 December, 1998.
125. Collins, "Maintaining a Jewish Identity in Scotland," p. 490.
126. *Jewish Chronicle*, 21 December, 2001.
127. Ehud Reiter, "Aberdeen's Synagogue Today," *Four Corners*, 15 (September 2007).
128. *Jewish Chronicle*, 31 December, 1909.
129. *Jewish Chronicle*, 14 November, 1910.
130. Collins, *Second City Jewry*, pp. 58-9; *Jewish Chronicle*, 2 September, 1881.
131. *Jewish Echo*, 23 April, 1954.
132. Minutes of the Aberdeen Hebrew Congregation, 3 May, 1992; Lionel P. Shrago to Rebecca Caplan, 7 July, 1992, Records of the Aberdeen Hebrew Congregation.
133. "Anti-Semitism Worldwide 1997/8," http://www.tau.ac.il/Anti-Semitism/asw97-8/united-kingdom.html. Last accessed August 2008.
134. *The Herald* (Glasgow), 6 March, 2002.
135. *Aberdeen Evening Express*, 8 March, 2005; *Aberdeen Press and Journal*, 8 March, 2005; *Aberdeen Press and Journal*, 3 February, 2005.
136. Daiches, "The Jew in Scotland," pp. 208-9.
137. Allan Junior, *The Aberdeen Jew* (Dundee and London: Valentine & Sons, 1927), p. 14.
138. Ditchburn, *Scotland and Europe*, p. 34.
139. Email to author, 22 April, 2005.
140. Collins, *Second City Jewry*, p. 63.
141. Newlands, "The Regional Economies of Scotland," p. 171.
142. *Jewish Echo*, 9 February, 1951.
143. Newlands, "The Regional Economies of Scotland," p. 178.
144. *Jewish Chronicle*, 25 June, 1982.
145. Teff, *O'er Vales and Hills*, p. 14.
146. Records of the Aberdeen Hebrew Congregation, 23 November, 1997, and 1 March, 1998.
147. *Jewish Chronicle*, 17 May, 1996.
148. "Aberdeen Jewish Community," Records of the Aberdeen Hebrew Congregation, n.d.

Chapter 2

1. *Jewish Chronicle*, 28 February, 1902.
2. *Jewish Chronicle*, 20 June, 1902.
3. *Jewish Chronicle*, 6 November, 1903.
4. Hirschman and Yates, *When Scotland Was Jewish*, p. 99.
5. Pollins, *Economic History of the Jews in England*, p. 56; H. Hamilton, "The Failure of the Ayr Bank, 1772," *Economic History Review*, 8:3 (1956), pp. 405-17.
6. "Ayr Hebrew Congregation," http://www.jewishgen.org/JCR-uk/Community/ayr/index.htm. Last accessed August 2008.
7. *Jewish Chronicle*, 21 October, 1960.
8. Collins, *Scotland's Jews*, p. 16.
9. *Jewish Chronicle*, 29 January, 1904.
10. *JYB, 1924*.
11. John Strawhorn and William Boyd, *The Third Statistical Account of Scotland: Ayrshire* (Edinburgh and London: Oliver & Boyd, 1951), p. 261.
12. *Jewish Echo*, 15 August, 1941.
13. Collins, *Scotland's Jews*, p. 26.
14. Home Office: Registered Papers, Supplementary HO 144/780/125837 Nationality and Naturalization: Dunetz, Joel (known as Joel Slonimsky), from Russia. Resident in Old Cumnock, Ayrshire. Certificate 15192 issued 27 March, 1905.
15. Iris Buten, "The Polson-Levansky-Buten-Serota Story," *Butenet*, http://www.buten.net/polyvensky/polyvensky.html. Last accessed July 2008.
16. Home Office: Registered Papers, Supplementary HO 144/16866, Nationality and Naturalization: Rosenbloom, Daniel, from Russia. Resident in Glasgow. Certificate AZ2309 issued 7 November, 1931.
17. Collins, *Go and Learn*, p. 75.
18. Smith, *The Making of Scotland*, p. 61.
19. John Strawhorn, *750 Years of a Scottish School: Ayr Academy, 1233-1983* (Ayr: Alloway Publishing, 1983), p. 102.
20. Collins, *Second City Jewry*, p. 153.
21. *Jewish Chronicle*, 1 September, 1871.
22. *Jewish Chronicle*, 7 February, 1871.
23. Braber, *Jews in Glasgow*, p. 91.
24. *Jewish Chronicle*, 25 July, 1890.
25. Collins, *Second City Jewry*, p. 79.
26. *Ibid.*, p. 79; *Jewish Chronicle*, 25 July, 1890.
27. *Jewish Chronicle*, 29 January, 1904.
28. *Jewish Chronicle*, 3 June, 1904.
29. Kaplan, "The Jewish Colonial Trust."
30. *Jewish Chronicle*, 15 July, 1904; *Jewish Chronicle*, 2 July, 1943; *Jewish Chronicle*, 13 October, 1905; *Jewish Chronicle*, 17 December, 1909.
31. *Jewish Chronicle*, 7 June, 1907.
32. *Jewish Chronicle*, 6 May, 1910; *Jewish Chronicle*, 16 December, 1910; *Jewish Chronicle*, 30 December, 1910.
33. *Jewish Chronicle*, 19 May, 1911.
34. *Jewish Chronicle*, 2 February, 1912; *Jewish Chronicle*, 2 February, 1912; *Jewish Chronicle*, 31 January, 1913; *Jewish Chronicle*, 28 February, 1913.

Notes—Chapter 2

35. J. Levy, letter to the Chief Rabbi, 22 May, 1916, ACC/285/4/2/111, Archives of the Office of the Chief Rabbi and the United Synagogue, London Metropolitan Archives (hereafter "LMA").
36. *Jewish Chronicle*, 19 October, 1917.
37. *Jewish Chronicle*, 1 February, 1918.
38. *Jewish Chronicle*, 6 April, 1917.
39. "Ministers' Subvention Fund, 1914–15," ACC/2805/4/5/3, LMA.
40. Letter to the Chief Rabbi, to 22 July, 1918, ACC/285/4/2/111, LMA.
41. *Jewish Chronicle*, 9 September, 1910.
42. *Jewish Chronicle*, 31 May, 1918; *Jewish Chronicle*, 14 June, 1918.
43. *Jewish Chronicle*, 28 February, 1919.
44. *Jewish Chronicle*, 20 May, 1927; *Jewish Chronicle*, 12 August, 1927; *Jewish Chronicle*, 14 June, 1929.
45. *Jewish Chronicle*, 23 March, 1923; *Jewish Chronicle*, 20 April, 1923.
46. *Jewish Chronicle*, 11 April, 1924; *Jewish Chronicle*, 14 April, 1922; *Jewish Chronicle*, 11 April, 1924; *Jewish Chronicle*, 28 July, 1922; *Jewish Chronicle*, 23 March, 1923; *Jewish Chronicle*, 20 April, 1923.
47. *Jewish Chronicle*, 15 September, 1922.
48. *Jewish Chronicle*, 31 October, 1924.
49. *Jewish Chronicle*, 14 April, 1922; *Jewish Chronicle*, 11 April, 1924; *Jewish Chronicle*, 28 July, 1922; *Jewish Chronicle*, 23 March, 1923; *Jewish Chronicle*, 20 April, 1923; *Jewish Chronicle*, 15 September, 1922; *Jewish Chronicle*, 11 April, 1924; *Jewish Chronicle*, 18 July, 1924; *Jewish Chronicle*, 15 September, 1922.
50. *Jewish Chronicle*, 22 January, 1926.
51. *Jewish Chronicle*, 22 May, 1924.
52. *Jewish Echo*, 29 May, 1931.
53. *Jewish Echo*, 30 August, 1929; *Jewish Chronicle*, 18 August, 1939; *Jewish Chronicle*, 25 August, 1939.
54. Joe Ross, *The Robert (Spilg) Spence Story* (unpublished ms. in author's possession, 1995), p. 25.
55. *Jewish Echo*, 1 October, 1937.
56. *Jewish Chronicle*, 12 February, 1926; *Jewish Chronicle*, 7 July, 1933; *Jewish Chronicle*, 4 February, 1938.
57. *Jewish Chronicle*, 2 March, 1951.
58. *Jewish Echo*, 5 May, 1933.
59. *Jewish Chronicle*, 30 April, 1926; *Jewish Chronicle*, 13 May, 1938; *Jewish Chronicle*, 27 October, 1939.
60. *Jewish Echo*, 8 October, 1937; *Jewish Echo*, 10 December, 1937; *Jewish Echo*, 29 April, 1938; *Jewish Echo*, 17 June, 1938; *Jewish Echo*, 1 July, 1938; *Jewish Echo*, 25 November, 1938; *Jewish Echo*, 23 December, 1938.
61. *Jewish Chronicle*, 1 October, 1937; *Jewish Chronicle*, 11 March, 1938; *Jewish Chronicle*, 22 April, 1938; *Jewish Chronicle*, 6 May, 1938; *Jewish Chronicle*, 22 July, 1938. *Jewish Chronicle*,

3 March, 1939; *Jewish Chronicle*, 6 October, 1939.
61. *Jewish Chronicle*, 3 November, 1939.
62. *Jewish Chronicle*, 8 December, 1939; *Jewish Echo*, 8 December, 1939; *Jewish Echo*, 5 July, 1940.
63. *Jewish Chronicle*, 16 February, 1940.
64. *Jewish Echo*, 16 May, 1941.
65. *Jewish Echo*, 11 July, 1941.
66. *Jewish Chronicle*, 25 July, 1941.
67. Records of the Ayr Hebrew Congregation, Scottish Jewish Archives Centre (hereafter "SJAC").
68. *Jewish Chronicle*, 3 November, 1944.
69. Benita Rosenstein (née Golombok), email to author, n.d.
70. *Jewish Echo*, 13 November, 1939.
71. *Jewish Echo*, 29 October, 1939; *Jewish Echo*, 24 November, 1939; *Jewish Echo*, 8 December, 1939; *Hashanah: The Scottish Jewish Year Book, 1955–56*.
72. Cyril Harris, *For Heaven's Sake* (London and Portland, OR: Vallentine Mitchell, 2001), p. 4.
73. *Jewish Chronicle*, 17 January, 1941; *Jewish Chronicle*, 7 February, 1941; *Jewish Chronicle*, 10 June, 1977.
74. *Jewish Chronicle*, 19 April, 1940.
75. *Jewish Chronicle*, 13 December, 1940.
76. *Jewish Chronicle*, 27 December, 1940.
77. *Jewish Chronicle*, 8 December, 1944.
78. *Jewish Chronicle*, 28 May, 1943.
79. *Jewish Echo*, 1 August, 1941.
80. *Jewish Echo*, 21 February, 1941.
81. *Jewish Echo*, 4 April, 1941.
82. John Strawhorn, *Ayrshire: The Story of a County* (Ayr: Ayrshire Archaeological and Natural History Society, 1975), p. 199; Strawhorn and Boyd, *The Third Statistical Account of Scotland: Ayrshire*, p. 261. Referring presumably to the opening of the new *shul*, Strawhorn and Boyd, however, incorrectly state that the synagogue was established in 1940.
83. *Jewish Echo*, 15 August, 1941.
84. *Jewish Echo*, 15 August, 1941.
85. *Jewish Chronicle*, 22 August, 1941.
86. *Jewish Echo*, 27 March, 1942.
87. Records of the Ayr Hebrew Congregation, 15 March, 1942, SJAC.
88. Records of the Ayr Hebrew Congregation, 19 April, 1942, SJAC.
89. *Jewish Echo*, 29 January, 1943.
90. Records of the Ayr Hebrew Congregation, 22 February, 1942, SJAC.
91. *Jewish Chronicle*, 29 November, 1940.
92. *Jewish Echo*, 13 March, 1942.
93. *Jewish Echo*, 13 June, 1941.
94. Harris, *For Heaven's Sake*, p. 5.
95. Moshe Silberhaft, "Eulogy Delivered at the Consecration of the Tombstone of the Late Chief Rabbi Cyril K. Harris," 4 July, 2006, http://www.africanjewishcongress.com/EULOGY.htm. Last accessed July 2007.

96. Ross, *The Robert (Spilg) Spence Story*, p. 23.
97. *Jewish Chronicle*, 19 July, 1946.
98. *Jewish Echo*, 10 September, 1948, and 4 November, 1949.
99. *Jewish Chronicle*, 10 April, 1953.
100. Strawhorn and Boyd, *The Third Statistical Account of Scotland: Ayrshire*, p. 261.
101. Benita Rosenstein (née Golombok), email to author, n.d.
102. *Ibid.*
103. Records of the Ayr Hebrew Congregation, 10 June, 1956, SJAC.
104. Records of the Ayr Hebrew Congregation, 10 August, 1958, SJAC.
105. Records of the Ayr Hebrew Congregation, 10 May, 1956, SJAC.
106. *Hashanah: The Scottish Jewish Year Book, 1955-56.*
107. Report Prepared by the Board of Deputies of British Jews on the Problems of the Smaller Jewish Communities, October 1959, ACC/2805/6/1/254, LMA; *Jewish Chronicle*, 25 May, 1951.
108. Records of the Ayr Hebrew Congregation, 23 October, 1961, SJAC.
109. *Daily Record*, 7 August, 2008. Ludovic Kennedy's *A Presumption of Innocence: The Amazing Case of Patrick Meehan* (London: Victor Gollancz, 1976), pp. 29, 63, 65-67, 22. For more detail on the robbery and the subsequent case, see Kennedy's book.
110. *Jewish Chronicle*, 11 October, 1974.
111. *Jewish Echo*, 26 March, 1975.
112. Records of the Ayr Hebrew Congregation, 30 August, 1959, SJAC; *Jewish Chronicle*, 1 June, 1984.
113. Strawhorn, *750 Years of a Scottish School*, p. 101.
114. Records of the Ayr Hebrew Congregation, 11 May, 1975, SJAC.
115. *Jewish Chronicle*, 3 November, 2006.
116. *Jewish Chronicle*, 23 December, 1983.
117. *Jewish Chronicle*, 8 March, 1991.
118. Allan Williams and Gareth Shaw, "Riding the Big Dipper: The Rise and Decline of the British Seaside Resort in the Twentieth Century," in *The Rise and Fall of British Coastal Resorts: Cultural and Economic Perspectives*, eds. Gareth Shaw and Allan Williams (London: Pinter, 1997), p. 6.
119. John K. Walton, *The British Seaside: Holidays and Resorts in the Twentieth Century* (Manchester and New York: Manchester University Press, 2000), p. 35.

Chapter 3

1. See M.K. Schuchard, *Restoring the Temple of Vision: Cabalistic Freemasonry and Stuart Culture* (Leiden: Brill, 2002), pp. 529-30.
2. Aronsfeld, "German Jews in Dundee," p. 15; Henry McGrady Bell, *Land of Lakes: Memories Keep Me Company* (London: Robert Hale Ltd., 1950), p. 37.
3. Bell, *Land of Lakes*, p. 38.
4. Collins, *Go and Learn*, p. 42.
5. Endelman, *The Jews of Britain*, p. 80.
6. *Ibid.*
7. Collins, "Growth and Development of Scottish Jewry, 1880-1940," pp. 4, 37; Aronsfeld, "German Jews in Dundee," p. 15; Salo Baron, Arcadius Kahan, et al., *Economic History of the Jews* (Jerusalem: Keter Press, 1975), p. 204; Albert Jacob, *The Day It Hit the Fan* (unpublished ms. in author's possession), p. 284.
8. Aronsfeld, "German Jews in Dundee," p. 15.
9. Bell, *Land of Lakes*, p. 38.
10. Aronsfeld, "German Jews in Dundee," p. 15; Eleanor Gordon, *Women and the Labour Movement in Scotland, 1850-1914* (Oxford: Clarendon Press, 1991), pp. 138-9.
11. Aronsfeld, "German Jews in Dundee," p. 15.
12. Aronsfeld, "German Jews in Dundee," p. 15.
13. Collins, *Second City Jewry*, p. 18.
14. Collins, "Growth and Development of Scottish Jewry, 1880-1940," pp. 4, 37.
15. MacDonald, "Discovering the Jews of Dundee," p. 18; Endelman, *The Jews of Britain*, p. 114.
16. MacDonald, "Discovering the Jews of Dundee," p. 22.
17. *Jewish Chronicle*, 31 December, 1875.
18. "Jewish Services in Dundee," *Dundee Courier*, 19 January, 1878.
19. *Dundee Courier*, 19 January, 1878.
20. *Dundee Courier*, 21 September, 1878.
21. Jacob, *The Day It Hit the Fan*, p. 276.
22. See, for example, *JYB, 1896*; Levy, *The Origins of Scottish Jewry*, p. 28; "Dundee Hebrew Congregation," http://www.jewishgen.org/JCR-UK/Community/dundee/index.htm; Collins, "Growth and Development of Scottish Jewry, 1880-1940," p. 37.
23. *Dundee Courier*, 27 May, 1920.
24. *Jewish Chronicle*, 9 September, 1904.
25. *Dundee Courier and Advertiser*, 26 February, 1965.
26. Audrey, *Multiculturalism in Practice*, p. 55; Kolmel, "German-Jewish Refugees in Scotland," p. 72.
27. *Jewish Chronicle*, 30 November, 1891; *Jewish Chronicle*, 4 December, 1891; *Jewish Chronicle*, 11 December, 1891; *Jewish Chronicle*, 1 January, 1892; *Jewish Chronicle*, 12 February, 1892.
28. Collins, *Second City Jewry*, p. 80; *Jewish Chronicle*, 16 September, 1892.
29. MacDonald, "Discovering the Jews of Dundee," pp. 22-23.

30. *Reports of the Dundee Female Jewish Association*, 1873, 1875, 1878, 1880, 1882, Dundee Central Library, Local Studies Collection.
31. *The Scotsman*, 17 May, 1910.
32. Ibid.
33. Gartner, *The Jewish Immigrant in England*, p. 92; Murray and Stockdale, *The Miles Tae Dundee*, 27; Robertson, ed., *An A-Z of Hilltown*, p. 31.
34. *Dundee Courier and Advertiser*, 26 February, 1965; Murray and Stockdale, *The Miles Tae Dundee*, pp. 26, 27.
35. Jacob, *The Day It Hit the Fan*, p. 285; *Dundee Courier*, 6 November, 1883; Collins, "Growth and Development of Scottish Jewry, 1880–1940," p. 37; Daiches, "The Jew in Scotland," p. 208.
36. This information is taken from http://www.dundeecity.gov.uk/photodb/index.html. Last accessed in May 2006, and the *Dundee Directory 1889–90*.
37. Sharman Kadish, *Jewish Heritage in England* (Swindon: English Heritage, 2006), p. 200.
38. Much of the following information is derived from letters between various parties in Dundee and the Chief Rabbi, held at the London Metropolitan Archives.
39. *Dundee Courier*, 6 November, 1883.
40. *Dundee Courier*, 6 November, 1883; the full correspondence of this dispute can be viewed at the Archives of the Office of the Chief Rabbi and the United Synagogue, London Metropolitan Archives.
41. *Dundee Directory, 1893–94*.
42. *Dundee Directory, 1894–95*; *Jewish Chronicle*, 3 May, 1895.
43. Jacob, *The Day It Hit the Fan*, pp. 285–86; *Jewish Chronicle*, 30 September, 1892.
44. *Jewish Chronicle*, 22 July, 1892.
45. Levy, *The Origins of Scottish Jewry*; Newland, "Immigrant Minorities in Dundee 1850–1914," p. 38.
46. *Jewish Chronicle*, 15 May, 1896.
47. *Jewish Chronicle*, 2 March, 1894.
48. *Jewish Chronicle*, 3 February, 1893; *Jewish Chronicle*, 6 November, 1893; *Jewish Chronicle*, 15 December, 1893.
49. *JYB, 1896*.
50. *Hashanah: The Scottish Jewish Year Book, 1955–56*; *Jewish Chronicle*, 26 January, 1888; Sidney Cramer, *Gravestone Inscriptions from Jewish Cemeteries* (Dundee: Dundee Central Library, 1953).
51. Collins, "Growth and Development of Scottish Jewry, 1880–1940," p. 37; *Hashanah: The Scottish Jewish Year Book, 1955–56*.
52. *Jewish Chronicle*, 6 September, 1895; *Dundee Directory, 1896–97*.
53. *Jewish Chronicle*, 6 September, 1895.
54. *JYB, 1896–1897*. There are no figures for 1895, as the *JYB* was not yet published.
55. *Jewish Chronicle*, 27 March, 1896; Collins, "Growth and Development of Scottish Jewry, 1880–1940," p. 37.
56. *The Scotsman*, 17 May, 10.
57. *Jewish Chronicle*, 14 April, 1899.
58. *Jewish Chronicle*, 3 January, 1902.
59. *Dundee Directory, 1903–4*.
60. Home Office: Registered Papers, Supplementary HO 144/462/B32428 Nationality and Naturalisation: Zacutta, Gabriel, from Russia. Resident in Liverpool. Certificate A11632 issued 25 August, 1900.
61. *Rules of the Dundee Hebrew Congregation, 1903* (7 September, 1902), SJAC.
62. *Jewish Chronicle*, 15 September, 1905.
63. *JYB 1904–1905*; *Jewish Chronicle*, 25 February, 1905.
64. Wolf Rothman, quoted in Graham R. Smith, "'None Can Compare': From the Oral History of a Community," in *The Dundee Book: An Anthology of Living in the City*, ed. Billy Kay (Edinburgh: Mainstream, 1990), pp. 191, 192.
65. *JYB 1905–1906*; *Jewish Chronicle*, 9 September, 1904; *Jewish Chronicle*, 16 September, 1904; *Jewish Chronicle*, 24 October, 1919.
66. Records held by the SJAC.
67. Kadish, *Jewish Heritage in England*, p. 200.
68. *Jewish Chronicle*, 17 February, 1911.
69. Joseph Rosensweig, letter to the Chief Rabbi Joseph Hertz, 20 November, 1919, LMA, ACC/2805/4/2/37.
70. *Jewish Chronicle*, 14 November, 1919.
71. Greg Lloyd and John McCarthy, "Dundee: A City Discovering Inclusion and Regeneration," in *Urban Regeneration in Europe*, eds. Chris Crouch, Charles Fraser and Susan Percy (Oxford: Blackwell, 2003), p. 56.
72. R.H. Campbell, *Scotland Since 1707: The Rise of an Industrial Society* (Edinburgh: John Donald, 1985), p. 188.
73. Aronsfeld, "German Jews in Dundee," p. 15; Murray and Stockdale, *The Miles Tae Dundee*, p. 25.
74. Jacob, *The Day It Hit the Fan*, p. 285.
75. *The Scotsman*, 3 May, 1915.
76. Fisher, email to author, 8 September, 2005; *Jewish Chronicle*, 17 February, 1911.
77. Collins, *Second City Jewry*, p. 152.
78. Braber, *Jews in Glasgow*, p. 99.
79. Ibid.
80. *Dundee Courier*, 27 May, 1920.
81. *Jewish Chronicle*, 25 February, 1921.
82. *Jewish Chronicle*, 8 February, 1924.
83. Collins, *Go and Learn*, p. 87.
84. Braber, *Jews in Glasgow*, p. 116.
85. *Jewish Chronicle*, 11 February, 1983; Collins, *Go and Learn*, p. 114.
86. *Jewish Chronicle*, 11 February, 1983.
87. *Jewish Chronicle*, 6 January, 1933.
88. Hal Kwalwasser, "My Mother: An Hon-

orary Ambassador," *Four Corners*, 14 (Summer 2007).
89. Collins, *Go and Learn*, pp. 123, 124, 125. See *Jewish Echo*, 15, 22, 29 November, 1955 and 6 December, 1955.
90. Block, "Jewish Students at the Universities of Great Britain and Ireland," p.184. See also Rubinstein, *A History of the Jews in the English-Speaking World*, pp. 475–6, n. 24.
91. Rubinstein, *A History of the Jews in the English-Speaking World*, p. 229.
92. Murray and Stockdale, *The Miles Tae Dundee*, 27; MacDonald, "Discovering the Jews of Dundee," 9.
93. *Jewish Chronicle*, 10 October, 1958; *Jewish Echo*, 17 May, 1940.
94. *Jewish Echo*, 10 March, 1939.
95. Ian Shein, email to author, 8 July, 2005.
96. *Jewish Chronicle*, 17 December, 1943; *Jewish Chronicle*, 31 March, 1944; *Jewish Chronicle*, 23 February, 1945; *Jewish Chronicle*, 22 November, 1940.
97. J.M. Green, *From Colditz in Code* (Hull: The Wilberforce Council, 1989), pp. 20, 22.
98. *Jewish Echo*, 3 January, 1941.
99. *Jewish Chronicle*, 19 November, 1943.
100. *Jewish Echo*, 20 January, 1939; *Jewish Chronicle*, 8 December, 1939; *Jewish Chronicle*, 22 March, 1940; *Jewish Chronicle*, 10 May, 1940; *Jewish Chronicle*, 7 April, 1944; *Jewish Chronicle*, 13 October, 1944.
101. *JYB, 1945, 1950*; *Jewish Chronicle*, 15 September, 1944.
102. Walter Fisher, email to author, 8 September, 2005.
103. Kwalwasser, "My Mother: An Honorary Ambassador."
104. Newlands, "The Regional Economies of Scotland," p. 169.
105. *Hashanah: The Scottish Jewish Year Book, 1957–58*.
106. *Jewish Chronicle*, 10 October, 1958.
107. Murray and Stockdale, *The Miles Tae Dundee*, p. 27; MacDonald, "Discovering the Jews of Dundee," p. 9.
108. *W.I.Z.O. Scottish Convention*, n.d.
109. *Hashanah: The Scottish Jewish Year Book, 1957–58*.
110. *Jewish Echo*, 28 February, 1958.
111. *Jewish Chronicle*, 18 September, 1959.
112. *Jewish Chronicle*, 18 September, 1959.
113. *Jewish Chronicle*, 27 November, 1959.
114. Ian Leveson, "Acknowledgements," in *Turning the Kaleidoscope: Perspectives on European Jewry*, eds. Sandra H. Lustig and Ian Leveson (New York and Oxford: Berghahn, 2006), p. ix.
115. William M. Walker, *Juteopolis: Dundee and Its Textile Workers, 1885–1923* (Edinburgh: Scottish Academic Press, 1979), pp. 118–119.
116. Dundee Oral History Project, DOHP 017/B/1, Dundee City Archives.

117. Gartner, *The Jewish Immigrant in England*, p. 60.
118. *Jewish Echo*, 15 January, 1960.
119. *JYB, 1962*.
120. S.M. Gillis to Julius Jung, 24 July, 1962, MS 167, Papers of Julius Jung, 1955–70, Hartley Library, University of Southampton (hereafter "Jung Papers").
121. Julius Jung's notes, 5 November, 1962, Jung Papers.
122. *Jewish Chronicle*, 29 November, 1963; *Jewish Echo*, 22 November, 1963.
123. *Jewish Chronicle*, 3 January, 1964.
124. *Jewish Chronicle*, 3 May, 1968.
125. Albert Jacob, "It's Quality, Not Quantity, That Counts!: The Dundee Jewish Community," *Four Corners*, 14 (Summer 2007).
126. *Jewish Chronicle*, 21 September, 1973.
127. Jacob, *The Day It Hit the Fan*, p. 288.
128. Kadish, *Jewish Heritage in England*, p. 200.
129. *Jewish Chronicle*, 12 January, 1979; *JYB, 1978*.
130. Kadish, *Jewish Heritage in England*, p. 200; idem, "Constructing Identity: Anglo-Jewry and Synagogue Architecture," *Architectural History*, 45 (2002), p. 404.
131. Much of this is based on the author's own observations, but I would like to thank Elkan Levy here for his useful comments on and insights into the Dundee synagogue.
132. Jacob, "It's Quality, Not Quantity, That Counts!"
133. Ibid.
134. *Jewish Chronicle*, 18 October, 1985; *Jewish Chronicle*, 25 October, 1985; *Jewish Chronicle*, 3 March, 1989.
135. *Jewish Chronicle*, 22 September, 1995.
136. Jacob, "It's Quality, Not Quantity, That Counts!"
137. *Jewish Telegraph*, 23 November, 2001.
138. *Jewish Chronicle*, 28 September, 2001.
139. *Jewish Telegraph*, 6 October, 2006.
140. *Jewish Chronicle*, 9 December, 2005; Hayden Krasner, email to author, 21 May, 2006.
141. Newlands, "The Regional Economies of Scotland," p. 171.
142. *Four Corners*, 12 (December 2006); *Four Corners*, 16 (December 2007).
143. *Four Corners*, 18 (July 2008).
144. Ian Shein, email to author, 8 July, 2005.
145. *Jewish Chronicle*, 21 April, 1950.
146. *Jewish Echo*, 24 April, 1942; *Jewish Echo*, 27 August, 1965.
147. Dundee Oral History Project, Dundee City Archives, DOHP 017/A/1.
148. *Jewish Chronicle*, 19 October, 1945; *Jewish Chronicle*, 23 November, 1945; *Jewish Chronicle*, 14 June, 1946.
149. *Jewish Chronicle*, 6 January, 1933.
150. Kwalwasser, "My Mother: An Honorary Ambassador."

151. Collins, *Go and Learn*, p. 125.
152. *Jewish Chronicle*, 21 September, 1973.
153. *Jewish Chronicle*, 2 September, 1973.
154. Dundee Oral History Project, DOHP 017/B/1.
155. *Jewish Chronicle*, 21 November, 1969.
156. Debby Taylor, email to author, 9 August, 2006.
157. *Jewish Chronicle*, 28 November, 1968.
158. *Jewish Chronicle*, 24 April, 1970.
159. *Jewish Chronicle*, 19 March, 1976; *Jewish Chronicle*, 2 April, 1976.
160. *Jewish Chronicle*, 11 November, 1977; *Jewish Chronicle*, 18 November, 1977; *Jewish Chronicle*, 16 December, 1977.
161. *Jewish Chronicle*, 16 December, 1977.
162. *Jewish Chronicle*, 9 March, 1979; *Jewish Chronicle*, 7 December, 1979.
163. *Jewish Telegraph*, 13 July, 2001; *Jewish Chronicle*, 13 July, 2001; *The Herald*, 13 July, 2001.
164. "Racial Tension in Tayside: A Regional Report Commissioned by Tayside Community Relations Council" (January 1987).
165. *Jewish Chronicle*, 4 March, 1966.
166. *Jewish Chronicle*, 17 June, 1977; *Jewish Chronicle*, 29 July, 1977.
167. Although some will argue that anti-Semitism and anti-Zionism is often one and the same thing, I will not enter into that discussion here; suffice to say that one can see two parallel trends in Dundee until they overlap in 1981.
168. *Jewish Chronicle*, 27 February, 1981; *The Times*, 23 March, 1981; *Jewish Echo*, 25 September, 1981; *Jewish Echo*, 27 March, 1981; Jacob, *The Day It Hit the Fan*, p. 343.
169. *Jewish Chronicle*, 10 April, 1981.
170. *Jewish Chronicle*, 10 July, 1981; *Jewish Chronicle*, 26 February, 1982.
171. *Jewish Chronicle*, 3 April, 1981; *Jewish Chronicle*, 27 March, 1981.
172. *Jewish Chronicle*, 27 November, 1981.
173. June Edmunds, *The Left and Israel: Party-Policy Change and Internal Democracy* (New York: Palgrave, 1999), p. 87; *Jewish Chronicle*, 16 July, 1982.
174. *Jewish Chronicle*, 22 April, 1983; *Jewish Chronicle*, 4 June, 1982.
175. *Jewish Chronicle*, 3 September, 1982; *Jewish Chronicle*, 15 April, 1983; *Jewish Chronicle*, 31 August, 1984.
176. Edmunds, *The Left and Israel*, p. 94.
177. *Jewish Chronicle*, 16 April, 1982.
178. Edmunds, *The Left and Israel*, p. 87.
179. *Jewish Chronicle*, 16 July, 1982.
180. *Jewish Chronicle*, 26 November, 1982.
181. *Jewish Chronicle*, 21 January, 1983.
182. *Jewish Chronicle*, 11 February, 1983.
183. *Jewish Chronicle*, 18 March, 1983; *Jewish Chronicle*, 20 January, 1984.
184. *Jewish Chronicle*, 18 March, 1983.
185. *Jewish Chronicle*, 10 April, 1981.
186. Jacob, *The Day It Hit the Fan*, p. 486.
187. *Jewish Chronicle*, 11 July, 1983; *Jewish Chronicle*, 25 May, 1985; *Jewish Chronicle*, 27 September, 1985.
188. "Racial Tension in Tayside."
189. *Jewish Chronicle*, 13 September, 1985.
190. *JYB, 1984, 1985.*
191. *The Independent*, 10 June, 1990.
192. *Jewish Chronicle*, 31 August, 1990; *Jewish Chronicle*, 9 November, 1990.
193. *Jewish Telegraph*, 13 July, 2001; *Jewish Chronicle*, 13 July, 2001; *The Herald* 13 July, 2001.
194. *Jewish Chronicle*, 13 July, 2001; *The Independent*, 13 July, 2002; *The Herald*, 27 August, 2001; *The Herald*, 12 July, 2001; *Daily Record*, 11 July, 2001; *The Express*, 11 July, 2001; *The Herald*, 11 July, 2001; *The Mirror*, 11 July, 2001; *The Scotsman*, 11 July, 2001.
195. *Jewish Telegraph*, 13 June, 2001.
196. *The Jerusalem Post*, 15 July, 2001.
197. *The Sunday Times*, 18 September, 2005.

Chapter 4

1. Robert Gourlay and Anne Turner, *Historic Dunfermline: The Archaeological Implications of Development* (Glasgow: Scottish Burgh Survey, 1978), pp. 5, 6.
2. Gourlay and Turner, *Historic Dunfermline*, p. 15.
3. W.T. Barr, *For a Web Begun: The Story of Dunfermline* (Edinburgh: Oliver & Boyd, 1947), pp. 141, 142.
4. *Jewish Telegraph*, 1 July, 2005.
5. Home Office: Registered Papers, Supplementary HO 144/1302/247470, Nationality and Naturalisation: Dorfman, Max, from Russia. Resident in Dunfermline. Certificate 24860 issued 5 March, 1914.
6. Edith Ruddick, *My Mother's Daughter: A Theatrical Autobiography* (Braunton: Marlin, 1995), p. 1.
7. Martin Eastwood, email to author, 9 March, 2006.
8. *Fife Trades Directory, 1914.*
9. *Jewish Chronicle*, 28 January, 1848.
10. *Jewish Chronicle*, 26 November, 1852.
11. Ruddick, *My Mother's Daughter*, p. 2.
12. Collins, *Go and Learn*, p. 75.
13. Collins, *Be Well!*, p. 37.
14. Collins, *Be Well!*, p. 37.
15. Ruddick, *My Mother's Daughter*, p. 1.
16. Jill Whitehead, "The Brown Family of Edinburgh," *Shemot*, 11:1, p. 16.
17. Collins, *Be Well!*, p. 37.
18. David Daiches, *Two Worlds: An Edinburgh Jewish Childhood* (Edinburgh: Canongate, 1997), p. 121.
19. Daiches, *Two Worlds*, p. 122.

20. Gartner, *The Jewish Immigrant in England*, p. 60.
21. Daiches, *Two Worlds*, p. 122.
22. Gartner, *The Jewish Immigrant in England*, p. 60.
23. Collins, *Aspects of Scottish Jewry*, p. 39.
24. *Dunfermline Directory, 1909, 1910–11.*
25. *Jewish Chronicle*, 16 October, 1908.
26. *Jewish Chronicle*, 27 November, 1908; *JYB*, 1911.
27. *Jewish Chronicle*, 27 September, 1912; *Jewish Chronicle*, 4 April, 191; *Jewish Chronicle*, 2 June, 1916; *Jewish Chronicle*, 16 February, 1917; *Jewish Chronicle*, 6 July, 1917; *Jewish Chronicle*, 7 September, 1917; *Jewish Chronicle*, 12 September, 1919; *Jewish Chronicle*, 19 December, 1919.
28. Ross, *The Robert (Spilg) Spence Story*, pp. 7, 8, 9.
29. W.I. Hodes, letter to the Chief Rabbi, 11 May, 1919, ACC/285/4/2/111, LMA.
30. H. Green, Letter to the Chief Rabbi, 8 July, 1919, ACC/285/4/2/111, LMA.
31. "Dunfermline Hebrew Congregation," http://www.jewishgen.org/jcr-uk/Community/Dunfermline/index.htm. Accessed August 2008.
32. *Jewish Chronicle*, 22 October, 1920.
33. Ruddick, *My Mother's Daughter*, p. 3.
34. Ruddick, *My Mother's Daughter*, p. 3.
35. See, for example, Harold Pollins, "The Jewish Community of Brynmawr, Wales," *The Jewish Journal of Sociology*, 50: 1 & 2 (2008), pp. 5–32.
36. *Jewish Echo*, 4 October, 1929.
37. Ruddick, *My Mother's Daughter*, p. 5.
38. Home Office: Registered Papers, Supplementary HO 144/1324/254227, Nationality and Naturalisation: Segal, Morris Symon, from Russia. Resident in Edinburgh. Certificate 25618 issued 24 October, 1914.
39. ACC/2805/1/4/3, LMA; ACC/2805/4/1/84, LMA.
40. Sonia Fodor, "Growing Up in Dundee," http://www.thorngent.eclipse.co.uk/exeshul/newsletter/dundee.htm. Last accessed August 2008.
41. Ruddick, *My Mother's Daughter*, p. 6.
42. *Ibid.*, p. 3.
43. *Ibid.*, p. 4.
44. *Ibid.*, p. 3.
45. *Ibid.*, p. 36
46. *Jewish Echo*, 24 March, 1933; *Jewish Chronicle*, 17 January, 1936; *Jewish Echo*, 17 January, 1936; *Jewish Chronicle*, 14 July, 1933.
47. *Jewish Telegraph*, 1 July, 2005; Ruddick, *My Mother's Daughter*, p. 5.
48. I am grateful to Doris Lewis (née Segal) for providing me with this information.
49. *Dunfermline Press*, 5 April, 1924.
50. I am grateful to Doris Lewis (née Segal) for providing me with this information.
51. Ruddick, *My Mother's Daughter*, pp. 4–5.
52. *Jewish Chronicle*, 15 December, 1939.
53. *Jewish Echo*, 23 May, 1941
54. Ruddick, *My Mother's Daughter*, p. 3.
55. *Jewish Chronicle*, 15 May, 1942; *Ibid.*
56. "Dunfermline's Jewish Connections," *Scottish Local History*, 67 (Summer 2006), p. 15.
57. *Dunfermline Press*, 2 March, 2006.
58 . *Jewish Chronicle*, 10 May, 1940; *Jewish Chronicle*, 15 May, 1942; *Jewish Echo*, 15 May, 1942. See also Doris Lewis in *Serving Their Country: Wartime Memories of Scottish Jews*, ed. Adele Conn (Glasgow: Glasgow Jewish Representative Council/Scottish Jewish Archives Centre, 2001), p. 38.
59. J.M. Green, *From Colditz in Code* (Hull: The Wilberforce Council, 1989), p. 143.
60. *Jewish Echo*, 17 August, 1945; *Jewish Chronicle*, 17 August, 1945.
61. Martin Sugarman, "Jewish POWs at Colditz," http://www.jewishvirtuallibrary.org/jsource/ww2/sugar6.html. Last accessed August 2008; *Jewish Chronicle*, 17 November, 1989.
62. *Canadian Press*, 3 July, 1945.
63. "Canadian Jewish Casualties in the Canadian Armed Forces," http://www.cjccc.ca/archives/casualtyinfo.php?info=496. Accessed September 2008.
64. *JYB, 1948*; "Dunfermline Hebrew Congregation," http://www.jewishgen.org/jcr-uk/Community/Dunfermline/index.htm. Accessed August 2008.
65. Smith, *The Making of Scotland*, p. 290.
66. *Jewish Chronicle*, 8 October, 1948.
67. Newlands, "The Regional Economies of Scotland," p. 171.
68. Jim White, email to author, 3 March, 2006.
69. *Jewish Echo*, 27 June, 1958; *Jewish Echo*, 29 April, 1960; *Jewish Echo*, 30 April, 1965.
70. I am grateful to Doris Lewis (née Segal) for providing me with this information.
71. *Jewish Echo*, 19 June, 1931; *Jewish Echo*, 6 May, 1932; *Jewish Echo*, 29 June, 1934.
72. *Jewish Chronicle*, 9 May, 1941.
73. *Jewish Chronicle*, 22 January, 1988.
74. *Jewish Chronicle*, 11 December, 1964.
75. *Jewish Chronicle*, 8 July, 2005; *Dunfermline Press*, 2 March, 2006.
76. Ruddick, *My Mother's Daughter*, p. 3.

Chapter 5

1. John Stewart, *Falkirk, Its Origins and Growth: A History of the Burgh* (Falkirk: F. Johnston, 1940), p. 181.
2. Smith, *The Making of Scotland*, p. 347.
3. Stewart, *Falkirk*, p. 182.
4. Collins, *Go and Learn*, p. 75.
5. Collins, *Go and Learn*, p. 75.
6. Collins, "Growth and Development of Scottish Jewry, 1880–1940," p. 39.

7. Lewis Lawson, *A History of Falkirk* (Falkirk: Falkirk Town Council, 1975), pp. 112-3.
8. *Jewish Chronicle*, 5 February, 1875; *Jewish Chronicle*, 21 May, 1875; *Jewish Chronicle*, 23 June, 1876.
9. Collins, *Scotland's Jews*, p. 26.
10. HO 144/304/B4914, Nationality and Naturalisation: Cohen, David, from Russia. Resident in Falkirk. Certificate A6026 issued 7 February, 1889.
11. HO 144/462/B32439, Nationality and Naturalisation: Cohen, Lewis Meyer, from Russia. Resident in Falkirk. Certificate A11609 issued 7 August, 1900.
12. HO 144/866/157544, Nationality and Naturalisation: Garbarski, Abraham Lewis (known as Abraham Lewis), from Russia. Resident in Falkirk. Certificate 17231 issued 24 January, 1908.
13. HO 144/1130/206113, Nationality and Naturalisation: Hassmann, Francis, from Germany. Resident in Falkirk. Certificate 20668 issued 8 September, 1911.
14. HO 144/1180/217422, Nationality and Naturalisation. Bulbin, Abraham, from Russia. Resident in Falkirk. Certificate 21315 issued 5 February, 1912.
15. Home Office: Registered Papers, Supplementary HO 144/1380/266809, Nationality and Naturalisation: Spilg, Max, from Russia. Resident in Falkirk. Certificate 1,469 issued 25 February, 1916.
16. Records held by the Falkirk Council Archives, Falkirk, A736.001.
17. Emmanuel Shinwell, *Conflict Without Malice* (London: Odhams Press, 1955), p. 21.
18. Avrom Saltman, "To Be Buried in Grimsby" (April 1998), http://www.jewishgen.org/jcr-uk/community/Gr/all.htm. Last accessed August 2008.
19. "Falkirk Synagogue," http://www.jewishgen.org/jcr-uk/Community/falkirk/index.htm. Last accessed August 2008.
20. *Jewish Chronicle*, 1 August, 1913.
21. Collins, *Go and Learn*, p. 85; Jerry White, *Rothschild Buildings: Life in an East End Tenement Block, 1887-1920* (London: Routledge, 1980), p. 116.
22. *Jewish Chronicle*, 31 October, 1913.
23. Ross, *The Robert (Spilg) Spence Story*, p. 2; Ken Waddell, "A Nickname Out of the Past," *Falkirk Herald*, newspaper clipping held by Falkirk Council Archives, n.d., c.1971; A390.01.
24. Collins, "Growth and Development of Scottish Jewry, 1880-1940," p. 39; Collins, *Scotland's Jews*, p. 16.
25. Ross, *The Robert (Spilg) Spence Story*, p. 2.
26. *Ibid.*, p. 3.
27. Waddell, "A Nickname Out of the Past."
28. *Ibid.*; Ross, *The Robert (Spilg) Spence Story*, p. 4.
29. Ross, *The Robert (Spilg) Spence Story*, p. 4.
30. *Ibid.*, p. 6.
31. *Ibid.*, p. 4.
32. *Ibid.*
33. Waddell, "A Nickname Out of the Past."
34. Ross, *The Robert (Spilg) Spence Story*, p. 6.
35. Waddell, "A Nickname Out of the Past."
36. Jackie Taylor, "A Communal Revival in Falkirk?" *Edinburgh Star*, 35 (February 2000), p. 6.
37. Letter from Marshall & Hunter, Solicitors, to the Chief Rabbi, 1 November, 1917, ACC/285/4/2/111, LMA.
38. Interview with Thomas Tate, 21 September, 1986, SJAC.
39. This photograph can be viewed at: http://www.falkirklocalhistorysociety.co.uk/images/falkirk47.jpg. Last accessed in August 2008.
40. Lawson, *A History of Falkirk*, p. 127.
41. Nat Dolan, email to author, 9 February, 2006.
42. Taylor, "A Communal Revival in Falkirk?" p. 6.
43. Lawson, *A History of Falkirk*, p. 128.
44. *Jewish Chronicle*, 24 July, 1914.
45. *Jewish Chronicle*, 11 September, 1914.
46. *Jewish Chronicle*, 14 January, 1916.
47. *Jewish Chronicle*, 27 October, 1916.
48. *Jewish Chronicle*, 9 November, 1917.
49. Letter from Marshall & Hunter, 1 November, 1917, LMA.
50. Collins, *Second City Jewry*, p. 192.
51. *Jewish Chronicle*, 22 January, 1923; *Jewish Chronicle*, 21 March, 1919; *Jewish Chronicle*, 25 July, 1919; *Jewish Chronicle*, 23 June, 1922; *Jewish Chronicle*, 16 June, 1933.
52. Kaplan, "The Jewish Colonial Trust."
53. Taylor, "A Communal Revival in Falkirk?" p. 6.
54. *Jewish Chronicle*, 19 December, 1930; *Jewish Chronicle*, 10 January, 1936; *Jewish Chronicle*, 28 February, 1936; *Jewish Chronicle*, 12 February, 1937; *Jewish Chronicle*, 13 May, 1938.
55. *Jewish Chronicle*, 24 April, 1936.
56. *Jewish Chronicle*, 30 December, 1938.
57. Nat Dolan, email to author, 9 February, 2006.
58. *Jewish Echo*, 21 February, 1936; *Jewish Echo*, 16 February, 1936.
59. *Jewish Chronicle*, 10 June, 1938.
60. Nat Dolan, email to author, 9 February, 2006.
61. *Ibid.*
62. *Jewish Chronicle*, 1 July, 1938.
63. *Jewish Chronicle*, 5 April, 1940.
64. *Jewish Chronicle*, 1 November, 1940.
65. Waddell, "A Nickname Out of the Past";

Taylor, "A Communal Revival in Falkirk?" p. 6.
66. *Jewish Chronicle*, 24 March, 1950.
67. *Jewish Chronicle*, 19 January, 1940; *Jewish Chronicle*, 3 September, 1948; *Jewish Chronicle*, 15 June, 1956; *Jewish Chronicle*, 15 February, 1957; *Jewish Chronicle*, 19 June, 1959.
68. *Jewish Chronicle*, 31 January, 1947.
69. *Jewish Chronicle*, May 26, 1961.
70. *Jewish Chronicle*, 13 October, 1961.
71. *Jewish Chronicle*, 11 December, 1964.
72. *Falkirk Directory, 1966–67*.
73. *Jewish Chronicle*, 10 September, 1971; *Jewish Chronicle*, 28 April, 1978.
74. *Jewish Chronicle*, 1 April, 1921; Collins, *Second City Jewry*, p. 220; Collins, *Be Well!*, p. 74.
75. *Jewish Echo*, 10 November, 1978.
76. *Ibid.*
77. *Jewish Chronicle*, 4 May, 1984.
78. *Jewish Chronicle*, 24 December, 1999.
79. Taylor, "A Communal Revival in Falkirk?" p. 6.

Chapter 6

1. Smith, *The Making of Scotland*, p. 448.
2. Collins, *Go and Learn*, p. 75.
3. Collins, *Second City Jewry*, pp. 65, 66.
4. Kadish, *Jewish Heritage in England*, p. 200.
5. Mark Smith, "The Last Jews of Greenock," *Edinburgh Star*, 26 (1997), p. 14.
6. Smith, "The Last Jews of Greenock," p. 14.
7. *Ibid.*
8. Hofman, *Mackerel at Midnight*, p. 1.
9. Collins, *Second City Jewry*, p. 71.
10. Smith, "The Last Jews of Greenock," p. 14–15.
11. Nicholas J. Evans, emails to author, 4 and 5 September, 2008.
12. Smith, "The Last Jews of Greenock," p. 14.
13. Collins, *Be Well!*, p. 146.
14. *Greenock Telegraph*, 9 November, 1874.
15. *Ibid.*
16. HO 144/374/B18147, Nationality and Naturalization: Weber, Alexander Carl, from Austria. Resident in Greenock. Certificate A8347 issued 21 May, 1895; HO 144/388/B20460, Nationality and Naturalisation: Ruhe, Adolph, from Germany. Resident in Greenock. Certificate A8978 issued 6 May, 1896; HO 144/398/B21973, Nationality and Naturalization: Scharina, Wilhelm Eduard Herrmann, from Germany. Resident in Greenock. Certificate A9785 issued 5 August, 1887; HO 144/455/B31385, Nationality and Naturalization: Heitmann, Carl Johann Julius, from Germany. Resident in Greenock. Certificate A11369 issued 8 March, 1900; HO 144/457/B31723, Nationality and Naturalization: Ohlms, William, from Germany. Resident in Greenock. Certificate A11418 issued 29 March, 1900; HO 144/650/B38193, Nationality and Naturalization: Wohlgemuth, John Frederick Charles, from Germany. Resident in Greenock, Renfrewshire. Certificate 12728 issued 14 April, 1902; HO 144/920/181661, Nationality and Naturalization: Baker, Wilhelm John Matisz, from Germany. Resident in Greenock. Certificate 18623 issued 8 December, 1909; HO 144/1067/189888, Nationality and Naturalization: Gaze, Wilhelm (known as William Gaze), from Germany. Resident in Greenock. Certificate 19025 issued 12 May, 1910; HO 144/1103/199397, Nationality and Naturalization: Hinrichs, Andreas Christian, from Germany. Resident in Greenock. Certificate 24597 issued 22 December, 1913; HO 144/1220/226154, Nationality and Naturalization: Bentz, Herman, from Germany. Resident in Greenock. Certificate 22435 issued 27 September, 1912.
17. John M. Hutcheson, *Notes on the Sugar Industry of the United Kingdom* (Greenock: James M'Kelvie, 1901), p. 69.
18. Harold Pollins, "Draft List of Jewish Residents in Greenock," September 1996, SJAC.
19. *Jewish Chronicle*, 9 March, 1883.
20. *Jewish Chronicle*, 28 July, 1882.
21. *Jewish Chronicle*, 29 September, 1893.
22. *Jewish Chronicle*, 2 November, 1894.
23. "Greenock Hebrew Congregation," http://www.jewishgen.org/jcr-uk/Community/greenock/index.htm. Last accessed August 2008.
24. Collins, *Second City Jewry*, p. 65.
25. Kadish, *Jewish Heritage in England*, p. 200.
26. "Greenock Hebrew Congregation," http://www.jewishgen.org/jcr-uk/Community/greenock/index.htm. Last accessed August 2008.
27. Smith, "The Last Jews of Greenock," p. 15.
28. *Jewish Chronicle*, 15 November, 1895.
29. *Jewish Chronicle*, 24 February, 1899.
30. *Jewish Chronicle*, 25 February, 1905.
31. *Jewish Chronicle*, 29 December, 1905.
32. "Authorisation for the Celebration of Marriage," issued by the Office of the Chief Rabbi, 3 January, 1906 (document in author's possession).
33. "Authorisation for the Celebration of Marriage," issued by the Office of the Chief Rabbi, 3 January, 1906; Marriage Register (both documents in author's possession); Home Office: Registered Papers, Supplementary HO 144/1064/189459 Nationality and Naturalization: Pinkus, Abram (known as Abram Levy), from Russia. Resident in Greenock. Certificate 18975 issued 20 April, 1910.

Notes—Chapter 6

34. *Jewish Chronicle*, 2 March, 1906.
35. Smith, "The Last Jews of Greenock," p. 15.
36. Kaplan, "The Jewish Colonial Trust" and "JCT" (unpublished documents in author's possession).
37. *Jewish Chronicle*, 14 December, 1906.
38. *Jewish Chronicle*, 21 December, 1906.
39. *New York Times*, 10 November, 1992.
40. *Jewish Chronicle*, 25 December, 1992.
41. *Jewish Chronicle*, 7 June, 1907.
42. *Greenock Telegraph and Clyde Shipping Gazette*, 4 June, 1907.
43. *Jewish Chronicle*, 7 June, 1907; *Greenock Telegraph and Clyde Shipping Gazette*, 4 June, 1907.
44. Alexandra Kirkpatrick, email to the author, 17 April, 2006.
45. Harvey Kaplan, "Jewish Burial Grounds in Scotland," unpublished document in author's possession, p. 3; see also "Jewish Cemeteries in Scotland," http://www.jgsgb.org.uk/bury03.shtml. Last accessed August 2008.
46. Harold Pollins, "An Archival Adventure in Scotland," *Oxford Menorah*, 142 (Winter 1996), pp. 13–14.
47. Smith, "The Last Jews of Greenock," p. 14.
48. Kadish, *Jewish Heritage in England*, p. 200.
49. *Jewish Chronicle*, 22 September, 1911; *Jewish Chronicle*, 28 August, 1914.
50. *Greenock Telegraph and Clyde Shipping Register*, 4 October, 1918; Pollins, "An Archival Adventure in Scotland," p. 13.
51. Kadish, *Jewish Heritage in England*, p. 200.
52. *Jewish Chronicle*, 14 April, 1922.
53. HO 144/639/B37524, Nationality and Naturalization: Banks, Harris, from Russia. Resident in Greenock. Certificate 12558 issued 22 May, 1902; HO 144/915/180028, Nationality and Naturalization: Fagerson, Ruben (known as Ruben Ferguson), from Russia. Resident in Greenock. Certificate 18509 issued 28 October, 1909; HO 144/1087/194401, Nationality and Naturalization: Blumberg, Edward, from Russia. Resident in Greenock. Certificate 19444 issued 2 September, 1910; HO 144/1283/241437, Nationality and Naturalization: Freedman, Abraham, from Russia. Resident in Greenock. Certificate 24149 issued 4 October, 1913.
54. HO 144/1655/247471, Nationality and Naturalization: Lopes, Joseph, from Italy. Resident in Greenock. Certificate 24839 issued 27 February, 1914.
55. Shinwell, *Conflict Without Malice*, p. 51.
56. *JYB, 1914, 1915*.
57. Collins, "Growth and Development of Scottish Jewry, 1880–1940," p. 38.
58. *Jewish Chronicle*, 10 August, 1917.
59. Interview with Thomas Tate, 21 September, 1986, SJAC.
60. Collins, "Growth and Development of Scottish Jewry," p. 38.
61. Pollins, "An Archival Adventure in Scotland," pp. 13–14.
62. Harold Pollins, email to Harvey Kaplan, 12 January, 2007 (copy in author's possession).
63. Pollins, "An Archival Adventure in Scotland," pp. 13–14.
64. *Jewish Chronicle*, 16 September, 1966.
65. *Jewish Chronicle*, 20 August, 1915; *Jewish Chronicle*, 19 June, 1908; *Jewish Chronicle*, 15 October, 1915; *Jewish Chronicle*, 2 June, 1916; *Jewish Chronicle*, 10 November, 1916; *Jewish Chronicle*, 20 April, 1917; *Jewish Chronicle*, 22 June, 1917; *Jewish Chronicle*, 27 July, 1917; *Jewish Chronicle*, 10 August, 1917; *Jewish Chronicle*, 7 September, 1917; *Jewish Chronicle*, 26 October, 1917; *Jewish Chronicle*, 1 September, 1916.
66. *Jewish Chronicle*, 4 March, 1921.
67. *Jewish Chronicle*, 25 March, 1921; *Jewish Chronicle*, 10 June, 1921; *Jewish Chronicle*, 26 August, 1921; *Jewish Chronicle*, 16 December, 192; *Jewish Chronicle*, 15 January, 1923; *Jewish Chronicle*, 6 April, 1923; *Jewish Chronicle*, 8 June, 1923.
68. L. Alexander Wolfe, letter to Harvey Kaplan, 10 December, 2001, SJAC.
69. *Jewish Echo*, 3 October, 1930. See also *Jewish Echo*, 28 September, 1928; *Jewish Echo*, 18 October, 1929.
70. *Jewish Echo*, 3 August, 1928.
71. Ronald S. (Roy) Friedman, email to author, 6 May, 2005.
72. *Jewish Chronicle*, 3 September, 1926.
73. Anthony Slaven, *The Development of the West of Scotland: 1750–1960* (London: Routledge, 1975), p. 199.
74. Slaven, *The Development of the West of Scotland*, pp. 199, 235.
75. *Jewish Chronicle*, 16 June, 1933.
76. *Jewish Chronicle*, 14 November, 1930; *Jewish Chronicle*, 22 November, 1935.
77. *Jewish Chronicle*, 22 November, 1935.
78. *Jewish Chronicle*, 18 March, 1949.
79. *Jewish Chronicle*, 14 November, 1930; *Jewish Chronicle*, 1 November, 1933; *Jewish Chronicle*, 22 November, 1935; *Jewish Echo*, 15 November, 1935.
80. *Jewish Echo*, 15 November, 1935.
81. *Jewish Chronicle*, 1 August, 1947.
82. Collins, "Growth and Development of Scottish Jewry," p. 38.
83. *Jewish Chronicle*, 24 January, 1936.
84. *Jewish Chronicle*, 1 October, 1937.
85. *Jewish Chronicle*, 4 June, 1937; *Jewish Chronicle*, 17 February, 1939; *Jewish Chronicle*, 2 February, 1940.
86. Ronald S (Roy) Friedman, email to author, 6 May, 2005.
87. Devine, *The Scottish Nation*, p. 545.

88. *Jewish Chronicle*, 20 November, 1942; *Jewish Chronicle*, 25 December, 1942.
89. Jessie Ritchie, "The Greenock Blitz: May 1941," http://www.bbc.co.uk/ww2peopleswar/stories/69/a2451269.shtml. Last accessed August 2008.
90. Smith, "The Last Jews of Greenock," p. 15.
91. *Ibid.*
92. *Jewish Chronicle*, 24 March, 1950.
93. *British Health Journal*, 12 August, 2000.
94. Alexandra Kirkpatrick, email to the author, 17 April, 2006; *Greenock Telegraph*, 30 June, 2000.
95. *Jewish Chronicle*, 14 May, 1965; *Jewish Telegraph*, 3 June, 2006.
96. *Jewish Chronicle*, 1 March, 1968.
97. *Jewish Echo*, 14 December, 1973.
98. *Jewish Echo*, 14 December, 1973.
99. *Jewish Echo*, 4 November, 1966.

Chapter 7

1. *Inverness Journal*, 5 March, 1830.
2. John Ross, email to author, 17 January, 2006.
3. *Jewish Chronicle*, 27 August, 1897.
4. John Ross, email to author, 16 January, 2006.
5. *Ibid.*
6. James Barron, *The Northern Highlands in the Nineteenth Century: Newspaper Index and Annals (from the 'Inverness Courier'), Vol. III, 1842–1856* (Inverness: Robt. Carruthers & Sons, 1913), p. 150.
7. *Jewish Chronicle*, 28 January, 1848.
8. *John O'Groat Journal*, 18 February, 1848.
9. *John O'Groat Journal*, 23 December, 1853.
10. *Jewish Chronicle*, 9 September, 1910.
11. John Ross, email to author, 16 January, 2006.
12. *John O'Groat Journal*, 22 October, 1841; *Inverness Journal*, 16 December, 1842; *Inverness Advertiser*, 16 April, 1850; *Inverness Advertiser*, 30 April, 1850; *Inverness Advertiser*, 12 December, 1855; *Inverness Advertiser*, 25 September, 1855; *John O'Groat Journal*, 23 May, 1845.
13. *Jewish Chronicle*, 9 March, 1883.
14. *Jewish Chronicle*, 10 November, 1911.
15. Simon Jackson, email to author, 14 and 15 February, 2006.
16. Gary Davis, email to Harvey Kaplan, 3 April, 2004.
17. *Jewish Chronicle*, 4 August, 1905.
18. *Jewish Chronicle*, 7 September, 1906.
19. *Jewish Chronicle*, 4 May, 1906.
20. *Jewish Chronicle*, 10 February, 1905.
21. Letter to the Chief Rabbi, 31 August, 1904, ACC/2805/01/01/105, LMA.
22. *Jewish Chronicle*, 10 February, 1905.
23. *Ibid.*
24. *Jewish Chronicle*, 12 April, 1907.
25. *Jewish Chronicle*, 16 December, 1938; Home Office: Registered Papers, Supplementary HO 144/2320, Nationality and Naturalisation: Arkush, Samuel, from Poland. Resident in Cardiff. Certificate B.556 issued 9 November, 1923.
26. *Jewish Chronicle*, 10 December, 1907.
27. *Jewish Chronicle*, 12 January, 1906.
28. *Inverness Courier*, 12 May, 1911.
29. *The Scotsman*, 26 June, 1911.
30. *The Scotsman*, 6 July, 1911.
31. *Inverness Courier*, 16 May,1911; *Inverness Courier*, 7 July, 1911. I am grateful to Harvey Kaplan for pointing this out to me.
32. *Jewish Chronicle*, 14 August, 1908; Collins, *Second City Jewry*, p. 140.
33. Home Office: Registered Papers, Supplementary HO 144/2320, Nationality and Naturalisation: Arkush, Esther. Child of Samuel Arkush. Certificate B.556.
34. Endelman, *The Jews of Britain*, p. 146.
35. *Jewish Chronicle*, 2 February, 1912.
36. *Jewish Chronicle*, 11 April, 1913.
37. *Jewish Chronicle*, 14 March, 1916.
38. S. Gerber, letter to the Chief Rabbi, 17 November, 1915, ACC/285/4/2/111, LMA. I am grateful to Dovid Katz for providing me with a translation here.
39. *Jewish Chronicle*, 28 March, 1919.
40. I. Ticktin, letter to the Chief Rabbi, 30 July, 1917; 14 August, 1918; and 7 December, 1918, ACC/285/4/2/111, LMA.
41. I. Ticktin, letter to the Chief Rabbi, 19 October, 1918, ACC/285/4/2/111, LMA. I am grateful to Dovid Katz for providing me with a translation here.
42. Isidore Wartski, letter to Reverend Feldman, n.d., c.1920, ACC/2805/4/2/2), LMA.
43. *Ibid.*
44. *Jewish Chronicle*, 27 July, 1906.
45. "The Chief Rabbi's Pastoral Tour," *Jewish Chronicle*, 7 September, 1917.
46. *Jewish Chronicle*, 4 March, 1921.
47. *Jewish Chronicle*, 12 April, 1929; *Jewish Chronicle*, 29 December, 1939; *Jewish Chronicle*, 18 August, 1944; *Jewish Chronicle*, 11 October, 1946.
48. *Jewish Chronicle*, 18 October, 1912; *Jewish Chronicle*, 28 June, 1912.
49. *Jewish Chronicle*, 4 October, 1912.
50. *Jewish Chronicle*, 29 November, 1918.
51. Collins, *Go and Learn*, p. 75.
52. Robert Gourlay and Anne Turner, *Historic Inverness: The Archaeological Implications of Development* (Glasgow: Scottish Burgh Survey, 1977), pp. 5, 7.
53. *Hashanah: The Scottish Jewish Year Book, 1955–56*.
54. *Jewish Chronicle*, 27 April, 1951.

55. *Inverness Courier*, 30 March, 1934.
56. Vicki Lazar, letter to author, n.d.
57. *Jewish Chronicle*, 7 August, 1931.
58. *Jewish Chronicle*, 18 January, 1924; *Jewish Chronicle*, 1 June, 1923.
59. *Inverness Courier*, 14 October, 1927.
60. *Inverness Courier*, 15 February, 1929.
61. *Inverness Courier*, 19 October, 1926; *Inverness Courier*, 7 April, 1928; *Inverness Courier*, 2 April, 1929.
62. *Inverness Courier*, 30 December, 2005.
63. John M. Matheson, letter to author, 26 January, 2006; *Inverness Courier*, 6 February, 1931.
64. *Inverness Courier*, 12 July, 1921.
65. D.N. Pritt, *The Autobiography of D.N. Pritt, Vol. 2* (London: Lawrence & Wishart, 1966), pp. 253–6.
66. Margaret Mulholland, email to author, 11 December, 2005.
67. Fiona MacLeod, email to author, 25 August, 2005; *Inverness Courier*, 31 January, 2006.
68. *Inverness Courier*, 28 March, 1930.
69. *Jewish Echo*, 29 October, 1937.
70. *Jewish Chronicle*, 23 November, 1934.
71. Kibblewhite and Rigby, *Fascism in Aberdeen*, p. 23.
72. *Inverness Courier*, 6 October, 1933.
73. *Inverness Courier*, 13 January, 1939.
74. *Jewish Chronicle*, 6 May, 1938.
75. *Jewish Chronicle*, 8 December, 1939.
76. *Jewish Chronicle*, 22 June, 1945; 23 February, 1945.
77. *Jewish Echo*, 24 May, 1940.
78. *Jewish Echo*, 25 May, 1940.
79. Ernest Elijs Jacobs, email to author, 13 January, 2006.
80. *Jewish Chronicle*, 30 March, 1973.
81. *Jewish Chronicle*, 13 July, 1945.
82. *Jewish Chronicle*, 11 November, 1946.
83. *Jewish Echo*, 12 June, 1953.
84. *Hashanah: The Scottish Jewish Year Book, 1955–57*.
85. *Jewish Chronicle*, 27 April, 1962.
86. Ken Morris, letter to author, 6 December, 2005.
87. L. Morris to Julius Jung, 31 October, 1962, Jung Papers.
88. L. Morris to Julius Jung, 8 October, 1964, and 31 October, 1962, Jung Papers.
89. *Jewish Chronicle*, 16 August, 1968.
90. This information is culled from a variety of (often conflicting) sources, including *The Jewish Year Book*, records held at the SJAC, and Collins, *Go and Learn*, pp. 74–5. With regards to Inverness, Abraham Levy wrote in 1958, "A small Jewish community existed in Inverness for a time but is now dissolved." He was obviously referring to the synagogue. See Levy, *The Origins of Scottish Jewry*, p. 29.
91. *Jewish Chronicle*, 30 March, 1973.
92. *Jewish Chronicle*, 29 August, 1975.
93. *Jewish Chronicle*, 9 August, 1973; *Jewish Chronicle*, 24 July, 1975; *Jewish Chronicle*, 7 July, 1978; *Jewish Chronicle*, 10 August, 1979; *Jewish Chronicle*, 4 July, 1980.
94. *Jewish Chronicle*, 7 August, 1981.
95. *Jewish Chronicle*, 11 November, 1927.
96. *Jewish Chronicle*, 4 November, 1921.
97. *Jewish Chronicle*, 1 June, 1923.
98. *Jewish Chronicle*, 28 January, 1944.
99. *Jewish Chronicle*, 10 March, 1944.
100. *Jewish Chronicle*, 29 December, 1950; *Jewish Chronicle*, 15 June, 1951.
101. L Gavin, letter to the Chief Rabbi, 6 December, 1919, ACC/285/4/2/111, LMA.
102. Richard Kearton, *With Nature and a Camera: Being the Adventures and Observations of a Field Naturalist and an Animal Photographer* (London: Cassell & Co., Ltd., 1898), p. 28.
103. Hunter, "Julius Quint," pp. 24–5. Photos of Quint can be viewed at: http://community.webshots.com/slideshow/94158009EtSjjE?mediaPosition=94159042.
104. Donald and Eileen Macleod, email to author, 15 January, 2006.
105. *Highland News*, 3 July, 1897.
106. *Highland News*, 31 January, 1917.
107. Donald Macleod, email to author, 26 January, 2006.
108. *Inverness Courier*, 17 July, 1879.
109. Hirschman and Yates, *When Scotland Was Jewish*, pp. 97–9.
110. *Jewish Chronicle*, 11 November, 1938.
111. Kadish, *Jewish Heritage in England*, p. 201.
112. *Stornoway Gazette*, 17 April, 2003; Per Kristian Sebak, *Titanic's Predecessor: The S/S Norge Disaster of 1904* (Lakesvaag: Seaward, 2004), chap. xi; Kaplan, "Jewish Burial Grounds in Scotland."
113. Kadish, *Jewish Heritage in England*, p. 201.
114. *The Scotsman*, 30 May, 1921.
115. "Moses Lewis Usher," *Canadian Jewish Casualties in the Canadian Armed Forces*, http://www.cjccc.ca/archives/casualtyinfo.php?info=4 5. Last accessed July 2008.
116. "Canadian Jewish Casualties in the Canadian Armed Forces," http://www.cjccc.ca/archives/casualtyinfo.php?info=501. Accessed September 2008.
117. "Canadian Jewish Casualties in the Canadian Armed Forces," http://www.cjccc.ca/archives/casualtyinfo.php?info=189. Accessed September 2008.
118. *Jewish Echo*, 23 January, 1964.
119. *Jewish Echo*, 6 February, 1981.
120. *Four Corners*, 10 (August 2006).
121. "VAF Capacity Building Grant—Report of Activity and Outcomes," Scottish Council of Jewish Communities, April 2006 (copy in author's possession), pp. 4–5.
122. *Four Corners*, 12 (December 2006).

123. Hofman, *Mackerel at Midnight*, p. 9.
124. *Ibid.*, pp. 9–12.
125. *Ibid.*, pp. 19–20.
126. *Ibid.*, p. 19.
127. *Ibid.*, p. 67.
128. *Ibid.*, p. 61.
129. *Ibid.*, p. 41.
130. Rather confusingly, from a statistical point of view, the Jewish Chaplain of the U.S. Army, Ivring Tepper, reported that three hundred soldiers arrived to swell the two hundred already assembled in the local Guildhall. *Jewish Chronicle*, 21 April, 1944.
131. *Shetland Times*, 14 April, 1944.
132. *Jewish Chronicle*, 23 February, 1945.
133. *Jewish Chronicle*, 24 July, 1975; *Jewish Chronicle*, 7 July, 1978; *Jewish Chronicle*, 10 August, 1979; *Jewish Chronicle*, 4 July, 1980; *Jewish Chronicle*, 7 August, 1981.

Conclusion

1. Teff, *O'er Vales and Hills*, p. 14.
2. Murray and Stockdale, *The Miles Tae Dundee*, p. 27.
3. Maitles, "Attitudes to Jewish Immigration in the West of Scotland to 1905," p. 48.
4. Audrey, "Glasgow Jewry," p. 7.
5. Pollins, *Economic History of the Jews in England*, p. 178.
6. Collins, *Go and Learn*, p. 75.
7. *Ibid.*
8. Teff, *Oe'r Hills and Far Away*, p. 17.
9. *The Scotsman*, 17 May, 1910.
10. Collins, *Go and Learn*, p. 114.
11. *Ibid.*
12. *Jewish Echo*, 9 December, 1988.
13. Lee Shai Weissbach, "East European Immigrants and the Image of the Jews in the Small-Town South," *American Jewish History*, 85:3 (1997), p. 243.
14. *Jewish Echo*, 23 May, 1941.
15. Robertson, ed., *A-Z of the Hilltown*, p. 31.
16. Records of Aberdeen Hebrew Congregation, 6 September, 1992.
17. *Dundee Courier and Advertiser*, 6 November, 1883; Collins, ed., "Growth and Development of Scottish Jewry, 1880–1940," p. 37; Daiches, "The Jew in Scotland," p. 208.
18. Jennifer Krase, "Jewish Community in Aberdeen: Developing Individual Identity," unpublished paper, University of Aberdeen, 2006, p. 7.
19. Aronsfeld, "German Jews in Dundee," p. 15.
20. *Ibid.*
21. Teff, *O'er Vales and Hills*, p. 14.
22. *Jewish Chronicle*, 25 February, 1905.
23. Collins, *Go and Learn*, p. 69; *Jewish Chronicle*, 25 February, 1905.

24. Lee Shai Weissbach's essay, "Small Jewish Communities in the Era of Mass Migration: The American Experience," in *Patterns of Migration, 1850–1914*, eds. Aubrey Newman and Stephen W. Massil (London: The Jewish Historical Society of England, 1996), pp. 159–74, has been very instructive here.
25. Lionel Shrago, interview by author, 4 July, 2005.
26. Shein, email to author, 8 July, 2005.
27. *Jewish Chronicle*, 22 March, 1940.
28. "VAF Capacity Building Grant," p. 1.
29. Weissbach, "East European Immigrants," pp. 244–5.
30. Hofman, *Mackerel at Midnight*, pp. 19–20.
31. Records of the Aberdeen Hebrew Congregation, 26 May, 1896.
32. Hofman, *Mackerel at Midnight*, p. 70.
33. Teff, *O'er Vales and Hills*, p. 15.
34. Harold Levy, 25 June, 1957, Aberdeen Hebrew Congregation Records.
35. *Ibid.*
36. Weissbach, "East European Immigrants," p. 256.
37. *Jewish Chronicle*, 21 May, 1993.
38. Shein to author, 8 July, 2005.
39. *Jewish Chronicle*, 12 March, 1926.
40. *Jewish Echo*, 7 May, 1976.
41. *Four Corners*, 10 (August 2006).
42. Kaplan, "The Jewish Colonial Trust."
43. *The Scotsman*, 17 May, 1910.
44. *Ibid.*
45. *Hashanah: The Scottish Jewish Year Book, 1957–58*.
46. David Cesarani, "The Transformation of Communal Authority in Anglo-Jewry, 1914–1940," in *The Making of Modern Anglo-Jewry*, ed. David Cesarani (Oxford: Basil Blackwell, 1990), p. 137.
47. Teff, *Oe'r Hills and Far Away*, p. 23. See also Daiches, *Two Worlds*, p. 26.
48. *Jewish Chronicle*, 13 February, 1970.
49. Audrey, "Glasgow Jewry," p. 48.
50. Ferguson, *Scotland*, p. 382.
51. Toland, *Reasons for Naturalizing the Jews in Great Britain and Ireland*, p. 188.
52. David McDougall, *In Search of Israel: A Chronicle of the Jewish Missions of the Church of Scotland* (London: T. Nelson & Sons, 1941), pp. 20–1.
53. Daiches, *Two Worlds*, p. 6.
54. Katz, *The Jews in the History of England*, pp. 236, 188.
55. William Kenefick, "Comparing Jewish and Irish Immigrants in Scotland," paper presented at the Symposium on Jewish Settlement, Development and Identities in Scotland, 1879–2004, Garnethill Synagogue, 17 October, 2004.
56. Devine, *The Scottish Nation*, p. 520.
57. *Dundee Courier*, 19 January, 1878.

58. *The Conversion of the Jews: A Series of Lectures Delivered in Edinburgh by Ministers of the Church of Scotland, John Johnstone* (Edinburgh, 1842), pp. x, xvii, xii. For more detail on these attitudes, see David Rose, "St Andrew's Jews: Attitudes to Jews in the Church of Scotland in the First Half of the Twentieth Century" (M.A. dissertation, University College London, 2003), p. 5.
59. *The Scotsman*, 17 May, 1910.
60. *Jewish Chronicle*, 29 May, 1936.
61. "VAF Capacity Building Grant," p. 2.
62. *Ibid.*, p. 3.
63. *Four Corners*, 13 (March 2007).
64. Ursula R. Henriques, "The Jews and Crime in South Wales Before the First World War," in *The Jews of South Wales*, ed. Henriques, pp. 69–83.
65. Weissbach, *Jewish Life in Small-Town America*, p. 8.
66. "Report Prepared by the Board of Deputies of British Jews on the Problems of the Smaller Jewish Communities," October 1959, ACC/2805/6/1/254, LMA.
67. *Jewish Chronicle*, 23 February, 1996.
68. "VAF Capacity Building Grant," p. 1.
69. *Ibid.*, p. 2.
70. Collins, *Go and Learn*, p. 69; *Jewish Chronicle*, 25 February, 1905.
71. Diana Pinto, "A New Jewish Identity for Post-1989 Europe," JPR policy paper, No. 1 (1996), p. 17.

Appendices

1. Gershom Scholem, *Sabbatai Sevi: The Mystical Messiah, 1626–1676* (London: Routledge, 1973), p. 348.
2. *Ibid.*
3. Michael McKeown, "Sabbatai Sevi in England," *Association for Jewish Studies Review*, 2 (1977), p. 141.
4. Scholem, *Sabbatai Sevi*, p. 349, n. 32.
5. Endelman, *The Jews of Britain*, p. 21.
6. Katz, *Philo-Semitism*, p. 156.
7. Peter Davidson, personal communication to author, 24 May, 2005.
8. *Ibid.*
9. Michael McKeon, *Politics and Poetry in Restoration England: The Case of Dryden's Annus Mirabilis* (Harvard University Press: Cambridge, MA, 1975), p. 208.
10. Williamson, "A Pil for Pork-Eaters," p. 249. See, for example, *New Letter Concerning the Jewes* (1666).
11. Scholem, *Sabbatai Sevi*, p. 332.
12. *Ibid.*, p. 349
13. *Ibid.*, p. 332.
14. *Ibid.*

Bibliography

Archival Primary Sources

Aberdeen Hebrew Congregation Records, Aberdeen Hebrew Congregation.
Archives of the Office of the Chief Rabbi and the United Synagogue, London Metropolitan Archives.
Ayr Hebrew Congregation Records, Scottish Jewish Archives Centre.
Census Records.
Dundee Central Library, Local Studies Collection.
Dundee Hebrew Congregation Records, Scottish Jewish Archives Centre.
Dundee Oral History Project, DOHP 017/B/1, Dundee City Archives.
Falkirk Council Archives, Callendar House.
Home Office: Registered Papers, Supplementary HO 144, National Archives.
Julius Jung Papers, 1955–70, Hartley Library, University of Southampton.

Published Primary Sources

Barron, James. *The Northern Highlands in the Nineteenth Century: Newspaper Index and Annals, Vol. III, 1842–1856* (from the *Inverness Courier*). Inverness: Robt. Carruthers & Sons, 1913.
Conn, Adele, ed. *Serving Their Country: Wartime Memories of Scottish Jews*. Glasgow: Glasgow Jewish Representative Council/Scottish Jewish Archives Centre, 2001.
Conversion of the Jews, The: A Series of Lectures Delivered in Edinburgh by Ministers of the Church of Scotland (Edinburgh, 1842).
Cramer, Sidney. *Gravestone Inscriptions from Jewish Cemeteries*. Dundee: Dundee Central Library, 1953.
Daiches, David. *Two Worlds: An Edinburgh Jewish Childhood*. Edinburgh: Canongate, 1987.
Fodor, Sonia. "Growing Up in Dundee," http://www.thorngent.eclipse.co.uk/exe shul/newsletter/dundee.htm.
Gammie, Alexander. *The Churches of Aberdeen: Historical and Descriptive*. Aberdeen: Aberdeen Daily Journal Office, 1909.
Green, J.M. *From Colditz in Code*. Hull: The Wilberforce Council, 1989.
Howell, James. *The Wonderful and Most Deplorable History of the Latter Times of the Jews*. London, 1653.
Junior, Allan. *The Aberdeen Jew*. Dundee and London: Valentine & Sons, 1927.
———. *Canny Tales Fae Aberdeen*. Dundee and London: Valentine & Sons, 1926.
Kearton, Richard. *With Nature and a Camera: Being the Adventures and Observations of a Field Naturalist and an Animal Photographer*. London: Cassell & Co., Ltd., 1898.
Kress, Walter. *From the Holocaust to the Highlands*. Aberdeen: Cauliay, 2007.
New Letter from Aberdeen in Scotland, Sent to a Person of Quality Wherein Is a More Full Account of the Proceedings of the Jewes Than Hath Been Hitherto Published, A. 26 October, 1665, reprinted by the *Jewish Chronicle*, 6 May, 1938.
Racial Tension in Tayside: A Regional Report Commissioned by Tayside Community Relations Council (January 1987).
Reports of the Dundee Female Jewish Association, 1873, 1875, 1878, 1880, 1882.
Ruddick, Edith. *My Mother's Daughter: A Theatrical Autobiography*. Braunton: Marlin, 1995.
Skene, William. *East Neuk Chronicles*. Aberdeen, 1905.

223

Strawhorn, John, and William Boyd. *The Third Statistical Account of Scotland: Ayrshire*. Edinburgh and London: Oliver & Boyd, 1951.
Toland, John. *Reasons for Naturalizing the Jews in Great Britain and Ireland, on the Same Foot with All Other Nations*. London, 1914.

Newspapers and Periodicals

Aberdeen Evening Express
Aberdeen Free Press
Aberdeen Journal
Aberdeen Press and Journal
Aberdeen Weekly Journal
British Health Journal
Canadian Press
Daily Record
Dundee Courier
Dundee Courier and Advertiser
Dunfermline Press
Edinburgh Star
The Express
Four Corners
Glasgow Herald
Greenock Telegraph
Greenock Telegraph and Clyde Shipping Gazette
The Herald
Highland News
The Independent
Inverness Advertiser
Inverness Courier
Inverness Journal
The Jerusalem Post
Jewish Chronicle
Jewish Echo
Jewish Telegraph
John O'Groat Journal
The Mirror
The New York Times
The Scotsman
Scottish Notes & Queries
Stornoway Gazette
The Sunday Times

Periodicals, Directories, and Encyclopedias

Aberdeen Almanac
Aberdeen Post Office Directory
Ayr and District Directory
Dundee Directory
Dunfermline Directory
Encyclopaedia Judaica
Falkirk Directory
Fife Trades Directory
Greenock Directory
Hashanah: The Scottish Jewish Year Book
Inverness Directory
The Jewish Encyclopaedia
Jewish Year Book
Northern Year Book
Transactions and Miscellanies of the Jewish Historical Society of England
The Universal Jewish Encyclopedia

Correspondents and Interviewees

Brown, Ramsay
Coull, J.R.
Davidson, Peter
Dolan, Nat
Dunitz, Alfred
Evans, Nicholas J.
Fisher, Walter
Friedman, Ronald S. (Roy)
Hay, Rona
Jackson, Simon
Jacobs, Ernest Elijs
Kirkpatrick, Alexandra
Krasner, Hayden
Lazar, Vicki
Levy, Elkan
Lewis, Doris
Macleod, Donald and Eileen
MacLeod, Fiona
Matheson, John M.
Morris, Ken
Mulholland, Margaret
Rosenstein, Benita
Ross, John
Shein, Ian
Shoshan, Etti
Shoshan, Yonni
Taylor, Debby

Secondary Sources: Books

Alderman, Geoffrey. *Modern British Jewry*, 2nd ed. Oxford: Clarendon, 1998.
Audrey, Suzanne. *Multiculturalism in Practice: Irish, Jewish, Italian and Pakistani Migration to Scotland*. Aldershot: Ashgate, 2000.

Baron, Salo, Arcadius Kahan, et al. *Economic History of the Jews*. Jerusalem: Keter Press, 1975.
Barr, W.T. *For a Web Begun: The Story of Dunfermline*. Edinburgh: Oliver & Boyd, 1947.
Bell, Henry McGrady. *Land of Lakes: Memories Keep Me Company*. London: Robert Hale Ltd., 1950.
Bergen, Amanda. *Leeds Jewry, 1930–1939: The Challenge of Anti-Semitism*. Leeds: Thoresby Society, 2000.
Bulloch, John Malcolm, ed. *The House of Gordon, Vol. II*. Aberdeen: New Sporting Club, 1907.
Braber, Ben. *Jews in Glasgow 1879–1939: Immigration and Integration*. London and Portland, OR: Vallentine Mitchell, 2007.
Brotherstone, Terry, and Donald J. Withrington, eds. *The City and Its Worlds: Aspects of Aberdeen's History Since 1792*. Glasgow: Cruithne Press, 1996.
Campbell, R.H. *Scotland Since 1707: The Rise of an Industrial Society*. Edinburgh: John Donald, 1985.
Cantor, Geoffrey. *Quakers, Jews, and Science: Religious Responses to Modernity and the Sciences in Britain 1650–1900*. Oxford: Oxford University Press, 2005.
Cesarani, David, ed. *The Making of Modern Anglo-Jewry*. Oxford: Basil Blackwell, 1990.
Coan, Peter Morton, ed. *Ellis Island Interviews: In Their Own Words*. New York: Checkmark Books, 1997.
Collins, Kenneth E. *Go and Learn: The International Story of Jews and Medicine in Scotland*. Aberdeen: Aberdeen University Press, 1988.
_____. *Scotland's Jews: A Guide to the History and Community of the Jews in Scotland*, 2nd edition. Glasgow: Scottish Council of Jewish Communities, 2008.
_____. *Second City Jewry: The Jews of Glasgow in the Age of Expansion, 1790–1919*. Glasgow: Scottish Jewish Archives, 1990.
_____, ed. *Aspects of Scottish Jewry*. Glasgow: Glasgow Jewish Representative Council, 1987.
Cross, Colin. *The Fascists in Britain*. London: Barrie & Rockliff, 1961.
Crouch, Chris, Charles Fraser, and Susan Percy, eds. *Urban Regeneration in Europe*. Oxford: Blackwell, 2003.

Davies, Grahame, ed. *The Chosen People: Wales and the Jews*. Bridgend: Seren, 2002.
Devine, Tom M. *The Scottish Nation 1700–2000*. London: Penguin, 1999.
_____, C.H. Lee, and G.C. Peden. *The Transformation of Scotland: The Economy Since 1700*. Edinburgh: Edinburgh University Press, 2005.
The Diced Cap: The Story of Aberdeen City Police. Published by the Chief Constable on behalf of the Corporation of the City of Aberdeen, 1972.
Ditchburn, David. *Scotland and Europe: The Medieval Kingdom and Its Contacts with Christendom, 1241–1560*. East Linton: Tuckwell, 2000.
Edmunds, June. *The Left and Israel: Party-Policy Change and Internal Democracy*. New York: Palgrave, 1999.
Endelman, Todd M. *The Jews of Britain, 1656 to 2000*. Berkeley: University of California Press, 2002.
Ferguson, William. *Scotland: 1689 to the Present*. Edinburgh: Oliver & Boyd, 1968.
Freedman, Murray. *Leeds Jewry: The First Hundred Years*. York: Jewish Historical Society of England, Leeds Branch, 1992.
Freud-Kandel, Miri J. *Orthodox Judaism in Britain Since 1913: An Ideology Forsaken*. London and Portland, OR: Vallentine Mitchell, 2006.
Gartner, Lloyd. *The Jewish Immigrant in England, 1870–1914*. London and Portland, OR: Vallentine Mitchell, 2001.
Gilbert, Martin. *The Routledge Atlas of Jewish History*, 7th ed. London and New York: Routledge, 2006.
Gordon, Eleanor. *Women and the Labour Movement in Scotland, 1850–1914*. Oxford: Clarendon Press, 1991.
Gourlay, Robert, and Anne Turner. *Historic Dunfermline: The Archaeological Implications of Development*. Glasgow: Scottish Burgh Survey, 1978.
____ and ____. *Historic Inverness: The Archaeological Implications of Development*. Glasgow: Scottish Burgh Survey, 1977.
Green, J.M. *From Colditz in Code*. Hull: The Wilberforce Council, 1989.
Harris, Cyril. *For Heaven's Sake*. London and Portland, OR: Vallentine Mitchell, 2001.

Henriques, Ursula R. Q., ed. *The Jews of South Wales: Historical Studies.* Cardiff: University of Wales Press, 1993.

Hirschman, Elizabeth Caldwell, and Donald N. Yates. *When Scotland Was Jewish: DNA Evidence, Archaeology, Analysis of Migrations and Public and Family Records Show Twelfth Century Semitic Roots.* Jefferson, NC, and London: McFarland, 2007.

Hofman, Ethel G. *Mackerel at Midnight: Growing Up Jewish on a Remote Scottish Island.* Philadelphia: Camino Books, 2005.

Hutcheson, John M. *Notes on the Sugar Industry of the United Kingdom.* Greenock: James M'Kelvie, 1901.

Hutt, Charlotte, and Harvey L. Kaplan. *A Scottish Shtetl: Jewish Life in the Gorbals, 1880–1974.* Glasgow: Scottish Jewish Archives Centre, 1974.

Hyamson, A.M. *A History of the Jews of England.* Oxford: Oxford University Press, 1941.

Hyman, Louis. *The Jews of Ireland form Earliest Times to the Year 1910.* Shannon: Irish University Press, 1972.

Josephs, Zoë. *Birmingham Jewry, Vol.2, Further aspects, 1740–1930.* Oldbury: Birmingham Jewish History Research Group, 1984.

Kadish, Sharman. *Jewish Heritage in England.* Swindon: English Heritage, 2006.

Katz, David S. *The Jews in the History of England, 1845–1850.* Oxford: Clarendon, 1996.

_____. *Philo-Semitism and the Readmission of the Jews to England, 1603–1655.* Oxford: Clarendon, 1982.

Kay, Billy, ed. *The Dundee Book: An Anthology of Living in the City.* Edinburgh: Mainstream, 1990.

Kennedy, Ludovic. *A Presumption of Innocence: The Amazing Case of Patrick Meehan.* London: Victor Gollancz, 1976.

Kibblewhite, Liz, and Andy Rigby. *Fascism in Aberdeen: Street Politics in the 1930s.* Aberdeen: Aberdeen People's Press, 1978.

Krausz, Ernest. *Leeds Jewry: Its History and Social Structure.* London: Heffer, 1964.

Lawson, Lewis. *A History of Falkirk.* Falkirk: Falkirk Town Council, 1975.

Levy, Abraham. *The Origins of Glasgow Jewry, 1812–1895.* Glasgow: A. J. Macfarlane, 1949.

Lipman, Vivian D. *A History of the Jews in Britain Since 1858.* Leicester: Leicester University Press, 1990.

_____. *The Jews of Medieval Norwich.* London: Jewish Historical Society of England, 1967.

_____. *Social History of the Jews in England, 1850–1950.* London: Watts & Co., 1954.

Livshin, Rosalyn D. *The History of the Harrogate Jewish Community.* Leeds: Leeds University Press, 1995.

Lustig, Sandra H., and Ian Leveson, eds. *Turning the Kaleidoscope: Perspectives on European Jewry.* New York and Oxford: Berghahn, 2006.

MacInnes, Ranald. *The Aberdeen Guide.* Edinburgh: Birlinn, 2000.

McDougall, David. *In Search of Israel: A Chronicle of the Jewish Missions of the Church of Scotland.* London: T. Nelson & Sons, 1941.

McKeon, Michael. *Politics and Poetry in Restoration England: The Case of Dryden's Annus Mirabilis.* Harvard University Press: Cambridge, MA, 1975.

Morawska, Ewa. *Insecure Prosperity: Small-Town Jews in Industrial America, 1890–1940.* Princeton, NJ: Princeton University Press, 1999.

Murray, Janice, and David Stockdale. *The Miles Tae to Dundee: Stories of a City and Its People.* Dundee: Dundee Art Galleries and Museums, 1990.

Newman, Aubrey. *Birmingham Jewry, Vol.1, 1749–1914.* Leicester: University of Leicester Press, 1980.

Phillips, Abel. *A History of the Origins of the First Jewish Community in Scotland-Edinburgh, 1816.* Edinburgh: John Donald Publishers, 1979.

Pollins, Harold. *Economic History of the Jews in England.* New Brunswick, NJ, and London: Associated University Presses, 1982.

Pritt, D.N. *The Autobiography of D.N. Pritt, Vol. II.* London: Lawrence & Wishart, 1966.

Robertson, Neil, ed. *An A-Z of Hilltown: A History of Dundee's First Suburb.* Dundee: Grey Lodge, 1994.

Roth, Cecil. *A History of the Jews in England,* 3rd ed. Oxford: Clarendon, 1964.

Bibliography

———. *The Rise of Provincial Jewry: The Early History of the Jewish Communities in the English Countryside*. London: Jewish Monthly, 1950.
Rubinstein, William D. *A History of the Jews in the English-Speaking World: Great Britain*. London: Macmillan, 1996.
Samuel, Judith. *Jews in Bristol: The History of the Jewish Community in Bristol from the Middle Ages to the Present Day*. Bristol: Redcliffe, 1997.
Scholem, Gershom. *Sabbatai Sevi: The Mystical Messiah, 1626–1676*. London: Routledge, 1973.
Schuchard, M.K. *Restoring the Temple of Vision: Cabalistic Freemasonry and Stuart Culture*. Leiden: Brill, 2002.
Sebak, Per Kristian. *Titanic's Predecessor: The S/S Norge Disaster of 1904*. Lakesvaag: Seaward, 2004.
Shaw, Gareth, and Allan Williams, eds. *The Rise and Fall of British Coastal Resorts: Cultural and Economic Perspectives*. London: Pinter, 1997.
Shinwell, Emmanuel. *Conflict Without Malice*. London: Odhams Press, 1955.
Skelton, Constance Oliver, and John Malcolm Bulloch. *Gordons Under Arms; A Biographical Muster Roll of Officers Named Gordon in the Navies and Armies of Britain, Europe, America and in the Jacobite Risings*. Aberdeen: New Spalding Club, 1912.
Skinner, Patricia, ed. *The Jews in Medieval Britain: Historical, Literary and Archaeological Perspectives*. Woodbridge: Boydell, 2003.
Slaven, Anthony. *The Development of the West of Scotland: 1750–1960*. London: Routledge, 1975.
Smith, John S., and David Stevenson. *Aberdeen in the Nineteenth Century: The Making of the Modern City*. Aberdeen: Aberdeen University Press, 1988.
Smith, Robin. *The Making of Scotland: A Comprehensive Guide to the Growth of Scotland's Cities, Towns and Villages*. Edinburgh: Canongate, 2001.
Sterne, Ernest C. *Leeds Jewry, 1919–1929*. Leeds: Jewish Historical Society of England, 1989.
Stewart, John. *Falkirk, Its Origins and Growth: A History of the Burgh*. Falkirk: F. Johnston, 1940.
Strawhorn, John. *Ayrshire: The Story of a County*. Ayr: Ayrshire Archaeological and Natural History Society, 1975.
———. *750 Years of a Scottish School: Ayr Academy, 1233–1983*. Ayr: Alloway Publishing, 1983.
Vice, Sue, ed. *Representing the Holocaust: Essays in Honour of Bryan Burns*. London and Portland, OR: Vallentine Mitchell, 2003.
Waddington, Raymond B., and Arthur H. Williamson, eds. *The Expulsion of the Jews: 1492 and After*. New York and London: Garland, 1994.
Walker, William M. *Juteopolis: Dundee and Its Textile Workers, 1885–1923*. Edinburgh: Scottish Academic Press, 1979.
Walton, John K. *The British Seaside: Holidays and Resorts in the Twentieth Century*. Manchester and New York: Manchester University Press, 2000.
Weissbach, Lee Shai. *Jewish Life in Small-Town America: A History*. New Haven and London: Yale University Press, 2005.
White, Jerry. *Rothschild Buildings: Life in an East End Tenement Block, 1887–1920*. London: Routledge, 1980.
Williams, Bill. *The Making of Manchester Jewry, 1740–1875*. Manchester: Manchester University Press, 1976.

Secondary Sources: Articles

Abrams, Nathan. "The Jews of Aberdeen: A Revolving Door Community Since 1893 and Its Antecedents," *Northern Scotland*, 27 (2007).
———, and Harvey Kaplan. "Jews in Scotland: Myth and Reality," *History Scotland*, 6:4 (July/August 2006).
"Anti-Semitism Worldwide 1997/8," http://www.tau.ac.il/Anti-Semitism/asw97-8/united-kingdom.html.
"Ayr Hebrew Congregation," http://www.jewishgen.org/JCR-uk/Community/ayr/index.htm.
Block, Geoffrey D.M. "Jewish Students at the Universities of Great Britain and Ireland–Excluding London, 1936–1939," *Sociological Review*, 34 (1942).
Braber, Ben. "The Trial of Oscar Slater (1909) and Anti-Jewish Prejudices in Edwardian Glasgow," *History*, 88 (2003).

"Bromberg, Ernest," *Scottish Screen Archive*, http://data.scottishscreen.com/personality/detail.php?id=10004.
Buten, Iris. "The Polson-Levansky-Buten-Serota Story," *Butenet*, http://www.buten.net/polyvensky/polyvensky.html.
"Canadian Jewish Casualties in the Canadian Armed Forces," http://www.cjccc.ca/archives/.
Cesarani, David. "The Transformation of Communal Authority in Anglo-Jewry, 1914–1940," in *The Making of Modern Anglo-Jewry*, ed. David Cesarani (Oxford: Basil Blackwell, 1990).
Collins, Kenneth E. "Maintaining a Jewish Identity in Scotland," in *Scottish Life and Society: The Individual and Community Life, a Compendium of Scottish Ethnology, Vol. 9*, ed. John Beech, Owen Hand, Mark Mulhern, and Jeremy Weston (Edinburgh: John Donald Ltd., 2005).
Cunningham, William. "Differences of Economic Development in England and Scotland," *Scottish Historical Review*, 13 (1916).
Daiches, Salis. "The Jew in Scotland," in *Records of the Scottish Church History Society, Vol. III*, ed. W.J. Couper and Robert McKinlay (Edinburgh: The Scottish Church History Society, 1929).
"Dundee Hebrew Congregation," http://www.jewishgen.org/JCR-UK/Community/dundee/index.htm.
"Dunfermline Hebrew Congregation," http://www.jewishgen.org/jcr-uk/Community/Dunfermline/index.htm.
"Dunfermline's Jewish Connections," *Scottish Local History*, 67 (Summer 2006).
"Falkirk Synagogue," http://www.jewishgen.org/jcr-uk/Community/falkirk/index.htm.
"Greenock Hebrew Congregation," http://www.jewishgen.org/jcr-uk/Community/greenock/index.htm.
Hamilton, H. "The Failure of the Ayr Bank, 1772," *Economic History Review*, 8:3 (1956).
Henriques, Ursula R. Q. "The Jewish Community of Cardiff, 1813–1914," in *The Jews of South Wales: Historical Studies*, ed. Ursula R. Q. Henriques (Cardiff: University of Wales Press, 1993).
_____. "The Jews and Crime in South Wales Before the First World War," in *The Jews of South Wales: Historical Studies*, ed. Ursula R. Q. Henriques (Cardiff: University of Wales Press, 1993).
Hunter, J. Albert. "Julius Quint: Shetland's Wandering Jew," *New Shetlander*, 159 (1987).
"Jewish Cemeteries in Scotland," http://www.jgsgb.org.uk/bury03.shtml.
Kadish, Sharman. "Constructing Identity: Anglo-Jewry and Synagogue Architecture," *Architectural History*, 45 (2002).
Kenefick, William. "Jewish and Catholic Irish Relations: The Glasgow Waterfront, c.1880–1914," *Jewish Culture and History*, 7:1–2 (Summer/Autumn 2004).
Levy, Abraham. "The Origins of Scottish Jewry," reprint of a paper read before the Jewish Historical Society of England, 13 January, 1958, place and date of printing unknown.
Levy, S. "Notes on Leicester Jewry," *Transactions of the Jewish Historical Society of England*, 5 (1902–05).
Lloyd, Greg, and John McCarthy. "Dundee: A City Discovering Inclusion and Regeneration," in *Urban Regeneration in Europe*, eds. Chris Crouch, Charles Fraser and Susan Percy (Oxford: Blackwell, 2003).
Maitles, Henry. "Attitudes to Jewish Immigration in the West of Scotland to 1905," *Scottish Economic & Social History*, 15 (1995).
_____. "Blackshirts Across the Border: The British Union of Fascists in Scotland," *Scottish Historical Review*, 82:1 (April 2003).
_____. "Jewish Trade Unionists in Glasgow," *Immigrants and Minorities*, 10:3 (1991).
McKeown, Michael. "Sabbatai Sevi in England," *Association for Jewish Studies Review*, 2 (1977).
Mellor, R.E.H. "Aberdeen—The Great Century," in *Aberdeen in the Nineteenth Century: The Making of the Modern City*, eds. John S. Smith and David Stevenson (Aberdeen: Aberdeen University Press, 1988).
"Moses Lewis Usher," *Canadian Jewish Casualties in the Canadian Armed Forces*, http://www.cjccc.ca/archives/casualtyinfo.php?info=45.
Newlands, David. "The Regional Economies of Scotland," in *The Transformation of Scotland: The Economy Since 1700*,

ed. T.M. Devine, C.H. Lee, and G.C. Peden (Edinburgh: Edinburgh University Press, 2005).
Pinto, Diana. "A New Jewish Identity for Post-1989 Europe," JPR policy paper, No. 1 (1996).
Pollins, Harold. "An Archival Adventure in Scotland," *Oxford Menorah*, 142 (Winter 1996).
———. "The Jewish Community of Brynmawr, Wales," *The Jewish Journal of Sociology*, 50:1 & 2 (2008).
Ritchie, Jessie. "The Greenock Blitz: May 1941," http://www.bbc.co.uk/ww2peopleswar/stories/69/a2451269.shtml.
Saltman, Avrom. "To Be Buried in Grimsby" (April 1998), http://www.jewishgen.org/jcr-uk/community/Gr/all.htm.
Silberhaft, Moshe. "Eulogy Delivered at the Consecration of the Tombstone of the late Chief Rabbi Cyril K. Harris," 4 July, 2006, http://www.africanjewishcongress.com/EULOGY.htm.
Smith, Graham R. "'None Can Compare': From the Oral History of a Community," in *The Dundee Book: An Anthology of Living in the City*, ed. Billy Kay (Edinburgh: Mainstream, 1990).
Smith, Mark. "The Last Jews of Greenock," *Edinburgh Star*, 26 (1997).
Sugarman, Martin. "Jewish POW's at Colditz," http://www.jewishvirtuallibrary.org/jsource/ww2/sugar6.html.
Taylor, Avram. "Breaking Free from 'A Scottish Shetl': The Life, Times and Jewishness of C.P. Taylor," in *Representing the Holocaust: Essays in Honour of Bryan Burns*, ed. Sue Vice (London and Portland, OR: Vallentine Mitchell, 2003).
Taylor, Jackie. "A Communal Revival in Falkirk?" *Edinburgh Star*, 35 (February 2000).
Tyson, Robert E. "The Economy of Aberdeen," in *Aberdeen in the Nineteenth Century: The Making of the Modern City*, eds. John S. Smith and David Stevenson (Aberdeen: Aberdeen University Press, 1988).
Weissbach, Lee Shai. "Unexplored Terrain: The History of Small Jewish Communities in Western Society," *Shofar*, 17 (Fall 1998).

———. "East European Immigrants and the Image of the Jews in the Small-Town South," *American Jewish History*, 85:3 (1997).
———. "Small Jewish Communities in the Era of Mass Migration: The American Experience," in *Patterns of Migration, 1850–1914*, eds. Aubrey Newman and Stephen W. Massil (London: The Jewish Historical Society of England, 1996).
Whitehead, Jill. "The Brown Family of Edinburgh," *Shemot*, 11:1 (2003).
Williams, Allan, and Gareth Shaw. "Riding the Big Dipper: The Rise and Decline of the British Seaside Resort in the Twentieth Century," in *The Rise and Fall of British Coastal Resorts: Cultural and Economic Perspectives*, eds. Gareth Shaw and Allan Williams (London: Pinter, 1997).
Williamson, Arthur H. "'A Pil for Pork-Eaters': Ethnic Identity, Apocalyptic Promises, and the Strange Creation of the Judeo-Scots," in *The Expulsion of the Jews: 1492 and After*, eds. Raymond B Waddington and Arthur H Williamson (New York and London: Garland, 1994).

Unpublished Material

Braber, Ben. "The Integration of Jewish Immigrants in Glasgow, 1880–1939" (Ph.D. dissertation, University of Glasgow, 1992).
Caplan, Sidney. "Jews in Scotland in Medieval Times" (ms. in author's possession).
Fleming, Linda. "Jewish Women in Glasgow, c1880–1950: Gender, Ethnicity and the Immigrant Experience" (work in progress).
Jacob, Albert. *The Day It Hit the Fan* (ms. in author's possession).
Kaplan, Harvey. "JCT" (ms. in author's possession).
———. "Jewish Burial Grounds in Scotland" (ms. in author's possession).
———. "The Jewish Colonial Trust" (ms. in author's possession).
———. "Review of *When Scotland Was Jewish: DNA Evidence, Archaeology, Analysis of Migrations and Public and Family Records Show Twelfth Century Semitic Roots*, by Elizabeth Caldwell Hirschman

and Donald N. Yates," *Jewish Culture and History* (forthcoming).

Kenefick, William. "Comparing Jewish and Irish Immigrants in Scotland," paper presented at the Symposium on Jewish Settlement, Development and Identities in Scotland, 1879–2004, Garnethill Synagogue, 17 October, 2004.

Krase, Jennifer. "Jewish Community in Aberdeen: Developing Individual Identity" (term essay, University of Aberdeen, 2006).

MacDonald, Ewan A. "Discovering the Jews of Dundee: With Particular Reference to German and Russian Jews" (Single Honours Dissertation, University of Dundee, 2005).

Newland, Katharyne C. "Immigrant Minorities in Dundee 1850–1914: The Irish and the Jews" (undergraduate dissertation, University of Dundee, n.d.).

Rose, David. "St Andrews' Jews: Attitudes to Jews in the Church of Scotland in the First Half of the Twentieth Century" (M.A. dissertation, University College London, 2003).

Ross, Joe. *The Robert (Spilg) Spence Story* (ms. in author's possession).

Taylor, Avram. "Remembering Spring Through Gorbals Voices: Autobiography and the Memory of a Community," paper presented at the Symposium on Jewish Settlement, Development and Identities in Scotland 1879–2004, 17 October, 2004.

Teff, Bennett. *O'er Vales and Hills: Some Reminiscences* (ms. in author's possession).

VAF Capacity Building Grant—Report of Activity and Outcomes, Scottish Council of Jewish Communities, April 2006 (ms. in author's possession).

Index

Aberdeen 1, 2, 7, 10, 11, 13, 14, 15–40, 44, 45, 46, 49, 50, 56, 72, 77, 93, 120, 124, 131, 132, 147, 148, 149, 158, 159, 164, 169, 170, 171, 173, 174, 175, 176, 177, 178, 179, 180, 181, 183, 187, 189–91, 192–5, 205n.42, 205n.55
Aberdeen Free Press 13
Aberdeen Hebrew Congregation 1, 21, 25, 29, 30, 33, 39, 58
Aberdeen Journal 21, 23
Aberdeen *shechita* case 22, 175
Adams, David 137, 183
Adler, Herbert M. 102, 118, 177–8
Adler, Dr. Hermann 11, 22, 23, 149, 177
Adolphus, Jacob 18
Amsterdam 65
Angus 87
anti-Semitism 14, 19, 22, 35–7, 53, 82, 90–4, 140, 153, 181–4, 213n.167
anti-Zionism 36, 90–4, 213n.167
Argyll and Bute Jewish Community 164
Arkush, S. 146, 147
Aronsfeld, C.C. 66, 172
Arran 162
Atkin, Minnie 139, 183
Austria 144
Ayr 1, 2, 10, 14, 41–64, 88, 100, 103, 116, 124, 126, 147, 159, 169, 171, 172, 174, 175, 179, 180, 184, 189–91, 205n.42
Ayr Hebrew Congregation 52, 59, 61, 63
Ayr Jewish Community Charitable Trust 63
Ayrshire 42–3, 46, 51, 53, 111

Bangor 149, 169
Bangor Hebrew Congregation 149
Baruch, Daniel 18
Battle of Stirling Bridge 7
Belfast 67
Berwick on Tweed 6, 7
Birmingham 9, 122
Bishop of Glasgow 5
Blair, Hugh 8
Bloch, Maurice 29, 49, 54, 55, 78
Board of Deputies 49, 55, 61, 93, 100, 104, 113, 118, 150, 171, 185
Braber, Ben 78
Bradford 67
British National Party (BNP) 94
British Union of Fascists (B.U.F.) 28, 156, 183
Brodie, Israel 157, 165
Brodum, William 18
Brown, David 8
burials 14, 49, 60, 72, 83, 105, 120, 131–2, 146–7, 161, 162, 164, 174–5, 194–5, 196, 197, 206–7n.54

Cambridge 7, 17
Canada 62, 88
Caplan, Sidney 7
Cardiff 147
Cardozo, Samuel 18
cemeteries 6, 8, 23, 72, 127, 131–2, 134, 146–7, 156, 164, 174–5
census 13, 20, 34, 41, 68, 73, 87, 95, 111, 114, 133, 154, 163, 164
Cesarani, David 180
charity 14, 21, 45, 51, 54, 67, 80, 81, 100, 108, 117, 120, 135, 149–50, 151, 179–81
Chief Rabbi 11, 22, 23, 44, 46, 71, 72, 76, 80, 101, 117, 127, 130, 145, 146, 148, 149, 150, 154, 157, 160, 171–2, 177
Churchill, Winston 76
Cohen, David 18
Colditz 104–5
Collins, Kenneth 1, 7, 9, 10, 13, 17, 21, 22, 23, 38, 42, 43, 44, 65, 98, 99, 113, 114, 123, 126, 134, 135, 137, 150, 173
Cromwell, Oliver 7, 16, 192
Cunningham, William 7
Cymbalist, David 154
Cymbalist, Mark 154
Cymbalist, Norris 154

Daiches, David 99, 182
Daiches, Rabbi Salis 5, 37, 78, 99, 102, 104, 159, 161, 178
Devine, Tom 182
Ditchburn, David 6, 37
Dumfries 61
Dundee 1, 2, 8, 10, 11, 14, 26, 31, 38, 39, 64, 65–94, 98, 99, 102, 106, 107, 109, 124, 125, 126, 132, 137, 147, 167, 169, 170, 171, 172, 173, 174, 178, 179, 180, 183, 187, 189–91, 213n.167
Dundee Courier 67, 68, 78
Dundee Female Jewish Association 69
Dundee Hebrew Congregation 68, 81, 84
Dunfermline 1, 2, 10, 31, 50, 80, 81, 95–109, 126, 137, 159, 169, 173, 174, 179, 183, 189–91, 205n.42
Dunfermline Hebrew Congregation 100, 108
Dunoon 43, 64, 163, 164

Edinburgh 1, 2, 7, 8, 10, 14, 15, 21, 23, 32, 41, 45, 46, 65, 70, 72, 78, 81, 82, 84, 88, 95, 97, 99, 100, 102,

231

Index

103, 104, 106, 107, 109, 110, 111, 112, 116, 120, 122, 124, 127, 136, 143, 147, 156, 158, 163, 167, 169, 171, 175, 176, 177, 181, 182, 183, 184, 186
Edinburgh Hebrew Congregation 33, 35, 178
Edward I 6, 7
Elgin 143
Endelman, Todd 9
England 1, 5, 6, 7, 9, 38, 53, 62, 73, 83, 89, 125, 162, 169, 192
Evans, Ann 95
Evans, Nicholas J. 37, 124
Expulsion of the Jews of England 5, 6

Fackenheim, Emil 27, 178
Fackenheim, Julius 27, 28, 30, 31, 38
Falkirk 1, 2, 10, 88, 100, 110–22, 126, 148, 159, 169, 174, 175, 179, 189–91, 198–200
Falkirk Hebrew Congregation 117
Fascism 27–8
Ferguson, William 8
Fife 87, 95, 98, 99, 104, 106, 107, 108, 109, 111
Finkelstein, Isaac 145, 146, 149, 150–3, 157, 158
France 66, 88, 101, 104
Fredinni, L. 67, 68
Freeman, Cecil 42, 44, 50, 63, 64
Freeman, Harris 42, 46, 48, 50, 51, 56, 57, 63
Freud-Kandel, Miri 9

Galloway, George 92
Gammie, Alexander 13
Garcia, Daniel 18
Garnethill 43
Gartner, Lloyd P. 99
Germany 8, 27, 66, 67, 111, 138, 142, 157, 161, 162, 167, 178
Gillis, Harold 87, 180
Glasgow 1, 2, 8, 9, 10, 11, 14, 15, 21, 23, 25, 26, 27, 29, 31, 32, 33, 35, 36, 41, 42, 43, 44, 45, 46, 47, 48, 49, 51, 52, 53, 54, 55, 57, 59, 60, 61, 62, 63, 65, 66, 71, 72, 77, 78, 81, 82, 83, 84, 88, 97, 99, 100, 101, 105, 106, 107, 108, 109, 110, 111, 114, 115, 116, 117, 119, 120, 121, 122, 123, 124, 125, 126, 127, 132, , 133, 134, 135, 136, 138, 139, 140, 141, 144,

146, 149, 150, 151, 154, 155, 157, 158, 159, 161, 163, 164, 165, 166, 167, 168, 169, 171, 175, 176, 177, 178, 179, 183, 184, 186, 204n.38, 205n.42
Glasgow Jewish Board of Guardians 126
Glasgow Jewish Representative Council 57, 87, 90, 163
Gorbals 62, 114, 150
Gourlay, Robert 95
Gourock 60, 136, 139, 141
Govan 62
Green, Julius 103, 104–5, 106
Greenock 1, 2, 10, 11, 44, 88, 123–41, 144, 149, 164, 167, 169, 174, 178, 179, 183, 189–91, 196, 205n.42
Greenock Hebrew Congregation 127, 135, 137, 138
Greenock Telegraph 124
Greenock Telegraph and Clyde Shipping Gazette 130
Greenwald family 164–5

Hamburg 66, 163, 164
Harris, Cyril 58
Henriques, Ernest 19
Henriques, Stella 19
Henriques, Ursula 12
Hilltown 67, 68, 69
Hirschman, Elizabeth Caldwell 6, 15, 161
Hofman, Ethel (née Greenwald) 123, 164–6
Hoppenstein, Reverend D. 45, 46, 50
Hull 59, 67, 14
Huntly 7, 158
Hyamson, A.M. 5

Invercloy Hotel 51, 53, 55, 56, 57, 58, 59, 60, 61, 62–3
Inverness 1, 2, 10, 13, 14, 44, 45, 49, 77, 88, 117, 132, 142–60, 165, 169, 174, 179, 183, 184, 189–91, 197, 205n.42, 219n.90
Inverness Courier 143, 154, 156, 161
Inverness Hebrew Congregation 145, 146, 147, 158, 166, 176
Ireland 123
Israel 30, 33, 38, 60, 61, 63, 81, 83, 86, 88, 90, 91, 93, 94, 107, 121, 139, 158, 164, 179, 183, 184, 186
Italy 133

Jacob, Albert 84, 86, 92, 94
Jacob, David 78, 80, 91
Jaffe, Daniel J. 66, 67
James IV 15
Jewish Chronicle 3, 12, 14, 15, 23, 24, 39, 40, 41, 43, 44, 45, 46, 47, 48, 49, 52, 54, 55, 56, 61, 63, 64, 67, 68, 71, 72, 73, 76, 81, 83, 88, 89, 91, 93, 98, 100, 102, 106, 107, 117, 118, 119, 121, 125, 126, 127, 130, 134, 136, 138, 144, 145, 149, 150, 151, 157, 179, 180, 186
Jewish Colonial Trust 21, 44, 73, 118, 128, 179
Jewish Echo 3, 12, 14, 30, 36, 40, 52, 55, 57, 58, 61, 62, 63, 64, 82, 88, 107, 108, 113, 120, 121, 135, 136, 137, 141, 155, 157, 159, 161, 165, 170, 173, 179, 183
Jewish National Fund (J.N.F.) 51, 54, 81, 102, 120, 137, 179, 180
Jewish Network of the Argyll and Highlands 10, 164, 187
Jewish Provincial Minister's Fund 46, 102
Jewish Telegraph 3, 40
Jewish Year Book 3, 12, 13, 14, 23, 31, 34, 41, 42, 45, 47, 52, 59, 61, 63, 73, 87, 100, 102–3, 104, 106, 113, 116, 120, 126, 127, 128, 130, 133, 134, 136, 138, 145, 146, 157, 164
Josippon 5
Jung, Julius 82, 158, 178
jute 65, 66, 72, 76–7

Kadish, Sharman 70, 76, 84, 123, 126, 131, 162
Kaplan, Harvey 1, 6, 9, 131
kashrut 22, 32, 53, 57, 60, 71, 72, 75, 76, 102, 103, 115, 120, 157, 164, 165, 170, 175
Katz, David 182, 192
Keith, Graham 206n.18
Kenefick, William 1, 9
Kilmarnock 43
King's College, Aberdeen 17, 18
Knox, John 7
Kress, Walter 27, 28

Laidlaw, Petra 206n.19
Largs 49, 52, 53, 58, 60
Latvia 97, 126, 154, 157
Leeds 9, 107, 121, 122, 124, 126, 136, 183
Leith 99, 112, 123, 164

Index

Lerwick 10, 25, 161, 162, 164, 165, 175, 176, 178
Levi, Hirsch 71, 173
Levy, Abraham 5, 6, 8, 18
Levy, Elkan 212n.131
Levy, Harold 178
Lewisohn, Benjamin 18
Lithuania 45, 72, 97, 102, 114, 126, 133, 140, 173
Liverpool 9, 43, 73
London 9, 17, 18, 21, 22, 32, 48, 53, 65, 70, 71, 76, 88, 89, 92, 119, 121, 124, 139, 153, 158, 159, 169, 171, 175, 183, 186, 192, 193
Lubon, Lazarus 19
Lyon, Benjamin 18
Lyon, Herman 8

MacDonald, Ewan 69
Maitles, Henry 1, 9
Manchester 9, 48, 67, 88, 89, 112, 124, 164, 176, 186
Marcus, Michael 78, 137, 183
Marischal College 7, 16, 17, 18, 183
Mary Queen of Scots 7
McKeown, Michael 192
medicine 17–19, 26–7, 65, 78, 79, 81, 113, 152, 169, 170, 181
Menassah ben Israel 7, 16
Merrens, Moses 144, 145, 146
Montefiore, Judah Israel 18
Morris, Lewis 153, 155–6, 158, 183
Mosley, Oswald 27, 156
Mossman, Isaac 7
Myers, Joseph Hart 8
Myers, Lazarus 19
Myres, Isaac 19

Nablus 91, 92, 93
Naftalin, Ephraim 45, 50
National Front 91, 94
Nazism 27, 82
neo-Nazism 91
New York 123, 124
Newcastle 6, 43
Newton Mearns 63, 64
SS Norge disaster 162

Office of Small Communities 11, 82
Orkney 163, 165
Otto, Julius Conradus 8
Oxford 17

Pacifico, Emmanuel 18
Palestine Liberation Organization (PLO) 91–4
peddling 25, 99–100, 114, 133, 142, 150, 160–1, 163, 168, 169
Pfingst, Dr. Gustav 31
Pinto, Diana 186
Poland 13, 20, 44, 51, 68, 72, 100, 102, 105, 111, 118, 125, 126, 141, 142, 143, 144, 146, 173
Pollins, Harold 9, 131, 132, 134, 135, 136
Prestwick 42, 49, 52, 59, 60, 169
Prussia 8, 20, 41, 42, 43, 66, 77, 117

Queen, Isaac 8
Quint, Julius 160

Rabin, Paulus Scialitti 8
Reform Judaism 67, 70, 79, 170, 177
religious education 31, 51, 52–3, 59, 72, 81, 82, 102, 104, 115, 117, 118, 119, 128, 147, 149, 177–9
Robert I 6
Romania 144
Ronder, Alex 50, 100, 103
Rosenberg, Alethia 19
Rosenberg, Harris 19
Ross, Abraham 60, 62, 184
Ross, Ernie 92, 94
Ross, Rachel 62, 184
Rosyth 95, 108
Roth, Cecil 5, 16
Rothesay 48, 49, 64
Rubinstein, William D. 9, 26, 79
Ruddick, Edith 101, 102, 103, 104
Ruddick, Jacob 97, 99, 103, 106
Russia 8, 13, 20, 22, 25, 26, 65, 66, 68, 72, 73, 78, 97, 98, 100, 102, 107, 111, 114, 125, 133, 144, 146, 162, 163, 173

St. Andrews 65, 78, 79, 82, 83, 87, 88, 91, 98, 170, 180
St. Kilda 160
Saltcoats 46, 49, 60
Sarmento, Jacob de Castro 18
Scholem, Gerhom 192–3
Schomberg, Ralph 18
Sclar, Isaac 50, 103, 107–8, 137, 183
Scotsman 13, 21, 25, 73, 77, 162, 179
Scottish Council of Jewish Communities 87, 109, 186
Scottish Jewish Archives Centre 2, 6, 75, 109, 131, 138
Scottish Jewish Year Book 61
Segal, Morris 81, 82–3, 102, 104, 105, 107, 109
Shabbetai Tsvi (Sabbatai Sevi) 16, 192
shechita 22, 35, 57, 70, 72, 75, 101, 175
Shetland Isles 10, 13, 25, 160, 161, 162, 163, 164–6, 169, 174, 175
Shinwell, Manny (Emmanuel) 111, 133, 137, 183
Skene, William 15, 19
Skinner, Patricia 6
Skye 10, 161, 163
Slater, Oscar 23, 48–9, 62, 184
Smith, Mark 123, 124, 126, 128, 131, 139
Solomon, Samuel 18
South Africa 26, 27, 29, 38, 58, 79, 88, 152, 167
Spicker, Paul 84, 87, 94, 180
Spilg, Gershon 114–5, 117, 126
Spilg, Reuben 49, 59, 101, 112, 113, 114–5, 120, 163
Stornoway 160, 161–2, 169
Suecus, Samuel 7, 16
Suero, Samuel 7, 16

Tain 143
Taub, Charles 144, 145, 146
Taylor, Debby (née Jacob) 90, 92
Temianka, Henri 127–8
Terret, Frank 51
Thomas fil Isaac 6, 15
Ticktin, Isaiah 148–9
Tiemianka, Israel 127, 128, 130, 134
Toland, John 5, 181
Trade Union Friends of Palestine 92–3
trades and occupations 24–7, 60, 66, 69, 80–1, 97–100, 101, 106, 112, 120, 125, 128–9, 133, 136, 137, 144, 150–4, 163, 167–70
Tranter, William 7
Troon 46, 48, 49, 52, 53, 59, 60

United Jewish Israel Appeal 11
United States 12, 26, 38, 62, 66, 67, 68, 78, 83, 88, 89, 99, 123, 138, 139, 152, 153, 162, 164, 167, 169, 181
University of Aberdeen 1, 7,

26, 27, 32, 34, 35, 36, 38, 39, 170
University of Abertay 88
University of Dundee 84, 87, 90, 91, 92, 103
University of Edinburgh 8, 113, 118, 152
University of Glasgow 92, 137, 140

Wales 9, 57, 98, 169, 184
Wallace, William 7
Wallach, Nathaniel 18
Wartski, Isidore 149
Weinberg, Julius 66, 67, 73, 77
Weisman, Malcolm 186

Weissbach, Lee Shai 12, 185
Wick 143
William of Newburgh 6
Williamson, Arthur 16
W.I.Z.O. 30, 55, 59, 81, 179, 180
Wolfe, Celia 133
Wolfe, David 131, 133, 139–40, 183
Wolfe, Isaac 139
Wolfe, Joseph 126, 128, 133, 135
Wolfe, Lenny (Leonard) 140
Wolfe, Walter 126
World War I 23, 25, 45, 76, 77, 100–1, 102, 120, 134, 148, 149, 163, 169, 184

World War II 10, 28–9, 35, 49, 52–9, 80, 83, 94, 103, 104, 107, 110, 120, 132, 138, 141, 156–7, 165–6, 167, 169, 172, 175, 183

Yates, Donald N. 6, 15, 161
Yiddish 69, 77, 99, 148, 168
York 5, 6

Zamek, Alexander 21, 22, 23
Zangwill, Israel 15
Zionism 14, 21, 30, 36, 42, 44, 51, 59, 61, 73, 81, 102, 118, 120, 128, 134, 137, 140, 147, 150, 179–81, 183

www.ingramcontent.com/pod-product-compliance
Ingram Content Group UK Ltd.
Pitfield, Milton Keynes, MK11 3LW, UK
UKHW041942140426
5217IPUK00014B/624

9 780786 442850